EURASIAN DISUNION
Russia's Vulnerable Flanks

By Janusz Bugajski and Margarita Assenova

D1565442

The JAMESTOWN
FOUNDATION

Washington, DC
June 2016

THE JAMESTOWN FOUNDATION

Published in the United States by
The Jamestown Foundation
1310 L Street NW
Suite 810
Washington, DC 20005
http://www.jamestown.org

For more information on this book of The Jamestown Foundation, email pubs@jamestown.org.

ISBN: 978-0-9855045-5-7

Library of Congress Cataloging-in-Publication Data

Names: Bugajski, Janusz, 1954- author. | Assenova, Margarita author.
Title: Eurasian disunion : Russia's vulnerable flanks / Janusz Bugajski and
   Margarita Assenova.
Description: Washington, DC : The Jamestown Foundation, 2016.
Identifiers: LCCN 2015034025 | ISBN 9780985504557 (pbk.)
Subjects: LCSH: Russia (Federation)--Foreign relations--21st century. |
   Russia (Federation)--Boundaries. | Geopolitics--Russia (Federation) |
   Geopolitics--Eurasia.
Classification: LCC JZ1616 .B839 2015 | DDC 327.47--dc23
LC record available at http://lccn.loc.gov/2015034025

Cover art provided by Peggy Archambault of Peggy Archambault Design.

Jamestown's Mission

The Jamestown Foundation's mission is to inform and educate policy makers and the broader community about events and trends in those societies which are strategically or tactically important to the United States and which frequently restrict access to such information. Utilizing indigenous and primary sources, Jamestown's material is delivered without political bias, filter or agenda. It is often the only source of information which should be, but is not always, available through official or intelligence channels, especially in regard to Eurasia and terrorism.

Origins

Founded in 1984 by William Geimer, The Jamestown Foundation made a direct contribution to the downfall of Communism through its dissemination of information about the closed totalitarian societies of Eastern Europe and the Soviet Union.

William Geimer worked with Arkady Shevchenko, the highest-ranking Soviet official ever to defect when he left his position as undersecretary general of the United Nations. Shevchenko's memoir *Breaking With Moscow* revealed the details of Soviet superpower diplomacy, arms control strategy and tactics in the Third World, at the height of the Cold War. Through its work with Shevchenko, Jamestown rapidly became the leading source of information about the inner workings of the captive nations of the former Communist Bloc. In addition to Shevchenko, Jamestown assisted the former top Romanian intelligence officer Ion Pacepa in writing his memoirs. Jamestown ensured that both men published their insights and experience in what became bestselling books. Even today, several decades later, some credit Pacepa's revelations about Ceausescu's regime in his bestselling book *Red Horizons* with the fall of that government and the freeing of Romania.

The Jamestown Foundation has emerged as a leading provider of information about Eurasia. Our research and analysis on conflict and instability in Eurasia enabled Jamestown to become one of the most reliable sources of information on the post-Soviet space, the Caucasus and Central Asia as well as China. Furthermore, since 9/11, Jamestown has utilized its network of indigenous experts in more than 50 different countries to conduct research and analysis on terrorism and the growth of al-Qaeda and al-Qaeda offshoots throughout the globe.

By drawing on our ever-growing global network of experts, Jamestown has become a vital source of unfiltered, open-source information about major conflict zones around the world—from the Black Sea to Siberia, from the Persian Gulf to Latin America and the Pacific. Our core of intellectual talent includes former high-ranking government officials and military officers, political scientists, journalists, scholars and economists. Their insight contributes significantly to policymakers engaged in addressing today's newly emerging global threats in the post 9/11 world.

Table of Contents

iv

Acknowledgements

We would like to extend our utmost thanks to all the people we consulted and debated in Washington and along each of Russia's vulnerable flanks in the Wider Europe and Central Asia. Our sincere gratitude to The Jamestown Foundation and its President Glen Howard for being at the forefront of prescient analysis on Russia and the "Eurasian" world. Finally, exceptional praise for Matthew Czekaj, Program Associate for Europe and Eurasia at The Jamestown Foundation, for his outstanding and rapid reaction editing.

Foreword

This monumental work dissects the international ambitions of the Russian government under the presidency of Vladimir Putin. Since he gained power over fifteen years ago, the former KGB colonel has focused his attention on rebuilding a Moscow-centered bloc in order to return Russia to global superpower status and to compete geopolitically with the West. As a result of the Kremlin's expansionist objectives, the security of several regions that border the Russian Federation has been undermined and, in some cases, the national independence and territorial integrity of nearby states has been violated.

Janusz Bugajski and Margarita Assenova's thoroughly researched volume not only assesses Moscow's ambitions, strategies and tactics, it also meticulously details the various tools used by the Kremlin to integrate or subvert its neighbors and to weaken NATO and the European Union. It examines five major flanks along Russia's borders that are particularly prone to Moscow's aggressiveness—from the Arctic and the Baltic to the Caspian and Central Asia—and analyzes the various instruments of pressure that Moscow employs against individual states.

No other work of this depth and breadth has been produced to date. At a time when Russia's revisionism and expansionism is accelerating, it is essential reading for policymakers and students of competitive geopolitics. In addition to examining Russia's assertive policies, the authors assess the future role of NATO, the EU, and the US in the Wider Europe and offer several concrete policy recommendations for Washington and Brussels that would consolidate a more effective trans-Atlantic alliance to ensure the security of states bordering a volatile Russia.

Glen Howard
President, Jamestown Foundation
May 2016

Executive Summary

Russia's attack on Ukraine and the dismemberment of its territory is not an isolated operation. It constitutes one component of a broader strategic agenda to rebuild a Moscow-centered bloc designed to compete with the West. The acceleration of President Vladimir Putin's neo-imperial project has challenged the security of several regions that border the Russian Federation, focused attention on the geopolitical aspects of the Kremlin's ambitions, and sharpened the debate on the future role of NATO, the EU, and the US in the Wider Europe.

This book is intended to generate a more informed policy debate on the dangers stemming from the restoration of a Russian-centered "pole of power" or "sphere of influence" in Eurasia. It focuses on five vulnerable flanks bordering the Russian Federation—the Baltic and Nordic zones, East Central Europe, South East Europe, South Caucasus, and Central Asia. It examines several pivotal questions including: the strategic objectives of Moscow's expansionist ambitions; Kremlin tactics and capabilities; the impact of Russia's assertiveness on the national security of its neighbors; the responses of vulnerable states to Russia's geopolitical ambitions; the impact of prolonged regional turmoil on the stability of the Russian Federation and the survival of the Putinist regime; and the repercussions of heightened regional tensions for US, NATO, and EU policy toward Russia and toward unstable regions bordering the Russian Federation.

The book concludes with concrete policy recommendations for Washington and Brussels in the wake of the escalating confrontation with Russia. The Western approach toward Moscow needs to focus on consolidating a dynamic trans-Atlantic alliance, repelling and deterring a belligerent Russia, ensuring the security of all states bordering Russia, and preparing for a potential implosion of the Russian Federation.

1. Introduction: Russia's Imperial Agenda

Russia's attack on Ukraine in February 2014 and the subsequent dismemberment of its territory is not an isolated operation. It constitutes one component of a much broader strategic agenda to rebuild a Moscow-centered bloc that is intended to compete with the West. The acceleration of Vladimir Putin's neo-imperial project, prepared and implemented after he assumed the office of President in December 1999, has challenged the security of several regions that border the Russian Federation, refocused attention on the ideological and geopolitical aspects of the Kremlin's ambitions, and sharpened the debate on the future role of NATO, the European Union, and the United States in the Wider Europe.

To enable more effective Western responses to the growing threats from Moscow, urgently needed is a comprehensive assessment of the dangers stemming from the attempted restoration of a Russian-centered "pole of power" or "sphere of influence" in a loosely-defined "Eurasia." This book is intended to generate a more informed policy debate by focusing on five regional flanks bordering the Russian Federation that remain vulnerable to Moscow's subversion—the Baltic and Nordic zones (northern flank), East Central Europe (western flank), South East Europe (southwestern flank), South Caucasus (southern flank), and Central Asia (southeastern flank).

The book chronicles the diverse tools applied by the Kremlin against targeted neighbors and examines several pivotal questions: the strategic objectives of Moscow's expansionist ambitions; the Kremlin's tactics and capabilities; the impact of Russia's assertiveness on the national security of its neighbors; the responses of vulnerable states to Russia's geopolitical ambitions; the impact of prolonged regional turmoil on the stability of the Russian Federation and the survival of the Putinist regime; and the repercussions of heightened regional tensions for US, NATO, and EU policy toward Russia and toward unstable regions bordering the Russian Federation.

Moscow's Ambitions

Following Putin's installment as Russia's President on December 31, 1999, legitimized in presidential elections in March 2000, the Kremlin has been controlled by a narrow group of senior military, defense industry, and security service leaders, together with loyal state bureaucrats and tycoons or oligarchs owning or managing key national industries. This ruling elite is presided over by the primary decision-maker, former KGB (*Komitet Gosudarstvennoy Bezopasnosti,* Committee for State Security) Colonel Vladimir Putin. The balance of power between different political factions has been a wellspring of speculation for Kremlinologists. Nonetheless, regardless of potential factionalism and diverse sectoral interests, Russia's foreign policy objectives have proved relatively consistent under Putin's rule. The narrow elite has exhibited no substantive dissenting voices, and key national decisions are reached within the presidential administration and not in the government cabinet. In this centralized and hierarchical context, it is valuable to consider the contours of Russia's external policy goals.

Some analysts have difficulties in explaining Putin's motives.[1] Is staying in power the only ultimate goal, as a few observers have suggested, or is the prolonged maintenance of power necessary in order to achieve certain broader objectives?[2] The notion that the Kremlin's domestic politics rather than its security calculations are at the root of Moscow's foreign policy revanchism is too narrow and simplistic, as internal and external policies are closely intertwined. The maintenance of domestic power may be undergirded by personal ambitions, but it also incorporates broader dimensions to be effective, whether populist, messianic, nationalist, or imperialist. Putin appears to harbor a messiah complex, convinced that he serves a noble historical purpose to restore Russia's glory and power.[3] For Putin and his entourage, Russia is an imperial enterprise.

Putin spent the first few years of his presidency amassing personal control through the "power vertical" and by constructing a "managed democracy" beholden to the Kremlin. In this system, central and regional governments are selected by the Kremlin, parliament rubber stamps presidential decisions, presidential and parliamentary elections are defrauded, and the political opposition is harassed, marginalized, or outlawed. Putin's presidential tenure has also been substantially extended. Under the amended constitution, Putin was elected for the third time on May 7, 2012, for six years and will be entitled to run again for President in 2018 for another six-year mandate.

The notion that Putin's only objective is to stay in power and amass a personal fortune regardless of the risk to Russia's national interests fails to explain Moscow's assertive and confrontational foreign policy. It can be argued that deeper cooperation with the West would bring more extensive economic benefits and international legitimacy that would in turn strengthen Putin's position inside Russia and expand his private assets. Engineering conflicts with neighbors and provoking disputes with Western governments can undermine the President's position by damaging economic development and undermining Russia's global standing even though, in the short term, the Kremlin is able to mobilize society against alleged external enemies to raise Putin's popularity and support government policy.

The primary objective of Moscow's foreign policy is to restore Russia as a major center or pole of power in a multipolar or multi-centric world.[4] Following the return of Putin to Russia's presidency in May 2012, after the Dmitry Medvedev interlude (2008–2012), the Kremlin reinvigorated its global ambitions and regional assertiveness. It also made more explicit the overarching goal to reverse the predominance of the United States within Europe and Eurasia. Kremlin officials believe that the world should be organized around a new global version of the 19th century "Concert of Europe," in which a handful of great powers balance their interests and smaller countries orbit around them. This constitutes multipolarity rather than multilateralism. In practice, such an approach would entail restoring the Yalta-Potsdam post–World War Two divisions, in which Moscow dominates Eurasia and half of Europe, but with a substantially diminished US presence in Europe. This would provide Russia with strategic depth in its active opposition to the West, including its professed values and security structures.

Western observers frequently repeat the observation that Putin is a tactician and not a strategist, but invariably fail to distinguish between the two. In essence, tactics are short-term methods while strategies are longer-term policies, and both are intended to achieve specific objectives. While its goals are imperial, Kremlin strategies and tactics are flexible and "pragmatic" and this can make them more effective than a rigid approach. They include enticements, threats, incentives, pressures, and a variety of subversive actions where Russia's national interests are deemed to predominate over those of its neighbors. By claiming that it is pursuing "pragmatic" national interests, the Kremlin engages in a combination of offensives by interjecting itself in neighbors' affairs, capturing important sectors of local economies, subverting vulnerable political systems, corrupting national leaders, penetrating key security institutions, undermining national and territorial unity, conducting propaganda offensives through a spectrum of media and social outlets, and deploying a host of other tools to weaken obstinate governments that resist Moscow.

Putin is often depicted in the West as an "opportunist" and not a strategist. However, opportunism is simply a means of benefiting from favorable circumstances and not an objective in itself. The question is what are Putin's objectives in creating or benefiting from opportunities to assert Russian power? Several analysts believe that the President may not have a coherent plan or goal to extend or revive the Russian empire, but may be simply acting out of spite to undermine security in neighboring countries and to obstruct Western enlargement.[5] Other analysts not only challenge the existence of any plans for imperial restoration, but also claim that the Kremlin simply acts defensively to protect its interests in neighboring states from an expanding and threatening West.[6]

There is some confusion in such assessments between Russia's ambitions and capabilities. While Moscow's goals remain fairly clear, as the government has consistently stated and acted to consolidate a predominant sphere of influence in territories designated as the "post-Soviet space," the regional extent of this Russian sphere, the response of each targeted country, and the ability to accomplish such a task without provoking substantial international resistance are much less predictable. Hence, the methods employed by the Kremlin require substantial flexibility, eclecticism, opportunism, and improvisation.

Since Russia's attack on Ukraine in early 2014, the term "hybrid war" has been widely employed to describe Moscow's subversion of a targeted neighbor.[7] While the concept generally signifies that the Kremlin deploys a mix of instruments against its adversaries, it fails to pinpoint the tactics, objectives, capabilities, and results of Moscow's offensive. It also assumes that the Kremlin has invented a novel form of warfare rather than pursuing a modern adaptation of traditional attempts to subvert the psychology, economy, polity, society, and military of specific states without necessarily engaging in a direct military offensive.

Russia's neo-imperial geopolitical project no longer relies on Soviet-era mechanisms vis-à-vis bordering states, such as strict ideological allegiance, the penetration and control of local ruling parties and security services, periodic military force, the permanent stationing of Russian troops, and almost complete enmeshment with the Russian economy. Instead, sufficient tools of pressure are applied to try and ensure the primary goal—for Moscow to exert predominant influence over the foreign and security policies of immediate neighbors so that they will either remain neutral or support Russia's international agenda and not challenge the legitimacy of the Putinist system. The ultimate goal is to establish protectorates around the country's borders, which do not forge close and independent ties with each other and do not enter Western institutions.

In this expansionist international context, it is useful to distinguish between Russia's national interests and its state ambitions. Moscow's security is not challenged by the accession to NATO of neighboring states. However, its ability to control the security dimensions and foreign policy orientations of these countries is challenged by their incorporation in the Alliance because NATO provides security guarantees against Russia's potential aggression.

While pursuing a neo-imperial agenda, Moscow has also calculated that if it cannot control the security policies of its neighbors, it is preferable to have uncertainty and insecurity along its borders. This enables the Kremlin to frighten its own public with perceptions of threat to Russia's stability and to undermine the NATO and EU accession prospects of several neighbors. An assertive foreign policy helps to distract attention from convulsions inside the Russian Federation. Putin's policy is presented as vital to national security by protecting Russia from internal turmoil, avowedly sponsored by Washington, in which NATO and EU enlargement is portrayed as evidence of aggressive "Russophobia."

In its eclectic ideological packaging, Putinism consists of a blend of Russian statism, great power chauvinism, pan-Slavism, pan-Orthodoxy, multi-ethnic Eurasianism, Russian nationalism (with increasing ethno-historical ingredients), social conservatism, anti-liberalism, anti-Americanism, and anti-Westernism. At the heart of this heady brew is the notion of restoring Russia's glory and global status that was allegedly subdued and denied after the collapse of the Soviet Union through a combination of Western subversion and domestic treason.

In reviving the image of greatness, Russia continues to live in the categories of World War Two. The officially promoted historical narrative of the "Great Patriotic War" has been employed as a source of national unity and loyalty to the state. The war is a key element in Moscow's self-glorifying propaganda. Russia is presented as a global power with a stellar history, while Stalinism is depicted as a necessary system that modernized the state and defeated Nazi Germany. This imparts the message that the current authoritarian regime can also violate human rights and capsize living standards, as long as it is determined to restore the glory of the "Russian World" *(Russkiy Mir)*. World War Two myths in Russia present two stark stereotypes: people who support the Kremlin are patriots and antifascists, while those who oppose are labeled as fascists regardless of actual political persuasions.[8]

The Putin administration believes that it can violate human rights and the integrity of neighboring states in the service of restoring Russia's glory. The "ideology of identity" has grown into a vital component of national populism, expressed in the concept of the "Russian World." This collectivist formula is both cultural and genetic and supposedly includes all Russian ethnics, Russian speakers, and descendants of both categories in any country. The term is underpinned by statist messianism, whereby the Russian government is obliged by history and divine fate to protect this broad community and defend it in particular against Western influences. Various elements of Soviet *chekism* (or the cult of state security) have also been revived and presented as a rebirth of national pride: "Growing reverence for the security apparatus reflects a broader trend toward reverence for strong statehood in Russia."[9] Putin is heralded as a *chekist* patriot who is restoring Russia's internal order and international stature.

Russia's Capabilities

As a resurgent neo-imperialist power that seeks to prove its robustness, Russia cannot display weakness toward the West. Hence, the country's economic limitations and escalating internal problems are disguised by state propaganda, while the recreation of a Eurasian bloc is supposed to demonstrate that Russia is a rising power and not a declining empire. Although Putin's ambition to create a new Moscow-centered Eurasian Union is unlikely to be successful, given Russia's ongoing economic decline and the resistance of most neighboring states, attempts to create such a bloc could destabilize a broad region along Russia's long flanks, particularly throughout Europe's East and in Central Asia.

As the largest Kremlin target, Ukraine serves as a valuable example of the impact of Moscow's imperial ambitions. After Putin returned to Russia's Presidency in May 2012, the Kremlin began to intensify its pressures on the former Soviet republics to participate in its integrationist projects. Moscow became fearful that the post-Soviet territories could drift permanently into either the Western or Chinese "spheres of influence." Putin's Eurasian alliance is thereby designed to balance the EU and NATO in the west and China in the east. Economic linkages are intended to reinforce political and security connections, making it less likely that Russia's neighbors can join alternative blocs.

To achieve its ambitions, Moscow needs to assemble around itself a cluster of states that are loyal or subservient to Russian foreign policy and security interests. Unlike the EU—where states voluntarily pool their sovereignty, decisions are taken by consensus, and no single state dominates decision-making—in Moscow's integrative institutions, countries are expected to permanently surrender elements of their sovereignty to the center. Since the collapse of the Soviet Union, the major multi-national organizations promoted by the Kremlin to enhance Eurasian integration have included the Commonwealth of Independent States (CIS), the Collective Security Treaty Organization (CSTO), the Eurasian Economic Community (EEC), the Customs Union (CU), and the Eurasian Economic Union (EEU). The EEU was formally established in January 2015 as the optimal multi-national format.[10]

The transition to the EEU has been described as the final goal of economic integration and is to include a free trade regime, unified customs and nontariff regulation measures, common access to internal markets, a unified transportation system, a common energy market, and a single currency. These integrative economic measures are to be undergirded by a tighter political and security alliance both through the CSTO and in bilateral arrangements with Russia.[11]

Putin was encouraged in his neo-imperial restorationist endeavors by favorable international conditions, most evident in the approach of President Barack Obama's administration. As a by-product of the White House accommodating "reset" policy toward Moscow, launched in early 2009, Washington curtailed its campaign to enlarge NATO and secure the post-Soviet neighborhood within Western structures. This increased the vulnerability of several states to Moscow's pressures and enticements and convinced Putin that his freedom of maneuver in the post-Soviet sphere was expanding. Belarus, Moldova, Ukraine, Georgia, Azerbaijan, and the Central Asian states were not priority interests for the White House, and some US policy makers appeared to approve of a Russian political and economic umbrella over these countries.

The net impact of the Obama approach was to convince Moscow that the US was withdrawing from international commitments after the Iraq and Afghanistan wars and had neither the resources, political will, nor public support to challenge Russia's re-imperialization. Moscow also concluded that despite the EU's Eastern Partnership outreach program, the European Union would remain divided and preoccupied with its internal problems and would not challenge Russia's economic hegemony among its immediate neighbors. Moscow's assumptions have been partly vindicated by the ease of its division of Ukraine, through the capture of Crimea, and the limited economic sanctions imposed by Western capitals. Nonetheless, Russia's assault on Ukraine has also unleashed protective measures in several neighboring states and revived calls for strengthening NATO's presence throughout Europe's East.

In the aftermath of the crisis over Ukraine, Moscow has reanimated the Western geopolitical scapegoat. It justifies its attack on Ukraine as a necessary offensive to counter Western subversion and destabilization. Russia's leaders depict the West as dangerous and unpredictable, and accuse the US of using "irregular warfare" such as NGOs and multinational institutions, including the International Monetary Fund (IMF), to conduct "color revolutions" and destabilize Russia. [12] Hence, any attempt at democratization along its borders makes Russia more vulnerable to Western machinations. Russia is also allegedly the victim of NATO expansion, whereby the incorporation of East Central Europe (ECE) in the North Atlantic Alliance was primarily intended to undermine Moscow. The next stage purportedly planned by Washington is to foster conflicts within the Russian Federation by using civil society, mass media, and human rights groups and by supporting Islamic insurgencies. Westernization is deemed a subversive weapon embodying many elements of Russophobia.

Putin has declared that Russia is under a growing multitude of outside threats emanating from the US and its allies. In particular, the West purportedly organized and provoked the Ukrainian crisis in 2014 in order to have an excuse to reinvigorate NATO and deploy Western forces closer to Russia's borders. Moscow will respond by deploying new offensive nuclear weapons aimed at Western nations, by updating its air and missile defense system, and by producing new precision-guided weapons.[13] Moscow is also determined to violate any treaty that obstructs its imperial agenda, including the December 1994 Budapest Memorandum on Security Assurances intended to guarantee the inviolability of Ukraine's borders.

Russia's new military doctrine signed by Putin in December 2014 describes an increasingly threatening international environment that can generate problems at home.[14] It claims intensifying "global competition" and direct threats emanating from NATO and the US in particular. The document contends that among the most serious regional hazards are conspiracies to "overturn legitimate government" in neighboring states and establish regimes that threaten Russia's interests. Such alleged American ploys are linked with the placement of Western forces in countries adjoining Russia and NATO's development of anti-ballistic missile (ABM), space-based, and rapid reaction forces. The new military doctrine also calls for Moscow to counter the use of communications technologies against Russia, such as cyber-warfare and social networks.

Moscow asserts that it will counter Western attempts to gain strategic superiority by deploying strategic missile defense systems.[15] It also reserve the right to use nuclear weapons in response to the use of nuclear or other weapons of mass destruction against Russia or its allies, and even in case of "aggression" against Russia with conventional weapons that would endanger the existence of the state.

The underlying geopolitical objective of the Eurasian Economic Union (EEU) is to create an alternative power center to EU integration.[16] However, the politically motivated EEU is a protectionist arrangement that will cost Russia substantial amounts of resources, harm its economy, and further alienate the country internationally. It may also retard the economic development of other integrated states. By contrast, the "deep and comprehensive free trade agreements" (DCFTA) offered by the EU to many post-Soviet states is based on the removal of tariff barriers and the adoption of a large part of EU regulations. The stimulus offered by the EU for integration into its internal market restricts Russia's opportunities to maintain political control over these states. It also promotes commitments to EU principles of legalism and governance and the application of regulatory standards in exchange for access to a market with a population of 500 million and with rapid growth potential.[17]

By contrast, EEU membership could mean lower energy prices, freer trade in the Eurasian space with a population of 170 million but with significantly lower purchasing power than in the EU, as well as slow economic restructuring and the strengthening of oligarchic and authoritarian management. In exchange for low energy prices and access to its domestic market, Russia intends to take over strategic sectors of the EEU economies and strengthen its influence within member states. This would guarantee that each state remains tethered to Russia regardless of leadership changes and the temptations of Western integration.

Through enhanced free trade agreements, the EU does not prevent further integration of the post-Soviet countries with each other, but once they become parties to Russia's Customs Union and the EEU, they are deprived of the opportunity to have bilateral agreements with the EU. Hence, each European capital needs to make a choice, as participation in customs agreements involving countries that have not harmonized their legislative framework with EU requirements precludes free trade with the EU. In sum, the EEU is incompatible with the core principles of the EU's external policy: it remains a project for trade simplification between non-liberal regimes.

Russia's escalating economic difficulties following the drastic fall in crude oil prices in 2014–2015 and the gradual impact of Western financial sanctions led to a ruble crisis and heightened the risk of maintaining close economic ties with Russia. All three of Moscow's EEU partners (Armenia, Belarus, and Kazakhstan) have been negatively affected by the collapse in value of Russia's currency.[18] For instance, the decline in the Russian market because of Western sanctions and the collapse of oil prices has cost the Belarusian economy almost $3 billion.[19] Moreover, the EEU is rife with internal divisions that will render it ineffective and unattractive to the broader region. In a sign of growing friction, after Moscow imposed retaliatory sanctions on EU agricultural produce in the summer of 2014, Belarus benefitted by re-exporting EU goods to Russia. The Kremlin reacted in November 2014 by banning the import of meat and dairy products from Belarus. In sum, divisions between an economically unstable Russia and its anxious neighbors will result in an ineffective and weak EEU.

The most grievous repercussions of Moscow's empire building have been witnessed in Ukraine, which remains the key prize in Kremlin plans to recombine the former Soviet republics. With control over Ukraine, Moscow could project its influence into Central Europe; without Ukraine, the planned Eurasian bloc would become a largely north Asian construct or a patchwork of states most susceptible to Moscow's pressures.

The anti-Ukrainian war launched in February 2014 was coordinated from the Kremlin, as only the President's office possesses the levers of control necessary to conduct such an operation. The Kremlin's main fear in Ukraine was not the avowedly endangered status of the Russian-speaking population. Its public paranoia was rooted in the prospect of Ukraine developing into a democratic, unified, and increasingly prosperous state that moves toward EU accession and eventual NATO membership. Such a model of development could become increasingly attractive for Russia's other neighbors and even for some of Russia's diverse regions. This would challenge the legitimacy and longevity of the kleptocratic and authoritarian Putinist system. For the Putinists, an independent and democratic Ukraine symbolizes everything that threatens their hold on power and disrupts plans to restore a Greater Russia. At the core of this deep hostility is the convenient conviction that Kyiv experienced a *coup d'état* camouflaged as a "color revolution" engineered by the West and ultimately designed to destroy Russia.

The various "color revolutions," whether Rose in Georgia (2003) or Orange in Ukraine (2004), are viewed in the West as indigenous attempts to prevent authoritarian backsliding, electoral manipulation, and popular disenfranchisement in the post-Soviet world. US and Western European organizations may have played supportive roles in these popular rebellions, but it was local activists who mobilized the public against the abusive elites. The ultimate outcome of such rebellions may be corroded or even reversed over time, but they provide hope that broader sectors of society can have a voice in the political process.

For Russian officials and pro-Kremlin analysts, "color revolutions" are negative phenomenon imposed from outside with unpredictable consequences. And if the results threaten to culminate in democratic reforms and Western integration, then the revolutions must be countered. Hence, the covert attack and partition of Ukraine are intended to prove that Ukraine is a failing state. Furthermore, in all post-Soviet countries, regardless of their political structures, the Kremlin seeks to limit national sovereignty by deciding on their foreign policy and security orientations.

In justifying foreign intervention, Aleksandr Bortnikov, head of the KGB successor, the Federal Security Service (*Federalnaya Sluzhba Bezopasnosti*, FSB), stated that his agency would react quickly and harshly to any attempt to overthrow existing regimes in the post-Soviet countries.[20] This indicates a pervasive fear in the Kremlin that the Ukrainian revolution against a government devoid of public trust could be replicated in Russia itself. Bortnikov claimed that "destructive forces" were financed by Western NGOs, thereby giving Russia's security services a license to target social activists, private institutions, and the liberal political opposition at home and to combat Western-inspired revolutions among its neighbors.

Arsenal of Subversion

Moscow employs diverse tools and methods to undermine its adversaries and to control its allies. It pursues various forms of subversion against specific states, with the exact recipe of policies dependent on the vulnerabilities and responses of targeted capitals. The Kremlin arsenal consists of a mixture of threats, pressures, enticements, rewards, and punishments, and it can be grouped into eight main clusters: international, informational, ideological, economic, ethnic, political, social, and military.

International

1. *Diplomatic Pressures:* High-level visits by Russian dignitaries or the deliberate snubbing of certain governments serve as standard diplomatic devices to extract concessions and voice approval or disapproval for specific foreign policies. Treaties and other inter-state agreements are highlighted, ignored, or rejected to exert pressure on specific governments. Even when bilateral treaties recognizing existing borders are signed with neighbors, their ratification by the parliament is deliberately delayed or their validity is overlooked. Sometimes, grander historical justifications are offered that purportedly invalidate an existing accord, as witnessed in the forceful annexation of Crimea from Ukraine in 2014.

The Russian parliament (*Duma*) also influences the political climate through combative statements and radical policy prescriptions by deputies that may make the government appear more moderate. This injects a sense of threat toward neighbors and raises regional anxieties. For instance, some *Duma* deputies have questioned the legality of the break-up of the USSR and the independence of the Baltic states and other former Soviet republics.

2. ***Deceptive Diplomacy:*** This can include offers of peace talks, mediation efforts, and conflict resolution at a time when Moscow is pursuing state dismemberment and other forms of subversion against specific neighbors. Deception, disinformation, and denial of responsibility for aggression are customary hallmarks of Russian foreign policy. Deception operations to mislead foreign political and military leaders are coordinated and conducted through diplomatic channels and government agencies in which false information is leaked and actual policy measures are camouflaged. Moscow also favors secret and bilateral meetings with US and EU representatives that can decide on some pressing questions in order to split any unified position by its Western adversaries.

3. ***Strategic Posturing:*** Instead of posing as a superior systemic and economic alternative to the West, as it did during the Soviet era, the Kremlin depicts Russia as an indispensable global partner. Supposedly, cooperation with Moscow is vital in resolving numerous international problems, including Iran's and North Korea's nuclear programs, the spread of *jihadist* terrorism, the proliferation of Weapons of Mass Destruction (WMD), global climate change, economic security, and a number of regional disputes. To underscore Russia's importance and gain advantages in other areas, officials engage in strategic blackmail by asserting that they can terminate their diplomatic assistance to Washington

or Brussels if they are opposed in some other policy domain. Conversely, the positive outcome of US-Russia cooperation may be stressed in various arenas to remove the spotlight from Moscow's attack on a neighbor, to discourage Western sanctions, and to encourage further collaboration. The overriding message is that Russia must be afforded a free hand in its post-Soviet neighborhood in return for its cooperation on matters of more vital concern to Washington and Brussels.

4. *International Self-Defense:* Russian leaders portray the country as the bastion of international law and the defender of independent statehood around the globe. Russia's "sovereign democracy" is displayed as a valid political model that can be emulated more widely, especially as protection against American imperialism. Washington is supposedly intent on severing economic ties between Russia and the EU in order to boost America's competitive position. It is also encircling Russia with loyal regimes, building a missile defense system to disarm Russia, and taking other aggressive measures to prevent Moscow from restoring its rightful role as a global power. Such policies are allegedly mirrored toward other emerging powers, particularly China. In an act of self-defense to counterbalance US political and economic hegemony, Moscow has formed the Eurasian Economic Union (EEU) and the Collective Security Treaty Organization (CSTO) on the former Soviet territories and is an active member of the Shanghai Cooperation Organization (SCO) and the BRICS (Brazil, Russia, India, China and South Africa) initiative. It casts itself as the bastion of global protection against the aggressive West and a hegemonic America.

5. *Ambassadorial Interference:* The appointment of high-ranking or Kremlin-connected Russian politicians as ambassadors to neighboring states engenders a more intensive involvement in domestic politics and resembles a quasi-colonial or protectorate relationship. In some cases, as in Serbia, Montenegro, and

Macedonia, Russian ambassadors have been publicly outspoken against NATO enlargement and pose as the defenders of incumbent governments against Western pressures and US interference. Conversely, some foreign diplomats stationed in Moscow and other Russian cities have been subject to verbal and physical harassment as well as media defamation with the evident approval of the authorities in Moscow.

6. *Espionage Enhancement:* A substantial increase in Russian embassy staff has been recorded in every Central and East European capital since Putin's assumption of power in 1999, indicating that espionage activities have greatly expanded through Russia's missions abroad. Russia has hundreds of intelligence officers at work in Europe, recruiting thousands of agents.[21] They are sometimes based at embassies and other diplomatic missions under official cover, but in many cases work as business people, academics, or students to penetrate targeted societies. Russia's three major espionage services have benefited from increasing funding during Putin's term: the Foreign Intelligence Service (*Sluzhba Vneshney Razvedki, SVR*); the Federal Security Service (*Federalnaya Sluzhba Bezopasnosti, FSB*), and the military intelligence service (*Glavnoye Razvedyvatelnoye Upravleniye, GRU*). SVR, FSB, and GRU operations against the West have expanded to levels reminiscent of the height of the Cold War. Many of the spies are younger and more educated than during the Soviet era and have an ideological commitment to restoring Russia's global status.

7. *Spy Recruitment:* Russia's espionage networks help identify corruptible or otherwise vulnerable politicians, officials, businesspeople, journalists, academics, and other public figures in the West. They also seek to recruit border guards and law enforcement personnel as informers. Moscow has also accumulated substantial experience in conducting "false flag"

operations, in which individuals are recruited under the guise of different causes, such as environmentalism, media freedom, minority rights, or campaigns against government surveillance in the West.

8. *Intelligence Penetration:* Former intelligence and counter-intelligence contacts in the former Communist states are utilized by Moscow, especially as some governments have possessed a limited new pool of agents and continue to employ professionals with ex-KGB connections. Western intelligence services remain concerned about Communist-era links and have demanded the protection of intelligence sources and a thorough screening of operatives, especially if a country aspires to NATO entry. Periodic revelations about the extent of Russia's espionage also serve Kremlin objectives by discrediting the trustworthiness and competence of government agencies in states canvassing for NATO accession or already Alliance members but supposedly penetrated by hostile foreign services.

9. *Creating Legal Chaos:* Russia is creating legal chaos in a number of neighboring countries where it has intervened to establish or occupy separate territorial units or to annex them. "Frozen conflicts" are *de facto* territories where these is legal confusion for local residents. By annexing Crimea, supporting separatism in Abkhazia and South Ossetia, backing secessionism in Transnistria, and propping up independence claims in the Donbas region of Ukraine, Russia creates legal pandemonium that may never be resolved.

The main legal problems resulting from these actions concern citizenship. In Crimea, a large share of the population retains Ukrainian citizenship and opposes Russia's annexation of the peninsula. In the Russian-occupied Georgian provinces of Abkhazia and South Ossetia, thousands of Georgians refuse to denounce their citizenship and face harassment and frequent detention by the self-proclaimed authorities.[22] In Moldova, the majority of Transnistria's residents hold Russian, Ukrainian, or some other passports besides Moldovan, as the Transnistrian document is not recognized internationally and is not valid for travel. However, in 2014, thousands of Transnistrian residents applied to obtain Moldovan passports to take advantage of Moldova's newly granted visa-free regime with the EU, despite Tiraspol's request to the Russian *Duma* to draft a law that would allow their territory to join Russia.[23] By the end of 2014, half of Transnistria's residents had confirmed their Moldovan citizenship.[24]

Moscow is finding it particularly difficult to bring Crimea into the common Russian legal space, because of differences in Ukrainian and Russian laws, penal codes, property deeds registration, benefits distribution, as well as the existing shortage of judiciary staff in the peninsula. According to Russian legal experts, even if a complete adaptation to Russian laws is concluded within two to three years, implementation will take much longer and the process will have an impact on Russia's own legal system.[25]

10. *Criminal Exploitation:* Russia's extensive international criminal networks are both a destabilizing socio-economic element and a tool of Moscow's political interests. The security services maintain close links with organized criminal syndicates, whereby the criminals obtain enhanced protection and the espionage network gains intelligence and wider access in targeted states. The Kremlin benefits from organized crime to penetrate neighboring economies, judiciaries, and political systems, and to operate as a shadow intelligence agency.[26]

Informational

11. *Cyberspace Warfare*: This includes systematic assaults and denial-of-service (DDoS) attacks on government sites by Kremlin-orchestrated hackers, as witnessed in Estonia, Georgia, and Ukraine during their confrontations with Moscow. It can also entail the monitoring of telecommunications and infecting targeted networks with various viruses. For instance, in 2014 a Russian hacking group exploited a previously unknown flaw in Microsoft's Windows operating system to spy on NATO, Ukraine's government, and other national security targets.[27] The group has been active since 2009, according to research by iSight Partners, a cyber security firm. Its targets in the 2014 campaign also included a Polish energy firm, a Western European government agency, and a French telecommunications company.

12. *Trolling Offensives:* The Kremlin recruits trolls either to write imaginary and inflammatory news reports or to disrupt the social media with provocative and disruptive comments.[28] The Kremlin's "troll army" reportedly includes hundreds of paid bloggers who saturate Internet forums, social networks, and comments sections of Western publications with diatribes lambasting the West and praising Putin. Kremlin-sponsored youth groups are believed to fund online trolling activities. Following its attack on Ukraine, Moscow substantially increased its trolling offensives; Ukrainian news outlets have published long lists of people and sites that featured the activities of pro-Kremlin trolls.

13. *Propaganda Attacks:* Russia's "information offensive" or overall propaganda assault on the West is widely organized and well funded. During the Cold War, Soviet authorities used the term "active measures" to denote a combination of propaganda and action by the KGB to promote Moscow's foreign policy objectives. Subversive propaganda seeks to create an alternative reality in

which all truth is relative and no information can be trusted, thereby disguising the facts about Moscow's regional aggression against countries such as Ukraine.[29] Nonetheless, such attacks also have a simple underlying narrative: that the US is seeking to rule the world and only Russia can stop Washington's drive for empire. This propaganda relies on four main tactics: dismissing the critic, distorting the facts, distracting from the main issue, and dismaying the audience.

14. *Media Controls:* Moscow's direct or indirect control over numerous television and radio outlets in Russia that broadcast programs to most former Soviet republics is a valuable instrument for influencing public opinion and political elites in neighboring states. This has been plainly evident in Belarus, Ukraine, and Moldova where a majority of citizens, and not only Russian ethnics, regularly watch and listen to the Moscow media, which is often more attractively packaged than local stations, in the form of "infotainment." The lack of professionalism and a penchant for sensationalism in much of the local media has also assisted Moscow's objectives in planting misleading information for political ends.

15. *Disinformation Campaigns:* More systematic and pinpointed disinformation campaigns are conducted against particular governments, politicians, or pro-Western political parties in nearby states. They can also target Western ambassadors in Moscow or other capitals. Through its smear campaigns, Russian state propaganda often combines facts with cleverly disguised falsehoods.[30] Moscow's message is given undue exposure due to an inability of some Western editors and journalists to distinguish between balance and objectivity, as well as the existence of a sizable constituency in the West, including businesspeople, academics, consultants, and journalists, whose jobs may depend on maintaining cordial relations with Russia. Disinformation can combine traditional media with the social media that help spread

hoax stories. It taps into the widespread propensity in all societies for repeating and believing conspiracy theories, however outlandish.

16. *Media Manipulation:* Russian outlets at home and abroad use the open Western media to create an environment favorable to Moscow by manipulating political and public opinion. This includes using intelligence operatives as journalists, bribing Western reporters, and presenting a diametrically opposed position to that of rivals to create the impression that the truth lies somewhere in the middle. For instance, Russian federal television and radio channels, newspapers, and online resources were employed in the concerted disinformation campaign against Ukraine in 2014–2015, in which the Kremlin denied any involvement in the war. Diplomats, politicians, political analysts, and representatives of academic and cultural elites supported this "disinformation front."[31] The Kremlin media also exploit Western commentators to validate the regime's messages. These "fellow travelers" fall into three categories: those who work or worked for the Kremlin but do not make their affiliations public; those who are apparently independent but support Russia's policies; and those who may not support Moscow's line, but whose words can be quoted in a way that appears to show that they do.[32]

17. *Media Creation:* Rival media outlets can be established in other states, including the television channel *RT* (formerly *Russia Today*), whose propagandists assert that the public is seeking an alternative and trustworthy source of information. The goal is to provide information and analysis that contrasts with the Western media, alleging that the latter is monolithic and serves government interests.[33] However, the stories covered are often skewered and incomplete in order to present Western officials in a negative light. The Kremlin has also enhanced its global outreach through its new *Sputnik* web and radio service that combines the print and

broadcast services of *Voice of Russia* with *RIA Novosti*. This propaganda outlet targets over 130 cities in 34 countries and will be available in at least 27 languages. All former Soviet republics will host a *Sputnik* hub that will broadcast in local languages and English. Moscow substantially increased spending for its foreign-focused media outlets for 2015, budgeting $400 million for its *RT* television channel and $170 million for *Rossiya Segodnya*, the state news agency that includes *Sputnik* News.

18. ***Psychological Operations:*** Russia's state-linked propaganda specializes in spreading confusion, fear, insecurity, panic, hysteria, and paranoia among targeted audiences abroad to deflate public morale, foster defeatism and demoralization, and reduce trust in national governments and international institutions. Propaganda can create uncertainty and ambiguity, thereby preventing any immediate response to Russia's aggressive actions. As part of Moscow's propaganda offensive to stoke fear and uncertainty along its borders, in June 2015 the Russian Prosecutor General's Office was asked by *Duma* deputies from the ruling United Russia party to examine whether the independence of the three Baltic states was legitimate according to the Soviet constitution.[34] Such a move served to question the sovereignty of all former Soviet republics and to legitimize Russia's interference in their domestic and foreign affairs.

19. ***Disarming Opponents:*** "Psychops" can purposively inculcate cynicism among the audience, convincing them that no government is truthful and that the Russian and Western positions deserve equal treatment. The ultimate goal of all psychological operations is to influence political decisions in other countries and to undermine the will to resist or oppose Moscow's policies. Russia's informational wars are often geared toward "reflexive control," in which under the influence of specially prepared information the adversary acts in a way that suits the

Kremlin, whether the response is defensive or aggressive. In the domestic context, state propaganda may also encourage public passivity and fear, so that the Russian population does not challenge government policy. Psychops also manipulate and channel resentments and grievances inside Russian society toward Western scapegoats who are deemed primarily responsible for the country's problems.

Ideological

20. *Claiming Victimization:* State propaganda depicts Russia as a victim of Western subterfuge and aggression and periodically heightens perceptions of threat and danger to confirm its assertions. Officials cultivate a sense of grievance and resentment against the West for Russia's alleged humiliation after the Soviet collapse.[35] According to Moscow's propagandists, the West either wants to eradicate Russia or to absorb it in the West: either way the purpose is to eliminate its uniqueness. Putin's rule has ensured that Russia will no longer retreat while under pressure from its adversaries and will not succumb to destructive Western enticements couched as democratization and globalization. Victimization provides justification for the maintenance of a strong state and an authoritarian leadership that intends to restore the country's military power, territorial reach, regional influence, and global ambitions.

21. *Alleging Encirclement:* Russia is surrounded by ostensible enemies and needs to pursue an aggressive posture to combat them. Moscow claims that NATO and the EU are encircling the country, pushing it into a corner, and forcing it to lash out. In an elaborate justification for its attack on Ukraine in 2014–2015, Moscow charges that Washington organized the overthrow of the legitimate government in Kyiv primarily to create an excuse for reinvigorating NATO and deploying American forces closer to

Russia's borders. In reality, NATO has been increasing its defensive presence in the region to deter Moscow's escalating threats against Alliance members.

Russia's leaders also contend that the US uses "irregular warfare" such as NGOs and multinational institutions, including the IMF, to conduct "colored revolutions" and destabilize Russia's dominions. The next stage planned by Washington is to foster conflicts within the Russian Federation by exploiting civil society, the liberal opposition, the mass media, and human rights groups, and by supporting Islamic insurgencies in the North Caucasus. The goal is to destroy Russia's unity, capture its territory, and exploit its natural resources.

22. *Imagining Russophobia:* Putin has made the struggle against "Russophobia" a cornerstone of his eclectic ideology, depicting Russians as an ostracized people despised by Western powers. Criticisms of Russian government policy by alleged Russophobes purportedly indicates a prejudicial disposition, a psychological illness, or a personality disorder. Some propagandists have sought to equate Russophobia with anti-Semitism thus depicting criticisms of Moscow's policies as a form of racism, which should be internationally condemned and outlawed. Almost any incident that casts Russia in an unfavorable light can be depicted as motivated by Russophobia. Hence, Kremlin spokesmen have portrayed the shooting down of a Malaysian passenger plane over Donbas on July 17, 2015, by a missile fired from an area controlled by pro-Moscow rebels as a Western plot to discredit Russia.

23. *Russian Supremacism:* Moscow's imperial ambitions are undergirded by the concept of the "Russian World" (*Russki Mir*). According to this notion, all ethnic groups living on the territory of the former Soviet Union form part of a distinct multi-national entity and should be brought within the same state or multi-state union. Several categories of people are included in the "Russian

World," including ethnic Russians, regardless of where they live; Russian-speakers and alphabet users, regardless of their ethnicity; and "compatriots" and their offspring who have ever lived on the territory of the Soviet Union or even in the Russian Empire.[36] Russian officials and the Kremlin's ideological preachers frequently stress the manifest destiny of the allegedly unique Russian culture and the deeply spiritual "Russian soul" infused with a "special morality." They deliberately ignore the deep demoralization evident in Russian society, as exemplified in its demographic trends including shorter life spans, declining fertility rates, and rising alcoholism. Russia's alleged spiritualty is supposed to compensate for its economic failures.

24. *Russian Unification:* The concept of a "Russian World'" is based on the assumption of a divided nation following the collapse of the Soviet Union. By promulgating Russian culture, education, language use, and political mobilization in neighboring states, Moscow tries to create the illusion in the West that these countries belong within Russia's cultural and political space. Hence, the government is simply pursuing a natural course of unification. The *Russki Mir* concept has been introduced into several laws creating the legal basis for protecting compatriots abroad. One of the laws provides for the legal right to use Russian troops in other countries to actively defend these compatriots.

25. *Pan-Slavism:* In Russia's official version of history, Ukrainians and Belarusians are considered to be offshoots of the Russian nation.[37] This is based on the historically incorrect idea that Kyivan Rus (9th to 13th centuries AD) was a "Russian" state. In fact, there were no distinct Russians, Ukrainians, or Belarusians during that period in history but numerous East Slavic tribes and tribal unions. After the 14th century, Muscovite Russians formed an enduring state entity that subsequently occupied Ukraine and Belarus for long periods and imposed the Russian language,

church, and culture on the local populations. As a result, Moscow believes it has the right to control all the East Slavic peoples and those that are opposed are dismissed as traitors, as is the case with many Ukrainians since the Maidan revolution. Russian pan-Slavism is also extended by its proponents to include selected South Slavic and West Slavic groups by appealing to those nationalist elements that traditionally view Moscow as a protector and liberator from Turkic, Germanic, and other occupying powers. This often includes Serbia and Bulgaria.

26. *Religious Invocations:* The Russian Orthodox Church is vocal in defending the allegedly endangered Christian Orthodox faithful in neighboring countries. It has a long tradition of serving as an instrument of government foreign policy before, during, and after the Communist interlude. The Moscow Patriarchate helps to maintain Russian influence within the former USSR among Orthodox believers and promotes anti-Western, illiberal, and anti-democratic values by stressing the divine nature of Russian nationalism and pan-Slavism.

Putin has revived Joseph Stalin's instrumentalization of the Orthodox Church and gained Patriarch Kirill's blessing for his trans-national "Russian World" concept.[38] Moscow steers the Patriarchate to exert its influence in states such as Ukraine, Belarus, Moldova, and Georgia in order to maintain pro-Russian sentiments and undermine any autocephalous Orthodox Churches that support independence and disassociation from Russia. The Moscow Patriarchate of the Russian Orthodox Church seeks to gather other Orthodox parishes under its jurisdiction. Many of these had transferred their allegiance from the Moscow Patriarchate to the Patriarchate in Constantinople after the Bolshevik takeover in 1917. Russian Orthodox churches have also been built or planned in several neighboring countries despite the misgivings of local officials.[39] These include a church in Tallinn, Estonia financed by sources linked to Vladimir

Yakunin, head of Russian Railways, and a church in Macedonia funded by a Russian businessman.

27. *Revising History:* To undergird its aim to rebuild a Greater Russia, Moscow is engaged in extensive historical revisionism. State-sponsored propagandists are rewriting the period of Soviet occupation as a progressive era of Russian benevolence rather than an era of retardation of Central and Eastern Europe's political and economic development through the imposition of a failed ideology, a one-party dictatorship, and an incompetent economic system. Moscow also claims that the Cold War ended in a stalemate, rather than admitting that the failed Soviet system disintegrated from within and could not compete with a more dynamic West

According to current historical rewriting, Russia naively tried to join the West during the 1990s but was rebuffed and ostracized. In reality, Russia failed to qualify for either EU or NATO membership because of its glaring inadequacies in the rule of law, democratic governance, and market competition, and its numerous conflicts with neighboring states. Officials contend that NATO and the EU captured the post-Communist countries when Russia was weakest, instead of conceding that these states were determined to join both institutions as protection against future empire building by the Kremlin. Distorted histories justify contemporary moves to revise borders and international alliances in order to rebuild a Russian sphere of dominance.

28. *War Cultism:* One central theme, which has virtually become state scripture in Russia, is the official narrative about the "Great Patriotic War" against Nazi Germany (1941–1945). By reviving history and developing myths about the war, Moscow is seeking to generate pride in Russia's achievements. It stresses the country's sacrifices and victories against the Third Reich and ignores such

facts of Moscow's active collaboration with Adolf Hitler in launching World War Two in September 1939, Stalin's decimation of the Red Army leadership, which left the country prone to Hitler's attack in June 1941 and resulted in millions of casualties, as well as the mass murders and ethnic expulsions perpetrated by Putin's *Chekist* predecessors in all territories occupied by the Red Army throughout Europe's East.

Wacław Radziwinowicz, the chief Moscow correspondent of Poland's daily *Gazeta Wyborcza*, has pointed out that the "cult of victory" has been converted into the basis of a civic religion. It has become "an indisputable dogma that the state, law and church guard with all their strength." [40] Putin's Russia lives in the categories of World War Two, and the officially promoted historical memory is a source of political unity against the Western enemy. A focus on the "Great Patriotic War" to define Russia's identity and legitimize the current regime also rehabilitates Stalin and glosses over his massacres and repressions. It likewise depicts the West as veering toward fascism in a purported replay of World War Two. The Kremlin funds international "anti-Nazi" organizations, claiming that fascists have penetrated several Western governments. The most notable is the "World Without Nazism" network, which includes about 140 organizations in 30 countries and organizes events to demonstrate Moscow's prominence in combating Nazism and fascism.

29. *Inciting Anti-Americanism:* The West in general and the US in particular are depicted as decadent and declining civilizations. But even as it allegedly deteriorates, America is charged with pursuing "democratic messianism," in which perverted Western values and political systems are forced upon defenseless states. All US administrations are accused of a multitude of imperialist designs, including unilateralism, militarism, undermining the independence of states, overthrowing governments, and breaking

up sovereign countries. The fate of Yugoslavia usually serves as the Kremlin's primary example, even though US administrations actually tried to steer clear of the conflict during the collapse of Yugoslavia in the early 1990s. The US also stands accused of being untrustworthy: by criticizing elected governments on the grounds of democratic shortcomings and other "ideological" misdemeanors, Washington purportedly challenges their survival and ignores the will of voters.

30. *Dividing the West:* In its propaganda assaults, Moscow seeks to drive a wedge between the "Anglo-Saxon" states of the US, Canada, and the UK, and continental Europe, with the latter viewed as more malleable, corruptible, and exploitable. The message is conveyed that American arrogance and hegemony limits the sovereignty of all EU member states. In the most poignant example, Washington allegedly pushes them into unwanted conflicts with Moscow by supporting "political adventures" in countries along Russia's borders. The Kremlin's objective is to divide the West and preclude any lasting trans-Atlantic solidarity against Russia and in support of Moscow's targeted neighbors.

31. *Promoting Anti-Europeanism:* Among the themes stressed by Kremlin propaganda outlets against the EU are: the degenerate nature of European liberalism; Western immorality and its alleged anti-religious and militant secularist campaigns; lack of sovereign state decision making; democratic paralysis and political chaos; recurring financial crises in the Eurozone; failed multiculturalism and uncontrolled immigration; and an inability to deal with radical Islamism and *jihadist* terrorism. In contrast, Russia is depicted as a bastion against Muslim extremism that is avowedly enveloping Europe because of the latter's liberalism and tolerance.

All these themes help Moscow to stimulate and influence a "fifth column" of movements and parties inside the EU that resembles the Communist International during Soviet times. In particular, Moscow exploits an assortment of radical right and ultra-conservative parties in numerous European states to reinforce its message of Western decadence and Russia's superiority. In addition, the Greek economic crisis and the country's potential ejection from the Eurozone currency union have proved beneficial to Moscow. Officials and propagandists can contend that the EU project is running out of steam and thereby raise the profile of Euroskeptics throughout the continent.

32. *Combative Traditionalism:* Russia's allegedly superior Eurasian civilization is starkly contrasted with the avowedly decadent Atlanticist civilization led by the US and the EU. It supposedly embodies the key moral foundations, including social traditionalism, "family values," religious conservatism, sexual "normality," cultural purity, and state patriotism. Russia is depicted to both domestic and Western audiences as the true defender of traditional values and social morals, while the West is allegedly deeply depraved through homosexuality, bisexuality, and other "deviations," while its governments seek to impose an intolerant secularist ethic on all societies. In this vein, a personality cult has been developed around President Putin, who is depicted as a patriotic and fully masculine heterosexual defender of traditional values and whose resolute stance is applicable to every culture. The traditionalist concoction is also impregnated with Islamophobia, anti-Semitism, and other forms of racism in order to appeal to Christian fundamentalist or white supremacist sentiments.

Economic

33. *Economic Enmeshment:* Moscow's objective is to enmesh specific states in a web of commercial and financial ties that buttress its political penetration. This is particularly evident in the case of the Eurasian Economic Union (EEU), established in January 2015 and intended to restore Russia's position as a global "pole of power." Moscow offers a range of incentives to induce neighbors to join the EEU, including cheaper gas, financial loans, and preferential trade benefits. It also tries to cajole states into the EEU through economic blackmail by instrumentalizing trade, energy, and other key factors.

On a broader scale, purchasing strategic economic sectors in European states, particularly in energy, banking, and telecommunications, helps Kremlin-connected companies to gain political clout. In addition, large debts owed to Russia provide opportunities for leverage, either by demands for prompt payment or debt forgiveness in exchange for ownership of strategic assets. Russia's business penetration also fosters corruption, non-transparency, links with organized crime, and various forms of political abuse. In the longer-term, some Russian officials and analysts believe that Moscow can attract a range of countries into the EEU, including current EU members Greece and Cyprus together with states rejected by the EU, such as Turkey.

34. *Energy Dependence:* As a substantial supplier of crude oil and natural gas to Europe, Moscow seeks to deepen the dependence of all nearby European states and various useful EU countries. The promotion of economic vulnerability through energy dependence is a mechanism for both financial profit and political leverage. Energy and other strategic resources can be decreased or severed at important junctures to exert pressure on particular capitals, or their price can be lowered or raised to gain political concessions.

Moreover, Russian company ownership of key energy infrastructure in Central, Eastern, and South Eastern Europe, such as pipelines, refineries, and storage sites, enables Moscow to exert additional political leverage.

35. *Energy Alliances:* Following Moscow's cancellation of the South Stream natural gas pipeline in December 2014, the Kremlin has tried to mobilize a small circle of allies to lay the groundwork for Turkish Stream, a projected alternative to South Stream that would enable it to maintain an influential position vis-à-vis the EU.[41] According to Putin's plan, Turkish Stream would traverse Turkey, Greece, Macedonia, Serbia, and Hungary toward the EU. However, doubts persist about the feasibility of the project, as Russia is sanctioned from obtaining Western capital, the transit countries are cash-strapped, Western companies are hesitant in investing in another unpredictable scheme, and Brussels will not finance a project that breaches legally binding contracts. Nevertheless, as long as there is some prospect that it will be built, Turkish Stream hampers rival projects by spawning uncertainty and making it more difficult to attract investors for other pipelines.

36. *Trade Disruptions:* Trade is used as a weapon by Moscow both as an enticement, through subsidies of various products and raw materials, and as a punishment, through partial or complete cutoffs in imports or the imposition of double tariffs on imported goods. In some instances, Moscow has reneged on fulfilling its trade agreements by refusing to pay for previous shipments on fictitious financial grounds. Moscow also uses its national ombudsman to prohibit imports, such as dairy products, fruits and vegetables, alcohol, and other beverages, from targeted neighbors in order to exert political pressure or to exact economic punishment. The trade bans are usually based on spurious health and safety pretexts.

Ethnic

37. *Cultivating Ethnic Discords:* A key instrument in Moscow's arsenal to weaken its neighbors is the promotion and perpetuation of ethnic conflicts. The authorities have numerous permutations at their disposal to entrap both friends and foes in such disputes. Targeted capitals become especially vulnerable if they are unprepared for subversion, if they fail to cooperate against Moscow's intrigues, or if they are seduced into supporting secessionism in neighboring countries on the grounds of defending their ethnic kindred. Moscow can encourage numerous demands for territorial autonomy and separatism in Europe's East, which is rife with potential ethnic disputes and national aspirations. The principal objective is to squeeze adversaries through threats of partition and to unsettle incumbent governments that resist Russia's regional policy.

38. *Meddling Mediation:* Russian media outlets and Kremlin spokesmen publicize a host of controversies between and within neighboring states in order to depict Russia as a defender of minority rights, calculating that some discontented factions will consequently support Moscow. Potentially pliable populations include disaffected non-Russian minorities and regional groups in neighboring countries that can be encouraged to oppose governments viewed as insufficiently friendly toward Moscow. Among numerous examples are the regions of Transnistria and Gagauzia (Moldova), Donbas, Transcarpathia, and Bukovyna (Ukraine), Ossetia and Abkhazia (Georgia), as well as Armenians in Georgia, Lezgins and Avars in Azerbaijan, and Poles in Lithuania.

39. *Inciting Russian Speakers:* The most obvious secessionist targets for the Kremlin are Russian ethnics in neighboring states, or Sovietized and russified populations that use Russian as their first

language and can be directly linked with the "Russian World." Over 25 million Russian ethnics and Russian-speakers reside in nearby countries, with Ukraine, Moldova, Estonia, Latvia, Belarus, and Kazakhstan being the principal hosts. Kremlin officials allege that in several neighboring states Russian populations suffer discrimination and are under constant threat from pro-Western governments. Claims of national humiliation are intended to mobilize society and to justify Russia's alleged retaliation in attacking its neighbors.

For instance, Moscow's propaganda deliberately conflates the marches of Baltic anti-Soviet World War Two veterans and their supporters with rising Nazism and preparations for genocide.[42] The purpose is to create an atmosphere of intimidation against Russian speakers and provide justifications for Moscow's intervention. Underlying this policy of interference is the fear that Russians will become fully assimilated in neighboring states and will no longer look toward Moscow for identity, support, or protection. To counteract such voluntary integration, Russia's Fund to Support and Protect the Rights of Compatriots Living Abroad (*Pravfond*) has been especially active in the Baltic states.

40. *Recruiting Local Subversives:* The Kremlin applies pressure to grant Russian-speakers enhanced political status, language rights, and dual citizenship. It thereby calculates that a loyal political corpus will be crafted to support its policies. Moscow thrusts itself forward as the arbiter in the separatist conflicts that it promotes, as most recently witnessed in eastern Ukraine. In reality, Kremlin assistance radicalizes minority leaders and makes conflict resolution more problematic. Supportive signals from Moscow encourage local militants to pursue their agendas in the belief that Russia will defend them. Kremlin-funded agencies reportedly conduct surveys of Russian-speaking populations in nearby countries to ascertain the extent of support for autonomy and

separatism. Subsequently, secessionist sentiments can be fanned, funded, or fabricated.

41. *Fostering Cross-Border Disputes:* Russian authorities manipulate inter-ethnic tensions between neighboring states in order to benefit from the ensuing cross-border conflicts. A major focus for secession is the ethnic kindred of states friendly toward Russia whose governments can be enticed to support collective rights across borders to undermine the integrity of targeted countries. For example, Russia has aided Armenia-backed separatists in Karabakh both to partition Azerbaijan, whose government is often perceived in the Kremlin as excessively pro-Western, and to reward Armenia for its close alliance with Moscow. Such support can be withdrawn if a government tries to veer away from a pro-Kremlin position.

In another conspicuous recent example, the Kremlin encourages Budapest to campaign for Hungarian minorities in nearby states. This has pressurized Ukraine in its western region of Transcarpathia, which contains a Magyar minority, and will potentially affect Romania in parts of eastern Transylvania. Serbs in Bosnia-Herzegovina, Montenegro, and Kosova are also supported by various Russian agencies to create constituencies for resistance against state integration into NATO and the EU.

42. *Challenging Borders:* By voicing support for minority rights or national self-determination in selected countries, the Kremlin can apply pressure on a government through pliable minority leaders seeking outside assistance. Nationalists and separatists on both sides of an ethnic divide can be covertly backed in order to intensify cross-border conflicts and give Moscow a greater role in mediating the ensuing conflict. By sponsoring inter-state disputes, Moscow can also claim that many of the post–World War Two borders in Central and Eastern Europe are illegitimate and should be altered in Russia's favor.

Political

43. *Fomenting Monochrome Revolutions:* Moscow is promoting protests to destabilize governments that it seeks to control, weaken, punish, or replace. Unlike the Western supported and indigenous "colored revolutions" that are intended to strengthen democratic rule and uncover the electoral or other abuses of incumbent governments, Moscow views street protests and riots as useful methods to weaken the democratic process and any progress toward Western integration. It has therefore funded individuals, parties, and movements to undermine administrations in several states, including Moldova and Montenegro. In Moldova, Moscow has financed movements that stage public protests against the pro-EU administration in an effort to replace it with a more Kremlin-friendly government. In Montenegro, Russian officials have supported disaffected groups and Serbian nationalist parties to try and unseat the government of Milo Djukanovic, which has pledged to attain NATO membership.

44. *Political Assassination:* Russia's spokesmen and media outlets question the trustworthiness of those Central and Eastern European officials who staunchly oppose Moscow's foreign policies. They stand accused of corruption, dishonesty, abuse of office, susceptibility to blackmail, various mental aberrations, and of maintaining contacts with foreign intelligence services. The latter charge is particularly troubling to NATO leaders where local officials are expected to deal with sensitive Alliance information. A wide array of mass media and social media outlets are mobilized by the Kremlin for purposes of political assassination. Provocative acts are also periodically staged on the territory of targeted states to discredit government officials or to accompany propaganda offensives. This can include bribery and blackmail accompanied by either genuine or falsified information leaked to the media.

45. *Funding Political Parties:* Russian sources have channeled funds to a broad spectrum of parties among their former satellites in order to purchase political influence. This has been most evident in the case of ultra-nationalist groups in Bulgaria and Hungary, but is not confined to one political stream. Radical leftists or even ideologically mainstream parties can be financed if it benefits Moscow. The Kremlin can assist parties with limited resources particularly during national election campaigns in return for a Moscow-friendly foreign policy. Companies tied to mother organizations in Russia have developed political lobbies in some countries and make campaign contributions to political parties who are either pro-Kremlin or anti-NATO in their orientation.

46. *Purchasing Political Support:* This includes the recruitment of politicians, businessmen, journalists, and other professionals to support Russia's foreign policy goals.[43] Over the past two decades, several politicians have been bribed or blackmailed into promoting Moscow's regional agenda, including the former Lithuanian President Rolandas Paksas, who was impeached and removed from office in April 2004. Kremlin agencies also possess volumes of personal information acquired during the Soviet era, which they can publicize and manipulate against uncooperative politicians. This compromising material, whether accurate or not, is referred to as *kompromat*. Former prominent Western politicians are also recruited with lucrative financial benefits to legitimize Russia's political and economic interests. The most glaring example was the hiring of former German Chancellor Gerhard Schroder in 2005 as Chairman of Nord Stream AG, the joint stock company that operates the undersea pipeline that supplies natural gas from Russia to Germany. Gazprom also unsuccessfully courted former Italian Prime Minister Romano Prodi to become Chairman of the planned South Stream pipeline's construction and operating consortium.

47. ***Endorsing Anti-Establishment Movements:*** An assortment of political parties, movements, networks, campaigns, and influential individuals in the West are openly or covertly courted and supported by Kremlin-connected organizations and media outlets. Moscow seeks to benefit from anti-establishment sentiments across the EU based on popular dissatisfaction with Brussels, whether among ultra-leftists, radical rightists, apolitical populists, or non-partisan militants. It has focused in particular on influential individuals and radical groups espousing anti-liberalism, anti-globalism, religious and ethnic intolerance, Islamophobia, and in some cases combative Christianity. Some personalities and parties are invited to Moscow for international conferences at which Russia is presented as the bastion of free speech for "traditional values" and the West is lambasted for its "moral bankruptcy."

48. ***Encouraging Nationalists:*** Kremlin support for a variety of ultra-nationalist parties throughout Europe is designed to undermine EU and NATO integration and even to divide targeted countries. This includes populist, ethno-nationalist, militant Christian, and other radical parties elected to the European Parliament, which criticize further EU enlargement, oppose the creation of a federal Europe, defend Russia's international policies, and vote against resolutions critical of Moscow. After the July 2014 EU parliamentary elections, approximately one fifth of deputies, many from radical rightist parties, reportedly opposed imposing any sanctions against Russia for its attack on Ukraine. Moscow also covertly backs ultra-nationalist and anti-Russian groups in neighboring states, which it can use to foster violence and instability, depict its political targets as tolerant of fascism, and discredit incumbent governments. For instance, the government in Kyiv has charged Russia's FSB with using ultra-right groups to destabilize Ukraine.[44]

Social

49. *Social Media Offensives:* Kremlin-sponsored campaigns use the freely available social media to mobilize supporters or paid Internet commentators to bombard various media outlets according to precise scripts. The extensive network of online contacts has helped Moscow gain a sizable number of fanatical supporters who are dynamic and aggressive, if not intelligent or well informed. Instead of operating through spontaneously formed discussion groups, these offensives are organized through vertical structures controlled by headquarters and commissioners.[45]

50. *NGO Promotion:* Russian agencies fund and establish NGOs among neighboring states to assist in Moscow's propaganda offensive and sometimes bribe Western experts to contribute. Such organizations include policy institutes, human rights formations, cultural clubs, and environmental groups. For instance, Romanian officials believe that *Gazprom* organized and financed anti-fracking movements and protests to prevent the development of alternative gas supplies in the country. Moscow's interference was also visible in Lithuania, where Chevron ran into a wave of fervent protests by activists, many of whom had previously shown little interest in environmental issues.[46] Other NGOs funded by Moscow have included veterans groups, historical societies, and an assortment of ethnic minority organizations.

51. *Establishing Policy Institutes:* Several branches of Kremlin-funded policy and analytical institutes have been established in Western states. They parody either financially independent American and European NGOs or Western organizations funded by governments but with analytical independence to provide reports and advice to administrations. The Russian equivalents

seek to attract various critics of Western policies and claim to provide alternative viewpoints. The most well-known outfit is the Russian Institute of Strategic Studies (RISS), directed by a former FSB general and close to the Kremlin's presidential administration.[47] The RISS has either established branches in several European capitals or funds joint programs with some Western institutions.

52. *Radicalizing Youth:* Lectures on the greatness of the Soviet Union, the threat of NATO enlargement, and the alleged insanity of Baltic politicians feature at camps in Russia attended by groups of young people from Lithuania, Latvia, and Estonia. The "Successors of the Victory" camp has been described as an "international educational congress of military-sports youth organizations and cadet corps."[48] Baltic security services believe that this may also be a training ground for future propagandists and saboteurs. The stated goal has been to awaken the "Soviet spirit" among Russian-speaking young people in the former Soviet republics.

53. *Propagating Disaffection:* Kremlin-linked ideologues and "political technologists" endeavor to appeal to a broad range of disaffected individuals and groups in Western societies. These may not openly or outwardly support Russia's policies but their opposition to Western governments or to capitalist economies can be useful for Moscow on various occasions. Such diverse groups may include anti-globalists, anti-capitalists, anti-liberals, ultra-leftists, environmentalists, radical religious sects, neo-Nazis, pacifists, nihilists, and anarchists. Moscow also benefits from the inherent weakness of civil societies in some post-Soviet countries in order to inflame social discontent. It fosters social divisions by funding groups and prominent individuals opposing major government policies that conflict with Moscow's objectives. The Kremlin could organize its own version of a "colored revolution" in a neighboring state whose government it seeks to replace. Social

unrest and government instability would then provide the pretext for a more direct Russian intervention.

Military

54. *Security Entrapment:* Moscow established the CSTO (Collective Security Treaty Organization) in April 1994 as a political-military structure of former Soviet republics and has forged asymmetrical bilateral military agreements with a number of CSTO states, including Belarus, Armenia, Kazakhstan, Kyrgyzstan, and Tajikistan. These arrangements enable Moscow to control the air defenses and borders of neighbors and to establish Russian military bases. Moscow pushes the idea of "equal security" to try and equalize NATO with the CSTO. At the same time, it calls on Ukraine and other countries to renounce their NATO aspirations, thus violating the principles of "equal security" in which every country presumably possesses the right to decide on its international alliances. To help defend its new security dominion, in 2009 Moscow initiated the Collective Rapid Reaction Forces (KSOR) within the CSTO whose avowed purpose is to "preserve the sovereignty, protect the constitutional order and restore the territorial integrity" of CSTO member states. [49] In effect, the Kremlin reserves the right to intervene militarily in the internal affairs of each CSTO member by mobilizing a collective assault that echoes its deployment of the Warsaw Pact against wayward allies during Soviet times.

55. *Military Threats:* These are periodically issued in response to policies pursued by neighbors but opposed by Moscow, such as NATO expansion or the installment of a NATO anti-ballistic-missile shield. According to its military doctrine, Russia reserves the right to conduct a preemptive military strike if it perceives a "distinct and inevitable military threat" to the country, or if Moscow feels threatened by reduced access to regions where it

possesses "crucial economic or financial interests."⁵⁰ Russia is also empowered to use its military within the former Soviet domain if a "complex and unstable situation develops" or if there is a direct threat to Russian citizens or ethnic Russians.

56. *Close Military Encounters:* Moscow uses its military to engineer close encounters with several Western states, especially NATO members, to raise levels of threat and tension and test the military and political responses of rival capitals.⁵¹ This can include aircraft overflights or navy incursions. Such threats are in themselves a form of psychological influence designed to demonstrate that the adversary is either weak or unprepared for a Russian offensive. They are deliberately confrontational to increase alarm in NATO capitals that an accidental crash or collision with Western aircraft or seacraft could result in loss of civilian life and even provoke an armed conflict, thus encouraging Western concessions to pacify Russia.

In the Baltic region in particular, Moscow conducts unscheduled combat alerts to test the reaction speed of Baltic units and has stationed missile systems that will affect the military balance of power: the *Iskander*-M ballistic system and the S-400 long-range anti-aircraft system.⁵² Moscow has built up its military capabilities in the Baltic Sea to be able to stage a rapid assault by regular forces, block air traffic, especially the arrival of support units from NATO, and hit the majority of land targets to deter the Alliance from intervening in a regional conflict.

57. *Active Provocations:* These may include personnel abductions, sabotage operations, acts of random terrorism, assassination of targeted officials, and other diversionary activities in order to promulgate public fear in pinpointed states and destabilize incumbent governments. Ukraine has been subjected to such attacks since the start of Russia's offensive in early 2014. It can also include intimidation and bribing of military and police officers,

with the objective of making them abandon their duties, as was evident in Crimea during Moscow's annexation of Ukraine's peninsula in early 2014.

58. *Intimidating Exercises:* Russian military exercises are notable for their magnitude and the frequency of "spot" exercises, involving the sudden and unannounced deployment of forces. Since 2012, Russia has conducted six major military exercises assembling between 65,000 and 160,000 personnel, dwarfing the size of all NATO maneuvers.[53] After launching its attack on Ukraine, Russia enhanced its capabilities in moving around sizable numbers of troops and equipment. The exercises have developed in quality, and the armed forces can perform increasingly complex joint operations. Moscow has also modernized its electronic and technical capabilities, enhanced command and control, and improved the use of a digital operational-tactical command system. Current reform and modernization programs are focused on developing a capability to intervene quickly and decisively in neighboring states by allocating resources to a small number of elite units, primarily airborne and special operations forces, that constitute the core of Russia's emerging Rapid Reaction Force.[54]

59. *Conjuring Confrontation:* A major military exercise in March 2015 assumed an especially threatening posture.[55] It covered several regions, including the Arctic, Baltic, and Black Seas and simulated a full-scale confrontation with NATO through the forward deployment of nuclear-armed submarines, theater ballistic missiles, and strategic bomber aircraft. Strategic weapon systems were also located near NATO's borders. By deploying Tu-22M3 bomber aircraft, Russia invoked the threat of nuclear confrontation and asserted that this was a response to potential military support from the West to Ukraine and in reaction to NATO beefing up its presence in the Baltic states.

60. **Nuclear Blackmail:** Kremlin officials have regularly warned that they will suspend various nuclear and conventional arms-control agreements and maintain tactical nuclear missiles along Russia's western borders. Such threats are combined with regular military exercises, including the annual *Zapad* maneuvers that have involved the simulated nuclear annihilation of neighboring capitals.[56] Russia's military doctrine provides for the first use of nuclear weapons under threatening circumstances. Such a posture also serves to divide the Alliance, as Europe, unlike the US, would be directly affected by the use of tactical or battlefield nuclear weapons. Russia uses the propaganda potential of its weapons deployments, snap exercises, and the destructive capabilities of newly developed weapons to induce anxieties among neighbors.

For instance, the periodically announced deployment of *Iskander* tactical missiles in the Baltic Sea and in Kaliningrad and Crimea are intended to demonstrate preparations for the use of nuclear delivery weapons. Moscow has also violated the Intermediate Nuclear Forces (INF) Treaty and Conventional Forces in Europe (CFE) Treaty and withdrawn from the Nunn-Lugar program for reducing nuclear threats. In June 2015, Putin announced that Russia would procure 40 new intercontinental ballistic missiles (ICBM) "capable of penetrating any possible enemy missile defense." NATO's Supreme Commander in Europe, US Air Force General Philip Breedlove, responded by accusing Putin of "ratcheting up nuclear tensions."[57]

61. **Tactical Compromises:** Russia's leaders seek advantages by partially stepping back from an initially aggressive stance and enticing Western concessions in accepting some of Moscow's gains. Western leaders then trumpet their evident success at averting a larger international crisis. The invasion of Georgia in August 2008 can be seen in the light of such calculations, where EU attention was riveted on dispatching monitors to the "buffer zones" carved out by Russian forces deeper in Georgian territory

rather than to the disputed regions of South Ossetia and Abkhazia, which Moscow recognized as independent states and where it emplaced its military units. Such a "stick and carrot" approach is also evident in Ukraine, where Russia's preparations for military action against Kyiv are interspersed with ceasefire initiatives to legitimize the separatist enclaves in the Donbas.

62. **Unconventional Offensives:** Russian analysts assert that the lines between war and peace are blurred. General Valery Gerasimov, Chief of the Military General Staff, describes how Russia can subvert and destroy states without direct, overt, and large-scale military intervention. [58] The Special Operations Forces of the Russian Federation (SOF) were established in March 2013 as a highly mobile group of forces of the Ministry of Defense designated for specific tasks abroad. [59] In addition to sabotage operations, the SOF create, train, and supervise foreign guerrilla movements. They were used during the seizure of the Crimean parliament on February 27, 2014, and subsequently in Ukraine's Donbas. Moscow is working to develop within a few years the capability to threaten several neighbors simultaneously on the scale of its operation in Ukraine. [60] This would give Russia the ability to carry out three such operations during the same timeframe without a major military mobilization that would allow the West time to respond.

63. **Disguised Subversion:** One overarching component of Moscow's unconventional assaults on neighboring states is its use of *maskirovka*, or disguised offensives. This combines several elements including surprise, camouflage, maneuvers intended to deceive, concealment, the use of decoys and military dummies, and disinformation to dupe the adversary. [61] Moscow's role in such low-scale military operations can either be denied altogether or depicted as a humanitarian or limited peace-making mission. This was evident in eastern Ukraine during the spring and summer of

2014 when Moscow dispatched hundreds of unchecked trucks allegedly to provide food and medical aid to the local population.

64. *Proxy Wars:* These are intensive operations against neighboring states designed to seize territory or topple national governments. Moscow engages in covert offensives in support of separatists. It creates fake insurgencies by financing and arming front groups; infiltrating the foreign territory using Russian special forces, mercenaries, and volunteers; corrupting local law enforcement bodies; inciting civil unrest; seizing public buildings; setting up road blocks and other barricades; disabling the functioning of police or military units; and declaring support for alternative authorities and security forces. Assistance to irregular fighters is designed to subvert and destabilize targeted countries and undermine the authority of the local and central governments.

65. *Sponsoring Separatists:* Even if majorities in targeted states do not support secession, local discontented individuals can always be found and funded by Moscow as new ethno-national leaders. The Kremlin relies on the passivity and fear of the silent majority in a specified region, while rebels are provided with weapons, recruits, finances, and media exposure. Russian specialists are infiltrated to provide leadership, weaponry, and organization, while crippling the capacity of national governments to protect the population. Moscow can also deploy a large conventional force along the borders to dissuade large-scale state action against the separatists that it has incited and supported.

66. *Conventional Intervention:* Regular forces can be deployed against neighbors in order to supplement unconventional or proxy wars, as witnessed in Georgia (2008) and Ukraine (2014–2015). Moscow may engage in a large-scale and direct military intervention to defeat or dislodge the military of a nearby state from a region that it has earmarked for partition or annexation.

Russian forces frequently train to increase the speed of their military actions so that the West has little time to implement a coherent response. Subsequently, the focus is on peace talks rather than reversing Russia's territorial advances. Moscow's involvement is preceded by the pretext that the local population is in danger of genocide and is desperate for military protection. This can be accompanied by armed provocations to elicit government retaliation, which in turn precipitates Russia's intervention, as was the case in Georgia in August 2008.

67. *Territorial Fragmentation:* This entails the invasion, occupation, and partition of neighboring states, the recognition of separatist entities as autonomous units or independent states, or Russia's outright annexation of conquered territories. In the case of Moldova and Ukraine, Moscow has been pushing its own version of federalism: in each case, the secessionist regions that Russia has nurtured are seeking a confederal arrangement with the central government and veto powers over the country's foreign and security policies in line with Kremlin interests.

An inadequate Western response to the partition of Ukraine and Georgia simply encourages Moscow to continue the process in other parts of the Wider Europe. In some cases, Moscow has pressed for territorial revisions by claiming that regions such as Crimea should be considered traditionally Russian and whose inclusion in a neighboring republic during Soviet times Russia denounces as unlawful. An additional underhanded method is the creeping "borderization" of neighboring countries. This has been evident in Georgia where Russian units have demarcated the border with Russian-controlled South Ossetia deeper into Georgian territory. Such actions are intended to demonstrate that Moscow can act with impunity in seizing nearby lands.

68. *Exploiting Frozen Conflicts:* Moscow supports the creation of "frozen conflicts" and the maintenance of "frozen states," as this paralyzes the central government and prevents Russia's neighbors from joining Western institutions. The Kremlin seeks international legitimacy for separatist enclaves that it has overtly or covertly sponsored and it acts as a mediator in avowedly resolving disputes with the central government that, in reality, are never resolved. This has been evident in several secessionist conflicts in the former Soviet Union, particularly in Moldova, Georgia, and Ukraine. Moscow indefinitely maintains several unresolved conflicts and prevents their resolution. It also holds in reserve the prospect of unfreezing these conflicts and unleashing further instability through renewed insurgency, intensified armed conflicts, and potential direct Russian military intervention. Such a threatening posture serves to convince Western governments to make compromises that favor Moscow

Vulnerable Flanks

In pursuit of a dominant "pole of power" position in Europe's East and in Central Asia, and in order to strengthen its revisionist "Russian World," Moscow is prepared to redraw international borders throughout the post-Soviet zone. The *de facto* annexation of Crimea in 2014 and the further division of Ukraine became a logical step after Russia's forced partition of Georgia, in August 2008, and the recognition of South Ossetia and Abkhazia as independent states, a move that brought no punishing international consequences. Putin's aggressive moves into Ukraine and the muted international response sent shockwaves throughout the broader neighborhood. States from the Baltic Sea to the South Caucasus and Central Asia felt under more direct threat of destabilization, dissection, and of being drawn involuntarily into Russia's imperial designs.

In sum, five of Russia's flanks are exposed to destabilization and armed conflict as a result of Moscow's revisionist and revanchist policies. Along Russia's northern flank, two of the three Baltic countries (Latvia and Estonia) contain significant ethnic-Russian populations and remain on alert for scenarios of subversion engineered by Moscow. Putin may decide on more direct and forceful measures to allegedly defend not only Russian ethnics but also "Russian-speaking" populations that were settled in these republics during the post–World War Two Soviet occupation.

Alternatively, Moscow may seek to carve out a land corridor across Lithuania to connect with its Kaliningrad exclave on the Baltic coast. The fact that this would mean direct action against a NATO member may prove attractive to Putin, as he could test Alliance unity and resolve in defending its territorial integrity. Even without direct attempts at partition and annexation, the Kremlin could pursue various destabilizing measures through energy pressures, trade embargoes, cyber attacks, incitement of ethnic unrest, or by staging sabotage or terrorist attacks on Baltic territory. This would also test NATO reactions to non-conventional attacks on a member state.

The Nordic non-NATO members, Sweden and Finland, are also growing increasingly concerned by Moscow's incursions along their borders and inside their territorial waters, which directly threaten their national security. They are assessing the possibility of entering the Alliance to protect their vital interests. Russia's attack on any of the Baltic states could draw Sweden or Finland into direct confrontation with Moscow.

Along Russia's western flank are several defensive flashpoints that could be triggered by Moscow's offensives. Poland could become embroiled militarily to protect its eastern borders and defend the besieged Ukrainian state, as well as its own co-ethnics in Ukraine. A Russian military invasion, occupation, and partition of mainland Ukraine would spark armed resistance and insurgency against Russian forces. Insurgent leaders might then appeal to Poland for military assistance. If Kyiv itself were bombed or captured, the Ukrainian government would likely seek refuge in Poland and draw Warsaw more directly into a confrontation with Moscow. Meanwhile, the rest of Central Europe would be exposed to a host of instabilities, ranging from energy cutoffs and trade disruptions to refugee outflows and military spillovers.

Belarus will seek to ensure its territorial integrity as the government of President Alyaksandr Lukashenka endeavors to shield itself from the prospect of Russia's expansionism. Moscow may claim parts of Belarus or view unification with Russia as the optimum solution. Lukashenka has not supported the annexation of Ukrainian territory for fear that this would set a precedent for the potential fracture of Belarus. Nonetheless, the Kremlin may call upon Minsk to provide "brotherly assistance" to Greater Russia, possibly within the framework of the Moscow-dominated Collective Security Treaty Organization (CSTO), or threaten political repercussions. In the most far-reaching scenario, if state integrity comes under increasing question, Belarus may break with Russia and appeal for international protection.

Romania can become more closely involved in supporting the territorial integrity and EU association of Moldova, a country threatened by Moscow-sponsored separatism in the Transnistrian and Gagauz enclaves. Emboldened by success in Crimea, Putin may push for a referendum on federalization or independence for Moldova's wayward regions. Concurrently with targeting Moldova, Moscow may forcefully establish an autonomous entity along Ukraine's Black Sea coast between Odesa and Crimea. This would create a direct territorial link between Crimea and Transnistria under Moscow's control and further challenge the pro-Western government in Kyiv. It would also provide Moscow with control over the entire northern coast of the Black Sea, including its maritime resources.

Along Russia's southwestern flank, NATO members Romania and Bulgaria are growing concerned about security in the Black Sea and the stability of the wider Balkan region. The seizure of Abkhazia from Georgia and Crimea from Ukraine and threats to truncate other countries has increased Russia's preponderance in the region. This heightens pressure on all littoral states, challenges NATO's presence and its deterrence projections in the Wider Europe, and provides Moscow with a stepping-stone toward Central Europe and the Balkans.

Moscow has also become more active among the post-Yugoslav states, seeking greater influence and leverage against Western interests and cultivating potential allies among countries that have yet to qualify for EU or NATO membership, particularly Serbia, or facing internal divisions, in the case of Macedonia and Bosnia-Herzegovina. Kremlin inroads through energy contracts, corrupt business deals, and the exploitation of local nationalisms undermine prospects for Western integration and place both NATO and the EU on the defensive.

Along Russia's southern flank, Moscow maintains pressure in the South Caucasus to undercut the region's Western connections. The governments in Georgia and Azerbaijan voiced dismay at the mild Western response to Russia's partition of Ukraine and what this could portend for their own territorial integrity. Benefiting from its substantial military presence in Armenia, Moscow could reanimate an armed conflict with Azerbaijan over the territory of Nagorno Karabakh, currently controlled by Armenia. It can also sever Georgia by forcibly creating a military corridor between Russia and Armenia. All these measures, in addition to reanimating an assortment of ethnic claims inside both Georgia and Azerbaijan, would have an adverse impact on the stability of both governments and may push them into an enforced Russian orbit.

Russia's offensives could also obstruct the construction of energy pipelines between the Caspian Basin and Europe or place these under

Moscow's control and handicap EU attempts to pursue energy diversity. This would also curtail US and European connections with Central Asia and reduce prospects for natural gas deliveries from the region to Europe. The Southern Gas Corridor (SGC) is planned as a network of pipelines that will connect gas fields in Azerbaijan with southern Italy via Georgia, Turkey, Greece, and Albania.[62] It is due to consist of three sections: the South Caucasus Pipeline (SCP), the Trans-Anatolia Natural Gas Pipeline (TANAP), and the Trans-Adriatic Pipeline (TAP). The SCP is already online and pipes Azerbaijani gas from the Caspian coast to the Georgian-Turkish border; TAP will pump gas directly into Italy; and TANAP, presently under construction, will link the SCP with TAP. TANAP is expected to be concluded by 2019 and TAP by 2020. The further development of the SGC could involve a broad energy infrastructure linking Europe, the South Caucasus, Central Asia, and the Persian Gulf that would exclude Russia.

Along Russia's southeastern flank, the Central Asian states are increasingly wary of Kremlin policy and growing political interference. They are also concerned about the impact of closer economic integration through the Eurasia Economic Union (EEU), where the cost may outweigh the benefits to their own economies. If coupled with an undercutting of state sovereignty and demands to "protect" Russian ethnics in Kazakhstan and elsewhere, this could raise nationalist voices in the region and precipitate more direct conflict with Moscow in opposition to the latter's integrationist agenda.

Central Asia faces escalating security challenges in the wake of NATO's withdrawal from Afghanistan, limited Western political and economic engagement, and Russia's growing aspirations. This can increase the appeal of local nationalists and propel some countries to develop closer ties with a more assertive China. Such relations could evolve into mutual defense arrangements as protection against a revisionist Russia.

The war between Russia and Ukraine has dramatically escalated the geostrategic competition between the Western states and a neo-imperial Russia. Moscow's invasion of Ukraine and annexation of Crimea demonstrates President Putin's geopolitical ambitions and the limitations of Western deterrents. It has challenged the independence of other nearby post-Soviet states and exposed America's newest NATO allies, NATO partners, and even the non-aligned European countries to the destabilizing regional repercussions of the Kremlin's assertiveness. Although Russia's military capabilities do not match those of its Soviet predecessor, the country presents a destabilizing presence in several key regions and employs numerous forms of subversion against targeted neighbors. The following five chapters systematically examine the threats confronted by Russia's vulnerable flanks and the responses of states that are targeted by Moscow.

Endnotes

[1] Consult Laurynas Kasčiūnas, Marius Laurinavičius and Vytautas Keršanskas, "Vladimir Putin's Pyramid of Rule: Who Really Governs Russia?" August 4, 2014, *Delfi*, Vilnius, Lithuania, http://en.delfi.lt/central-eastern-europe/vladimir-putins-pyramid-of-rule-who-really-governs-russia.d?id=65432116.

[2] Power and wealth are manipulated by the Kremlin's PR as potent symbols of President Putin's alleged strength. Hence, campaigns against his acquisition of substantial wealth may simply reinforce Putin's public image as a powerful Russian leader in the Tsarist and Soviet traditions.

[3] A valuable analysis of the "Putin Doctrine" can be found in Leon Aron, "Putinology," *The American Interest*, July 30, 2015, http://www.the-american-interest.com/2015/07/30/putinology.

[4] For previous analysis by Janusz Bugajski concerning Russia's state ambitions and strategies see *Georgian Lessons: Conflicting Russian and*

Western Interests in the Wider Europe, CSIS Press, 2010; *Dismantling the West: Russia's Atlantic Agenda*, Potomac Books, 2009; *Expanding Eurasia: Russia's European Ambitions*, CSIS Press, 2008; and *Cold Peace: Russia's New Imperialism*, Praeger/Greenwood, 2004.

[5] Check Jakub Grygiel,"The Geopolitical Nihilist," *The American Interest*, December 10, 2014, http://www.the-american-interest.com/2014/12/10/the-geopolitical-nihilist.

[6] See the extract from Richard Sakwa's book *Frontline Ukraine: Crisis in the Borderlands*, January 15, 2015, http://theibtaurisblog.com/2015/01/15/extract-frontline-ukraine.

[7] For a critique of the term "hybrid war" see Jānis Bērziņš, "Russian New Generation Warfare is not Hybrid Warfare," in Artis Pabriks and Andis Kudors (Eds.), *The War in Ukraine: Lessons for Europe*, The Centre for East European Policy Studies, University of Latvia Press, Rīga, 2015, pp. 42–43, http://eng.appc.lv/?p=642.

[8] Konstantinas Ameliuškinas, "Lithuanian Historian: Moscow Does Not Have Moral Right to Host End of WWII Celebrations," Vilnius *Delfi*, February 11, 2015, http://en.delfi.lt/lithuania/society/lithuanian-historian-moscow-does-not-have-moral-right-to-host-end-of-wwii-celebrations.d?id=67143936.

[9] Julie Fedor, *Russia and the Cult of State Security: The Chekist Tradition, from Lenin to Putin*, London and New York: Routledge, 2013, p. 130.

[10] Putin's own description of the EEU initiative can be found in Vladimir Putin, "Novyi Intergrationnyi Proekt dlia Evrazii," *Izvestia*, October 3, 2011, http://izvestia.ru/news/502761.

[11] A useful analysis of the EEU can be found in Nicu Popescu, "Eurasian Union: The Real, The Imaginary and The Likely," Chaillot Papers, 132, September 2014, Paris: European Union Institute for Security Studies, http://www.iss.europa.eu.

[12] For a concise examination of Kremlin perceptions of the West see Janis

Berzins, "NATO: Russia's Main Geopolitical Enemy," in Andris Spruds and Karlis Bukovskis (Eds.), *Ten Years in the Euro-Atlantic Community: Riga Conference Papers 2014,* Latvian Institute of International Affairs, Riga, 2014, pp. 21–31.

[13] Pavel Felgenhauer, "Kremlin Sees Ukraine Crisis as Part of Overall US-led Assault on Russia," *Eurasian Daily Monitor,* September 11, 2014, Volume 11, Issue 159.

[14] Paul Goble, "Putin's New Military Doctrine Says Russia Faces More Threats Abroad -- and at Home," December 27, 2014, *Window on Eurasia,* http://windowoneurasia2.blogspot.com/2014/12/window-on-eurasia-putins-new-military.html; and http://news.kremlin.ru/media/events/files/41d527556bec8deb3530.pdf.

[15] Pavel Podvig, "New Version of the Military Doctrine," Russian Strategic Nuclear Forces, December 26, 2014, http://russianforces.org/blog/2014/12/new_version_of_the_military_do.shtml.

[16] Consult *Eurasian Union: a Challenge for the European Union and Eastern Partnership Countries,* Eastern Europe Studies Centre, 2012-12-19, Vilnius, Lithuania, http://www.eesc.lt/2012-7.html.

[17] *Ibid,* p. 28.

[18] Joseph Dobbs, *The Eurasian Economic Union: A Bridge to Nowhere?* Policy Brief, European Leadership Network, March 4, 2015, http://www.europeanleadershipnetwork.org/the-eurasian-economic-union-a-bridge-to-nowhere_2498.html.

[19] *Interfax,* Minsk, June 1, 2015, www.interfax.com.

[20] Paul Goble, "A Mini-Brezhnev Doctrine? -- FSB Promises to Block Revolutions in CIS Countries," June 7, 2014, *Window on Eurasia – New Series,* http://windowoneurasia2.blogspot.com/2014/06/window-on-eurasia-mini-brezhnev.html.

21 For a synopsis see Edward Lucas, "Russia's *Sub Rosa* Statecraft," *The American Interest*, Vol. 10, No. 3, December 10, 2014, http://www.the-american-interest.com/2014/12/10/russias-sub-rosa-statecraft.

22 Interviews by the authors in in Tbilisi, Georgia in July 2015.

23 "Moldova's Trans-Dniester region pleads to join Russia," *BBC*, March 18, 2015, http://www.bbc.com/news/world-europe-26627236.

24 "Transnistria," in *Freedom in the World 2015*, Freedom House, 2015, https://freedomhouse.org/report/freedom-world/2015/transnistria.

25 Paul Goble, "Moscow Faces Problems In Absorbing Crimea Into Russian Legal Space," *Window on Eurasia*, May 15, 2014, http://www.interpretermag.com/moscow-faces-problems-in-absorbing-crimea-into-russian-legal-space/; Ekaterina Dyatlovskaya, "Вхождение в Закон," (Getting into Law), *Novie Izvestia*, May 14, 2014, http://www.newizv.ru/politics/2014-05-14/201465-vhozhdenie-v-zakon.html.

26 Martin McCauley, *Bandits, Gangsters and the Mafia: Russia, the Baltic States, and the CIS,* Harlow, England: Longman, 2001, p. 75. According to McCauley, nine major *mafia*-like organizations have emerged controlling approximately half of the Russian economy.

27 Ellen Nakashima, "Russian Hackers use 'Zero-Day' to Hack NATO, Ukraine in Cyber-Spy Campaign," October 13, 2014, http://www.washingtonpost.com/world/national-security/russian-hackers-use-zero-day-to-hack-nato-ukraine-in-cyber-spy-campaign/2014/10/13/f2452976-52f9-11e4-892e-602188e70e9c_story.html.

28 Paul Goble, "How Russian Trolls are Recruited, Trained and Deployed," January 29, 2015, *Window on Eurasia -- New Series*, http://windowoneurasia2.blogspot.com/2015/01/how-russian-trolls-are-recruited.html.

29 Ben Nimmo, "Anatomy of an Info-War: How Russia's Propaganda Machine Works, and How to Counter it," May 15, 2015, Central European

Policy Institute, http://www.cepolicy.org/publications/anatomy-info-war-how-russias-propaganda-machine-works-and-how-counter-it.

[30] Paul Goble, "Hot Issue – Lies, Damned Lies and Russian Disinformation," Jamestown Foundation, August 13, 2014, http://www.jamestown.org/single/?tx_ttnews[tt_news]=42745#.VWnrFKb9oVU.

[31] Jolanta Darczewska, "The Anatomy of Russia Information Warfare: the Crimean Operation, a Case Study," *Point of View*, No.42, May 2014, Centre for Eastern Studies, Warsaw, Poland, p.5, http://www.osw.waw.pl/en/publikacje/point-view/2014-05-22/anatomy-russian-information-warfare-crimean-operation-a-case-study.

[32] Ben Nimmo, 2015, op. cit.

[33] Johan Wiktorin, 'Time for a Counterattack on the Kremlin," September 12, 2014, http://20committee.com/2014/09/12/time-for-a-counterattack-on-the-kremlin.

[34] Anna Dolgov, "Baltics React With Indignation to Reports of Russia Questioning Their Independence," *The Moscow Times Online*, July 1, 2015, http://www.themoscowtimes.com. Instead of reacting defensively and playing into Kremlin hands, the Baltic governments could simply turn the tables on Moscow by questioning the legitimacy of the Russian Federation that was assembled through conquest, mass murder, and forcible expulsions during the Tsarist and Soviet eras.

[35] Lilia Shevtsova, "Russia and the West: Humiliation as a Tool of Blackmail," *The American Interest*, June 2, 2015, http://www.the-american-interest.com/2015/06/02/humiliation-as-a-tool-of-blackmail.

[36] Speech by Andrei Illarionov at NATO PA Session in Vilnius," *The Lithuanian Tribune*, June 16, 2014, http://www.lithuaniatribune.com/69155/speech-by-andrei-illarionov-at-nato-pa-session-in-vilnius-201469155/.

[37] Paul Goble. "Ukrainians and Belarusians are Not 'Byproducts' of Russian Ethno-National Development," *Window on Eurasia – New Series*, April 28, 2014, http://windowoneurasia2.blogspot.com/2014/04/window-on-eurasia-ukrainians-and.html.

[38] Hannah Gaiis, "Putin, Stalin, and the Church," *First Things*, May 20, 2015, http://www.firstthings.com/web-exclusives/2015/05/putins-taking-his-cues-on-religion-from-an-unlikely-source.

[39] Elisabeth Braw, "Mixed Feelings In Macedonia As A Russian Orthodox Church Rises," *Radio Free Europe/Radio Liberty*, June 25, 2015, http://www.rferl.org/content/macedonia-russian-orthodox-church-skopje/27093507.html. Estonian intelligence agencies allege that some of the money earmarked for construction of the church was channeled to pro-Moscow politicians.

[40] Wacław Radziwinowicz, "Niepokalane Rosyjskie Zwycięstwo," *Gazeta Wyborcza*, Warsaw, April 4, 2015, http://wyborcza.pl/magazyn/1,144507,17700646,Niepokalane_rosyjskie_zwyciestwo.html.

[41] Krisztina Than and Michael Kahn, "New South Stream Will Be Russia's 'Route of Friendship,'" Brussels, *EurActiv.com*, February 25, 2015, http://www.euractiv.com/sections/energy/new-south-stream-will-be-russias-route-friendship-312401.

[42] Vladislav Maltsev,"March of the Deadheads; Neo-Nazis in the Baltic States Are Not Yet Encountering Resistance," Moscow, *Lenta.ru*, March 18, 2015, http://lenta.ru.

[43] "Pro-Russian Pseudo-Elections in the East of Ukraine Disclose Russian Agent Network in Europe," November 7, 2014, http://eurasianintelligence.org/news.php?new=165&numm. A number of EU citizens were present during the illicit elections in occupied Donbas on November 2, 2014. To obtain observer status they had to be licensed by representatives of the Russian Command overseeing the militia groups in occupied Ukrainian territories. In effect, these EU citizens are collaborators with Russia's intelligence agencies.

[44] Paul Goble, "Putin Using Far Right to Destabilize Ukraine, Poroshenko Says," *Window on Eurasia – New Series,* September 3, 2015, http://windowoneurasia2.blogspot.com/2015/09/putin-using-far-right-to-destabilize.html.

[45] Jolanta Darczewska, op.cit., May 2014, p. 29, http://www.osw.waw.pl/en/publikacje/point-view/2014-05-22/anatomy-russian-information-warfare-crimean-operation-a-case-study.

[46] Andrew Higgins, "Russian Money Suspected Behind Fracking Protests," November 30, 2014, http://www.nytimes.com/2014/12/01/world/russian-money-suspected-behind-fracking-protests.html.

[47] Official site of the Russian Institute for Strategic Studies: http://riss.ru.

[48] Sarunas Cerniauskas: "What Are 'Cadets' From Lithuania Being Taught in Russian Military Camp?" *Delfi,* Vilnius, October 9, 2014, http://en.delfi.lt/lithuania/society/lithuanian-school-students-are-taken-to-russian-paramilitary-camps-according-to-media-reports.d?id=66071036.

[49] Roger McDermott, "Russia Hosts CSTO Exercises in Western Military District," *Eurasia Daily Monitor,* September 1, 2015, Volume 12, Issue 156.

[50] RFE/RL, *Newsline,* Vol. 7, No. 190, Part I, October 6, 2003, and Denis Trifonov, "'Ivanov Doctrine' Reflects Moscow's Growing Confidence in the CIS and Beyond," *Central Asia-Caucasus Institute Analyst,* Johns Hopkins, Washington, D.C., November 19, 2003, http://old.cacianalyst.org/?q=node/1657.

[51] Jonathan Marcus, "Russia's 'Close Military Encounters' with Europe Documented," *BBC News,* November 10, 2014, http://www.bbc.com/news/world-europe-29956277. The London-based European Leadership Network produced a detailed study of assertive Russian activity entitled: "Dangerous Brinkmanship: Close Military Encounters Between Russia and the West in 2014." It chronicles almost 40 specific incidents, which "add up to a highly disturbing picture of violations

of national airspace, emergency scrambles, narrowly avoided mid-air collisions, close encounters at sea and other dangerous actions happening on a regular basis over a very wide geographical area," including harassment of reconnaissance planes, close over-flights over warships, and mock bombing raid missions. The targets include several NATO members.

52 Kaarel Kaas, "Russian Armed Forces in the Baltic Sea Region," *Diplomaatia*, Estonia, August 7, 2014, http://www.diplomaatia.ee/en/article/russian-armed-forces-in-the-baltic-sea-region/. *Iskanders* were reportedly deployed to the 152nd Missile Brigade in Kaliningrad. These missile systems provide Russia with the capacity to strike strategically important targets, including airports, ports, railway junctions, and command centers, from southern Poland to central Finland.

53 Melinda Haring, "The West's Strategy Toward Putin Promises Conflict and Increases Danger of Wider War: Ian Brzezinski," http://www.atlanticcouncil.org/blogs/new-atlanticist/the-west-s-strategy-toward-putin-promises-conflict-and-increases-danger-of-wider-war.

54 Douglas Mastriano and Derek O'Malley (Eds.), *Project 1704: A US Army War College Analysis of Russian Strategy in Eastern Europe, an Appropriate US Response and the Implications for US Landpower*, March 26, 2015, http://www.strategicstudiesinstitute.army.mil/pubs/display.cfm?pubID=1274.

55 "Russia Targets NATO With Military Exercises," March 19, 2015, *Stratfor*, p. 6, https://www.stratfor.com/analysis/russia-targets-nato-military-exercises.

56 On July 22, 2014 President Putin addressed the Russian Security Council and terminated cooperation between Russia and NATO. His response to NATO's moves to reinforce the security of members close to Russia was the deployment of the *Iskander*-M tactical ballistic missile system along Russia's western borders and in Kaliningrad. See Roger McDermott, "Russia-NATO: No 'Business as Usual,'" *Eurasia Daily Monitor*, July 29, 2014, Volume 11, Issue 138.

[57] Pavel Felgenhauer, "Website Publishes Purported Detailed Russian Invasion Plan of Eastern Ukraine," *Eurasia Daily Monitor*, June 18, 2015, Volume 12, Issue 114.

[58] "The 'Gerasimov Doctrine' and Russian Non-Linear War," *Military-Industrial Kurier*, February 27, 2013, http://inmoscowsshadows.wordpress.com/2014/07/06/the-gerasimov-doctrine-and-russian-non-linear-war/.

[59] Vitalii Usenko and Dmytro Usenko, "Russian Hybrid Warfare: What are Effects-Based Network Operations and How to Counteract Them," http://euromaidanpress.com/2014/11/05/russian-hybrid-warfare-what-are-effect-based-network-operations-and-how-to-counteract-them.

[60] According to Lieutenant-General Ben Hodges, commander of US Army forces in Europe, in Adrian Croft, "Russia Could Soon Run Multiple Ukraine-Sized Operations: US General," January 16, 2015, *Reuters*, http://www.reuters.com/article/2015/01/16/us-nato-russia-idUSKBN0KP1F620150116. Russian Defense Minister Sergei Shoigu has claimed that Moscow will maintain its modernization plans estimated to cost more than 20 trillion rubles ($300 billion) by 2020.

[61] For a summary of *maskirovka* operations see Lucy Ash, "How Russia Outfoxes Its Enemies," *BBC News*, January 28, 2015, http://www.bbc.com/news/magazine-31020283.

[62] Emanuele Scimia, "Southern Gas Corridor's Advances Cool off Energy Cooperation Between Italy and Russia," *Eurasia Daily Monitor*, August 3, 2015, Volume 12, Issue 145.

2. Northern Flank: Baltic and Nordic

The Baltic Sea occupies a pivotal position in Moscow's plans to consolidate the northern flank of its expansionist Eurasian project. It provides a vital trade route to Russia's second largest city, St. Petersburg, hosts the Nord Stream natural gas pipeline between Russia and Germany, and is the location of the Baltic fleet, headquartered in the Kaliningrad exclave. Despite Kremlin opposition, over the past two decades the Baltic Sea has become largely a NATO lake, with six member states having located along its coast: the traditional members, Denmark and Germany, and relative newcomers Poland, Estonia, Latvia, and Lithuania. In addition, since Russia's assault on Ukraine, the remaining two neutral states, Sweden and Finland, are moving closer to NATO in an effort to protect their security in an increasingly unpredictable region.

Russia's northern flank consists of two sets of countries that have experienced growing pressures from Moscow: the Baltic and the Nordic. The three Baltic states (Estonia, Latvia and Lithuania) occupy the most vulnerable position, especially Latvia and Estonia, which contain significant ethnic-Russian and Russian-speaking populations. Each state has campaigned for more effective NATO protection to counter attempts to unsettle their internal security. In the wake of Russia's attack on Ukraine, the Baltic states formally requested NATO to deploy several thousand troops as a permanent deterrent. They are seeking a brigade-size unit of approximately 3,000 soldiers so that every Baltic country would have at least one battalion stationed on its territory. The successful defense of any NATO member in deterring

Moscow's many-pronged assaults will be a crucial test for the credibility of the Alliance over the next decade. If any NATO member is dismembered by Russia, then Moscow will not only exact revenge for losing the Cold War, it will also have in effect dismantled the Western Alliance.

The Nordic non-NATO members, Sweden and Finland, have also become increasingly concerned by Moscow's activities along their borders. Events in Ukraine in 2014 threw into sharp focus the absence of Nordic capabilities following years of drawdowns and a focus on crisis management operations instead of territorial defense.[1] Two decades of underinvestment in defense and substantial force reductions have hollowed out territorial defense capabilities. Northern Europe has been left dangerously exposed to military coercion at a time of mounting uncertainty. If regional stability was threatened because of Russia's actions, both Sweden and Finland could petition for NATO membership, thus expanding the rupture between Washington and Moscow and intensifying Russia's justifications for its regional aggressiveness.

In the event that Moscow decides to directly attack Estonia, Latvia, or Lithuania, in an alleged defense of its national interests, it will seek full military maneuverability in the Baltic Sea and to restrict NATO's response. In flexing its military muscles through large-scale maneuvers, the construction of new bases, and frequent violations of the air space and coastal waters of littoral states, Moscow has been aiming at several objectives. First, the military buildup is supposed to demonstrate that Russia is again a great power and can create an environment of uncertainty in the Baltic and Nordic regions. Second, Moscow is testing NATO's political and military responses and adjusting its own tactics and operations in potential preparations for armed conflict. And third, in the case of Estonia, Latvia, and Lithuania, the Kremlin's military pressures are part of a broader multi-pronged offensive to weaken their governments, stir social and ethnic disputes, and demonstrate that NATO will not be able to defend them in the event of war.

Baltic Front

The Putin administration has persistently tried to demonstrate that the independence of the three Baltic states is an "abnormality" as compared to the period when the region was under Russian or Soviet rule.[2] Russia's post-Soviet narrative has depicted the Baltic countries as a platform for expanding US interests in Belarus, Ukraine, and Russia itself on the pretext of democratization and promotion of human rights. Lithuania, Latvia, and Estonia are on NATO's front line, and each capital fears that in the aftermath of Russia's attack on Ukraine, the Kremlin may engage in several forms of incursion to demonstrate its strength and underscore Western impotence.

While Russia's ambitions toward the three Baltic states are clear, its pretexts for intervention and its strategies of subversion are varied. In terms of objectives, the Kremlin follows two overarching goals. First, it seeks to marginalize and isolate the three countries and reduce their influence in the post-Soviet neighborhood. It calculates that neutralized governments will not challenge attempts to establish a Eurasian bloc among the remaining post-Soviet states. Russia's officials understand that the Baltic nations cannot be incorporated in its regional organizations, but they want to prevent them from supporting any initiatives for a wider EU or NATO that would undermine the Eurasian alternative. Despite Moscow's pressures, all three Baltic capitals remain internationally active in support of Ukraine, Georgia, Moldova, and other countries that have resisted the Kremlin.

Second, Russia wants to emasculate NATO, especially along their common border in Europe's East. By regularly challenging the Baltic countries through troop maneuvers, air space violations, threats of invasion, or nuclear annihilation, Putin's officials are intent on demonstrating that if Russia decides to attack, the Balts will be helpless to resist and NATO's common defense doctrine will prove worthless. In effect, the Kremlin's ambition is NATO "rollback," in which Estonia, Latvia, and Lithuania may formally remain part of the Alliance but are unable to oppose Russian policy and NATO does not emplace its infrastructure on Baltic territory.

Moscow has two main pretexts for pressuring the Baltic countries: the status of Kaliningrad and the position of Russian-speaking minorities. The Kremlin seeks exclusive control over a transit corridor across Lithuania to its exclave of Kaliningrad, a slither of territory on the Baltic coast that Russia annexed from Germany at the close of World War Two. Officials claim that the region is being isolated through international sanctions against Russia, introduced after its assault on Ukraine during 2014. They have issued warnings that Kaliningrad could be deliberately cut off by Vilnius in an attempted takeover of the territory.

A more likely scenario is a rising movement for autonomy in Kaliningrad, demanding closer links with the EU, similar to Ukraine's aspirations, which the Kremlin will be determined to thwart. Kaliningrad's population is showing signs of frustration with economic stagnation and Moscow's neglect, and long-term Western sanctions will further diminish living standards. However, Lithuanian officials calculate that Russia could stage a provocation along Kaliningrad's border, claim that the local population is in danger of isolation, encirclement, or attack, and dispatch a troop convoy to open a direct military corridor from Russia across Lithuanian territory.

Moscow has tried to benefit from political, ethnic, and social turbulence in the region in order to keep the Baltic countries off balance. It has exploited the Russian minority question to depict the Baltic governments as failing to meet European standards for minority protection. The Kremlin claims the right to represent and defend the interests not only of Russian ethnics but all "Russian-speakers" in order to raise the number of alleged victims of Baltic repression. Assertions by officials that Baltic governments discriminate against Russians, despite the conclusions of international human rights organizations, contribute to heightening tensions.

Latvia and Estonia contain sizable Russian-speaking populations. Although the greater share of these residents are integrated in the state through citizenship, political participation, and economic opportunity, a considerable minority have avoided naturalization and may be susceptible to manipulation by Moscow's agitprop offensives. According to the 2011 census, out of two million people in Latvia, 26.9% were Russians, although the pool of "Russian speakers" remains larger. Of these, about 290,000 are currently non-citizens, as they have not passed an elementary naturalization test or have not applied for citizenship. In Estonia, according to the 2011 census, out of a population of almost 1.3 million, 24.8% were Russians, with a larger number of "Russian speakers," of which nearly 90,000 are currently non-citizens.

In both countries, non-citizens benefit from all EU-harmonized civil rights, aside from being unable to vote in Latvia in line with norms evident in other EU states. However, in Estonia non-citizens are permitted to vote at the local level. As permanent residents, all non-citizens can freely travel to all EU territories and live and work anywhere in the country. Nonetheless, a small minority remains susceptible to an intense Moscow-directed campaign to manufacture or exploit grievances in order to divide Latvian and Estonian societies. Conflicts can be incited by spreading anti-government disinformation through widely watched Russian television channels and by infiltrating these countries using Russian special forces to organize local provocateurs. Officials in Moscow can subsequently intervene to allegedly protect Russian compatriots. As in Ukraine, the aggressor can thrust himself forward as the peacemaker and mediator.

Numerous pressures have been applied over several years against the Baltic states by various arms of the Russian government. In addition to direct military threats and the exploitation of ethnic divisions, Moscow has used energy embargos, economic sanctions, political influences, financial corruption, cyber wars, NGO activism, and media disinformation campaigns to engender social divisions and confrontations and weaken the Baltic authorities. In the aftermath of events in Ukraine, Latvia and Estonia have remained on alert for another scenario of partition engineered by Moscow on the grounds of defending Russian compatriots. Kremlin ambitions may be bolstered by its relative successes in Ukraine, especially as the Western response proved inadequate in preventing partition. The Baltics also have relatively small and weak military forces. As a consequence, each state has sought more effective NATO protection of their borders, territories, and political institutions to counter attempts to unsettle internal security.

As the major energy supplier in the region after the demise of the Soviet Union, Moscow has periodically sought to disrupt the Baltic economies in order to gain political advantage. Each government has tried to reduce its dependence on Russian energy and its exposure to blackmail. Moscow also endeavors to control energy transit routes, as this is both financially and politically profitable. Energy supplies are used as leverage to purchase shares in local refining and transportation systems. Moreover, periodic threats to reduce or halt supplies are intended to induce concessions for Russian investments in local economies. Another customary form of political pressure involves targeted trade sanctions against the Baltic states. For instance, in June 2015 Russia's Federal Veterinary and Phyto-Sanitary Oversight Service prohibited the transit of fish and fish products from the Baltic countries across Russia to Kazakhstan.[3]

Estonia

According to the 2011 census, Estonia had 1,294,236 permanent residents, of whom 68.7% defined themselves as Estonian, 24.8% as Russian, and 4.9% as other nationalities.[4] Approximately 85% of the total are citizens, 8% are non-citizens, and 7% are Russian citizens, with the total number of non-citizens decreasing significantly since the country regained independence in 1991. The reluctance of some Russian-speakers to integrate into Estonian society has caused socioeconomic and political problems, most visibly in major industrial areas such as Ida-Viru county, bordering Russia in the northeast of the country, and in the capital Tallinn.

The city of Narva and the wider Ida-Viru county is reportedly receptive soil for Moscow's information war because of the number of Russians distrustful of the central government and experiencing tough economic conditions.[5] Many residents feel marginalized and excluded from national development. In 2013, a third of the population in Ida-Viru (33.7%) lived in relative poverty, while Estonia's average was 22%. Only 52% of the county's working-age population was gainfully employed and the unemployment rate stood at 13% in Ida-Viru in 2014, almost twice the national average. 54% of Ida-Viru residents are Estonian citizens; 17% do not have any citizenship, and 28% are Russian citizens.

However, the Russian-speaking community is not as homogeneous as it was at the start of the 1990s. Differences have widened in attitudes toward the Estonian state and in the ability to adapt to changing economic conditions. According to a study conducted in 2011 by Marju Lauristin, professor of sociology at the University of Tartu, the Russian-speaking population is split roughly into two: approximately half are successfully integrated, the rest much less so or not at all. The assimilated sector consists mostly of younger people born and educated in Estonia, possessing Estonian citizenship, having a good command of the language, able to cope economically, and valuing the benefits of EU membership. Most live in Tallinn and other larger cities. Although there are no Russian ethnic parties in Estonia's parliament, the Center Party appeals mostly to assimilated Russians and includes the mayor of Tallinn. The least integrated Russian sector is made up of older people brought up in Soviet times with no command of Estonian, as well as blue-collar workers, the unemployed, and rural residents.[6] The national estrangement of members of the unintegrated sector has pushed them deeper into Russia's sphere of influence.

For many years, the advice from Russia to its Baltic diaspora was not to accept the host country's citizenship. Moscow could then use non-citizens to discredit the Baltic governments in international organizations, accusing them of human rights violations. Despite the fact that Estonia prohibits dual citizenship, Moscow allowed its "compatriots" (the term for Russians living outside the country) to become Russian citizens in an expedited manner. Moscow downplayed the fact that non-citizen residents of Estonia benefit from all rights except voting at national level and running for political office, in line with EU norms. They can travel freely in the Schengen area and do not need visas to visit Russia. The Kremlin also manipulates the question of Russian-language education. The reform of state schools was designed to expand education in the Estonian language, a policy opposed by some Russian activists and older teachers who retain a Soviet mentality and refuse to integrate.

Another source of pressure against Estonia revolves around Russia's manipulation of Finno-Ugric aspirations. Estonians form part of the distinct Finno-Ugric language group of northeastern Europe that also includes Finns, Hungarians, Mordvins, Sami, Komi, and Mari people. Leningrad Governor Aleksandr Drozdenko has claimed that the Izhors, a Finno-Ugric group numbering 26,000, some of whom support the creation of an autonomous republic in northwestern Russia, are a threat to the country's territorial integrity.[7] This could be a signal to Estonia and Finland to terminate their support for the cultural revival of Finno-Ugric populations in Russia or face another pretext for Russia's multi-pronged interventions to allegedly defend Russian interests.

Moscow has tried to influence politics in Estonia by supporting the largely Russian minority Center Party. In the March 1, 2015, parliamentary elections, the Reform Party gained 27.7% of the vote and won 30 out of 101 seats. The Center Party, reportedly linked to Putin's United Russia party, came second with 24.8% and 27 seats.[8] In the county of Ida-Viru that includes Narva, the Centre Party won 58% of the vote. Over 90% of Narva's 60,000 residents, on the border with Russia, reportedly identify themselves as Russian-speakers. The liberal-centrist Reform Party and the Center Party shared a coalition government in the past, but the relationship was spoiled by the Center Party's stance on Ukraine. Party leader Edgar Savisaar stirred controversy when he openly backed Russia's annexation of Crimea. In addition, military maneuvers conducted by Moscow on Estonia's border just days ahead of the elections were intended to intimidate voters and encourage the Russian vote.

The main target of Russian state propaganda in Estonia is the older generation, whose level of education is low and whose command of Estonian or other languages is insufficient to benefit from the foreign-language media. However, some young and educated Estonian Russians have also supported Putin and Kremlin revisionism and demanded that Russian become the country's second official language. Estonian analysts believe that the government has not placed sufficient emphasis on conditions among many Russian-speakers, leaving them little option but to immerse themselves in Russia's sphere of information. The Russian media incites conflict by presenting a biased picture of the Western world, including the Baltic states, alleging that it threatens Russia. It also deliberately provokes Estonian nationalism to promote ethnic tensions, while claiming that Estonians are "Russophobes." For instance, in April 2007, Moscow capitalized on the government's relocation of a bronze statue to Red Army "liberators" from the center of Tallinn to a nearby military cemetery, by fanning local demonstrations and publicizing them as evidence of anti-Russian repression.

Moscow supports several local NGOs that are critical of the Estonian government and supportive of the Kremlin. For example, the Legal Information Center for Human Rights (LICHR) dispenses advice to ethnic minorities and produces reports condemning Estonia's treatment of the Russian minority.[9] Estonia's security services have classified the LICHR as a Russian agent. Its human rights reports are financed by the Kremlin-sponsored Fund to Support and Protect the Rights of Compatriots Living Abroad (the Compatriot Fund, or *Pravfond*), which together with the *Russkiy Mir* Foundation provides funding for the LICHR's operations. Other pro-Kremlin NGOs include Estonia Without Nazism and the Integration Media Group. A few radical Russian organizations and individuals are also either favored by Moscow or espouse support for an imperial Russia.[10]

On the cyber security front, Estonia had direct experience of cyber warfare in April 2007, when government and private websites came under massive attack from sources believed to be linked with the Russian government. Moscow used the pretext of the removal of the bronze statue, which to most citizens of Estonia represented half a century of Soviet occupation and repression. Since that time, the Estonian government has taken precautions to limit any future damage from cyber attacks and in 2008 opened a NATO Cooperative Cyber Defense Center of Excellence, in the capital Tallinn. Its goal is to research, educate, and help develop cyber security for the Alliance. Estonia's Police and Border Guard Board have also prepared a cyber crime unit to take charge of Internet-related crime from the start of 2016.[11]

In terms of national security, Estonia has no binding border treaty with Russia, as the current draft is awaiting the approval of President

Putin.[12] The treaty passed the first reading in the Estonian parliament in April 2014 and the MPs decided the second reading will be scheduled only once Russia has also begun proceedings. Delays in ratification create a climate of uncertainty in the country regarding potential border violations by Russia. Estonia possesses a highly professional police, security, and border protection force, even though much of the 130 kilometers of border with Russia is porous. It also has highly competent local-level institutions that presumably cannot be easily overtaken by separatists, as was the case in eastern Ukraine. In addition, the military displays high morale and motivation to resist any Russian intervention.[13]

Estonia's energy vulnerabilities have significantly decreased in recent years. Even though the country remains dependent on Russian natural gas for 100% of its supplies, gas only constitutes 9% of the total energy mix. Although it has fewer energy levers, Russia can engage in other forms of sabotage such as interrupting or severing underwater fiber optic cables between Estonia and Sweden and Finland.

Moscow also engages in periodic direct provocations against Estonia. For example, a Russian unit abducted Eston Kohver, an officer of Estonia's Internal Security Service, near the Russian border, on September 5, 2014.[14] The abduction occurred shortly after President Obama visited Tallinn to pledge protection against Russia's aggression and on the eve of the NATO summit in Wales. Kohver's kidnapping was intended to signal that Moscow was capable of penetrating the territory of all three Baltic states and that NATO would not be in a position to respond.[15] On August 19, 2015, a court in Russia sentenced Kohver to fifteen years in prison for espionage and other charges. [16] Estonian Prime Minister Taavi Rõivas condemned the trial as "a clear and grave violation of international law." Officials maintain that Kohver was apprehended when investigating smuggling operations involving Russian officials. On September 26, 2015, Kohver was exchanged for a Russian spy, a former officer in Estonia's security police found guilty of passing secret information to Moscow.

Estonia's reactions to Moscow's subversion have involved a spectrum of initiatives. According to Estonian President Toomas Hendrik Ilves in his Victory Day speech on June 23, 2014, Estonia has a battle-ready defense force with high morale.[17] Internal Affairs Minister Hanno Pevkur asserted that internal security spending should be raised from 1.7% to 2% of GDP, similarly to defense spending.[18] It would focus on containing potential riots, buttressing rapid reaction forces, equipping border guards, and improving communication capabilities. Tallinn is also increasing its military expenditures beyond NATO requirements of 2% of GDP.

Estonia has formulated a new National Defense Act to better prepare the country to counter modern security threats.[19] The legislation gives the Prime Minister a greater role in planning and managing national defense. It sets out different levels of nationwide preparedness, from general defense readiness in time of peace to martial law and mobilization in periods of war. It lays down a common planning model that identifies the duties and activities of all official agencies. Minister of Defense Sven Mikser underscored that the threats facing Estonia are much more diverse than a purely military attack. Hence, military defense is simply one element in the concept of comprehensive national defense.

During his visit to Estonia in September 2014, Obama announced plans to create a US-Baltic-Nordic air force training center at Amari base, in addition to the NATO Baltic air policing capabilities already based there.[20] The government hopes to make the presence of NATO fighter jets at Amari a permanent fixture of the Alliance's military planning system. According to Foreign Minister Urmas Paet, Estonia wants NATO to increase its presence in the Baltic region to become permanent on the sea, land, and air.[21]

President Ilves has called for a permanent NATO ground force in

Estonia, as the current Alliance contingent is a temporarily stationed US infantry company with only 150 soldiers.[22] Russian troops could reach Tallinn from the border in just four hours. By the time NATO would be ready to launch any significant action it would be too late. Estonia has a standing army of 5,300 troops and relies on NATO to police its airspace. Although NATO quadrupled its policing mission over the Baltic states from four to 16 fighter jets in 2014, this is a small fraction of Russia's combat aircraft numbers.

Various measures have been undertaken to improve Estonia's military preparedness. In late April 2015, Estonia and the US held five days of joint military exercises.[23] The main goal was to increase combat readiness in a conventional war. In May 2015, the *Siil* 2015 exercises involved 13,000 conscripts, reservists, and members of the *Kaitseliit* (Estonian Defense League) paramilitary organization. *Siil* 2015 also included NATO soldiers that were already deployed in Estonia. In December 2014, the defense ministers of the Baltic republics agreed to establish a joint body for security data coordination.[24] Estonia has been installing mobile monitoring systems on the border with Russia with assistance from the EU External Borders Fund (EBF), which supports EU border protection.[25] As there is no border monitoring inside the Schengen zone, the security of external borders is a concern for all states. Cameras have also been installed on the Herman Fortress in Narva to monitor the transborder river shared with Russia. Surveillance systems were also renewed in Lake Peipu and several other key locations.

On the minority front, in 2014 Estonia decided to create a Russian-language TV channel to counter Moscow's propaganda. The station was due to begin broadcasts in the fall of 2015. Estonian Public Broadcasting (ERR) and Latvian Public Service Television (LTV) also concluded an agreement in March 2015 to cooperate in developing their Russian-language TV channels.[26] An increasing number of Russian-language broadcasts have featured on Estonian stations. For instance, in January 2015, Estonia's public broadcasting company

ERR launched a weekly news magazine in Russian called "AK+" to be broadcast on a national television channel and a commercial television channel.[27] In addition, the TEDX free internet network is spreading to Russian-inhabited areas and enabling easier communication and expression of local needs and grievances to both local and central governments.[28]

Latvia

Latvia has confronted an extensive Russian media campaign designed to discredit the country internationally. [29] Successive Latvian governments have been accused of reviving fascism and promoting Russophobia. Moscow was especially interested in blackening Riga's reputation during its presidency of the EU Council, in the first six months of 2015. Officials and analysts also fear that Russia's special services may conduct various destabilizing provocations to test NATO's resolve in defending Latvia. Additionally, Moscow has engaged in divisive tactics between the Baltic states to weaken their common front vis-à-vis Russia.[30] This involves trying to engender conflicts over territory and resources. For instance, Janiz Kruzinis, a Latvian activist of the Association Against Nazism, which follows Moscow's line, launched an Internet petition campaign to seek "the return of the territory of Palanga" from Lithuania along the Baltic coast. Within a week, 10,000 people reportedly signed the petition.

On the energy front, Moscow's leverage with Latvia has decreased in recent years, as Riga continues to diversify its sources and forms of energy, including Liquefied Natural Gas (LNG) from Poland and Lithuania and gas interconnectors with neighbors. If Russia terminated all its agreements with Latvia, including energy supplies, Latvia's GDP would reportedly suffer a 10% contraction. However, the current amount of gas reserves would suffice for a year and alternative supplies are becoming available through the Klaipėda gas terminal in Lithuania.[31] The opening of the terminal in December 2014 was one of the most important steps in strengthening security for the Baltic states, as demonstrated by Moscow attempting to convince a Norwegian company not to take part in the project.[32]

Russia can apply other economic pressures, as 10% of Latvia's GDP is earned from the transit of goods to Russia, which makes up 80% of the total freight turnover of Latvian Railways. Moscow's imposition of an embargo on EU agricultural produce, in August 2014, damaged the cargo transit sector.[33] Russia's ban on food imports from the EU hit the Baltic countries the hardest since Russia's share in the structure of their exports is larger than in other EU countries, especially in agriculture. [34] An additional economic tool is available through political corruption, as Russian state-connected money is present in various industries, while the absence of liberalization in the gas market has favored corruption.

In order to influence Latvian politics and ensure a government in Riga that does not oppose Russia internationally, Moscow has supported the predominantly ethnic Russian Harmony Party. In the September 17, 2011 elections, Harmony gained a majority of votes among Russian-speakers but was left out of the governing coalition by a combination of Latvian parties amidst fears that it could veer Latvia away from the West. Russian organizations also gathered signatures to hold a referendum on making Russian an official second language. The initiative was defeated on February 18, 2012, by over 74.8% of voters. Just 24.88% of citizens voted in favor, and only in the eastern region of Latgale did a majority vote for the constitutional change.[35]

According to Foreign Minister Sergei Lavrov, Moscow will continue to expand the Russian World project and this includes assistance for "compatriots in their struggle for political rights" in Latvia.[36] The 2011 census showed that 62.1% of the population were Latvians (1,285,136) and 26.9% Russians (557,119).[37] The Russian total has dropped from 34% since the 1989 census. Approximately 288,000 of the Russians are non-citizens, mostly monolingual elderly people. This figure has significantly decreased, having stood at about 700,000 in 1994.[38] In October 2013, the law was amended to allow citizenship for people born to non-citizens. In the past two decades of independence, citizenship has been steadily made more inclusive as Latvians feel more confident about their national and state survival following half a century of Soviet occupation, ethnic expulsion, Russian colonization, and compulsory russification. Applying for citizenship takes about nine months and requires minimal language proficiency. However, even non-citizens have various benefits, and as permanent residents they can travel to both the EU and Russia without visas.

Latvia lacks a common forum for inter-ethnic reconciliation, and there is little dialogue between the two communities regarding Latvia's occupation under Tsarism and Sovietism. Russian authorities exploit these divisions and reportedly monitor public opinion to assess Latvia's vulnerabilities.[39] One important component is support for a federalized Latvia and for an autonomy movement in the eastern region of Latgale, populated heavily by Russians.

Latgale is vulnerable to separatist appeals, as it is less developed economically, conducts significant trade and business with Belarus and Russia, and the Russian media predominates, particularly television. In the language referendum in February 2012, 60% of the region's population voted for Russian as a second state language. The move was rejected by a clear Latvian majority, which viewed the language proposal as threatening the use of Latvian. The danger also exists that too many concessions that raise the status of the Russian language or broader minority rights could animate Latvian nationalist groups, as distrust of Russia has increased since its intervention in Ukraine during 2014. Nationalist polarization suits Moscow and provides pretexts for potential intervention.[40] Nonetheless, according to opinion polls, the majority of Russians are loyal and integrated in Latvian society, especially those that have lived in the country for generations.

Russia's officials have attacked the Preamble to the Latvian Constitution, passed by Latvia's parliament in June 2014, claiming that it gives a privileged position to the titular nation over ethnic minorities and will facilitate further inter-ethnic splits.[41] The preamble states that the Republic of Latvia has been established by uniting the territories historically inhabited by Latvians and based on the Latvian nation's desire for sovereignty and to ensure the existence and development of the Latvian nation, its language and culture.

Russia's representatives frequently complain about conditions in Latvia despite the wide array of minority rights in line with EU standards that the Russian Federation itself fails to guarantee. They accuse Latvian officials of neo-Nazism and xenophobia to justify Moscow's interference in the country's affairs. Despite such attacks, Riga grants extensive group rights to Russians, including schools, media, culture, and language use at the local level wherever Russians form over 20% of population, in addition to the full array of civic rights benefiting all citizens.

Nils Ušakovs, the Mayor of Riga and leader of Harmony Center, the largest single party in the country, is an ethnic Russian. Harmony has tried to appeal to Latvian ethnics as a social democratic formation and downplayed its links with Putin's party, United Russia. Nonetheless, many Latvians view Harmony with suspicion and consider it potentially disloyal to Latvian statehood. Moscow's attack on Ukraine contributed to undermining Harmony's reputation.[42]

Russian intelligence services remain active in Latvia to foster pro-Kremlin sentiments and operate under the cover of local governments, businesses, and non-governmental organizations.[43] The Russian embassy in Riga delivers books to Russian schools each year and their content is not checked.[44] The Russian Orthodox Church exerts an influential role, and some students travel to Russia for scholarships. The Russian media uses entertainment for political propaganda purposes, and a substantial number of Latvians who speak Russian also watch Russian TV. Moscow is helping to develop a broad array of groups, including fraternities, Afghan war veterans, conservationists, and historical societies tied to a Russian heritage. It has also tried to radicalize elements of the minority through persistent propaganda, youth camps, and business lobbies.

Latvia's ruling coalition remained in power after winning a majority of seats in the October 4, 2014, elections. Harmony received 23.3% of votes, earning 25 seats in the 100-seat legislature, six fewer than in previous ballots. The center-right coalition led by Prime Minister Laimdota Straujuma's Unity party, which includes the National Alliance and the Union of Greens and Farmers, totaled 61 seats after receiving 57% of the vote.

A Russian Union (RU) was established in May 2014 as a more radical formation that could take support away from the Harmony Party. Led by Tatiana Zdanek, the Union declared its backing for Russia's annexation of Crimea and for the pro-Kremlin separatist "people's republics" of Donetsk and Luhansk. The Union obtained over 5% of the vote in the European elections of May 22–25, 2014, and Zdanek became one of the eight representatives from Latvia in the European parliament. The RU claims that Harmony is too moderate and accommodating and openly supports the Russian World concept. Although it underperformed in Latvia's general elections in October 2014, gaining less than 2% of the vote and no parliamentary seats, it has the potential for mobilizing the most alienated and radicalized elements of Latvia's Russian population.[45] It emphasizes conservative traditionalism against the liberal EU and seeks to exploit any grievances among minority groups.

Latvian officials claim that a Ukraine-type scenario would be difficult for Moscow to engineer because of better intelligence, more effective internal security and law enforcement capabilities, and competent border-control mechanisms. Nonetheless, about 10% of Russian ethnics could be persuaded to support separatism, whether actively or passively.[46] According to Riga political analyst Aleks Grigoryevs, after the events in Donbas, a majority of Russians in Latgale would not welcome intervention by Moscow, but a small fraction of 10–20% might be prepared to. If they were armed, they could create major problems for Latvia, particularly as the media could blow such a revolt out of proportion.[47]

In January 2015, pro-Moscow groups launched websites for a Latgale People's Republic in southeastern Latvia and a Vilnius People's Republic around the capital of Lithuania.[48]

The People's Republic of Latgale was proclaimed on the Internet in late January 2015. Latvian intelligence services traced the initiators as provocateurs in Russia.[49] Although these messages did not represent real movements they created propaganda headaches for the two governments. If they ignore the provocation it could stimulate local nationalism and ethnic strife, but if they act tough against the Internet sites, this will undermine claims that Latvia and Lithuania are stable and tolerant democracies.

Scenarios of destabilization can be outlined for Latvia.[50] They may include the holding of local referenda and the installation of autonomist or separatist local governments in Latgale, where Russians account for approximately 40% of the population. The goal would be to create trouble spots, triggering a government crackdown that would engender local resentments, foster ethnic division, and provide more pretexts for Moscow's intervention. Alternatively, Riga may seek to pacify the minority by lifting all restrictions on citizenship and language use, thus raising the political profile of Russians in decision-making. Either reaction can encourage moves toward regional autonomy in Latgale and even herald the unilateral dispatch of a Russian "peacekeeping" operation to consolidate the new local governments, push out Latvian ethnics, and establish a predominantly Russian zone protected by Russian military units.

Moscow officials, together with some Russian activists in Latvia, have tried to exacerbate ethnic tensions by supporting sympathetic NGOs. According to *Re:Baltica*, a Latvian non-profit organization, the Russian government is massively funding NGOs in all three Baltic countries to influence political discussions and push Moscow's political line.[51] *Re:Baltica* published a major study of the NGO sector in September 2015, entitled "Kremlin's Millions: How Russia Funds NGOs in Baltics." The study reveals that there are more than 40 such organizations in the region. Those in Latvia and Estonia have received at least €1.5 million since 2012. Two thirds of them are connected to pro-Moscow political parties in the Baltic states and may even be a mechanism for funneling money to those parties. They frequently present themselves as "anti-fascists" and aim to influence the public debate against the West and in favor of Moscow. Latvia has seven major pro-Moscow NGOs receiving Russian funds,

For instance, Latvian officials suspect that the Latvian Human Rights Committee coordinates its actions with Moscow.[52] On March 26, 2015, Russia's *Duma* held a roundtable on the problems of non-citizens in Latvia and Estonia, at which Aleksander Gaponenko, head of the NGO Parliament of the Unrepresented or Congress of Non-Citizens, appealed for Moscow's help.[53] Gaponenko was the main initiator of the referendum on Russian as Latvia's second official language and remains under criminal investigation for inciting ethnic hatred.[54]

The Latvian media has reported that pro-Russian agitators have visited houses, schools, and public institutions in the Latgale region and instigated local inhabitants to seek the region's incorporation into Russia.[55] They allegedly offered money to officials to join them in the campaign for autonomy. The Institute of European Studies, in Riga, receives Russian government funding. The group has conducted several projects with *Russkiy Mir* and the Compatriot Fund and focuses on the plight of Russians in Latvia. Solvita Āboltiņa, chairman of the Latvian parliament's security committee, believes that about

100 local NGOs receive money from Moscow and conduct activities hostile to the state, including its independent status.[56] In March 2015, *GVD Baltija*, an NGO suspected of aiding pro-Russia separatists in eastern Ukraine, was banned from staging a rally in Riga.[57] In mid-January 2015, Latvian Security Police raided their offices and the home of the NGO's founder, Stanislavs Bukains. The searches were conducted as part of a criminal probe into recruiting people for terrorist acts, as well as the illegal purchase and possession of firearms.

Latvian commentators believe that Russian-language media controlled by the Russian government and NGOs connected with Moscow have cultivated dissatisfaction among Russian-speakers."[58] On July 3, 2014, Prime Minister Laimdota Straujuma stated that Russia was waging an "information war" in Latvia.[59] To help counter Moscow's disinformation, Riga sought EU funding to launch a Russian-language television network. The new channel is to feature news and entertainment programs, an advantage Russia's television stations currently maintain over Western outlets, which broadcast only news. Latvia was prepared to have it operate under EU direction and to include the other two Baltic states in the endeavor.[60]

Latvian analysts believe that the most effective way to oppose provocative propaganda is to improve the quality of state and local government services in all regions, combat official corruption, and provide high-quality education.[61] Latvia's public media should long ago have established a studio in Latgale to produce local stories, report on the mood of local residents, and discuss the activities of local government employees and private businessmen.

According to a public opinion survey commissioned by the government in 2014, about 75% of non-Latvians felt that they belonged in Latvia, and 64% declared themselves to be patriots of Latvia.[62] Meanwhile, 38% of respondents also believed that Russian-speaking residents are more loyal toward Russia than Latvia. Nonetheless, Andrei Neronskiy, director of Moscow's Center of

Latvia's Russian Culture, claimed that events in Ukraine's Donbas could be repeated in the Baltic states.[63] According to Neronskiy, 500 militiamen would be sufficient to fracture the Latvian state into several enclaves. Riga is not sufficiently prepared to suppress national uprisings, the police do not possess the necessary skills for full-fledged combat actions, while the limited NATO forces based in the Baltic area would be unable to perform internal security functions. In addition, municipal police officers in Latvia's eastern regions may start switching sides as they did in eastern Ukraine.

Putin's press secretary Dmitry Peskov threatened that if "radical nationalists" came to power in Riga and if Brussels recognized them as it did in Ukraine in 2014, then "Latvian citizens of Russian origin would rise in revolt."[64] The comments indicate that Moscow has worked out a crisis scenario in Latvia in which some components of its strategy in Ukraine could be applied. The Kremlin may portray various political developments in Latvia as an existential threat to the Russian population and necessitating direct intervention.

General Adrian Bradshaw, deputy commander of NATO forces in Europe, has warned that Putin might try to seize NATO territory.[65] Moreover, this could be an open invasion rather than a concealed occupation if Moscow calculates that NATO would be unwilling to escalate the conflict. Russia could capitalize on one of its frequent unannounced military drills near the Baltic borders to launch an invasion. Indeed, military exercises in 2009 and 2013 emulated the occupation of the territory of the Baltic states. Since the war in Ukraine, Russia's military activities near Baltic borders have intensified dramatically. Russian warships and submarines either entered Latvia's Exclusive Economic Zone or patrolled near its territorial waters more than forty times during 2014 alone.

Russia has rebuilt its military base in Ostrov, only 32 kilometers from the Vecumi parish in Latvia; it is now home to the 15th Army Aviation Brigade with one hundred new battle helicopters and attack helicopters.[66] Russian helicopters can reach Riga in approximately one hour. As a result of these and other provocative moves, Latvia's Foreign Minister Edgars Rinkevics called for the permanent presence of NATO forces in the region.[67] During a visit to the US, Latvian Defense Minister Raimonds Vējonis also informed officials about Russia's increased military activities near the country's borders.[68] Aleksander Grushko, Russia's envoy to the North Atlantic Alliance, condemned Latvia, Lithuania, and Estonia for requesting permanent NATO forces, claiming that this violated key provisions of the 1997 Russia-NATO Founding Act.[69] It purportedly displayed NATO's efforts to build up its military potential along its eastern flank.

In terms of domestic security, experts and veterans of Latvia's National Guard believe that its fighting capabilities and weaponry need to be updated.[70] A discussion has also raged on whether to introduce compulsory military service to strengthen the country's national defense forces. The defense ministry plans to have available 6,000 regular army troops, 7,000 fully trained National Guards, and 4,000 well-trained and equipped reserve soldiers by 2018.[71]

Latvian Interior Minister Ricards Kozlovskis has asserted that the state needed to better protect itself from intruders, as the number of people illegally entering Latvia was increasing.[72] Kozlovskis believes that strengthening the eastern border, stretching for 450 kilometers, is a priority by completing border demarcations and installations, including the construction of a 12-meter-wide border area, where people will not be allowed to enter. In addition, Latvia's parliament introduced a bill on suspending temporary residence permits to Russian investors.[73] Latvia's justice minister Dzintars Rasnačs stated that due to Russia's aggression in Ukraine steps should be taken to terminate Latvian residence permits for Russian citizens, most of whom have acquired expensive properties. Some pose a security threat, as a parallel society is emerging in several towns where wealthy Russians are able to corrupt local politicians.[74]

In September 2014, Latvia opened a NATO-accredited Strategic Communications Center, in Riga, amid fears of negative Kremlin influences on the country's Russian minority.[75] The Center analyzes information warfare and psychological operations waged by Moscow in order to help strengthen NATO's strategic communications capabilities. Lawmakers also backed legislation that will more than double defense spending to the NATO-recommended minimum of 2% GDP by 2020, from 0.91% of GDP in 2014.

Lithuania

Moscow focuses on several themes to weaken Lithuania's pro-Western governments, particularly the military transit question to Kaliningrad and the position of Lithuania's Russian-speaking minorities. It also targets episodes from Lithuanian history that can provoke territorial disputes with Russia or Belarus.[76] In the Vilnius region, historical ownership rights are claimed by some Russian and Belarusian sources, providing Moscow with opportunities to incite Lithuanian-Belarusian frictions. Claims that the Lithuanian capital was Belarusian for 600 years and illegally became Lithuanian provide valuable historical cover for a potential military incursion to convince soldiers that they were not occupying but liberating and protecting historic Russian-Belarusian lands. In addition, a key message of Russia's propaganda is that NATO has launched an arms race and is seeking a confrontation with Russia. Hence, Lithuania's membership of NATO allegedly poses a threat to the security of both Russia and Belarus.

Kaliningrad is a brewing source of instability for Lithuania. Vilnius supervises all military transport to Kaliningrad across its territory and rejects any extra-territorial agreements with Russia.[77] However, Moscow may demand unilateral control of such a corridor or stage a provocation against a Russian convoy to justify intervention. It could also claim that Kaliningrad has been severed from outside supplies by

Lithuania, which allegedly does not recognize it as Russian territory, and then move to unblock the exclave. The military in Kaliningrad could itself stage a provocation against Lithuanian territory. [78] Ominously, officials in Kaliningrad have accused participants of Ukraine's Maidan revolution of infiltrating the region through Poland and Lithuania.[79]

Plans for a unified energy network among EU states may have serious consequences for Kaliningrad by breaking up the electric grid between Russia and the EU at its borders.[80] The unification of the electric grids of Lithuania, Latvia, and Estonia with the rest of the EU would exclude Kaliningrad from the Baltic energy system. This could lead to electricity shortages and may be used as a pretext for Moscow to pursue the construction of a nuclear power plant there opposed by EU neighbors or even to forcibly create a land corridor across Belarus and Lithuania. Indeed, exercises conducted in Kaliningrad on a regular basis revolve around an offensive scenario to carve out a corridor between Kaliningrad and Russia.

The prospect of power shortages and territorial isolation may also motivate local activists seeking an independent fourth Baltic republic or transforming Kaliningrad into an EU-linked Euro-region. This could provoke a crackdown and provide additional ammunition for Moscow's intervention across Lithuanian territory. Russian ultra-nationalist groups also campaign for expanding Kaliningrad's borders to the prewar frontiers of Germany's East Prussia and incorporating the Lithuanian port of Klaipėda.

In recent years, Kaliningrad has witnessed intensive military activity with the deployment of S400 air defense systems and a powerful radar that covers the whole of Europe and the Northern Ocean waters and may be capable of paralyzing the air space over the entire Baltic Sea.[81] Moscow has also threatened to deploy *Iskander* tactical missiles carrying nuclear warheads in the region; some reports indicate that they are already positioned in Kaliningrad.

Russia's military exercises near the Lithuanian border are viewed in Vilnius as direct threats. For instance, the *Zapad* exercises in the fall of 2013 simulated the creation of a land link between Russia and Kaliningrad, thus involving the invasion of both Lithuania and Latvia and cutting off Lithuania from Poland. Russian forces have also rehearsed a nuclear strike on Warsaw. Lithuania remains under pressure to allow for a permanent military transit corridor under Moscow's control to Kaliningrad. During 2014 and 2015 there was also a surge in violations of Baltic air space by Russian aircraft despite NATO's reinforcing mission.[82] Most takeoffs were made by fighter jets to escort Russian warplanes flying from northern Russia to Kaliningrad.

Russia's navy has conducted exercises off the coast of the Baltic states and violated Lithuania's exclusive economic zone. Russian naval vessels have ordered commercial ships to change routes and obstructed the laying of an undersea power connection cable between Sweden and Lithuania.[83] Since early 2015, the laying of the *Nordbalt* cable has been disrupted four times by the Russian navy, which claims that it is protecting its "military exercise zones."[84] The incursions of a suspected Russian submarine inside the Stockholm archipelago, in October 2014, alerted Vilnius to enhance the security of its new LNG terminal in Klaipėda.[85] Observers noted that saboteurs could stage an incident near the entrance to the port in order to close it.[86]

On the economic warfare front, Moscow has consistently applied energy sanctions against all three Baltic states, whether by cutting off supplies of fossil fuels or raising prices. Vilnius is active in energy diversification, by opening an LNG terminal in 2014, limiting dependence on Russian natural gas, and constructing a gas interconnector with Poland. This will help meet about two thirds of Lithuanian energy needs. Vilnius also wants to plug into the Nordic market, synchronize its electricity grid with the EU and disconnect it from the post-Soviet zone. A lessened dependence on Russia will also help bring down heating prices over the next decade.

In weaning itself off Russia's energy supplies, Vilnius has faced additional pressures. Plans to build a nuclear power plant in Lithuania caused Moscow to announce the construction of two plants – in Belarus and Kaliningrad. When Vilnius stopped the project, the Russian proposals were shelved. The Kremlin wants to block initiatives that enable Lithuania to break out of its remaining energy dependence on Russia. By raising the cost of energy imports, Moscow also seeks to impact on social grievances over rising fuel bills. Additionally, it has supported and funded environmentalist and rural movements opposed to shale gas exploration—a potential alternative to gas imported from Russia.[87]

According to Lithuanian Prime Minister Algirdas Butkevičius, If Russia completely closed all roads for goods from Lithuania, it would cost the country up to 4% of GDP.[88] There are also concerns that some business ventures in the energy field have connections with the Kremlin and provide Putin with political levers against Vilnius.[89] Lithuania has direct experience of previous attempts to purchase its government leaders. A case of direct political subversion in which influence was bought by Russian businessmen tied to Kremlin intelligence services unseated Lithuania's President Rolandas Paksas in April 2004 and placed other officials under suspicion of collaboration.

Russia's espionage activities have intensified in recent years. Lithuania's intelligence agencies reported that about one third of Russian diplomats worked for spy agencies.[90] They are increasingly interested in Lithuania's military infrastructure, especially in Šiauliai, home to a NATO air base for policing Baltic skies, and the LNG terminal in Klaipėda, which opened in January 2015.[91] Russian and Belarusian special services have also been active along the border with Lithuania, reportedly trying to recruit border guards as informers. The spies are especially interested in Lithuania's law enforcement institutions and border security infrastructure.[92] Several of Russia's neighbors have reported the potential threat posed by the allocation of land plots near military facilities to Russian companies or wealthy citizens who appear to be working with the Kremlin. For instance, the Russian company Rail Skyway Systems sought to purchase land near the Zokniai NATO air base but was rebuffed after the intervention of Lithuanian security services.[93]

Vilnius has reinstated limited conscription as anxieties have mounted over Russian military activities. [94] President Dalia Grybauskaitė unveiled a plan for 3,500 men between the ages of 19 and 26 to be drafted for a nine-month period every year, starting in the fall of 2015. Lithuania abolished conscription in favor of a professional army in 2008, four years after it joined NATO. Conscription would help fill gaps in units and train extra reservists for the armed forces consisting of 8,000 professional soldiers.

Grybauskaitė stated that the Baltic states must be prepared to independently resist a military conflict with Russia for at least three days until NATO allies arrive.[95] Conscription sends a clear message that, if attacked, Lithuania would defend itself. The authorities have also conducted security exercises without NATO allies in order to improve coordination between the country's institutions. [96] For instance, the Iron Sword 2015 national exercises in May 2015 involved over 3,000 personnel from the Lithuanian Armed Forces and the Defense, Internal Affairs, and Health Ministries, as well as from municipal governments and the Lithuanian Riflemen's Union. Among other scenarios, the authorities simulated threats against the LNG terminal in Klaipėda.

The Kremlin tries to spread its influence in Lithuania via public organizations, education institutions, television, Internet, and other widely accessible information channels. Vilnius created the Cyber Defense Law and a coordination center to help investigations by trained police officers. Analysts believe that informational wars should be viewed with the same seriousness as cyber attacks, with the involvement of all targeted institutions, whether cultural, educational, economic, or political.[97] Lithuanian analysts contend that Russian sources spread conspiracy theories on the most varied topics and by involving people in discussing conspiracies it distracts them from real information.[98]

In its national security strategy, Lithuania has included information attacks as a looming threat. In a telling example of an informational offensive, on February 4, 2015, Lithuanian army commanders issued public assurances that conscripts would not be sent to international missions abroad, refuting rumors spread by the Russian media aimed at discrediting the restoration of conscription.[99] Russia's media also disseminated false information that the projected Lithuanian-Polish-Ukrainian brigade could become a pretext for sending conscripts to fight in Ukraine.

Russia's *Pravfond*, which helps implement Moscow's "compatriots policy," directly finances at least three organizations in Lithuania, nine in Latvia, and nine in Estonia.[100] According to intelligence sources, they are active in spreading disinformation about the Baltic countries and creating a broad pro-Moscow network. One of the key Kremlin-funded operatives is Rafael Muksinov, who was included in the joint list of candidates of the Polish Electoral Action and Russian Alliance parties during the 2015 local government elections and was elected to the Vilnius City Municipality Council. He is also the leader of the Compatriots Council at the Russian Embassy in Vilnius. One of his associates is Algirdas Paleckis, head of the Lithuania Without Nazism association funded by Moscow and linked with the World Without Nazism group, registered in France with branches in all three Baltic countries, Moldova, Germany, the UK, and the US. Another suspected implant is Karlis Bilansas, funded by *Pravfond* to run the Independent Human Rights Centre.

Russian state TV exerts influence over the older generation, while the youth is reached mostly through the Internet. Russia's television channels are viewed by almost 16% of the population, or by over 400,000 people.[101] Social networks also exert a significant influence in Lithuania. Hacking of Internet portals and sites and posting false information has developed into a major problem. Vilnius temporarily closed three Russian TV channels in the summer of 2014 because they were broadcasting hate speech and war propaganda during the Russia-Ukraine war.[102]

Most of the Polish population in Lithuania, the largest minority in the country, also inhabits the Russian information sphere, especially older Sovietized and russified citizens not under Poland's influence. The Polish minority numbered 200,317 people, according to the Lithuanian census of 2011, or 6.6% of the population. [103] It is concentrated in the Vilnius and Šalčininkai regions in the south of the country. Russian ethnics totaled 176,913 people, or 5.8% of the population.

The Electoral Action of Poles in Lithuania (EAPL), headed by Valdemar Tomaszevski (Waldemar Tomaszewski, in Polish), has demonstrated pro-Kremlin positions over Ukraine, is suspected of receiving funds from Moscow, and cooperates closely with leaders of Lithuania's Russian minority.[104] A report leaked in November 2013 by Lithuania's State Security Department revealed that representatives of the EAPL and the Russian Alliance had visited the Kremlin. [105] Moscow fosters disagreements between Vilnius and the Polish minority, as this harms the country's reputation in the West and negatively affects ties with Warsaw. During the October 2012 parliamentary elections, the EAPL combined with the Russian Alliance, an arrangement fostered by the Russian embassy in Vilnius.

The EAPL possesses eight seats in Lithuania's parliament and is run as a hierarchical organization with little opposition. It also controls two local governments in Vilnius and Šalčininkai and periodically has representatives in the central government. It has focused on various grievances of the Polish minority such as the lack of bilingual place names and the inability to use the Polish alphabet in the documents of Poles.[106] Some critics contend that making concessions to the EAPL will simply escalate its demands to make Polish a second state language. Others complain that successive Lithuanian governments have allowed Polish and Russian leaders to isolate their communities. Poles need to be better integrated into Lithuanian society and Poland itself needs to be more active to pull the Polish population away from Russia's information sphere. Alternative Polish parties and NGOs need support and Lithuanian parties must be more engaged in minority affairs. Joint projects with Poland in the Vilnius and Šalčininkai regions could counterbalance Russia's influences, and investments are especially needed in infrastructure and job creation.[107]

Russian minority leaders are also active thanks to Moscow's assistance. Rafael Muksinov, Chairman of the Coordinating Council of Russian Compatriots in Lithuania, contends that the minority needs Russian kindergartens, schools, and universities, as well as "a fully-fledged information and cultural space."[108] A more radical Russian movement, Be Together, spreads pro-Moscow propaganda, anti-Americanism, and traditionalism to try and capture support from other conservative movements.[109]

The Russian embassy reportedly funds several local NGOs, including environmentalists, groups looking after the graves of Russian soldiers, and several historical societies. Lithuania's National Security and Defense Committee is also convinced that individuals have been sent to Lithuania to organize fake trade unions. Yevgeniy Sivaykin, an avid Putin supporter, has formed several professional unions and organized rallies claiming that workers are abused in Lithuania.[110] The incitement of ethnic or social dissatisfaction is useful for Moscow in unsettling the central government.

Russia's secret services finance historical reconstruction clubs that enact war games from the Tsarist period in Lithuania. Lectures on the greatness of the Soviet Union, the threat of NATO, and the allegedly inane Baltic politicians are given in "international educational camps" in Russia attended by young people from Lithuania, Latvia, and Estonia.[111] Such indoctrination events have the goal of awakening the "Soviet spirit" among Russian-speaking young people from the former Soviet countries. Moscow is also suspected of encouraging groups among Russia's population who actively support and collect funds for the proxy separatists in Ukraine's Donbas.[112] Such activities can be qualified as financing terrorism and recruitment for terrorist activities.

According to senior Lithuanian military officers, in response to the Ukrainian war Vilnius must step up its capabilities to prepare for unconventional challenges, such as the incitement of ethnic minorities or the incursion of armed persons without identification signs.[113] In one scenario of subversion, leaders of the Polish and Russian minorities could ask Moscow to support a referendum on the autonomy of the Vilnius and Šalčininkai regions. Lithuania's military and internal security units require improved equipment, means of communication, and transportation. Reports periodically surface that the Lithuanian counterintelligence service is not effective enough to cope with Russia's subversion. For instance, it has failed to sufficiently monitor and investigate the activities of Russian agents in Lithuania's energy, finance, and transportation sectors.[114]

Lithuania's Minister of the Interior Dailis Alfonsas Barakauskas was instrumental in establishing a pan-Baltic expert coordination committee to foster collaboration between institutions in charge of public order and internal security. The interior ministers of Lithuania, Latvia, and Estonia reached agreement on the establishment of such a committee in September 2014, amid growing concerns over Russia's provocations.[115] The Ministry of Defense also prepared a brochure with information on how citizens should act in a war situation.[116] It describes the social and psychological challenges involved. In the event of conflict, the media would announce a state of greater readiness and a national headquarters would provide concrete instructions for citizens.

On November 1, 2014, Vilnius activated a new rapid-reaction force designed to resist unconventional security threats. Henceforth, 2,500 troops would be placed on high alert to counteract attacks by unmarked combatants, like those in eastern Ukraine.[117] The force, accounting for about a third of Lithuania's 7,000-strong military, would take from two to 24 hours to be fully mobilized. The core of the force consists of two mechanized battalions, each with 700 to 800 members, joined by logistical support, a special operations unit, and an air contingent.[118] It would be activated in the initial, self-defense phase and allow for NATO forces to be deployed from outside the country.

The defense ministry also tabled legislation that would enable the President to authorize the use of military force in a defined territory without first declaring martial law. In December 2014, the standby units of the army, including the rapid-response force, were placed on a higher state of preparedness because of the increased activities of Russian forces in Kaliningrad and in western parts of the Russian Federation.[119]

All three Baltic capitals fervently supported the creation of NATO's new "spearhead force," announced at the Alliance summit in Wales, in September 2014, which is to consist of 3,000 to 4,000 troops. An interim force was to become operational by the close of 2015, with a permanent force scheduled for 2016. Speed is essential in countering unconventional threats, as Russia's military can move into an area rapidly and establish a foothold before conventional armies can react. A NATO command center, or force integration unit, was established in Lithuania in the summer of 2015, with about 40 officers. The center would serve to coordinate and help equip NATO's advanced units in the event of war with Russia.

In addition, Lithuania earmarked military assistance for Ukraine to better defend itself against Russia's ongoing attack; this included the supply of weapons and training. [120] Russia's Foreign Ministry vigorously protested such moves. In case of a Russian assault on Lithuania, Polish Special Forces, which have worked closely with their Baltic counterparts in the former Yugoslavia, Afghanistan, and Iraq, are reportedly prepared to come to the country's assistance. [121]

Nordic Front

The Nordic non-NATO members, Sweden and Finland, are growing increasingly concerned by Moscow's pressures along their borders and direct threats to their security, as witnessed in periodic Russian military penetration of their air space and territorial waters. Fears over Putin's ambitions have escalated among the security services in Stockholm and Helsinki, as well as among NATO members Norway and Denmark. Swedish intelligence agencies have expressed serious concerns that Moscow is supplementing its spying efforts in Scandinavia and even preparing for war. Wilhelm Unge, the chief counter-intelligence analyst for the Säkerhetspolisen (Säpo) agency has stated that the escalating crisis in Europe's East posed a significant security threat. [122]

In conducting military incursions, Moscow has several objectives. First, it is testing the military and political response of targeted countries. Second, it is sending messages to a largely pacifist public in Sweden and Finland that any moves toward NATO membership will result in heightened military risks and confrontations with Russia. Third, it is discouraging further military cooperation, including joint exercises, with NATO states in the Baltic zone. And fourth, it seeks to demonstrate to the entire Baltic region that NATO's commitment to defend its members is merely a paper declaration that Russia could easily overturn.

The Kremlin wants to maintain both Sweden and Finland as neutrals and preclude them from assisting any NATO operations to defend the Baltic states. A variety of pressure points are thereby exploited: military threats, territorial violations, diplomatic moves, propaganda attacks, and disinformation campaigns to cower Finnish and Swedish societies. Further measures are threatened if Helsinki or Stockholm progress toward NATO accession, including the confiscation of investments, banning flights across Russia, and enabling illegal immigrants to cross the long Russian-Finnish border.

In a demonstration of Russia's military contingency plans, in March 2015, Russian forces rehearsed the invasion of Norway, Finland, Sweden, and Denmark during a military exercise involving 33,000 troops. [123] The maneuvers were based on the assumption that a Western-backed uprising against Putin was taking place in Moscow. Russia responded by launching a simulated assault on four states by seizing northern Norway, Finland's Aland Islands, Sweden's Gotland Island, and Denmark's Bornholm Island. The capture of these territories would enable Russia to seal off shipping lanes and isolate the three Baltic states. The occupation of any Finnish or Swedish territory would also be intended to disqualify both countries from NATO accession.

To protect themselves against possible attack, both Finland and Sweden are expanding their military cooperation. They are also strengthening security ties with NATO members Norway and Denmark through consultations and exercises. Russia's Foreign Ministry warned, on April 12, 2015, that closer ties between NATO and Finland and Sweden were of "special concern" for Moscow. This was a response to a joint declaration by the defense ministers of Sweden, Norway, Finland, Denmark, and Iceland, on April 9, 2015, asserting that northern Europe must prepare for possible crises because of Russia's grievous violations of international law. [124] In retaliation, the Kremlin complained that a new Nordic defense pact signified a "confrontational approach" toward Russia.[125] The defense ministers stated that they would boost defense sector cooperation; share intelligence on maritime and airspace activities; take joint steps on cyber defense; conduct military drills; consider launching a new air-police mission called Northern Flag; share air bases; and explore their engagement in joint military acquisitions.[126]

Nonetheless, all such measures will not be sufficient to shield either Finland or Sweden from Russia's pressure or to prevent their embroilment in a future Baltic-wide war if Putin decides to strike. Washington itself should not push for NATO enlargement in two countries that still treasure their non-alignment, as this risks aggravating latent anti-American sentiments. Instead, it should allow Moscow's provocations to convince Helsinki and Stockholm that their security is best assured inside the North Atlantic Alliance and alongside their Nordic and Baltic compatriots.

In the wake of its attack on Ukraine, Russia's military activities around the Baltic Sea accelerated and become more unpredictable during 2014 and 2015. In large measure, the assault on Ukraine has been a psychological operation in order to demonstrate Moscow's reach and capabilities. [127] Finnish and Swedish airspaces are strategically important to NATO; hence, Russia's military testing is designed to indicate how the two countries will react under pressure. An important military component of security in northeastern Europe is the closest possible integration of Sweden and Finland into NATO planning and deployments. It would be more difficult to defend the Baltic states without their help, as they possess important military capabilities and intelligence services.[128]

Moscow's security threats aimed at the Nordic states may be a staged diversion or a ploy to test their reactions and dissuade them from cooperating with NATO in defense of the Baltic states. However, if regional stability seriously deteriorated because of Russia's assertiveness toward Estonia, Latvia, or Lithuania, both Sweden and Finland could petition for NATO membership. This could increase tensions throughout northern Europe and further widen the rupture between Washington and Moscow.

Finland

Calls to consolidate Finland's defenses have grown since Russia's attack on Ukraine and the regular violation of Finnish airspace by Russian aircraft. General Jarmo Lindberg, commander of Finland's Defense Forces, has asserted that Europe needs to be prepared for a sudden deterioration along its eastern frontier, where Finland shares the EU's longest border with Russia.[129] Moscow may be concerned that Finns would come to the aid of nearby Estonia in case the latter is attacked. It could offer NATO its land, air, and sea facilities to defend an Alliance member and supply weapons and other equipment to assist Tallinn. Unlike Sweden, Finland has maintained a respectable defense sector with a sizable conscript base army. Helsinki also has direct experience of Russia's aggression, having stymied attempts by Moscow to occupy the country during World War Two.

To heighten Helsinki's anxieties, Moscow announced in the fall of 2014 that it would place its most advanced S-400 missile system in the Kola Peninsula adjoining Finland. The system is able to intercept stealth fighters and cruise missiles with a maximum range of 400 kilometers.[130] Russia has six missile troop bases in the Kola Peninsula and has reopened the Alakurtti base, close to the Finnish border, as part of its deployment of military units along the Arctic Circle, from Murmansk to Chukotka. Putin announced that Russia would build a network of military facilities on its Arctic territories to host troops, advanced warships, and aircraft to protect its interests and borders.[131] Moscow is pressing ahead to develop the Arctic territories, including hydrocarbon extraction and opening a Northern Sea Route, as an alternative to traditional passages from Europe to Asia. The region will become a growing source of competition with the US, Canada,

Norway, and Denmark. Indeed, Foreign Minister Lavrov claimed that NATO's presence in the Arctic was unnecessary.

Russia's military periodically violates Finnish air space and territorial waters. On April 27, 2015, the Finnish navy fired warning shots at a suspected Russian submarine detected in waters close to the capital.[132] In line with its pressures against any country engaged in military sales to Ukraine, Russia's Foreign Affairs Ministry complained against Helsinki's supplies of laser range-finders, accusing Helsinki of undermining peace and stability in Ukraine.[133]

In addition to military pressure, Helsinki's national interests were harmed by serious data security breaches in the Foreign Ministry's communications network. Finland's secret services, *Supo*, reported in July 2014 that "foreign state actors" were believed to be behind the attacks, which were very advanced and difficult to detect.[134] In the second attack, investigated as "aggravated espionage," the spyware software was linked to a website hosted by a foreign state. *Supo* confirmed that large amounts of material were taken from the Foreign Ministry and had potentially damaged national interests.

A group of Finnish analysts published a report in March 2015 on the impact of Russian networks of influence in the country.[135] *Lustraatio* (Lustration) highlights the need for the establishment of a "truth commission" to investigate Soviet networks of influence in Finland during the Cold War and the importance of unmasking current collaborators. Another vexing question has been the purchase of land and real estate by Russian citizens close to military bases, radar stations, air traffic control systems, flight training sites, and ammunition dumps.[136] As a result of "systematic land acquisitions," large plots of land on the Finnish coast and extensive water areas have been transferred to Russian ownership—mostly businessmen close to the Kremlin. The headquarters of the Finnish Navy in Turku is one of the targets of Russian companies. They have offered high prices for nearby land and stated that they intend to build "recreational areas."[137]

An article in December 2014 by Charly Salonius-Pasternak, a senior researcher at the Finnish Institute of International Affairs, caused consternation in Helsinki.[138] The author claimed that by occupying a couple of Finland's Åland Islands, Russia could control most of the airspace in the Baltic Sea. The Åland Islands are an autonomous and demilitarized region of Finland once occupied by Tsarist Russia. Moscow could demand a naval base from Finland, claiming that saboteurs threatened to blow up the Nord Stream pipeline and Russian oil tankers.[139] The Russian navy can blockade the Gulf of Finland, thus severing the bulk of Finland's trade. Moscow could also announce that it was assuming responsibility for the security of the Baltic Sea because terrorists were attempting to cut off its raw material exports.

Officials in Moscow periodically manipulate the Karelian question to increase pressure on Helsinki. The Karelian region was annexed by Soviet Russia from Finland after World War Two and most of the territories form a Karelian Republic along Finland's borders. In March 2015, Nikolai Patrushev, head of Russia's Security Council, charged Finnish nationalists with increasing agitation in Karelia and recruiting local people to destabilize the republic.[140] Patrushev claimed that Finland's government had also intensified its support for Karelian nationalists. According to local analysts, Moscow's campaign against alleged nationalists was more vigorous than the latter's activism. Locals feared this could be the harbinger for abrogating the EU-Russia agreement on border cooperation, which has brought funds to the northern border region but has also enabled many Karelians to see their impoverishment in comparison to Finns on the other side of the frontier.

In a major diplomatic incident at the beginning of July 2015, Alexei Pushkov, head of the Russian *Duma's* foreign affairs committee, raised the possibility of imposing sanctions against Finland for its denial of entry visas to *Duma* Speaker Sergey Naryshkin and five other

Russian citizens planning to attend an OSCE meeting in Helsinki.[141] All six Russian citizens are on the EU sanctions list imposed after Moscow's attack on Ukraine. A broad range of measures could be taken by Moscow against Helsinki, including a freeze on trade agreements and changes to customs tariffs.

Moscow's efforts to portray Finland as the primary loser in EU sanctions against Russia, most evident through its Finnish-language *Sputnik* network, has had limited impact on the public. Indeed, Finnish perceptions of Russia became more negative after the latter's attack on Ukraine. According to an opinion poll carried out by the National Defense University and the Police University College in the fall of 2014, 74% of respondents admitted that their views of Russia had become more negative.[142] In another survey of Russian speakers living in Finland, 66% of the respondents felt that the Ukraine conflict had negatively impacted on Russo-Finnish relations, while 21% said Finnish attitudes toward Russian-speakers had changed for the worse.[143] Close to one third of respondents claimed they had experienced negative attitudes in Finland because they were Russian speakers.

Moscow's propaganda in Finland has significantly expanded and operates through various avenues. The Finnish authorities established a working group with the heads of communications from each ministry to pinpoint Russia's subversive disinformation in the media and other outlets.[144] For example, Moscow sources claims that the Russian minority in Finland, numbering under 60,000 out of 5.4 million people, is under pressure of assimilation and discrimination and the Russian government must take steps to protect them.[145]

In response to Moscow's attack on Ukraine and threats against Finnish territory, President Sauli Niinistö urged greater defense spending in order to maintain a credible military deterrent.[146] In March 2015, the majority of Finns favored increasing the defense budget during the current parliamentary term: 27% strongly supported this position and 32% "somewhat agreed." [147] Finland maintains an armed force of about 30,000, but the military has undergone budget cuts since 2012, with reservists reduced from 350,000 to 230,000 troops, several garrisons shuttered, and materiel acquisitions delayed. Defense Minister Carl Haglund warned that Finland would have to make "difficult and expensive" decisions about upgrading the country's aging defense hardware. He also called for the government to develop the ability to wage cyber warfare. [148]

The Defense Ministry has been working on a feasibility study looking at renewing the air defense system and replacing the existing fleet of Hornet fighter jets. Finland remains the only Nordic country that can generate substantial amounts of trained combat troops, but the bulk of the Finnish army lacks modern equipment and only a small fraction of the planned eleven wartime brigades are adequately equipped. [149] In the context of Russia's assertiveness along Finland's borders, Helsinki has laid out plans for a Finnish "spearhead force" mirroring NATO's reaction force. Additionally, Haglund announced that Helsinki would step up surveillance of its airspace following several violations by Russian aircraft. [150] In June 2015, 8,000 reservist troops underwent a large-scale exercise in the eastern region of Pielinen Karelia, near the Russian border. [151] Finland and Sweden also prepared joint submarine hunt exercises, the sharing of military bases, and other measures to tighten defense connections. [152]

Finland and Sweden are also increasing their military cooperation with NATO. A framework was agreed during NATO's Wales Summit in September 2014. The Host Nation Support Memorandum of Understanding includes 50 to 60 "Mutual Objectives," with a protocol under which either country could invite NATO to deploy land, naval, and air force assets on their territories. [153] Following this agreement Aleksey Pushkov, chair of the Russian *Duma's* Foreign Affairs Committee, claimed that both countries were surrendering their neutrality and moving toward NATO accession. [154]

Military cooperation between Finland and Estonia has steadily developed.[155] A radar station was opened at Toikamae near Otepaa in south Estonia, which Estonia bought as part of joint procurement with Finland. It will refine monitoring of the Pskov garrison, the training center of Russia's Special Forces. Estonian soldiers will visit Finland for regular training, Tallinn will buy CV-90 armored infantry fighting vehicles from the Netherlands, and the Finns will teach Estonian troops how to operate them. Washington has also urged Helsinki to participate in Estonia's air defenses.

In the aftermath of Russia's military intervention in Ukraine, support for Finland's NATO membership expanded among citizens. The sense of security has been evaporating and a debate was launched on the pros and cons of NATO accession.[156] According to Mika Aaltola, of the Finnish Institute of International Affairs, growing backing for NATO entry shows that Finns see the Alliance as a necessary counterweight to Russia's hardening position, as they are unsure whether Finland could respond to regional crises on its own.[157] A quarter of respondents in August 2014 believed Finland should become a member of NATO, 9% higher than in November 2013. Although 58% of those polled continue to oppose NATO membership, 56% of all respondents view Russia as a threat to Finland, up from 39% in March 2014.[158] Supporters of the conservative National Coalition Party were the most strident supporters of NATO entry, and a further third of NATO backers described themselves as Finns Party voters. The Left Alliance and Social Democrat constituencies were the largest groups still opposing NATO entry.

Prime Minister Alexander Stubb believed that Finland belongs in NATO, although his governing coalition officially opposed membership.[159] Stubb asserted that Finland should not join NATO simply because of Russia, but to enhance its overall security. He stressed that Finland no longer exists in a gray zone but is a part of the West.[160] The Defense Ministry strongly supports NATO membership, calculating that this would enhance the country's capabilities, but has not actively campaigned for accession. Opponents of joining NATO contend that this would aggravate relations with Russia and damage trade and energy linkages. Moscow could impose trade bans and customs fees with damaging economic impact, as Russia was Finland's third largest importer and the biggest exporter, supplying 25% of Finland's electricity. Trade figures also indicate that Finland is more exposed to economic losses stemming from a weaker Russian economy than any other euro country. Moscow could also confiscate Finnish investments, declare Finnish products as unsafe, cut transportation links, ban Finnair from using Russian airspace, mount cyber attacks on government sites, terminate nuclear security cooperation, and fan fears about the safety of Russian nuclear reactors.

At the end of May 2015, Finland's new center-right coalition included the option of applying for NATO membership "at any time" in its Joint Policy Position statement. [161] Prime Minister Juha Sipilä's administration also drafted a new foreign and security policy with a special segment calculating the monetary costs and implications of Finland's potential NATO accession.

Proponents of NATO entry argue that the significance of the Alliance for Finland's security is evident in two ways: the economy is dependent on a maritime connection to Europe through the Baltic Sea; and in a possible crisis, the greatest challenge is to obtain necessary military material including missiles and spare parts. During a confrontation with Russia, Finland must maintain a sea connection with Europe through NATO, which would require a powerful navy and air force. In a crisis, Finland's weapons and ammunition supplies would rely largely on the US, which plays a crucial role in the country's security. [162] Finland cannot be militarily self-sufficient and can only be included in NATO decision-making through membership.

NATO has sent signals to both Helsinki and Stockholm that they would be well-qualified candidates. If they decided to apply, the negotiation stage could proceed fairly rapidly, with Finland in particular meeting most requirements and its military forces already being more NATO compatible than some member states. Nonetheless, membership will require majority public support, whereas surveys still indicate that only a third of Finns are strongly in favor. In contrast, based on a survey carried out in June 2014 by the Officers' Union among its members, 76% of generals and colonels in active service are in favor of NATO membership.[163]

President Sauli Niinistö has claimed that the treaty-based post–Cold War arrangement was broken by Moscow, and, therefore, Finland's international position has changed: "In a certain way, we are an opponent of Russia because we support the EU."[164]

During the Cold War, Finland's foreign policy avoided open opposition to the Soviet Union and claimed to be neutral. The most urgent question is how the Kremlin would react to Finland's NATO membership and whether staying outside the Alliance actually increases or decreases Finland's security. The new coalition government formed by the Center Party and the nationalist Finns Party after the April 19, 2015, elections has avoided the question of NATO membership for the near future, given Moscow's ominous saber-rattling. Nonetheless, Helsinki remained committed to increasing its defense spending, and the question of NATO accession will depend on the country's sense of security and vulnerability.

Sweden

Sweden has experienced increasing surveillance and military pressure from Moscow since the onset of the Ukrainian war. Even before this conflict, Stockholm was vehemently criticized by Moscow as a collaborator with Poland in pushing the EU's Eastern Partnership program allegedly designed to tear the post-Soviet states away from Russia.[165] According to Russia's ambassador to Sweden, "We are not the ones who started the military escalation in the Baltic Sea area, it is a response to NATO's increased activities."[166] According to Putin advisor Sergey Markov, Sweden is one of the most Russophobic countries in Europe, and any moves toward its NATO membership would aggravate security throughout the region.

Russia's intelligence agencies have redoubled their efforts to recruit spies in Sweden, and Russia's military has increased flight exercises against simulated Swedish targets. Stockholm's military leaders have been criticized for failing to mobilize any jets in response to Russian flights along the Swedish border. Moscow has engaged in numerous security provocations, especially in airspace and maritime incursions. In the most egregious incident in October 2014, a Russian submarine traveled close to Stockholm, prompting Sweden to mobilize its troops and ships.[167] Submarine and aircraft infiltrations are designed to affect Sweden's population and test its air and sea defenses, which have been significantly weakened through budget cuts over the past twenty years. This presents Stockholm with a starker choice in increasing its defense spending and petitioning for NATO entry to enhance its security.

Russia's submarine intrusion may also have been a diversionary operation in order to focus Swedish attention and resources on one area while potentially striking in another zone. Conversely, Moscow simply wanted to demonstrate Swedish impotence under the newly installed red-green coalition government led by Prime Minister Stefan Löfven.[168] One litmus test for the new administration will be the Host Nation Support agreement, initialed with NATO prior to the elections in September 2014. Moscow's threatening actions may have been designed to delay ratification and implementation of this NATO accord.

Russia's fleet has tripled its exercise time on the Baltic Sea in recent years, and its air force is more active, with fighter planes flying closer to Swedish borders. In June 2014, NATO held a large BALTOPS international exercise near southern Sweden. The American fleet with a Swedish officer as deputy commander led the exercise, involving 30 vessels and 52 airplanes from 14 participating countries. This large-scale presence of NATO forces contributed to eliciting a more aggressive posture by Russian commanders. They have tried to demonstrate their strength by testing the latest fighter planes and cruise missiles and simulating air attacks off the island of Gotska Sandön. No Swedish planes were dispatched in response, thus indicating Stockholm's low level of readiness for an attack. Moscow also conducted exercises by dropping paratroopers on the beaches of Kaliningrad, across the Baltic Sea from Sweden, which could be difficult for Russia to defend in the event of a war with NATO.

Russia's Air Force has simulated action inside Swedish borders in a possible war scenario in which Sweden belongs to an enemy bloc. In May 2014, the previous Swedish government decided to give priority to its military presence on the Baltic Sea, as Foreign Minister Carl Bildt emphasized how important it was for Sweden to demonstrate its solidarity as a NATO partner.[169] Stockholm confirmed that it would allow NATO to use Swedish territory in the event that the Baltic states were attacked by Russia.[170]

In October 2014, Sweden's signals intelligence leaked a photo of a Russian fighter jet flying only about 30 feet away from a Swedish military intelligence plane; also, armed NATO fighter jets followed Russian fighters above the Swedish island of Öland.[171] Increased military activity in the airspace above the Baltic Sea has heightened the risk that a civilian passenger plane could collide with a Russian military plane. Such a crash between an SAS passenger aircraft and a Russian reconnaissance plane was narrowly averted in March 2014.[172] The planes were only 90 meters apart and the SAS flight from Copenhagen to Italy had 130 passengers aboard. Russian aircraft frequently fly with their transponders turned off so they cannot be detected by radar and thereby pose a danger for commercial aviation. A conflict could rapidly develop if a collision with a passenger airplane occurred and Moscow attempted to deflect blame by charging NATO with causing the incident.

In the mid-1990s, Stockholm reduced its sizeable conscription-based military trained for territorial defense. The Army was cut by almost 90% and the Navy by 70%; only the Air Force largely maintained its resources. In 2009, the center-right government decided that Sweden would abandon conscription and territorial defense to focus on limited international operations. Currently, Sweden has just over 14,000 active duty troops plus a reserve of only 9,000 responsible for protecting a country the size of California. In reality, Sweden is unable to defend itself, and even a massive increase in military spending would do little to improve capabilities in the short-run as the country has lost a generation of combat commanders.[173]

Some analysts have posited the idea that Russia could seriously test and thwart NATO by occupying the Swedish island of Gotland, located about 50 miles from Sweden's coast and only 80 miles from Latvia.[174] Given its location at the center of the Baltic Sea, Gotland could become critical in defending the Baltic states from a Russian attack. By occupying Gotland and using it for military operations, Moscow could prevent the Alliance from sending troop reinforcements and equipment to the Baltic states or using the island as a base to hunt Russian submarines. Although Gotland's strategic importance has increased since the Baltic states joined NATO, Sweden has reduced its military presence and only maintained a Home Guard battalion there. It is also important to remember that the Alliance would be under no obligation to defend Gotland, as Sweden is not a NATO member.

In January 2015, Sweden's military Supreme Commander Sverker Göranson requested a substantial budget increase in order not to fall further behind Russia and other countries in the region.[175] This would include a greater number of full-time employees, more resources to conduct training, and personal equipment for soldiers. Sweden's defense budget in 2014 amounted to only 1% of GDP; plans were initiated for a steady increase by 2020, but only to 1.2% of GDP. In March 2015, Defense Minister Peter Hultqvist asserted that Sweden would raise defense spending by €677 million ($720 million) and re-establish a permanent military presence on Gotland.[176] Most of the money allocated between 2016 and 2020 would be spent on modernizing ships that could detect and intercept submarines.

However, a credible deterrent would take Sweden much longer to achieve. According to analysts, ten to fifteen years are needed to construct a defense capable of protecting Sweden after a decade of cutbacks. According to opinion polls, 45% of Swedes think that defense spending should increase, while 36% believe it must remain the same.[177] In one important step, Stockholm brought back the option of using reservists to boost its military force. Defense Minister Hultqvist argued that the move was necessary against the backdrop of Russia's rearmament. Sweden's military also upgraded its cooperation with neighboring NATO member Denmark, in which the two countries would henceforth exchange confidential information, have free access to each other's air and naval bases for refueling, enhance cooperation in air and maritime surveillance, and be able to use each other's airspace when incidents occurred.[178]

In early May 2015, NATO held one of its largest anti-submarine exercises, Dynamic Mongoose, in the North Sea, with the participation of Sweden for the first time. NATO simulated detecting and attacking foreign submarines. Stockholm also decided to expand its role in the annual NATO Baltic exercises.[179] In June 2015, Swedish forces participated in antisubmarine exercises with NATO in connection with the naval exercise BALTOPS-2015 in the coastal waters off Denmark, Poland, and Sweden. The drills engaged about 40 ships and aircraft from 15 member states and NATO partners and involved maneuvering, warship escorting, air defense, antiterrorism measures, location and neutralization of mines, and artillery fire. The goal was to improve the interoperability of national forces.

Sweden has also sharpened its rhetoric, with Prime Minister Loefven asserting after the October 2014 submarine hunt that Sweden would defend its "territorial integrity with all available means." An opinion poll published in January 2015 found that 73% of Swedes were concerned about developments in Russia, compared to only 45% a year earlier.[180] For the first time, the annual poll also found more Swedes were generally in favor of NATO membership (48%) compared to those opposed (35%). In another poll in January 2015, the proportion of Swedes supporting NATO membership jumped by five percentage points.[181] In an April 2014 survey, 33% considered accession a good idea, up from 28%, while 47% were opposed, a drop from 56%.

The NATO debate has intensified in Sweden, despite the fact that the country has traditionally sought neutrality and nonalignment. However, credible nonalignment necessitates the ability to defend oneself or to deter potential threats—the principle on which Swedish security policy was based during the Cold War, with sizable defense appropriations and a more extensive domestic defense industry. But after the Soviet collapse, Swedish defense capabilities were dramatically reduced.

The non-socialist parties are becoming more receptive to NATO membership.[182] In effect, a campaign is underway for Sweden to apply for NATO entry: the Center Party and the Christian Democrats have changed their positions on NATO and the Moderate Party also started to push the membership issue. Nevertheless, political opinion against NATO remains strong within the red-green parties; the Social Democrats have given little indication that they are softening their opposition while in coalition with the pacifist Environment Party. Moscow endeavors to maintain contacts and influence with the leftist parties to undermine any pro-NATO sentiments. While opponents warn that tensions will increase in the region if Russia feels more squeezed by Swedish membership, advocates point out that NATO membership will make Sweden's defense more credible. Paradoxically, the pacifist opponents of NATO entry will need to support greater defense spending to justify staying outside the Alliance, unless they intend to surrender to Moscow's demands.

Proponents of Alliance membership argue that Sweden was never neutral during the Cold War, as all previous Social Democrat governments cooperated with the US, and defense planning was based on defense against the Soviet Union.[183] Moreover, Sweden has been a member of NATO's Partnership for Peace for twenty years, participated in NATO missions from Kosova to Afghanistan, and has hosted NATO exercises. The government has stated that Sweden would not remain passive if an EU or Nordic country were attacked militarily and that Stockholm expected the same assistance. In addition, Sweden and Finland view themselves as a tandem, whereby NATO accession by one would mean membership for both. While Stockholm debates its options, Russia's ambassador to Sweden, Viktor Tatarintsev, tried to frighten its politicians and public by declaring that NATO membership would precipitate a military response by Moscow.[184]

Norway and Denmark

In February 2015, Norway's Defense Minister Ine Eriksen Søreide asserted that the West's attitude toward Russia would never be the same after the war in Ukraine and there was no way back to a normalized relationship.[185] Relations between Oslo and Moscow grew frosty after Putin's seizure of Crimea. Norway cut military and political communications with the Kremlin and started modernizing its airbases.

The Barents Sea, which borders both countries, is strategically important to the Kremlin, providing its only direct ice-free access to the Atlantic.[186] A large proportion of Russia's submarines—of which at least 22 are nuclear-powered—are based close to the Norwegian border. Norway's continuing military vulnerability was acknowledged in September 2014, when Søreide announced that defense will have to be radically upgraded as a direct result of increased concern over Russia's actions.[187]

According to Lieutenant-General Kjell Grandhagen, Norway's military intelligence chief, Putin's Russia is more aggressive and unpredictable, including in areas close to Norway.[188] In 2014, Norway intercepted 74 Russian warplanes off its coast, 27% more than in 2013, scrambling F-16 fighters from a military air base in Bodo.[189] The US pledged to pre-position Abrams M1A1 main battle tanks and other armored vehicles in Norway to boost the country's security. Oslo was also tasked with providing facilities for a NATO detachment and deployment of airborne early warning systems at the Air Force Base in Ørland.

Norway's defense minister stated that Oslo would increase military spending in 2015 by 3.3% and the military was being restructured to deal more effectively with the new risks. Russia has also sharply increased snap military exercises near Norwegian territory, in violation of established procedure, either announced at the last minute or kept fully secret. Russia is particularly focused on Svalbard, demilitarized Norwegian-controlled islands in the high Arctic that Moscow believes serve as a platform for eavesdropping and other covert NATO activities.

The bulk of Russia's strategic nuclear capacities are deployed close to Norway's borders; hence, Moscow could seek to secure its nuclear weapons by directly intervening on Norwegian territory. The Kola Peninsula bordering Norway is particularly important for stationing a large proportion of its nuclear weapons that would be used in a conflict with the US. According to Norwegian intelligence, Russia's upgrades in areas near Norway consist primarily of new submarines and surface vessels, an extra brigade, a new air defense system and nuclear missiles, and a renewal of air force planes with upgraded weapons systems. Norwegian fighter jets are dispatched weekly to identify Russian military aircraft flying close to Norway's territorial borders, some of which appear to be armed.[190] Russia's strategic air force capable of carrying missiles with nuclear weapons has been more active since the start of the Russia-Ukraine war.

Neighboring Denmark, another NATO member, has also been subject to Moscow's threats. Mikhail Vanin, Russia's ambassador to Denmark stated on March 21, 2015, that Moscow's nuclear missiles could target the country's navy if it joins NATO's anti-missile defense shield.[191] The threat sparked an angry reaction among Danish officials. NATO's missile shield is due to be fully operational in parts of Central Europe by 2025. Copenhagen has pledged to supply frigates equipped with advanced radar to track incoming missiles. It was also reported that, in June 2014, Russian jets simulated a nuclear attack on Denmark's Bornholm Island, timed to coincide with an annual festival involving the country's entire political leadership.[192]

As the Arctic or High North has grown in importance for future resource extraction and shipping, Russia has declared the region as its largest sphere of economic investment. Undiscovered reserves of crude oil and natural gas in the Arctic are estimated at 13% and 30% of the world's total, respectively. Russia is vying for control of the region's fossil fuels and rare metals with other "polar nations," thus making the region a potential flashpoint. Moscow is constructing new military bases in the Arctic and intends to restore the region's Soviet defense infrastructure. Russia's Federal Agency for Special Construction (*Spetsstroy*) is installing air defense bases and combat aviation guidance posts along the Arctic Ocean coastline.[193] The stage is set for confrontation, as the West does not recognize a large portion of the Arctic shelf as Russian, while Moscow claims that NATO seeks to advance its interests with military force.

The Kremlin is developing a unified command structure

to coordinate military operations in the Arctic and has established a new government entity to execute Russia's policy in the region.[194] It is constructing a combined naval, air, ground, and nuclear defense in the Arctic in anticipation of a future NATO threat and to project its claimed economic and strategic interests.

However, during 2014 and 2015, further exploration in the Arctic became problematic for Moscow because US and EU sanctions curbed the sale of equipment for oil and gas drilling. A poll taken in August 2014 indicated that 63.3% of Norwegians backed the economic measures against Moscow, while only 17.5% disapproved.[195] Putin's special envoy to the High North, Artur Tsjilingarov, visited Norway in December 2014 and asserted that the country risked major financial losses by following EU policy of sanctions against Russia.[196] Norwegian oil companies were evidently in danger of losing the competition for major contracts in the High North. Moscow has also threatened to scale down its cooperation with the eight-member Arctic Council, claiming that the Nordic countries were acting provocatively toward Russia.[197] While Moscow's feuds with the three Baltic states intensify conflicts with the Nordic countries, disputes over the Arctic will further exacerbate tensions with northern Europe and North America.

Endnotes

[1] Stefan Forss and Pekka Holopainen, "Breaking the Nordic Defense Deadlock," February 2015, Strategic Studies Institute and US Army War College Press, www.StrategicStudiesInstitute.army.mil.

[2] Agnia Grigas, "Anatomy of Russia's Information Warfare in Baltic States," Vilnius, Delfi.lt, December 29, 2014, http://en.delfi.lt/lithuania/foreign-affairs/russias-information-warfare-in-the-baltic-states-ii.d?id=66778660. Moscow's armed occupation of the Baltic countries after World War Two is

depicted in official statements as a voluntary act of joining the Soviet Union.

[3] *Interfax*, Moscow, June 4, 2015, www.interfax.com.

[4] "Population and Housing Census 2011," Estonia.eu, http://estonia.eu/about-estonia/country/population-census-2011.html.

[5] Kristina Kallas, "Dangerously Forgotten Ida-Viru," Tallinn, *Eesti Paevaleht*, March 12, 2015, http://epl.delfi.ee.

[6] Katja Koort, "The Russians of Estonia: Twenty Years After," *World Affairs*, July-August 2014, http://www.worldaffairsjournal.org/article/russians-estonia-twenty-years-after.

[7] Paul Goble, "Leningrad Governor Attacks Finno-Ugric Groups as Threats to Russia's Territorial Integrity," *Window on Eurasia -- New Series*, March 4, 2015, http://windowoneurasia2.blogspot.com/2015/03/leningrad-governor-attacks-finno-ugric.html.

[8] Kristopher Rikken, "Ruling Reform Party Wins Estonian Election, Fending Off Challenge From Archrival Center," Tallinn, *ERR News*, March 1, 2015, http://news.err.ee.

[9] Elisabeth Braw, "The Kremlin's Influence Game," *World Affairs*, March 10, 2015, http://www.worldaffairsjournal.org/blog/elisabeth-braw/kremlin%E2%80%99s-influence-game.

[10] For a diatribe by a "Holy Russia" fanatic see the interview with Yiriy Zhuravlev, head of the Russians in Estonia Movement by Mariya Solnceva, "Russians in Estonia: Estonia is in Deep NATO, as They Say." According to Zhuravlev, the Russian people will never tolerate "Western liberal fascism." Evidently, "true Russians, genuine patriots of Russia, today, as always, are on all the battlefields of the Holy Liberation Battle. 2007 in Estonia. 2008 in South Ossetia, Abkhazia. 2013, 2014, 2015 in Crimea, Luhansk, Donbas, Novorossiya... Ahead are 2016, 2020," Tallinn, *Baltija Online*, April 20, 2015, www.baltija.eu.

[11] "Estonian Police to Create Cyber Crime Unit," Tallinn, *BNS,* July 14, 2015, www.bns.ee.

[12] "Border Treaty Waiting for Putin's Decision, MP Says," Tallinn, Estonian Public Broadcasting, *ERR News,* June 25, 2014, http://news.err.ee.

[13] Based on the author's discussions with Estonian government officials and independent analysts in Tallinn in September 2014.

[14] *CNN,* September 5, 2014, http://www.cnn.com/2014/09/05/world/europe/estonia-russiaabduction/index.html?hpt=hp_t2.

[15] Sarunas Cerniauskas: "Linkevicius: Abduction in Estonia Is a Reminder to Baltic Countries," *Delfi*, Vilnius, September 5, 2014, www.delfi.lt.

[16] "Russia Jails Estonia Security Official Eston Kohver," *BBC News,* August 19, 2015, http://www.bbc.com/news/world-europe-33986733.

[17] "President: Estonia's Freedom Deserves Defending, Preserving," Tallinn, *Baltic News Service*, June 25, 2014, http://www.bns.ee.

[18] "Internal Security Expenditure Should Also Reach 2% of GDP, Says Minister" Tallinn, Estonian Public Broadcasting, *ERR News*, July 14, 2014," http://news.err.ee.

[19] "New Estonian Bill to Replace National Defense in Estonia," Tallinn, *Baltic News Service*, July 22, 2014, http://www.bns.ee.

[20] "Amari Sees Fulfillment of Obama Promise," Tallinn, *Postimees.ee*, December 22, 2014, http://news.postimees.ee.

[21] "Estonia Wants NATO Fighters to be Permanently Stationed at Amari Air Base," Tallinn, *Baltic News Service,* June 25, 2014, www.bns.ee.

[22] "Estonia President Toomas Ilves Seeks Permanent NATO Force," April 12, 2015, *BBC News,*

http://www.bbc.com/news/world-europe-32274170.

[23] *Interfax*, Tallinn, April 20, 2015, www.interfax.com.

[24] "Baltic Armies to Create Coordination Network," *Interfax*. Tallinn, December 12, 2014, http://www.interfax.com.

[25] "EU to Help Install Mobile Monitoring Systems on Estonian-Russian Border," *Interfax*, Tallinn, December 20, 2014, http://www.interfax.com. The EBF allotted €1.9 billion in 2007–2013, including €27 million for programs in Estonia.

[26] "Estonian, Latvian Russian-Language TV Channels Plan Cooperation," Tallinn, *ERR News*, March 31, 2015, www.news.err.ee.

[27] "Estonian Public Broadcaster To Launch Weekly News Magazine in Russian," Tallinn, *BNS*, December 23, 2014, http://www.bns.ee.

[28] Based on discussions by the authors with Estonian government officials and analysts in Tallinn in September 2014.

[29] Paul Goble, "Russia Seen Expanding Active Measures and Media Campaign Against Latvia in 2015," January 5, 2015, *Window on Eurasia – New Series,* http://windowoneurasia2.blogspot.com/2015/01/window-on-eurasia-russia-seen-expanding.html.

[30] Paul Goble, "Moscow Brings Its Traditional Divide-and-Rule Approach Back to the Three Baltic Countries," *Window on Eurasia – New Series,* July 4, 2015, http://windowoneurasia2.blogspot.com/2015/07/moscow-brings-its-traditional-divide.html.

[31] "Latvia's GDP Would Suffer 10% Reduction if Russia Terminated All Agreements With Latvia," *Leta,* Riga, August 18, 2014, http://www.leta.lv.

[32] Uldis Smits, "Lithuania Stronger," Riga, *Latvijas Avize,* November 3, 2014.

[33] Aleksandr Nosovich: "Where Will Dreams Lead If Russian Business Leaves Baltic Countries?"
Kaliningrad, July 16, 2014, www.rubaltic.ru.

[34] "Analyst: Russia's Sanctions to Hit Baltic Countries Hardest," Tallinn, *BNS*, August 7, 2014, www.bns.ee.

[35] "Latvian Constitutional Referendum, 2012,"
https://en.wikipedia.org/wiki/Latvian_constitutional_referendum,_2012.

[36] Gundars Reders, "Russian World Project Bound to Expand," Riga, *LSM.lv*, January 12, 2015, http://www.lsm.lv.

[37] Population Census 2011 - Key Indicators, October 3, 2013,
http://www.csb.gov.lv/en/statistikas-temas/population-census-2011-key-indicators-33613.html.

[38] Artis Pabriks, a former foreign and defense minister, noted that by 2014 the number of Latvian residents without citizenship had dropped to 12% from 36% in the early 1990s. See Alison Smale, "Latvia's Tensions With Russians at Home Persist in Shadow of Ukraine Conflict," *New York Times*, August 23, 2014.

[39] Based on discussions by the authors with Latvian government officials and analysts in Riga in September 2014.

[40] Ibid.

[41] "Preamble to Latvian Constitution will Facilitate Ethnic Split - Russian ForMin," Moscow/Riga, *Baltic News Service*, June 21, 2014.

[42] Bens Latkovskis, "What To Do With Harmony?" *Neatkariga*, Riga, August 15, 2014.

[43] Linda Bagone, "Partners of Latgale Municipalities—NGOs Linked With Russian Intelligence Services," Riga, *LSM.lv*, December 14, 2014. According to Latvian intelligence services, four non-governmental organizations in Russia—*Russkaya Baltika* in Kaliningrad, the St. Petersburg-based

International and Regional Policy Center, the Russian-Baltic Media Center, and the Russian Strategic Study Centre—are used as platforms for the activities of Russia's special services in Latvia.

[44] Based on discussions by the authors with Latvian government officials and analysts in Riga in September 2014.

[45] Interview with Miroslav Mitrofanov, co-chair of the Russia Union by Aleksandra Rybakova, "Is Russian Issue Still Actual in Latvia?" Kaliningrad, *rubaltic.ru*, October 8, 2014, www.rubaltic.ru.

[46] Based on discussions by the authors with Latvian government officials and analysts in Riga in September 2014.

[47] Paul Goble, "A Small Number of Russians in Latgale Can Create Big Problems for Riga, Grigoryevs Says," *Window on Eurasia – New Series,* February 23, 2015, http://windowoneurasia2.blogspot.com/2015/02/a-small-number-of-russians-in-latgale.html.

[48] Paul Goble, "Pro-Moscow Groups Launch Websites for 'Peoples Republics' in Latvia and Lithuania," January 30, 2015, *Window on Eurasia – New Series,* http://windowoneurasia2.blogspot.com/2015/01/pro-moscow-groups-launch-websites-for.html.

[49] Carol J. Williams, "Latvia, With a Large Minority of Russians, Worries About Putin's Goals," *Los Angeles Times,* May 2, 2015, http://www.latimes.com/world/europe/la-fg-latvia-russia-next-20150502-story.html#page=1.

[50] "On Findings As For Special Operation Planned in Latgale," *Situation Reports,* December 12, 2014, Center for Eurasian Strategic Intelligence, http://eurasianintelligence.org/news.php?new=213&num.

[51] Paul Goble, "Moscow Massively Funding Pro-Russian NGOs in Baltic Countries," *Blog on Russia and Eurasia,* The Jamestown Foundation, September 11, 2015, http://www.jamestown.org/blog.

52 Elisabeth Braw, "The Kremlin's Influence Game," *World Affairs*, March 10, 2015, http://www.worldaffairsjournal.org/blog/elisabeth-braw/kremlin%E2%80%99s-influence-game.

53 Paul Goble, "Moscow Faces Obstacles in Deepening its Involvement with Ethnic Russians in Latvia," *Window on Eurasia – New Series*, March 27, 2015, http://windowoneurasia2.blogspot.com/2015/03/moscow-faces-obstacles-in-deepening-its.html.

54 "Latvia's Russian Rights Activist Was Detained as Part of Probe Into Ethnic Incitement," *BNS*, Tallinn, May 27, 2015, http://www.bns.ee.

55 Dovydas Pancerovas, "Latvia is Concerned With Activities of Pro-Russian Agitators, What Is the Situation in Lithuania?" Vilnius *15min.lt*, November 25, 2014, http://www.15min.lt.

56 Paul Goble, "Moscow Using Russian Organizations to Destabilize Latvia, Riga Officials Say," *Window on Eurasia – New Series*, March 9, 2015, http://windowoneurasia2.blogspot.com/2015/03/moscow-using-russian-organizations-to.html.

57 "Pro-Russia NGO Banned From Staging Multiday Rally in Riga," Tallinn, *BNS*, March 5, 2015, http://www.bns.ee.

58 Paul Goble, "Moscow Has Already Begun Hybrid War Against Latvia, Riga Journalist Says," *Window on Eurasia – New Series*, March 3, 2015, http://windowoneurasia2.blogspot.com/2015/03/moscow-has-already-begun-hybrid-war.html.

59 "Latvian NATO Center to Counter Russia 'Propaganda,' " Riga, *AFP*, North European Service, July 3, 2014, http://www.afp.com/en/home.

60 Paul Goble, "Latvia Seeks EU Funding for Full Service Russian-Language TV Channel," *Window on Eurasia – New Series*, December 29, 2014, http://windowoneurasia2.blogspot.com/2014/12/window-on-eurasia-latvia-seeks-eu.html.

[61] Juris Vilums, "Informational (In)security in Latgale," Riga, *Delfi*, December 17, 2014, http://www.delfi.lv.

[62] Voldemars Krustins, "When Morality Not Present," Riga, *Latvijas Avize*, September 2, 2014.

[63] "Expert: 500 Russian Militiamen Enough to Stop Existence of Latvia," Kaliningrad, *newsbalt.ru*, July 2014. Neronsky asserted that the preconditions for division were in place, as "discrimination against the Russian community is intensifying... The West is closing its eyes to this, the patience of Russians is not unlimited, and the example of Crimea and the Donbas may push them to decisive actions." See also Paul Goble, "500 Donetsk-Type Militants Could End Latvia's Existence as Unified State, Moscow Expert Says," *Window on Eurasia – New Series*, July 15, 2014, http://windowoneurasia2.blogspot.com/2014/07/window-on-eurasia-500-donetsk-type.html.

[64] Paul Goble, "Peskov Says Ethnic Russians in Latvia Would Revolt if Radical Nationalists Came to Power in Riga," *Window on Eurasia – New Series*, November 21, 2014, http://windowoneurasia2.blogspot.com/2014/11/window-on-eurasia-peskov-says-ethnic.html.

[65] Aivars Ozolins, "Putin's Next Target - Baltic States," Riga, *TVNET*, February 26, 2015, http://www.tvnet.lv.

[66] Gunars Nagels, "National Security," Riga, *Latvijas Avize*, July 15, 2014.

[67] "Latvian Formin Calls for Decision on Lasting Presence of Allied NATO Forces in Baltic," Tallinn, *Baltic News Service*, June 25, 2014, www.bns.ee.

[68] "Latvian Def Min Urges US To Support Permanent Presence of Allied Forces in Baltics," Tallinn, *Baltic News Service*, July 7, 2014, www.bns.ee. US forces maintain a rotational presence in the region. For instance, in October 2014, soldiers of the 1st Cavalry Division were deployed to Latvia to replace members of the US Army Europe's 173rd Infantry Brigade Combat Team.

See "Latvia Highly Appreciates US Troops' Presence—Military Official," Tallinn, *BNS*, October 14, 2014, www.bns.ee.

69 *Interfax*, Moscow, June 2, 2015, www.interfax.com.

70 Ugis Libietis, "Latvian Security Challenges—Unfulfilled Homework and 'Sprats Value,' " Riga, *LSM.lv*, September 2, 2014, www.lsm.lv.

71 Aidis Tomsons, "Experts Discuss Need To Introduce Compulsory Military Service," Riga, *Latvijas Radio Online*, March 9, 2015, http://www.latvijasradio.lv.

72 "Ricards Kozlovskis, 'Latvian Eastern Border Should Be Strengthened,' " Riga, *Radio Latvijas*, August 14, 2014.

73 "Latvian Parliament To Continue Discussing Ban on Residence Permits to Russian Investors," Tallinn, BNS, November 20, 2014, http://www.bns.ee.

74 Uldis Smits, "Green, Black," *Latvijas Avize*, Riga, October 14, 2014, p. 3, http://www.la.lv.

75 "NATO Strategic Communications Center of Excellence in Riga Accredited," Tallinn, *BNS*, September 2, 2014, http://www.bns.ee.

76 Dovydas Pancerovas, "Five Targets in Lithuania: Which of Them is Russian Propaganda Going to Target This Year?" Vilnius, *15min.lt*, January 5, 2015, http://www.15min.lt.

77 Based on discussions by the authors with Lithuanian government officials and analysts in Vilnius in September 2014.

78 Ibid.

79 "Accusations Against Lithuania From Lips of Russian Official," Vilnius, July 3, 2014, www.lrytas.lt.

80 Paul Goble, "EU Energy Plan Puts Kaliningrad at Risk, Moscow Paper Says," *Window on Eurasia – New Series*, April 20, 2015,

http://windowoneurasia2.blogspot.com/2015/04/eu-energy-plan-puts-kaliningrad-at-risk.html.

[81] Jevgenijus Bardauskas and Joana Lapėnienė, "Defense Expert: We Cannot Rule Out the Possibility That Russia Is Planning a Corridor From Kaliningrad to Belarus Through Lithuania," *LRT.lt*, August 31, 2014, http://www.lrt.lt.

[82] "Polish Airmen Guarding Baltic Skies: Russian Activity Growing With Every Year" *Šiauliai*, Vilnius, Lithuania, July 28, 2014, *Baltic News Service*, www.bns.ee.

[83] Based on discussions by the authors with Lithuanian government officials and analysts in Vilnius in September 2014.

[84] "Russian Warships Disrupt Swedish Cable Laying," Stockholm, *The Local*, May 2, 2015, www.thelocal.se. The 400-kilometer-long (250 miles) cable runs from Klaipeda, Lithuania, to Nybro, on Sweden's east coast. Its purpose is to improve Lithuanian and Scandinavian trading on electricity markets and to increase the security of power supplies to Lithuania.

[85] "Reserve Officer: Situation Near Swedish Coast Might Be Repeated Near Lithuanian Coast," *alfa.lt*, Vilnius, October 20, 2014, www.alfa.lt.

[86] Vaidas Saldžiūnas and Gediminas Pilaitis, "Is Lithuania Capable of Defending Itself Against Underwater Guests?" *lrytas.lt*, Vilnius, October 21, 2014, www.lrytas.lt.

[87] Based on discussions by the authors with Lithuanian government officials and analysts in Vilnius in September 2014.

[88] "Russian Blockade of Lithuanian Goods, Services Could Cost up to 4 Percent of GDP - Lithuanian Prime Minister," Vilnius, *Elta*, November 27, 2014, www.elta.lt.

[89] Rūta Janutienė, "Finnish Goodness With Strong Russian Smell," Vilnius, 16 June 2014, www.lrytas.lt. One such company is the Finnish *Fortum*. Arturas Paulauskas, head of parliament's National Security and Defense

Committee claimed possible ties between *Fortum* and the Kremlin. A portion of Lithuania's heating sector has to be given to private business, where *Fortum* is the sixth largest investor in this field in Europe. It is linked with oligarch Genadyi Timchenko, who has Putin's patronage and Finnish citizenship, and was on a list of individuals sanctioned by the West after Russia's invasion of Ukraine in 2014.

[90] "Lithuania Claims One-Third of Russian Diplomats Are Spies," Paris, March 30, 2015, *AFP (North European Service),* http://www.afp.com/en/home.

[91] "Lithuania Detains Military Officer Suspected of Spying," Vilnius, December 31, 2014, *AFP (North European Service),* http://www.afp.com/en/home.

[92] Dovydas Pancerovas, "Lithuanian Officers' Reports Show Russian, Belarusian Spies' Attempts To Recruit Them," Vilnius, *15min.lt,* April 17, 2015, http://www.15min.lt.

[93] Paulius Gritėnas, "Why Are Russian-Capital Companies Interested in Land Plots Surrounding Military Bases?" *lrytas.lt,* Vilnius, October 16, 2014, www.lrytas.lt.

[94] "Lithuania to Reinstate Army Conscription Amid Russia Fears," February 24, 2015, Vilnius, *AFP (North European Service),* http://www.afp.com/en/home.

[95] "Baltics Facing Real Threat - Lithuanian President," Vilnius, March 4, 2015, *BNS,* http://www.bns.ee.

[96] "Lithuanian Military Will Carry Out Exercises Without NATO Allies," *lruytas.lt,* Vilnius, April 21, 2015, www.lrytas.lt.

[97] Artūras Paulauskas, Head of Parliamentary National Security, Defense Committee: "What Will We Do Next in Fight Against Information War?" Vilnius, *Delfi,* July 22, 2014, www.delfi.lt.

[98] Monika Garbaciauskaite Budriene, "Interview With Journalist Peter Pomerantsev: How Russian Collective Consciousness Formed: Fear, Conspiracy Theories, Tearing of Wounds," Vilnius, *Delfi*, February 9, 2015, www.delfi.lt.

[99] "Conscripts Not To Be Sent to Foreign Missions - Lithuanian Defense Chief," Vilnius, *BNS*, March 4, 2015, www.bns.ee.

[100] Sarunas Cerniauskas, Dovydas Pancerovas, "Special Investigation: Money From Kremlin's Fund Are Going Into Lithuanian, Latvian, Estonian Pockets," Vilnius, *15min.lt*, June 8, 2015, www.15min.lt.

[101] Rasa Pakalniene, "Propaganda: New Level, Greater Influence," Vilnius, December 10, 2014, *Lietuvos Zinios*.

[102] Based on discussions by the authors with Lithuanian government officials and analysts in Vilnius in September 2014.

[103] For Lithuania's 2011 census figures see http://osp.stat.gov.lt/en/2011-m.-surasymas.

[104] Based on discussions by the authors with Lithuanian government officials and analysts in Vilnius in September 2014.

[105] Valdas Tamosaitis, "Polish Knot of Russia," Vilnius, July 17, 2014, www.bernardinai.lt.

[106] Karolis Jovaisas, "Do Not Ask Who Helped Valdemar Tomasevski To Become Popular. We Did," Vilnius, *Delfi*, June 19, 2014, http://www.delfi.lt.

[107] Romualdas Bakutis, "How To Save Lithuanian Poles From Tomasevski's 'Patronage,'" Vilnius, November 19, 2014, www.alfa.lt. A significant portion of Poles evidently do not want to vote for the LLRA but are being pushed away by radicals in several Lithuanian parties.

[108] Marija Larisceva, "Conference Platform," Vilnius, *Litovskiy Kuryer*, July 9, 2014, www.kurier.lt.

[109] Based on discussions by the authors with Lithuanian government officials and analysts in Vilnius in September 2014. Lithuanian officials consider it important to defend local conservatism and traditionalism from Putin's attempts to appropriate these values.

[110] Evelina Valiuškevičiūtė, "Mission To Find Weak Spots of Lithuanian State," Vilnius, *lrytas.lt*, February 23, 2015, www.lrytas.lt.

[111] Sarunas Cerniauskas, "What Are 'Cadets' From Lithuania Being Taught in Russian Military Camp?" Vilnius, *Delfi*, September 9, 2014, www.delfi.lt.

[112] Dovydas Pancerovas, "Latvia Is Concerned With Activities of Pro-Russian Agitators, What Is the Situation in Lithuania?" Vilnius, *15min.lt*, November 25, 2014, www.15min.lt.

[113] "It Is Important To Train Army Units, Prepare for Unconventional Challenges - General Zukas," Vilnius, *Baltic News Service*, June 19, 2014, www.bns.ee.

[114] Kastytis Braziulis, "Yakunin: Task Has Been Completed, Your Excellency Mr. President," *alfa.lt*, August 20, 2014, www.alfa.lt.

[115] "Baltics To Cooperate on Dealing With Threats to Internal Security," Vilnius, *BNS*, October 2014, www.bns.ee.

[116] Dovydas Pancerovas, "What Should We Do, if Weight of Russian Aggression Fell on Lithuania?" *lrytas.lt*, Vilnius, September 29, 2014, www.lrytas.lt.

[117] "Lithuania Creates Response Force to Prevent Ukraine Scenario," *AFP, North European Service*, Paris, October 13, 2014, www.afp.com.

[118] Rick Lyman, "Ukraine Crisis in Mind, Lithuania Establishes a Rapid Reaction Force," December 19, 2014, *The New York Times*, http://www.nytimes.com/2014/12/20/world/europe/lithuania-assembles-a-force-as-it-readies-for-whatever-russia-may-bring.html?_r=0.

[119] "Lithuania's Standby Army Units Put on Higher State of Preparedness - Media," Vilnius, December 8, 2014, www.bns.ee.

[120] "Kiev - Lithuania Pledges Military Aid for Ukraine," Kyiv, November 24, 2014, *AFP (North European Service)*, www.afp.com.

[121] Interview with Roman Polko, former commander of the Polish Army's GROM Special Forces, "Former Polish Special Forces Commander: Polish Soldiers Would Defend Lithuania," Vilnius, *Delfi*, March 16, 2015, www.ru.delfi.lt.

[122] Adam Withnall, "Russia's 'Preparations for War on Sweden' Lead to Security Service Concerns," *The Independent*, April 8, 2014, http://www.independent.co.uk/news/world/europe/russias-preparations-for-war-on-sweden-lead-to-security-service-concerns-9246749.html.

[123] Edward Lucas, *The Coming Storm: Baltic Sea Security Report*, CEPA, June 2015, p. 9, http://www.cepa.org//sites/default/files/styles/medium/Baltic%20Sea%20Security%20Report-%20%282%29.compressed.pdf.

[124] *EurActiv*, April 13, 2015, http://www.euractiv.com/sections/global-europe/russia-concerned-finland-and-swedens-nato-rapprochement-313709.

[125] Andrew Rettman, "Russia Concerned by Finland and Sweden's NATO Rapprochement," *EU Observer*, Brussels, April 13, 2015, https://euobserver.com/foreign/128297.

[126] Sveinung Berg Bentzrod, "Russian Aggression: Nordic States Extend Their Military Cooperation," Oslo, *Aftenposten.no*, April 9, 2015, www.aftenposten.no.

[127] "Saber Rattling? The Fact is that to Russia the Baltic Opens a Way out to the World," Helsinki, *Suomen Kuvalehti Online*, December 22, 2014, www.suomenkuvalehti.fi.

[128] Written testimony to the House of Commons Foreign Affairs

Committee, September 3, 2014, by Edward Lucas, Senior Fellow, Center for European Policy Analysis, Washington, DC, and
Senior Editor, *The Economist,*
https://docs.google.com/document/d/1nLdiU4jRMYlVgtrX6JXs4L8vxwlN2NpVh8ndUgbYH94/mobilebasic?pli=1.

[129] Kati Pohjanpalo, "Finland Says NATO an Option After Russia 'Violates' Border Laws," August 26, 2014,
http://www.bloomberg.com/news/2014-08-26/finland-says-nato-an-option-after-russia-violates-border-laws.html.

[130] Jarmo Huhtanen, "Russia Will Bring Its Most Advanced Missile System to Kola Peninsula Near Finland," Helsinki, *HS.fi*, November 21, 2014, www.hs.fi.

[131] *RIA Novosti*, Moscow, October 21, 2014, http://ria.ru.

[132] "It Is Necessary To be Prepared for Surprises Also in Finland's Territorial Waters," Helsinki, *HS.fi*, April 29, 2015.

[133] Ministry of Foreign Affairs of the Russian Federation, Moscow, March 2, 2015, www.mid.ru.

[134] "Secret Services: Cyber Spies Twice Penetrated Foreign Ministry," Helsinki, *YLE.fi*, July 3, 2014, www.yle.fi.

[135] "Russia Experts Call for Lustration in Finland," March 2, 2015, http://lustraatio.fi/lustration.

[136] Tuula Malin, "Welcome of Coffee and Biscuits for Putin," *Iltalehti*, April 7, 2015. Some analysts believe these Russian citizens could jam radars and communications systems during an inter-state conflict.

[137] Paulius Gritėnas, "Why Are Russian-Capital Companies Interested in Land Plots Surrounding Military Bases?" *lrytas.lt*, Vilnius, October 16, 2014, www.lrytas.lt.

[138] Laura Halminen, "Tuomioja: Researcher Wrote With 'Ulterior Motive,' " Helsinki, *HS.fi*, December 30, 2014, www.hs.fi.

[139] Charly Salonius-Pasternak, James Mashiri, Michael Moberg, "Could This Happen?" Helsinki, *Suomen Kuvalehti Online*, February 27, 2015.

[140] Paul Goble, "Patrushev Says Helsinki Stirring Up Nationalists in Karelia," *Window on Eurasia - New Series*, March 20, 2015, http://windowoneurasia2.blogspot.com/2015/03/patrushev-says-helsinki-stirring-up.html.

[141] "Russian Politicians Raise Possibility of Sanctions Against Finland," *YLE.fi*, Helsinki, July 3, 2015, www.yle.fi.

[142] Laura Halminen, "Opinion Poll: Russia's Reputation Collapsed in Finland -- Still Few in Favor of NATO Membership," Helsinki *HS.fi*, October 10, 2014, www.hs.fi.

[143] "Yle Survey: Russian-Finnish Relations Significantly Weakened by Ukraine Crisis," Helsinki, *YLE.fi*, January 4, 2015, www.yle.fi.

[144] Information from meetings by the authors with officials and analysts in Helsinki, April 27–28, 2015.

[145] Information from meetings by the authors with officials and analysts in Helsinki, April 27–28, 2015.

[146] "President Emphasizes Western Outlook in New Year Speech," Helsinki *YLE.fi*, January 1, 2015, www.yle.fi.

[147] Juha-Pekka Raeste, "HS Poll: Majority in Favor of Increasing Defense Budget," Helsinki, *HS.fi* March 16, 2015, www.hs.fi.

[148] "Defence Minister Wants Finland Cyber Warfare-Ready," Helsinki, *YLE.fi*, February 11, 2015, www.yle.fi.

149 Stefan Forss and Pekka Holopainen, *Breaking the Nordic Defense Deadlock*, Strategic Studies Institute and US Army War College Press, February 2015, p. 39, www.strategicstudiesinstitute.army.mil.

150 "Haglund Toughens Stance on Russian Airspace Violations," Helsinki, *YLE.fi*, August 29, 2014, www.yle.fi.

151 "Finland Plans Large-Scale Military Exercise on Russian Border," Helsinki, *YLE.fi*, August 30, 2014, www.yle.fi.

152 Elina Kervinen, "Finland and Sweden Plan to Have Joint Submarine Hunt Exercises," Helsinki, *HS.fi*, January 12, 2015, www.hs.fi.

153 Gerard O'Dwyer, "Sweden And Finland Pursue 'Special Relationship' With NATO," *Defense News*, October 10, 2014, http://www.defensenews.com/apps/pbcs.dll/article?AID=2014310100032.

154 "Russian Politico: Finland and Sweden No Longer NATO-Neutral Countries," Helsinki, *YLE.fi*, August 28, 2014, www.yle.fi.

155 Kaja Kunnas, "Finland Does Not Shy Away From Cooperation With NATO-Member Estonia,' Helsinki *HS.fi*, February 8, 2015, www.hs.fi.

156 Wolfgang Hansson, "Putin's Scare Tactics Backfired Completely," Stockholm, *Aftonbladet Online*, June 10, 2014, www.aftonbladet.se.

157 "Analyst: 'Finns Right To Be Concerned About Russia,' " Helsinki, *YLE.fi*, August 9, 2014, www.yle.fi.

158 "Poll: Ukraine Crisis Fuelling Support for Joining NATO," *YLE.fi*, Helsinki, August 9, 2014, www.yle.fi.

159 Interview with Finnish Prime Minister Alexander Stubb, "Stubb Wants to Step up Pressure on Russia," Stockholm, *DN.se*, July 5, 2014, www.dn.se.

160 "PM Stubb: NATO Is Like the EU, Membership Is Long Term," Helsinki, *YLE.fi*, August 9, 2014, www.yle.fi.

[161] Gerard O'Dwyer, "New Finnish Government Raises NATO Stakes," May 24, 2015, *Defense News,* http://www.defensenews.com/story/defense/policy-budget/warfare/2015/05/24/finland-new-government-nato-membership-russia-sweden-tension-ukraine-baltic/27710113.

[162] Kari Huhta, "Ukrainian Crisis Emphasizes Finland's Relationship With the United States," Helsinki *HS.fi,* June 23, 2014.

[163] Petri Valkki, "Finnish Debate on NATO Membership Benefits, Disadvantages Summarized," *Suomen Sotilas,* June 26, 2014.

[164] Ville Pernaa, "Russia Has Returned to Power Politics and Spheres of Interest," Helsinki, *Suomen Kuvalehti Online,* June 19, 2014. President Sauli Niinistö warned that Western countries confront a new Cold War with Russia but demonstrate a consistent softness when dealing with Moscow's actions. See Simon Tisdall, "Finland Warns of New Cold War over Failure to Grasp Situation in Russia," November 5, 2014, *The Guardian,* http://www.theguardian.com/world/2014/nov/05/finland-warns-cold-war-russia-eu.

[165] Information from meetings by the authors with officials and analysts in Stockholm, April 29–30, 2015.

[166] Interview with Viktor Tatarintsev, Russia's ambassador to Sweden, by Michael Winiarski, "People Cannot Treat Us Like Infants," Stockholm, June 14, 2014, www.dn.se.

[167] "Russian Submarine Reportedly Found Within 31 Miles Of Stockholm, Sweden Mobilizes Troops," *News/Inquisitor,* October 19, 2014, http://www.inquisitr.com/1548959/russian-submarine-reportedly-found-within-31-miles-of-stockholm-sweden-mobilizes-troops/#OhGIeScyh6UrcZyt.99.

[168] Claes Arvidsson, "Government's First Crisis Is Here," *Svenska Dagbladet Online,* Stockholm, October 20, 2014, www.svd.se.

[169] Mattias Carlsson and Josefin Sköld, "Power Game in Baltic Sea," Stockholm, June 14, 2014, www.dn.se.

170 Information from meetings by the authors with officials and analysts in Stockholm, April 29–30, 2015.

171 Hugo Anderholm, "Why is Russia Getting so Aggressive Toward Sweden?" October 20, 2014, http://www.vice.com/read/why-is-russian-military-hanging-out-on-swedish-territory.

172 Tomas Augustsson, "Sweden May Start Following Russian Planes," Stockholm, *Svenska Dagbladet Online*, July 14, 2014, www.svd.se.

173 Elisabeth Braw, "Bully in the Baltics: The Kremlin's Provocations," *World Affairs*, March/April 2015, http://www.worldaffairsjournal.org/article/bully-baltics-kremlin%E2%80%99s-provocations.

174 Elisabeth Braw, "Gotland Island, the Baltic Sea's Weak Link," January 14, 2015, *World Affairs, In the Blogs*, http://www.worldaffairsjournal.org/blog/elisabeth-braw/gotland-island-baltic-seas-weak-link.

175 "Supreme Commander: Defense Needs Several Billion," Stockholm, *DN.se*, January 12, 2015, *Dagens Nyheter*, http://www.dn.se.

176 "Sweden Raises Military Spending Amid Concerns Over Russia," Stockholm, March 12, 2015, *AFP (North European Service)*, www.afp.com.

177 "Assertive Russia Causes Military Rethink in Sweden," December 12, 2014, Stockholm, *AFP*, www.afp.com.

178 Olle Nygards, "SvD Reveals: Sweden in Military Cooperation With Denmark," Stockholm, *Svenska Dagbladet Online*, February 27, 2015, www.svd.se.

179 Jonas Gummesson, "Armed Force Heavily Involved in NATO Exercise," Stockholm, *Svenska Dagbladet Online*, May 13, 2015, www.svd.se.

[180] "Sweden Confirms Second 'Submarine' Sighting," Stockholm, January 11, 2015, *AFP (North European Service),* www.afp.com.

[181] "More Swedes Show Support for NATO," Stockholm, *The Local,* January 9, 2015, www.thelocal.se.

[182] Ewa Stenberg, "Social Democratic Party Holds Key to Membership," *Dagens Nyheter,* Stockholm, *DN.se,* January 9, 2015, www.dn.se.

[183] "With the Alliance for Freedom," *DN.se,* Stockholm, October 20, 2014, www.dn.se.

[184] "Russia Warns Of 'Risks' Should Sweden Join NATO," *Dagens Nyheter,* Stockholm, June 18, 2015, http://www.thelocal.se/20150618/russia-warns-of-risks-should-sweden-join-nato.

[185] Ole Ask, "Defense Minister Sharpens Tone Toward Russia," Oslo, *Aftenposten.no,* February 26, 2015, www.aftenposten.no.

[186] Louise Callaghan, "Norway on Alert as Putin Prowls," London, *Sunday TimesOnline,* April 19, 2015, www.thesundaytimes.co.uk.

[187] Stefan Forss and Pekka Holopainen, *Breaking the Nordic Defense Deadlock,* Strategic Studies Institute and US Army War College Press, February 2015, p. 23, www.strategicstudiesinstitute.army.mil.

[188] Interview by Rune Thomas Ege with Norwegian military intelligence chief Lieutenant-General Kjell Grandhagen, "The Norwegian Intelligence Service Chief in a Major 'VG' Interview: Russia is More Unpredictable," Oslo, *VG Nett,* December 6, 2014, www.vg.no.

[189] Andrew Higgins, "Norway Reverts to Cold War Mode as Russian Air Patrols Spike,"April 1, 2015, *New York Times,* http://www.nytimes.com/2015/04/02/world/europe/a-newly-assertive-russia-jolts-norways-air-defenses-into-action.html?_r=0.

[190] Nina Berglund, "Russian Jets Signal 'Return to Arctic,' " *Views and News from Norway,* October 14, 2014, Oslo, www.newsinenglish.no.

[191] "Denmark Could Face Nuclear Attack if Joins Missile Shield: Russian Ambassador," Copenhagen, March 21, 2015, Paris, *AFP (North European Service)*, http://www.afp.com/en/home. NATO's European missile defense system was headquartered in Ramstein, Germany, in 2012. It includes US missile destroying warships in Spain, Patriot anti-missile systems in Turkey, ship-borne radar systems deployed by several member countries, and planned missile interceptors in Romania.

[192] David Blair, "Russian Forces 'Practiced Invasion of Norway, Finland, Denmark and Sweden," June 26, 2015, *The Telegraph*, http://www.telegraph.co.uk/news/worldnews/europe/russia/11702328/Russian-forces-practised-invasion-of-Norway-Finland-Denmark-and-Sweden.html.

[193] For details on Moscow's military plans in the Arctic see Aleksey Krivoruchek, "Russia Will Reestablish Air Defense Systems and Airfields in the Arctic: Reestablishment of Discarded Aviation Infrastructure Will Cost R6 Billion," Moscow, *Izvestiya Online*, July 2, 2014, www.izvestia.ru.

[194] Matthew Bodner and Alexey Eremenko, "Russia Starts Building Military Bases in the Arctic," *The Moscow Times Online*, Moscow, September 8, 2014, www.themoscowtimes.com.

[195] Kirsten Karlsen, "The Russians Will Feel the Economic Sanctions," *Dagbladet.no*, Oslo, August 31, 2014, www.dagbladet.no.

[196] "Russia Warns Norway Over Sanctions," *The Norway Post*, December 22, 2014, www.norwaypost.no.

[197] Adam Hannestad, "Ukraine Casting Shadow Over Arctic Conference," Copenhagen, *Politiken.dk*, April 17, 2015, www.politiken.dk.

3. Western Flank: East Central Europe

Russia's Western flank includes a broad swath of territory that can be divided into two regions: East Central Europe (ECE) and South East Europe (SEE). However, both politically and geographically, it is difficult to demarcate precise boundaries between them. East Central Europe includes two sets of countries, in terms of their recent national developments: the Visegrad Group in Central Europe and the neighboring Intermarium zone between the Baltic Sea and the Black Sea.

The Visegrad Group was based on an agreement forged between three states in February 1991, following the collapse of the Soviet bloc and the Warsaw Pact. After the splintering of Czechoslovakia in January 1993, it became known as the Visegrad Four (V4), consisting of the Czech Republic, Hungary, Poland, and Slovakia. The fundamental idea behind the Visegrad initiative was for the four re-emerging ECE democracies to coordinate their policies in striving for NATO and EU accession. Government officials believed that by speaking with one voice in various multi-national formats they were more likely to be heard and no country would fall behind in its membership aspirations. All four countries qualified for entry into NATO and the EU between 1999 and 2004. Subsequently, the diversities among the four capitals grew more evident—and became particularly blatant during Russia's attack on Ukraine in 2014.

The Intermarium region encompasses three states, Belarus, Ukraine, and Moldova, which formed part of the Soviet Union and whose sovereignty and international alliances continue to be directly challenged by a revisionist and expansionist Moscow. East Central Europe also includes Romania, which was part of the Soviet bloc but maintained some leeway in its foreign policy. It is included in this chapter because of its close links with both sub-regions. Romania has close historical, cultural, and political connections with Moldova, a state directly confronting Moscow's neo-imperial restoration. And as a NATO and EU member, Romania has significant commonalities with Poland and the other Visegrad states.

Visegrad Front

East Central Europe provides opportunities for Russian inroads toward pan-European and transatlantic institutions through economic, political, and intelligence penetration. Russia's officials focus on influencing political decisions in each capital through a combination of diplomatic pressure, personal and professional contacts, economic enticements, and energy dependence. Reports regularly surface in Slovakia, Hungary, and other states that old comrade networks continue to operate between local politicians and Moscow. These are based on financial benefits rather than ideological or political convictions. It enables the Kremlin to exert political influence over certain officials and governments, challenges unified EU and NATO positions, and assists Moscow's international aspirations. Lucrative business contracts, donations to political campaigns, and various forms of financial corruption allow Moscow to exert political leverage and convince key politicians to favor Russian investments.

Moscow also endeavors to benefit from political, ethnic, religious, and social turbulence in ECE in order to keep governments off balance. Putin's Kremlin appeals to both the leftist old guard and the ultra-nationalist hyper-conservative Euroskeptics. Any democratic regression in ECE combined with the growth of nationalism and populism can favor Russia's regional objectives by weakening democratic institutions, engendering EU divisions, and undermining NATO's effectiveness.

The ECE region does not form a unified bloc. Differences have been evident between Poland and its Visegrad neighbors in terms of their Eastern policy and reactions to Russia's attack on Ukraine. Warsaw is more assertive in focusing EU and NATO policy on the Intermarium zone, and has viewed transatlantic relations as paramount. In contrast, Hungary, Slovakia, and the Czech Republic are more circumspect. During the Russia-Ukraine war, all three governments were hesitant in supporting sanctions against Moscow partly for economic reasons, especially where there is high dependence on Russia's energy supplies. In some cases, political leaders may either benefit from corrupt Russian business deals, have some sympathy toward a more authoritarian political model, or view Russia as a potential source of assistance in their foreign policy and national ambitions, as the case of Hungary demonstrated.

Some Visegrad governments focus on their immediate national interests rather than on more significant longer-term strategic calculations. Pacifying Moscow through opposition to EU sanctions may result in reciprocal economic favors from the Kremlin, but it also encourages Putin to be more ambitious in restoring Russia's hegemony in East Central Europe. Russia's attack on Ukraine did not convince Hungary to terminate the contract with *Rosatom* for the modernization and extension of the nuclear power plant in Paks, as Prime Minister Viktor Orbán studiously avoided any confrontation with Moscow. The same principle held true for the Czech Republic. Prime Minister Bohuslav Sobotka declared that the Czech Republic had not called for strengthening NATO forces in Europe.[1] Slovakia also adopted a weak stance on the Ukrainian crisis. Slovak Prime Minister Robert Fico even protested against the idea of America's stronger military presence in Central Europe.

As a result of the Russia-Ukraine war, the Visegrad Group has been weakened, as has the Weimar Triangle, established as a consulting mechanism between Germany, France, and Poland. Warsaw has been largely sidelined, while Berlin and Paris pursue their own attempts with Moscow to resolve the conflict over Ukraine by, in effect, freezing the conflict in Donbas. In addition, the informal creation of a new ECE regional grouping may benefit Putin and further undermine Visegrad. Prague is tightening its ties with Austria and a Slavkov Triangle has emerged that also includes Slovakia.[2]

The Slavkov Triangle is intended to better coordinate infrastructure, transport, and energy security between the three countries. Moreover, in contrast with the V4, the Slavkov Triangle will become institutionalized, with a permanent tripartite working group on the level of deputy foreign ministers.[3] This model of cooperation may become an incentive to include other countries, such as Slovenia and Croatia in regional economic projects. On January 30, 2015, Czech Prime Minister Sobotka, Slovak Prime Minister Fico, and Austrian Chancellor Werner Faymann met at Slavkov, near Brno, in the Czech Republic. They adopted a joint position against tightening sanctions on Moscow, claiming that all sanctions are ineffective and should be lifted. The Slavkov initiative is a tactical victory for Putin, because a new crack has appeared in EU policy toward Russia that cuts across Central Europe.

Poland

The strategic rivalry between Poland and Russia revolves around two core questions: Poland's international alliances and the position of intermediate territories that have been a part of either Russia or Poland in various historical periods.[4] Moscow lost Poland and the rest of East Central Europe as satellite states when Communism and Sovietism collapsed in the late 1980s and early 1990s. However, under the Putin administration, Russia has tried to restrict the impact of

Poland's NATO membership by periodically threatening the country with military attack and thereby challenging NATO's defense guarantees. It has also sought to undermine Poland's influence among countries that were once part of the Soviet Union and which Moscow seeks to assimilate in a new Russo-centered dominion, especially Ukraine and Belarus.

For Poland, NATO and EU membership and a strategic partnership with the US are viewed as cornerstones for the defense of its independence. In order to deepen this protective cover, each Polish government has endeavored to build a strategic buffer along its eastern borders by helping its immediate neighbors move closer toward the EU and NATO, or at the very least to curtail Moscow's dominant position on these territories.

In recent years, a confluence of factors toned down the Russo-Polish geostrategic conflict: NATO's enlargement momentum waned, Washington relegated Europe in its order of national security priorities, Ukraine declared itself neutral, and Georgia lost a war and two of its regions to Russia. During 2007, the Donald Tusk government altered Warsaw's geotactics cognizant of Poland's vulnerability in ECE as a consequence of lessened US engagement. Foreign policy was redesigned to improve relations with both Russia and Germany. Officials argued that this would make Poland more secure than at any time in its history by consolidating its position inside the EU and NATO and lessening prospective conflicts with Moscow. Cordial ties with Russia also boosted Poland's stature inside the EU, as Warsaw was no longer perceived as a "Russophobic" troublemaker, an image promoted by Moscow in order to reduce Polish influence.

However, the sources of bilateral competition between Russia and Poland were not resolved and flared on several occasions. The death of President Lech Kaczyński and 95 other people in a plane crash in Russia, on April 10, 2010, contributed to souring relations between

Warsaw and Moscow when Russian investigators failed to return the fuselage to Poland and issued a tendentious report on the causes of the crash. In the wake of a popular revolution in Ukraine in February 2014 that ousted President Viktor Yanukovych, Warsaw was at the forefront in condemning Moscow's aggressive reaction. Russian forces invaded Ukraine, annexed the Crimean peninsula, and manufactured a separatist conflict in the Donbas region. Moscow was intent on destabilizing Ukraine to prevent its Western integration. Poland intensified its role as the primary campaigner within the EU and NATO for Ukraine's national interests and territorial integrity. This repositioned Warsaw in its long-term geostrategic competition with Moscow, as Poland faced the destabilizing prospect of the collapse of the Ukrainian state. Even though Berlin and Paris subsequently sidelined the Polish authorities in negotiations with Russia over the armed conflict in eastern Ukraine, Warsaw continued to play a supportive role for Kyiv in international institutions.

The ongoing conflict with Moscow could provoke a more assertive Polish foreign policy following the country's recent parliamentary elections. The victory of the rightist Law and Justice (PiS) party on October 25, 2015, may inject a stronger nationalist element in dealing with Moscow. On the positive side, this could be manifest in a more activist role in support of Ukraine and other states threatened by Russia's subversion. This can include more visible diplomatic activity, increased funding and involvement in strengthening Ukraine's institutions, and closer military cooperation.

On the negative side, a more forceful Polish policy toward Russia that is not coordinated with the larger EU states could prove beneficial for the Kremlin in its attempts to preclude a common Union strategy toward its "eastern partners." Moreover, a more conservative Euroskeptic stance by the PiS government could contribute to isolating Poland and disabling a more assertive approach toward Russia. An upsurge of nationalist passions in Warsaw would likely create rifts with Germany, as the latter painstakingly avoids being drawn into open conflicts with Russia. PiS could also contribute to Kremlin attempts to expand fissures in Central Europe if it more vehemently supports the collective rights of Polish minorities in Lithuania and Ukraine and criticizes the governments in Vilnius and Kyiv.

Poland has no sizable Russian-speaking population, and Moscow cannot invade on the pretext of defending its compatriots. Small autonomist movements among Silesian and Kaszubian regionalists have no partiality toward Russia, Poland's Ukrainians would not follow Moscow's script, and the only option for the Kremlin are Belarusians living in a contiguous area of Podlasie in eastern Poland.[5] Moscow could claim it was defending them as part of the Russian and Orthodox world, but the support of Minsk would be needed. This seems unlikely, as President Alyaksandr Lukashenka is himself concerned about Russian-sponsored separatism in Belarus.

Another possibility for conflict is a manufactured territorial dispute along the border with Kaliningrad *oblast*. Three-quarters of Germany's former East Prussia is in Poland, with the remainder belonging to Russia. The division of these lands after World War Two can be used as a provocation on grounds of retrospective illegitimacy. Moscow could claim some of the territory in Poland as historically part of Kaliningrad and stage a provocation involving Russian-speakers sent into the region or engineer the demolition of border crossings that would provoke a Polish reaction and a direct conflict with Russia.

The Kremlin has cultivated peripheral but noisy pro-Russian groupings in Poland, as it has in most other states. Although these have marginal public support and limited political prospects, their very existence is beneficial for Moscow's propaganda of deception, and they perform a vocal nuisance role against the Polish administration. In 2015, Mateusz Piskorski, a former parliamentary deputy for the populist agrarian Self-Defense party, created a new formation titled *Zmiana* (Change). It called for close cooperation with Russia and is reportedly funded by Moscow.[6] Piskorski formerly served as a commentator for the Kremlin-funded television station *Russia Today* (today rebranded as *RT*), defending Moscow's policies, and he appears regularly on *Sputnik*-Poland to criticize the Warsaw government and assert that Polish and Russian national interest must be fully aligned.

Piskorski also monitored the illegitimate Crimean referendum on March 16, 2014, organized by Russian proxies and special services. His party advocates Poland remaining in the EU but limiting cooperation with the US and orienting itself toward Moscow and Beijing. It is likely to appeal to a narrow group of ultra-rightists espousing a pan-Slavic nationalist heritage whose strands date back to the pre–World War Two National Democrats. In a script that appeared to be written in the Kremlin, Piskorski called for Poland's exit from NATO, refused to live in a Europe controlled by the US, favored a "pragmatic" relationship with Moscow, looked back with nostalgia at the Soviet bloc, and yearned for a Eurasian pole of power that would compete with the US and China.[7]

Another Putin advocate in Poland, Konrad Rękas, deputy leader of *Zmiana*, launched a campaign for property restitution or compensation payments by the government in Kyiv for Poles formerly resident in Ukraine.[8] The aim was to sour relations between Poles and Ukrainians and isolate Kyiv. The Russian media praised the initiative and afforded it substantial publicity. Moscow has also supported some Polish policy NGOs. For instance, the European Center of Geopolitical Analysis (ECGA), a think tank based in Szczecin and co-founded by Piskorski, is under suspicion of working for the Kremlin.[9] It publishes pro-Russian analyses, including interviews with members of the Donetsk People's Republic. Following the launch, in February 2015, of the Polish-language version of the *Sputnik* Russian news agency over radio airwaves in Warsaw and via its website, Foreign Minister Grzegorz Schetyna asserted that pro-

Russian propaganda in Poland was a new phenomenon that needed to be closely monitored.[10]

According to an April 2015 government report on cyber security, Poland experienced a record number of hacker and cyber attacks in 2014: 7,498 compared to 5,670 in 2013 and 457 in 2012.[11] In addition, their level of sophistication significantly increased, indicating the backing of a state. They included a series of high-profile hacking and denial-of-service (DoS) attacks against key state and financial websites, including the homepage of Poland's President and the Warsaw stock exchange. An online group calling itself Cyber Berkut claimed responsibility and asserted that they were retaliating against Warsaw's support for Kyiv. The information war against Poland via the Internet includes the dissemination of disinformation by bloggers and contributors to online discussion forums.

One objective of Moscow's information offensive is to exacerbate tensions between Poland and its neighbors. In early 2015, the now customary "people's republics" were announced on Facebook—for Lithuania's Vilnius and Ukraine's Lviv regions. The instigators called for referenda to separate these heavily Polish-populated areas that were part of Poland before World War Two. Such "cyber states" may not pose a threat to either country targeted by the Kremlin, but they are components of a propaganda exercise to stir anxiety and suspicion and create frictions between Poles, Lithuanians, and Ukrainians.

The revival of Polish-Russian political confrontations over Ukraine contains a strong security dimension. During 2014 and 2015, Russian military aircraft significantly increased their approaches toward Polish airspace to signal Moscow's displeasure with Warsaw in assisting Ukraine.[12] Incidents of espionage have also risen: in one such example, four Russian diplomats were expelled following the arrest of two Poles, including a military colonel charged with collaborating with a foreign intelligence service.[13] The officer had access to NATO secrets. The Russian nationals included two military intelligence officers from the Main Intelligence Directorate (GRU) who handled the suspected spies. For the Kremlin, Poland is an intelligence priority, as a NATO member sharing a border with Russia and Belarus. According to Polish counter-intelligence, aside from traditional intelligence work, Russian spies are also involved in "lobbying activities" and economic espionage.[14]

There was a significant shift in Poland's strategic thinking during 2014, illustrated in the new National Security Strategy approved in October 2014. For the first time in more than 20 years, it stated that Poland was threatened by war and named Russia as an aggressor in Ukraine.[15] The document called for higher military spending, more reservists, the reinforcement and modernization of garrisons in eastern Poland, and the preparation of uniformed services and the public administration to operate in crisis situations. The government drafted a bill calling for increasing military spending from 1.95% to at least 2% of GDP, starting in 2016.

In March 2015, General Stanisław Koziej, Head of the National Security Bureau, warned that Poland must be ready for the possibility of a "hybrid" war, similar to the one in eastern Ukraine.[16] Apart from military forces, various sectors of Polish society would be needed in the event of such a conflict, including the police and firefighters. In January 2015, the Polish Ministry of National Defense announced that it would provide military training to any civilian who volunteered. Tomasz Siemoniak, Poland's Defense Minister also planned to establish a Territorial Defense Force to include the best recruits from paramilitary associations and other volunteers to create a force resembling the US National Guard.[17] A territorial defense unit would be stationed in every voivodship within the framework of the existing National Reserve Force (NSR).

Operational forces would need the support of these local units in the event of a conventional war. The Polish military numbers 120,000 troops, with about half this number combat capable. The primary task of the territorial defense force is to slow the enemy's advances. NATO's rapid response force could not reach Warsaw within the two to three days that it would take Russia's military. As Polish troops would be unable to hold the front line, a fast retreat would be essential to avoid being surrounded and eradicated. Many Polish brigades require up to three months to achieve full mobilization, while Russian forces have become more mobile and deployable. In such demanding conditions, the speed of a Russian invasion could be limited by territorial defense units, which would engage the enemy in irregular warfare, allowing military forces more time to deploy. These troops would need modern equipment, including communications devices in order to coordinate their actions with operational forces, as well as night vision devices and anti-tank weapons.

Poland's military plans to purchase attack helicopters and drones, strengthen the navy with submarines armed with cruise missiles, and build a medium-range missile defense shield styled as *Wisla*. Poland's selection of the Patriot air defense system for its missile defense program will strengthen defense cooperation with the US.[18] The Patriot selection is the core of Poland's military modernization. Approximately $10 billion will be spent on upgrading air and missile defense systems, with about half allocated to missile defense. In sum, Warsaw intends to spend $37 billion on military modernization by 2022, making it the leading NATO spender in the ECE area. Poland's projected expenditures are equivalent to that of all other states that joined NATO after 1999.

Warsaw is also seeking to enhance regional security by bolstering its domestic weapons industry and selling weapons to nearby allies, with credit offered for buyers.[19] The hardware will include GROM antiaircraft systems, radar, transporters, firearms, radio transmitters, and drones. The Defense Ministry is also developing a system to defend virtual space with the construction of a cybernetic operations center. Increased spending is intended to provide the military with the power of "defensive deterrence."[20] Poland is also urging NATO to press ahead with a broader missile shield system that is due to be completed in 2020, with significant elements in Poland and Romania.[21]

Sizable military exercises, codenamed *Anakonda 2014*, were held at several military training grounds in Poland during September and October 2014. They involved 12,500 soldiers, including 750 troops from allied military forces. The core of the Polish units consisted of mechanized forces, plus chemical and reconnaissance regiments, a fleet of ships, and a tactical and transport air squadron. Soldiers practiced scenarios in which NATO's rapid response forces are deployed to Poland following an attack from the East.[22] In an unprecedented contribution, 2,000 German soldiers took part in NATO's "Saber Strike" exercises on Polish soil in Drawsko Pomorskie in June 2015.[23] A total of 10,000 soldiers participated. Berlin's initiative is part of a broader plan for tightening military cooperation with Poland in the face of threats from Russia. Work was also underway to incorporate one German battalion (500–1,000 men) in a Polish brigade and a Polish battalion in a German brigade. This arrangement is modeled on the French-German brigade, established in 1987 by President François Mitterrand and Chancellor Helmut Kohl, while a Polish-German division might be formed in the future.

Despite Washington's reassurances, a poll conducted in March 2015 revealed that 49% of Poles believed that NATO allies would not respond if Russia invaded Poland.[24] The opposition of the German and French governments to establishing permanent NATO bases in Poland for fear of antagonizing Putin reinforced the distrust of Poles. The number of skeptical citizens has increased since the 2014 figure of 45%. Following President Obama's "European Reassurance Initiative," announced in June 2014, NATO planned to pre-position hardware along its eastern flank and establish bases or storage locations for military hardware, ammunition, and fuel.[25] At a meeting of NATO defense ministers in Brussels on February 5, 2015, a decision was made to emplace such depots in Poland, Romania, Lithuania,

Latvia, Estonia, and Bulgaria, staffed by about 40 officers at each site. In the event of armed conflict, these units would become NATO's rapid reaction force command centers. Currently, NATO reaction forces have a 30-day readiness period, whereas by 2016 the new units would be able to respond within three days.

NATO's Very High Readiness Joint Task Force (VHRJTF) will involve a brigade task group with about 5,000 soldiers plus an aviation regiment, assault helicopters, and special-forces elements. Poland will host the new force's command-and-control center at NATO's Multinational Corps Northeast headquarters, in Szczecin, on the Baltic Sea. This spearhead force, earmarked to defend Poland and the Baltic states, is planned to be ready by 2016. However, because of Russia's aggressive stance, NATO foreign ministers decided that more immediate response units with a few hundred soldiers would also be readied.[26] This would enable the US to deploy troops more quickly to act as a tripwire to deter any impending Russian invasion.[27]

By establishing depots of ammunition, fuel, and equipment, Poland would not have to wait six months for the deployment of US hardware to Europe.[28] While Washington has talked about a "permanent rotational presence" of American troops in Poland, officials in Warsaw want to transform this into a permanent presence. President Andrzej Duda, elected on May 24, 2015, has strongly supported direct US military engagement and NATO infrastructure and harbors no illusions about Moscow's ambitions. He declared that he would focus his presidency on enhancing relations with states across Central and Eastern Europe that view Putin's Russia as a common threat.

To assist Ukraine in its Western aspirations, Warsaw, Kyiv, and Vilnius signed an agreement in July 2015 on the creation of a Ukrainian-Polish-Lithuanian military brigade. Its predecessor, the *UkrPolBat* (Ukrainian-Polish Peace Force Battalion), was formed in 1998 as part of NATO's peacekeeping missions and was mostly composed of mechanized units. The 4,500 strong *LitPolUkrBrig* brigade will have its headquarters in Lublin, in southeast Poland, and each country will contribute four battalions. [29] Warsaw and Kyiv intend to use the new brigade in crisis situations and peacekeeping missions conducted by the EU. This initiative will contribute to Ukraine's adaptation to western military standards and strengthen its military potential.

On the information front, Poland's authorities have confronted Moscow in a sensitive domain—the interpretation of history. President Bronisław Komorowski decided to make Westerplatte, where World War Two began with the German invasion of Poland on September 1, 1939, the location for celebrating the 70th anniversary of the end of the war on May 8, 2015. [30] Komorowski underscored that the victory of the Allies, in May 1945, did not bring freedom to all the European nations, as the eastern part of the continent fell under Soviet Communism. This is a direct blow to Russia's self-assertions about its allegedly liberating role during and after World War Two. The war culminated in a clash between two totalitarian powers, Germany and the Soviet Union, which first collaborated to subjugate Central Europe. Subsequently, the Soviets cooperated with the West to defeat Nazi Germany and to seize territories in Europe's East.

Czech Republic

The Visegrad administrations have been divided in their response to the Russia-Ukraine war. Czech and Slovak center-left government leaders have proved timid in their reactions, although several government and opposition politicians called Russia's intervention an act of aggression. Their primary concern was to maintain cordial relations with Moscow and not damage economic and energy connections and other material interests. The prominent Czech analyst Jiri Pehe believes that Putin found his Trojan horse in a region with parochial horizons. [31] The gap between Poland and the other Central European countries visibly widened during the Ukrainian crisis, and the three smaller V4 states found a common language with a traditionally opportunistic Vienna. In addition, Pehe believes that influential "fifth columns" still exist in these countries 25 years after the fall of Communism, while Russia's intelligence and criminal networks intensively operate on their territories.[32]

Policy makers advocating close cooperation with Poland are reportedly losing influence in Prague and are being replaced by officials who want to reorient the country closer to Austria.[33] The "special bond" between Prague and Warsaw was based primarily on personal contacts between Presidents Václav Havel and Aleksander Kwaśniewski and efforts made by Prime Ministers Mirek Topolánek and Donald Tusk, who pushed for the installation of a US missile defense shield in the region. In addition, the founders of the Eastern Partnership—Sweden, Poland, and the Czech Republic—worked together to bring the post-Soviet states closer to the EU, but Prague has largely withdrawn from this process since 2014. The Czech government increasingly emphasizes the Vienna-Bratislava-Prague triangle when coordinating Eastern policy with respect to Ukraine and Russia.

After assuming office in March 2013, Czech President Miloš Zeman pledged to promote closer political and economic ties with Russia. During 2014, he condemned the EU's sanctions against Moscow and dismissed the Ukrainian conflict as a "civil war."[34] One of Zeman's closest friends and confidants is an ex-KGB officer blacklisted by the US, and some reports indicated that the President was susceptible to political influence after receiving financing for his election campaign from Martin Nejedlý, head of the Czech *Lukoil* office. Zeman's pronouncements provoked a conflict between the Czech Ministry of Foreign Affairs and the presidency, undermining the country's foreign policy. Ukraine's Ministry of Foreign Affairs also summoned the Czech ambassador on November 20, 2014, to inform him that the President's statements were unacceptable to Kyiv.

Prime Minister Bohuslav Sobotka, leader of the Czech Social Democratic Party (CSDP), who assumed office in January 2014, also rejected Zeman's proposal for the "Finlandization" of Ukrainian foreign policy, or its subordination to Moscow's interests. [35] He asserted that the term "Finlandization" was connected with the Cold War era and its spheres of influence, which deprived countries of free decisions and the term should not be used in contemporary international politics.

The political opposition has challenged presidential appeasement of Russia. Senators from the Christian Democratic Union–Czechoslovak People's Party (KDU-CS) criticized Zeman for his accommodating stance and his refusal to perceive Russia's aggression toward Ukraine and other neighbors, which was "weakening and threatening vital relations with our allies in the EU and the US." [36] They issued a statement claiming that Zeman was devaluing the paramount importance of human rights in the name of alleged economic interests of Czech companies. Zeman broke with the EU and attended the Victory Day celebrations in Moscow on May 9, 2015. He was received by Putin in the Kremlin who thanked him for his "independent position" in opposing Western sanctions. [37]

Czech left-wing politicians are normally more prone to cooperate with Russia, in contrast with center-right governments critical of Putin, including former Prime Minister Mirek Topolánek. Premier Sobotka stated that the Czech Republic could not cut its trade ties with Russia over Ukraine, although Czech exports to Russia amount to less than 4% of its total, compared with some 80% to the EU. Moscow has steadily courted Prague and offered investments for Czech companies in engineering, construction, energy, agriculture, and other sectors.

The opposition parties TOP 09 and the Civic Democrats have criticized Sobotka for questioning the effectiveness of EU sanctions against Moscow. [38] Karel Schwarzenberg, TOP 09 chairman and former Minister of Foreign Affairs, asserted that Russia was at war with the EU because it intervened in Ukraine when Kyiv prepared to sign an Association Agreement with the Union. According to Schwarzenberg, the war in Ukraine requires sacrifices and the Czech Republic should stand in the front line of countries resisting Russia's aggression. Despite or possibly because of Prague's lukewarm approach toward sanctioning Moscow, the Czech Republic was viewed as a soft target for Russian espionage. For instance, in March 2015, three Russian diplomats were expelled as spies, while Moscow responded by expelling four Czech diplomats.[39]

Moscow's actions in Ukraine raised public concerns about Czech security. According to a STEM opinion poll conducted in October 2014, 65% of Czechs stated that Russia may prove a future threat to their country.[40] At the same time, 80% agreed that the war in Ukraine endangered European peace, while 71% supported the territorial integrity of Ukraine. According to an extensive poll conducted in April 2015, 68% of Czechs were afraid of Russian secret service activities, 61% feared a military attack on the Baltic states, and 63% did not support President Zeman's stance on Russia.[41] Of those polled, 62% believed that the Czech Republic should strengthen its relations with NATO allies. In reaction to Moscow's threatening posture, the Czech military decided to establish a new special unit to include combat commandos and IT and psychological experts.[42] The unit's task will be to reinforce Czech special forces in offensive operations: it will be deployed in 2017 and contain 200 specialists.

Slovakia

Moscow considers Slovakia to be another weak link in Central Europe and makes intensive efforts to sway public opinion and the political elite in its favor.[43] It has sponsored a number of public events in Bratislava and issues voluminous material with a pro-Kremlin content on various websites. It capitalizes on lingering pan-Slavic sentiments among some Slovak politicians and intellectuals. The pro-Kremlin camp includes orthodox communists, euroskeptics, radical nationalists, populist extremists, and various anti-Westerners. In the wake of rising anti-immigrant sentiments, many ardent nationalists declared themselves as Putin supporters.

When it assumed office in April 2012, Robert Fico's government promised to improve relations with Russia, a policy sharply criticized by the opposition. The center-right parties consider Fico pro-Russian because of his close relations with officials in Moscow and positive expressions about Putin. Both Prime Minister Fico and outgoing President Ivan Gašparovič were lukewarm on applying EU sanctions against Russia. Fico dismissed sanctions as gestures with no real impact, but also failed to support stronger measures. He reserved the right to veto further EU sanctions if it harmed Slovakia's economic interests. Both leaders expressed worries that a tough stance toward Moscow could damage Slovak business, including energy imports and car exports.

The opposition and mass media harshly criticized Fico after he claimed, on a visit to the Kremlin in June 2015, that there were no disputes between Slovakia and Russia. [44] Underlying Fico's accommodating position was his fear that Russia's planned Turkish Stream gas pipeline would circumvent Ukraine and strip Slovakia of sizable revenues from gas transit to Europe.

President Andrej Kiska, elected in March 2014, at the outset of the Ukraine-Russia war, differed with Fico and considered sanctions against Moscow as necessary and effective.[45] He also supported closer military cooperation with the other Visegrad countries. [46] Additionally, Kiska underscored that Slovakia had to meet its pledge to spend 2% of GDP on defense. Between 2009 and 2014, defense spending had been reduced by 27%, no major military hardware was modernized, and Slovakia's air-defense system remained dependent on the delivery of spare parts from Russia. [47] Critics also berated serious shortcomings in strategic and defense planning, the absence of comprehensive projects for armaments, and long-term instability in personnel.[48] As a result, Slovakia lagged behind most allies in military preparedness as well as in the quality of its equipment.

Premier Fico, in contrast to his Polish and Baltic counterparts, has been opposed to the permanent stationing of a multi-national NATO force on Slovak territory, evidently fearing that this would be provocative for Moscow.[49] He even compared NATO, a voluntary alliance, with Czechoslovakia's enforced occupation by Soviet forces by claiming that: "Slovakia has historical experience with the presence of foreign armies on its territory."[50] Not surprisingly, he came under vociferous attack from the opposition for acting like a Russian stooge and defending Moscow's interests above those of the EU. According to Pavol Frešo, leader of the opposition Slovak Democratic and Christian Union–Democratic Party (SDKU-DS), Fico's approach undermined Slovakia's trustworthiness for both the EU and NATO.[51]

Yet, the Fico government agreed to build a logistics base that could be used by NATO in Poprad, in the Presov region in eastern Slovakia.[52] According to Defense Minister Martin Glvac, ammunition could be stored at the facilities if required by a NATO operation. Bratislava also offered for Alliance use an airport in Sliac and a training facility in Lest, both in the Banska Bystrica region of central Slovakia. The V4 countries had also previously agreed to form a battle group of 3,000 to 4,000 soldiers that Slovakia evidently remained committed to.

In the energy sector, Slovakia is fully dependent on natural gas supplies from Russia, which constitute about a quarter of its total energy mix. Major Russian investments in Slovakia were undertaken under the center-right government of Mikuláš Dzurinda in 2002–2006. These included the privatization of the oil pipeline company *Transpetrol* by Russia's *Yukos* and the privatization of *Cargo Slovakia* by other Russian investors. The opposition has been sharply critical of the most controversial Slovak-Russian joint project, a broad-gauge railway. The SDKU has also issued warnings about growing Russian influence in the energy sector, particularly in *Slovenske Elektrarne* (Slovak Power Plants) and extraordinary loans provided by a Russian bank to a major Slovak energy company.

Former Slovak Prime Minister Iveta Radičová believes that Czech President Miloš Zeman and Slovak Prime Minister Robert Fico make pro-Russian statements in order to appeal to people who feel some nostalgia for communist times.[53] Nonetheless, the majority of the public is supportive of Ukraine. In a survey carried out by the Focus agency for the Institute for Public Issues (IVO) and the daily *Sme* in June 2014, 83% of Slovak citizens responded that Ukrainians should democratically elect their future for themselves and Moscow should not interfere.[54] More than 60% disagreed that Ukraine formed part of the Russian sphere of influence.

Hungary

The government of Prime Minister Viktor Orbán has become the most accommodating of the four Visegrad states toward Moscow. Its pro-Russian foreign policy orientation followed controversial legislative changes by the ruling Fidesz party since its election in April 2010. These changes spurred confrontation with EU institutions, which charged Orbán with backtracking on democracy. Closer ties with Russia were evidently intended to balance Budapest's Western orientation and help protect it from criticism. Paradoxically, while in opposition between 2002 and 2010, Fidesz accused the Socialist government of pursuing pro-Russian policies, when former Socialist Prime Minister Ferenc Gyurcsány was criticized for signing on to the South Stream pipeline project.

In domestic politics, Orbán has claimed that he intends to abandon liberal democracy in favor of an "illiberal state," citing Russia and Turkey as examples. According to one prominent critic, Orbán has openly renounced Western-style democracy for the nationalist authoritarianism of Putin's Russia. Orbán's speech on July 26, 2014, about the terminal decline of liberal democracies declared his preference for an "illiberal state" in which he was prepared to "stand up" to Hungary's enemies, such as the EU and Western banks.[55] The fact that the speech was delivered to Hungarians in Romania may also indicate that Orbán was fantasizing about leaving a legacy in reconstructing the historical Hungary state. Punitive measures by the EU could even prompt Budapest to exchange full EU membership for a limited partnership. Orbán would then be hailed among Euroskeptics of various political stripes as the first leader to effectively resist Brussels. This could also earn him hero status among officials in Moscow.

Orbán's party was re-elected, in April 2014, for a second consecutive four-year term. The Prime Minister has repeatedly clashed with EU officials for replacing the heads of independent institutions, including the country's courts, with allies, for tightening control over the media, and changing election rules to help Fidesz retain a constitutional majority in parliament. Orbán claimed that more centralized control was needed to confront multinational companies such as banks and energy firms in order to protect Hungarians from becoming an EU "colony."[56]

Orbán has declared the liberal, welfare-based systems to be obsolete and a new labor-based "non-liberal" model was supposedly needed. However, it remains unclear exactly what sort of a state he wants to construct, thus enabling his critics to level an assortment of charges against him. Opposition parties have expressed concern about the "Putinization of Hungary," in which Orbán would turn the country into Russia's mirror image and puppet state.[57] Orbán's policies toward Moscow have also alienated Hungary from its traditionally close ally Poland.[58] Relations markedly deteriorated during Russia's annexation of Crimea and destabilization of eastern Ukraine, when Budapest raised the issue of granting autonomy to the Hungarian minority in Transcarpathia, in western Ukraine. Putin's February 17, 2015, visit to Budapest underscored Orbán's divorce from Warsaw, and the dispute has made Prague and Bratislava uncertain with regard to the future of the V4.

In response to Washington's criticisms of Orbán's policies and the imposition of an entry ban on six Hungarian officials, including the head of the national tax office over alleged corruption, anti-US statements became commonplace in Budapest and relished in the Kremlin.[59] On December 23, 2014, Orbán accused Washington of meddling in the internal affairs of Central European countries, claiming that its allegations of corruption among Hungarian officials were simply a "cover story." Orbán also asserted that Cold War–like conditions were developing between the US and Russia over the conflict in Ukraine and that Budapest wanted to remain neutral. The Prime Minister was parroting the Kremlin line that Washington was seeking to draw ECE into a conflict with Russia.

Orbán's government was hesitant to criticize Russia following its covert attack on Ukraine in early 2014. Although Hungary signed on to the EU position regarding Russia's aggression, Orbán's focus has been on the security of the Magyar minority in Ukraine rather than on the fate of Ukraine itself. Relations between President Putin and Premier Orbán have remained close throughout the Ukrainian crisis. Putin has declared Hungary one of Russia's most important political, trade and economic partners, while Foreign Minister Lavrov praised Hungary as an EU and NATO state behaving responsibly by favoring dialogue rather than political pressure.[60] In opposing the EU sanctions against the Kremlin, Orbán is intent on forming a pro-Russia bloc inside the Union to prevent it pulling away from Russia over the crisis in Ukraine. Evidently, his biggest concern was that isolating Russia would damage the Hungarian economy.[61]

Putin's visit to Budapest on February 17, 2015, gave Orbán the opportunity to reiterate that sanctions against Russia were not in anyone's interest. He underlined Hungary's need to renew a gas supply contract with Moscow, which was expiring in 2015. Russia's nuclear giant *Rosatom* indicated that it was following through on a contract signed in January 2014 to build two new nuclear reactors in Hungary and would loan Budapest €10 billion despite Russia's financial problems.

Russia is Hungary's largest trading partner outside the EU and Moscow has enticed Budapest with the prospect of becoming a Central European hub for natural gas distribution. Budapest relies on Russia for 80% of its gas and oil needs and has also expanded Moscow's energy interests in the region. Hungary's state-owned MOL energy company has been embroiled in a struggle with the Croatian government to gain control of INA (*Industrija Nafte*), Croatia's main energy company. By early 2014, MOL had obtained 47% of the shares, but Zagreb refused to cede full control to Budapest.[62] MOL was also negotiating to sell its shares in INA to *Gazprom*, brushing aside opposition by EU and US officials. Hungary's opposition believes that Orbán has also proposed to store Russian gas in Hungarian underground tanks. This would help Moscow undermine Ukraine's status as a transit country, as it would be easier to turn off gas supplies for Ukraine without risking cut-offs to the EU

In the spring of 2014, Budapest signed a €10 billion preferential loan deal with Moscow for *Rosatom* to expand Hungary's only nuclear plant at Paks. *Rosatom* agreed to build two new power units by 2023 and to pay for 80% of the expenses. The Paks power plant provides approximately 40% of Hungary's energy usage, and by 2023 it is supposed to cover all of Hungary's electric energy requirements. Hungary can be a major stumbling block in EU objectives to establish a single gas market in Central Europe. Multi-billion dollar projects with Russia are attractive for Orbán because they offer a way to distribute money domestically and cement political loyalties.[63] Orbán is also eager to develop economic ties with Moscow in sectors other than energy. Moscow demonstrated its approval of the Orbán government by promising to lift selected sanctions that it imposed on all EU agricultural imports in August 2014. Hungary's pork products were to be among the first exemptions.[64]

Moscow has also benefited from Hungarian sensitivities to its kindred residing in neighboring states, particularly in the Transcarpathian region of western Ukraine. The Orbán administration and Hungarian nationalists have manipulated the minority question to score domestic political points in purportedly defending their compatriots at a time when Ukraine was under attack from Moscow's proxy separatists in Donbas after Russia annexed Crimea.

Transcarpathia (also known as Subcarpathia) contains a population of 160,000 Magyars out of a regional population of 1.25 million, where the Hungarian Democratic Federation of Ukraine (UMDSZ) has protested over the partial mobilization of males to defend Ukraine's integrity. It claimed that reserve officers called up were not adequately trained or equipped to fight against separatists in eastern Ukraine. Hungary's radical nationalist Jobbik, (formally called the Movement for a Better Hungary), the third largest party in the National Assembly, demanded that Budapest clearly demonstrate its support for Hungarians in Ukraine, as "the war in Ukraine is not one for a Hungarian cause."[65]

In seeking to depict Ukraine as a failing state, Moscow claimed that Kyiv was facing increasingly serious problems in Transcarpathia, where Ruthenians (Rusyns) and Hungarians were allegedly actively opposing the policies of the Ukrainian authorities. Russia's propagandists propagate the notion that Ruthenians in western Ukraine are Russians, rather than Ukrainians or a distinct ethnic group. Anatoliy Sava, a member of the World Council of Subcarpathian Rusyns, called on Hungary to protect the people of Transcarpathia against possible "genocide" by Ukraine's authorities. He claimed that Kyiv should recognize the results of the Transcarpathian autonomy referendum of December 1991 because otherwise the region will secede from Ukraine unilaterally.[66] In March

2015, Moscow's media outlets spread unsubstantiated reports that Ruthenian organizations were demanding autonomy and quoting Petro Getsko, styled as the "prime minister of Subcarpathian Rus," who has not been seen in the region for years.

In reality, mainstream Ruthenian or Rusyn organizations have supported Ukraine's path toward European integration. Nonetheless, a minority of Transcarpathian autonomists view Russia and Hungary as their strategic partners. A congress of Rusyns and Hungarians was held in Budapest at the beginning of August 2014.[67] The organizers established a "coordinating council" of the Rusyn and Hungarian communities of Transcarpathia. Its main task was to protect people from being recruited to fight in Kyiv's war with separatists. Hungarians account for about 12% of Transcarpathia's population, while Ukrainians, of which self-declared Rusyns form a small proportion, make up 80%. Rusyn autonomists also appealed to Slovakia and the Czech Republic for assistance, as both countries also contain Rusyn populations.

In March 2015, Budapest announced that it distributed Hungarian citizenship papers to 94,000 people in Transcarpathia, an action that may have been coordinated with Moscow to create more headaches for Kyiv.[68] It clearly suits Moscow to recruit Hungary to place additional pressure on the Ukrainian government. Some Russian officials have even urged Budapest to recognize some kind of Transcarpathian republic similar to their Luhansk and Donetsk creations in Ukraine.

Intermarium Front

The three post-Soviet states in East Central Europe between the Baltic and Black Seas, Ukraine, Belarus, and Moldova, remain especially vulnerable to Russia's pressures. The reintegration of this "post-Soviet space" under Moscow's dominance became a priority under President

Putin, as it gave credence to Russia's aspirations as the pre-eminent Eurasian power. The Kremlin opposes any significant foreign military presence in these countries and any aspirations to enter NATO. It also obstructs the creation of regional alliances or initiatives that may inhibit Russian inroads and pursues the integration of its immediate neighbors in Eurasian organizations. Russian officials also oppose EU entry for these countries, viewing such a process as damaging their political, economic, and business interests.

The Black Sea has become a vital arena of opportunity for Russia to increase pressure and leverage on littoral states and to limit and even reverse NATO's presence in the region. The first stage of containing NATO in the Black Sea was accomplished in the summer of 2008 following the invasion and partition of Georgia and the recognition of Abkhazia as a separate state. Since that time, Russian forces have boosted their presence in Abkhazia and constitute a constant threat to Georgian stability and territorial integrity, while effectively freezing Tbilisi's progress toward NATO accession.

The second stage of Russia's Black Sea policy was the Ukrainian operation launched in 2014, with the capture of Crimea, the incorporation of Sevastopol and Russia's Black Sea fleet within Russia itself, the proxy insurgency in the Donbas region of eastern Ukraine, and the attempted destabilization of the pro-Western Ukrainian government. Such maneuvers and Russia's militarization of the Black Sea have significant implications for European security and NATO operations. They challenge the North Atlantic Alliance's presence in the Black Sea, curtail further NATO enlargement, weaken NATO's extended deterrence in Europe, and present a stepping-stone westward for Russia toward the Balkans and Central Europe.

Russia is using the Black Sea as a more advantageous method of revisionism than extensive land conquests. Control of ports and sea-lanes delivers several benefits: it threatens to choke the trade and energy routes of wayward states, prevents NATO from projecting sufficient security for Black Sea members, and gives Moscow a larger stake in exploiting fossil fuels in maritime locations. The Black Sea strategy allows for a disruption of energy supplies through pipeline connections between the Caspian Basin and Europe and obstructs EU attempts to pursue energy diversity. This would further curtail US and European connections with Central Asia and undermine prospects for future natural gas deliveries from Turkmenistan and Azerbaijan to Europe.

Moscow claims privileged interests in the broader Intermarium region, while asserting the right to provide "comprehensive protection of rights and legitimate interests of Russian citizens and compatriots abroad."[69] The Kremlin asserts that only Russia is entitled to "stabilize the post-Soviet territory."[70] It believes that all three countries should have limited sovereignty under Russia's stewardship, while offering incentives and imposing sanctions in order to develop closer asymmetrical ties.[71] The inducements include cheap energy, a growing market, employment for guest workers, visa-free travel, diplomatic support, and assistance in developing their security sectors. The pressures on neighboring governments involve the exploitation of Russian minority populations through the defense of their allegedly endangered interests, support for oppositionist parties and pro-Russian movements, energy embargoes, trade sanctions, political demands, security threats, covert institutional penetration, territorial subversion, and in some cases outright military actions.

Another intrusive mechanism was inaugurated in May 2008 with the creation of the Federal Agency for CIS Affairs in Moscow.[72] It was attached to the foreign ministry and mandated to deal with "soft security" questions in Moscow's relations with neighbors, especially in assisting Russian citizens resident in the post-Soviet countries, whose conditions serve as a primary justification for intervention. Russian officials also seek to enlist national elites by enticing them with lucrative business contracts and diplomatic support in return for their political loyalty.[73] The urgency of this strategy was highlighted in the aftermath of the "colored revolutions" in Ukraine (2004) and

Georgia (2003) that moved both countries closer to Western institutions. Those popular developments were perceived as direct confrontations with the West that could spark a similar pro-democracy revolution in Russia itself.

By aiding and abetting the secessionist regions of neighboring states, the Kremlin keeps the national governments off balance and hinders their entry into Western institutions. Moscow's ideal solution is the federalization or confederalization of Ukraine and Moldova, and potentially Georgia, Belarus, and Azerbaijan. In such an arrangement, the autonomous entities would maintain veto powers over the foreign and security policies of the central governments and indefinitely keep each country outside of NATO and the EU and keep the US at a distance.

A new "frozen conflict" in the Donbas region of Ukraine will have repercussions for a much broader region. It can encourage ethno-territorial secessions elsewhere in former Soviet territories, undermine Western security guarantees, and challenge Europe's existing borders. It will also generate disputes within NATO and the EU on how to handle split states and quasi-independent entities from which Moscow will seek to profit. Moscow indefinitely maintains a variety of unsettled conflicts and holds in reserve the prospect of unfreezing them. It thereby threatens unpredictable instability through a renewed insurgency, further bloodshed, and potential direct Russian military intervention. Such a posture serves to convince Western governments to make political compromises to accommodate Moscow.

Moscow views the EU as a strategic threat not only because it can divert the trade of post-Soviet states away from Russia due to its superior market, but also because its legal principles, democratic standards, and transparent business practices undermine the core ingredients of the Putinist system. Such fears have been evident in

Kremlin attempts to block Ukraine, Moldova, and Georgia from signing Association Agreements with the EU.

Russian state propaganda also claims that the entry of any post-Soviet country into NATO would irrevocably damage its political, economic, and social ties with Russia and even fracture the state. Such threats increased in the wake of the NATO summit in April 2008, following the Alliance's declaration that Ukraine and Georgia would eventually become NATO members even though they had not even received Membership Action Plans (MAPs) to prepare them for potential accession.[74] Moscow has sought to develop an alternative alliance to NATO, designed to embrace all former Soviet republics and styled as the Collective Security Treaty Organization (CSTO). The CSTO was created in 2012, but by 2015 it only included Russia, Armenia, Belarus, Kazakhstan, Kyrgyzstan, and Tajikistan, after Azerbaijan, Georgia, and Uzbekistan withdrew from the alliance, fearing Moscow's military and political dominance.

Ukraine

Russia's elites have an imperialistic and patronizing posture toward Ukraine, denying the existence of a separate and distinct Ukrainian history and national identity. Ukraine is considered to be an ethnic patchwork and an artificially created country that is Russia's "younger brother," destined to perpetually remain in a close union dominated by Moscow. When Kyiv has misbehaved by petitioning for closer links with NATO or the EU, officials in Moscow have employed a range of subversive weapons to bring Ukraine back into line.

Moscow's pursuit of supranational integration challenges the independence of neighboring states, as they are constrained from freely choosing their international alliances. This was clearly evident in the case of Ukraine. President Viktor Yanukovych sought to straddle Western and Eastern assimilation by reassuring Ukrainians that he could pursue close ties with both Europe and Moscow. However, Putin made this precarious balancing act increasingly difficult through his persistent pressure on Kyiv to abandon the EU project and join the Moscow-centered Customs Union, the precursor to the Eurasian Economic Union (EEU). Yanukovych's withdrawal from signing an Association Agreement at the EU's Eastern Partnership Summit in Vilnius, on November 28–29, 2013, sparked a popular uprising in Kyiv that led to his ouster in late February 2014 and sparked Russia's direct attack on Ukraine's sovereignty and territorial integrity.

In order to return Kyiv more firmly under its control, Moscow has engaged in various forms of pressure and subterfuge. These have included energy blackmail, an intensive media barrage, corrupting or discrediting pro-Western politicians, manipulating ethnic and regional grievances, and raising territorial claims. Russia's military doctrine also bestows Moscow with the right to intervene in neighboring states containing large Russian populations. The Russian or Russophone minority, constituting about a third of the Ukrainian total, has been exploited by Moscow to apply political pressures on Kyiv and promote proxy separatism in the Donbas area of eastern Ukraine.

The Kremlin fears Ukraine is slipping out of its grasp as the new government of President Petro Poroshenko and Prime Minister Arseniy Yatseniuk pursues closer ties with the West. Paradoxically, Putin himself has intensified Ukrainian patriotism and national identity through his attack on the country. Such expanding sentiments will damage Russia's agenda for assembling the EEU or any other multi-national imperium, as Ukraine will vehemently resist integration. This will also undermine pan-Slavism as one binding ideology of the Russian state. Additionally, Moscow is anxious about democratic contagion and a reformist model from Ukraine that could challenge Putin's authoritarian regime or unseat allies in other post-Soviet states such as Belarus or Armenia. Hence, Kyiv's success could become Moscow's failure. In allegedly defending Ukraine against a perceived Western-sponsored takeover, Russia's leaders believe they are fighting to secure their own political survival as well as the integrity of Russia and its dominions.

Despite Moscow's insistence that the war in Ukraine was an internal affair, on February 24, 2015, the Russian newspaper *Novaya Gazeta* published an official government strategy document outlining the invasion of Ukraine. It was prepared weeks before the Yanukovych administration collapsed in February 2014.[75] The overall strategy included breaking Ukraine into autonomous sectors, attaching southeastern Ukraine to Moscow's Customs Union, and a longer-term plan for annexation. Moscow would activate its agents and informers in the security and military services, deeply embedded during the Yanukovych era, in order to neutralize Ukraine's military responses. The strategy document also called for a public relations campaign to justify Russia's intervention. The strategy paper contradicted the Kremlin's claim that it annexed Crimea as a reaction to its residents feeling threatened by Ukrainian nationalists.

While Moscow's objectives have been clear-cut, its strategies and tactics proved more flexible and adaptable, generally consisting of two simultaneous offensives since the start of the war in early 2014: political and territorial. The Kremlin mounted a political assault claiming that the government was illegitimately installed through a *coup d'état*, asserting that the general elections in October 2014 were only partly legitimate, and seeking a commitment to federalize Ukraine through constitutional amendments. For the Kremlin, federalization means a divided state that blocks Kyiv's international ambitions and prevents Ukraine from making progress toward EU association.

Ukraine's government rejected Moscow's demands for debilitating federalization. However, during the summer and fall of 2015, Kyiv was pressured by Washington, Berlin, and Paris to implement constitutional amendments that would expand Ukraine's decentralization. By including a provision in the constitution stating that Kyiv will formulate a new law governing local administrations in certain portions of Donetsk and Luhansk *oblasts,* parliament left the door open to providing a special status for the occupied Donbas territories.

Western leaders also sought to convince Kyiv to include the rebel-held areas in the October 25, 2015, local elections, even though the government did not control these territories and the elections would fall far short of any democratic standards. However, leaders of the non-recognized Donetsk and Luhansk People's Republics indicated that they would organize their own local elections outside of Kyiv's jurisdiction and scheduled them for February 2016. In response, Western mediators, led by Berlin and Paris, pressured Kyiv to validate the separatist elections by incorporating them in special legislation. The inclusion of these regions within Ukraine but without Kyiv's control will reinforce Moscow's drive to federalize the country with Western support by bestowing legitimacy on its proxies. As elected regional representatives, the rebels could be empowered to negotiate constitutional amendments with Kyiv to gain some form of self-determination. Instead of a military occupation of Ukraine, Russia is banking on concessions by the West that could contribute to paralyzing the central government without need for war.[76]

In its territorial offensive, Russia has partitioned and annexed Crimea, where just under 60% of the population are ethnic Russians, according to recent estimates. Moreover, Moscow has instigated proxy separatism in the Donbas region to test the prospects for further division. It dispatched its special forces and recruited assorted mercenaries to engineer conflict and establish secessionist governments in the Donetsk and Luhansk *oblasts.* Similar tactics in other cities, such as Kharkiv and Odesa, failed to spark any armed rebellions or a civil war. According to the 2012 census, the ethnic Russian population amounted to 17.3% of Ukraine's 45.4 million people. In addition to Crimea, the majority inhabited the eastern *oblasts*, although their share in any region other than Luhansk (39%) and Donetsk (38%) did not exceed 30%.[77] In the bigger picture, about a third of Ukraine's population use Russian as their primary language and are therefore viewed as part of the "Russian World" in addition to Russian ethnics.

The attempted separatist offensive to sever the bulk of southeastern Ukraine only registered limited success in a handful of districts in Donetsk and Luhansk *oblasts*. Opinion polls indicated that only a small minority of the Donbas population supported federalization or secession. In the absence of sufficient public enthusiasm for autonomy or partition, and given the successful Ukrainian military counter-offensive to reclaim occupied territories in the summer of 2014, Putin intervened more directly with Russian troops at the end of August 2014 to shore up rebel gains. However, Moscow avoided a large-scale invasion and potentially costly occupation.

Having decided not to annex the Donbas, as this would further drain a faltering Russian economy that was already supporting a bankrupt Crimea, the Kremlin has been pushing for a split state in Ukraine. Its model resembles that of Moldova or Bosnia-Herzegovina, in which autonomous regions not controlled by the central government either disqualify the country from meeting the criteria for EU or NATO entry or they actively block central government policymaking by holding veto powers.

The Kremlin also sought to legitimize the separatist leaders by making them a party to various ceasefires and peace talks with Kyiv, Moscow, the EU, and the Organization for Security and Cooperation in Europe (OSCE). This was especially evident in the Minsk agreement, codified in two documents, Minsk I in September 2014, which was violated by Russia's proxies, and Minsk II signed in February 2015.[78] The armistice negotiations included leaders of the two rebel regions—the Luhansk People's Republic and the Donetsk People's Republic.

Although some voices in Kyiv calculated that surrendering the rebel regions to Russia could bring a lasting peace, government officials were convinced that this would simply encourage Moscow to push the war deeper into Ukraine in order to further fracture and destabilize the country. Such a maneuver would also entail abandoning the majority of citizens in the Donbas who opposed secessionism and thus erode the credibility of the administration.

Putin has also favored a policy that is reminiscent of the post–Orange Revolution (2004) scenario: state subversion. This entails fanning social and regional unrest; corrupting or discrediting Ukraine's new officials; making deals with local oligarchs; spreading disinformation to promote political divisions; inciting nationalist radicals through FSB penetration of their organizations; threatening military intervention so that Kyiv maintains a large and expensive standing army; and waiting for a major economic crash as Ukraine undertakes deep structural and budgetary reforms. The net effect would be another round of public unrest culminating in the overthrow of the pro-Western government and disqualification from Western integration. At the same time, the Kremlin calculated that Western sanctions against Moscow would be eased and Putin will be praised in Western capitals for not pursuing the military option and further dismembering Ukrainian territory.

To preclude the Kremlin scenario of instability, it is imperative for the Ukrainian administration elected on October 26, 2014, to conduct effective structural and fiscal reforms, move closer to Western institutions, maintain sufficient national cohesion, and resist Moscow's pressures and enticements. Russia's attack has underscored the importance for all Ukrainian parties of maintaining national unity and steering the country away from dependence on an unreliable and aggressive Russia. In a key economic move, during 2015, Ukraine significantly reduced its dependence on *Gazprom* for natural gas supplies.[79] Kyiv is pursuing supply diversification with the backing of the European Commission. Ukraine's business practices in the gas trade are also changing. The current political leaders have no personal interest in the gas business or depend on interest groups linked to the energy sector. Talks with Moscow on gas supplies are becoming less political and more business oriented, handled by the Ministry of Energy and *Naftohaz*, Ukraine's national oil and gas company.

Nonetheless, Russia continues to exert energy pressures on Ukraine at a difficult financial juncture. During 2015, it demanded that Kyiv pay for gas bills estimated at over $5 billion, dating back to 2013, and threatening to cut supplies until all payments were received. Several EU countries have pledged to supply Ukraine with gas to cover its most urgent needs. From supplying nearly all of Ukraine's gas imports, since mid-2014 *Gazprom's* share has dropped dramatically and Kyiv procured the remainder through reverse flows from Europe. With the diversification of supplies, by mid-2015 the consumption of Russian gas was reduced from 28.1 bcm to 19.9 bcm and the Russian share of total gas imports fell from 90% to 37%. Moreover, legislation was adopted to establish transparency in gas contracts.

Ukraine's economic problems, stemming from years of mismanagement and corruption, have been compounded by the war in Donbas, whose economic production accounted for about 10% of Ukraine's GDP in 2013.[80] Moscow has also imposed tough trade sanctions so that Kyiv's exports to Russia have fallen by half since the start of the Russian offensive, equivalent to 12% of total exports. This caused Ukraine's GDP (excluding Crimea) to shrink by 6.8% in 2014 and was projected to drop by a further 9% in 2015. Unfortunately, the EU has failed to fully open its markets to Ukrainian exports despite signing an Association Agreement and a Deep and Comprehensive Free Trade Agreement with Kyiv; indeed, the implementation of the latter has been delayed under pressure from Moscow. Although the IMF agreed, in 2015, on a $40 billion bailout designed to keep Ukraine solvent it is only providing under half of that sum and Ukraine is experiencing problems raising the rest.

Both Moscow and Kyiv appear to be waiting for the collapse of each other's economies and the subsequent impact on foreign policy. The fate of the separatist controlled regions has hung in the balance with Kyiv applying economic pressure on the rebels by cutting state subsidies for pensions, local authorities, health, and education, and withdrawing support for the banking system. Without state subsidies from Kyiv or Moscow, the rebels seem barely competent in governing territories where infrastructure has been destroyed, factories have closed, and revenues have shrunk. Moscow does not want these regions to collapse economically but cannot afford to fully subsidize them and seeks to place the burden on Kyiv. The local elections would evidently oblige Kyiv to maintain its subsidies to the occupied regions and support the very structures that are pulling Ukraine apart.

On the religious front, on May 24, 2015, Moscow Patriarch Kirill officially declared that the Ukrainian Orthodox Church of the Moscow Patriarchate was no longer obligated to obey the "godless" Ukrainian authorities.[81] This pronouncement was a direct challenge to Ukrainian sovereignty and demonstrated that Kirill was a Kremlin collaborator in the offensive against Kyiv. However, since 2011, the number of Ukrainians who declared themselves members of Churches subordinate to the Moscow Patriarchate has fallen from 25.9% of the population to 20.8%. [82] In an indication of the strengthening of Ukrainian national identity involving religious affiliation, in June 2015 a merger was announced between the Ukrainian Autocephalous Orthodox Church and the Ukrainian Orthodox Church of the Kyiv Patriarchate, two of the three largest Orthodox denominations in Ukraine. This will significantly undermine the authority and influence of the Russian Orthodox Church and the Russian state inside Ukraine.

In addition to Transcarpathia (*see Hungary section*), another area of potential separatist agitation is the Danubian basin, bound by the Black Sea to the east, Moldova to the west, and Romania to the south. Reports have circulated about the emergence there of a "Bessarabian

People's Republic," modeled on the Donetsk and Luhansk secessionists. Bessarabia is the historic name of an area comprising the current territory of Moldova, without the breakaway Transnistria region, and some territories in Ukraine's Odesa region. Southern Bessarabia has a large percentage of ethnic minorities, including Bulgarians, Moldovans, Gagauz, and Russians. The Kremlin possesses the means to induce Gagauz politicians on both sides of the Ukrainian-Moldovan border to join forces and stir problems, while some residents of the Bessarabia region are susceptible to Kremlin propaganda and nationalist enticements.

On April 6, 2015, a People's Council of Bessarabia (PCB) in southwestern Ukraine and an Odesa People's Republic (OPR) in the Black Sea port announced their existence. [83] Reportedly, the PCB was established to press for the status of a national-territorial autonomous unit within Ukraine, while the OPR declared itself fully independent of Kyiv. Although these moves appeared to be largely propaganda initiatives orchestrated by a few local activists with Kremlin support, they needed to be carefully monitored by Kyiv. Information about the creation of the PCB was posted on its website, which was registered in Moscow. [84] Dmytro Zatuliveter, chairman of the Union of Transnistrian Inhabitants of Ukraine, became the self-declared leader of the PCB. Ukrainian police reported that the "founding congress" took place in a restaurant with no foreign guests.

Ukraine's genuine minority organizations stated that they had no connection with the separatist initiative that was designed to destabilize the Bessarabian region. The Gagauz national-cultural society Birlik and the Association of Ukrainian Bulgars described the creation of the "people's council" as a sham and a provocation. Nonetheless, in a region where there has been little economic development since independence, there is some potential in stirring unrest that does not require majority support.

Another key domain of Russia's attack on Ukraine has been

cyberspace.[85] The objective is to wear down the opponent and push him to change political course. Russia has employed various forms of cyber assaults, including but not limited to denial of service attacks against government institutions, monitoring of Ukrainian telecommunications, and infecting Ukrainian networks with various viruses. Cyber attacks and cyber espionage can inflict serious harm on a country's defense capabilities.

On the military front, Russia's invasion and occupation of Ukraine has necessitated deep security sector reforms by Kyiv. On April 9, 2015, the government formulated a new security doctrine setting its sights on joining NATO.[86] Oleksander Turchynov, the Secretary of Ukraine's National Security and Defense Council (NSDC), concluded that Russian aggression was a "long-standing factor" and NATO membership was "the only reliable external guarantee" of the country's sovereignty and territorial integrity. Public support for NATO membership has skyrocketed since Russia's attack on the country, and stood at 64% by August 2015.[87]

At the end of August 2015, Ukraine's government approved a draft of the new Military Doctrine that clearly defined the Russian Federation as the country's main enemy and aggressor. Kyiv has also pursued closer bilateral military ties with individual NATO states to assist in the process of security modernization. For example, 300 US Army paratroopers were deployed to Ukraine in April 2015 to help train 900 national guardsmen. Predictably, the initiative was condemned by Moscow as provoking regional instability. Ukraine also decided to curtail its exports of military components to Russia, including advanced engines and elements used in the production of numerous types of military equipment. Given Moscow's dependence on Ukrainian supplies, this could seriously dent Russia's military export earnings and even lead to a collapse of its arms industry.

According to the deputy head of Ukraine's anti-terrorist operation, Colonel Sergiy Galushko, by July 2015 Russia had massed roughly

54,000 troops along Ukraine's border. [88] This force reportedly consisted of 45 battalion tactical groups and 17 company tactical groups. There is frequent speculation in Kyiv about a full-scale Russian military invasion, with evidence allegedly leaked from the Russian General Military Staff. It serves Moscow's interests to encourage rumors about imminent invasions as this engenders fear and uncertainty in Ukrainian society and distracts political attention from vital economic and structural reforms.

Moscow is also suspected of engaging in terrorism and sabotage operations to destabilize various parts of Ukraine and weaken the central government. In January 2015, Ukraine's Security Service (SBU) extended counterterrorist measures to the Zaporizhzhya region after a railway bridge was blown up on the Kamysh Zarya-Rozovka line. [89] The number of bomb alerts and terrorist attacks has been on the rise, especially in regions where the public mood is more heterogeneous and some pro-Moscow sentiments are present. [90] The objective is to probe for weaknesses, undermine the local authorities, and intimidate the population. On February 22, 2015 a bomb was detonated at a rally in support of national unity in Ukraine's second-largest city of Kharkiv, causing several fatalities. [91] There have been other bomb attacks in Kharkiv, with Moscow-backed rebels threatening to expand their operations. Terrorism remains a lethal tool in Moscow's arsenal of subversion and destabilization.

Belarus

Russia's challenge to Ukraine's independence and territorial integrity may push its ally Belarus westward, although Russia's leaders are unlikely to remain passive if President Alyaksandr Lukashenka cultivates closer Western connections. Moscow may seek an alternative leader after the presidential elections held on October 11, 2015: not a pro-European democrat but a pro-Russian loyalist. The Kremlin is capable of engineering a political coup in Minsk, as the country is heavily penetrated by Russia's security services, in order to replace Lukashenka with a more compliant figurehead. Alternatively, Moscow could exploit nationalists and other radicals to stage protests in Minsk, mimicking Ukraine's Maidan revolution, and then intervene on the pretext of restoring law and order while implanting a new leader in Minsk.

Conditions for such a coup may become favorable if the economy seriously deteriorates, with Minsk remaining heavily dependent on Moscow's subsidies and bearing the consequences of Russia's economic contraction. However, too much Kremlin pressure is also risky for Moscow, as Lukashenka may decide to move closer to the West for political protection.[92] For instance, the release of Nikolay Statkevich and five other political prisoners, in August 2015, appeared to be a bridging act with the West, as both Washington and Brussels had been calling for clemency for several years.

In an indication of growing fears of Russia's dominance, Aleksey Yanukevich, leader of the Belarusian Popular Front Party, stated that Lukashenka was "a lesser evil" in comparison to Kremlin imperialism.[93] As a result, the Belarusian Popular Front, despite its opposition to Lukashenka, did not intend to field a candidate against him in the October 2015 presidential elections. Yanukevich believed that anything that destabilizes Belarus, including a popular rising such as the Ukrainian Maidan, would only benefit the Kremlin. According to the opposition, Moscow's "fifth column" in the country threatens the independence of Belarus and its survival far more than Lukashenka through his links with Russia. Vladimir Borodac, a former Belarusian security service officer, asserts that Moscow can seize the country whenever it wants because the majority of Belarusian *siloviki* are prepared to take orders from Moscow, and replacing Lukashenka may be easier for the Kremlin as he is relatively isolated in Europe.[94]

Belarusian political analysts claim that Minsk expects Moscow to offer financial aid in exchange for an increase in Russia's military presence.[95] According to Russia's Defense Minister Sergei Shoigu, Moscow planned to increase the number of its aircraft stationed at Belarusian air bases. Four Su-27M3 fighter aircraft were deployed at the Lida air base near the Belarus-Lithuania border during 2014.[96] By the end of 2014, Baranovichi air base housed a regiment of 24 aircraft of Su-27M3 fighters. This doubled the number of Russian fighter aircraft stationed near the borders of Lithuania and Poland.

Russian authorities also planned to build a separate air force base in Babruysk, in the Mogilev region of central Belarus, by 2016, and pressured Minsk to approve its construction. The location of such a base would be a perennial threat to Poland, Lithuania, and Ukraine and could enable Moscow to pull Belarus into a war with a neighboring state. There are indications that Lukashenka has opposed the base, and if Moscow persists in its construction this may have the unintended consequence of raising resistance against Russia's dominance and even weakening Lukashenka's domestic position.[97] Quite possibly, Moscow may intentionally seek to make him more pliable or even replace him with a more predictable state leader.

Moscow is capable of rapidly turning Belarus into a forward base by incorporating it in Russia's Western Military District, which would constitute a direct challenge to Ukraine, Lithuania, and Poland.[98] The presence of Russian forces and bases could embroil Belarus in military conflicts launched by the Kremlin. Questions remain whether the Belarusian military is capable of resisting Russian armed forces given that the two militaries are closely interlinked, as evident in their joint anti-air defense system. To effectively resist Russia's aggressive moves, Belarus would need to develop a sizable mobile national guard that could engage in partisan warfare.[99]

In an indication of close collaboration between security services in Moscow and Minsk, Lithuania's State Security Department disclosed that Belarus' security services cooperate with their Russian counterparts against Lithuania.[100] Following the disintegration of the USSR, Moscow maintained its covert presence in the security agencies of former republics and has deployed non-Russians against third countries where locals are less suspicious of their actions than they would be of Russians. According to the Vilnius report, Belarusian agents in Lithuania focus primarily on the activities of the Belarusian opposition. However, they are also recruiting agents and collecting information about military and strategic civilian infrastructure sites, which they most probably share with Russian services.

With regard to the crisis in Ukraine, there are contrasting interpretations of Minsk hosting meetings of the Contact Group, involving Kyiv, Moscow, the OSCE, and the two rebel groups from Donbas. On the one hand, it benefits Lukashenka to host senior European leaders and gain credit as a peacemaker. On the other hand, it is advantageous for Moscow to host such talks in an allied state and enable separatist leaders from Luhansk and Donetsk to participate as legitimate interlocutors. Throughout the war in Ukraine, the Belarusian President has avoided any actions that alienate him further from the West. For instance, Minsk did not back the Russian embargo imposed against Ukraine, Georgia, and Moldova, which signed Association Agreements with the EU during 2014; and unlike Putin, Lukashenka viewed the new authorities in Kyiv as legitimate.

Most Belarusians are exposed to regular Russian TV channels and many view Ukraine through the prism of Moscow's interests and Kremlin propaganda. Moreover, government officials imply that any attempts at organizing demonstrations similar to Kyiv's Maidan revolt would result in destabilization and possible Russian intervention. The war in Ukraine had an impact on public opinion in Belarus. While the majority of Belarusian citizens want to avoid a bloody Ukrainian scenario, an increasing number were also opposed to unification with Russia.

WESTERN FLANK | 181

Analytic reports published by the Belarusian Independent Institute of Socioeconomic and Political Studies (IISEPS) include the results of national opinion polls.[101] In a poll conducted in June 2014, if a referendum were held on Belarus-Russia state unification, 24.8% of respondents would vote positively whereas 54.8% would vote against. In December 2007, the opponents of unification accounted for only 31.6%. The number of citizens who think that Belarus and Russia should be one state with one president, government, army, flag, and currency only reached 9.8%. After the annexation of Crimea, many people evidently grew concerned that Belarus could become an object of Moscow's expansionism.

As insurance against greater Russian interference in Belarus, Lukashenka has emphasized Belarusian identity and language and the country's distinct national interests. In January 2015, the state media announced a policy of "de-russification" of schools to revive the Belarusian language. At a press conference on January 29, 2015, Lukashenka underscored that Belarus was an independent state and not part of the Russian World.[102] To avert aggression, the Belarusian army was reportedly developing mobile units "that could deal a blow to the aggressor." Lukashenka also publicly regretted that nuclear weapons were surrendered by Belarus in 1994, because "he who possesses brute force is right."

Belarus introduced legislation on martial law on February 1, 2015, and adjusted its definition of invasion to take account of Putin's actions in Ukraine.[103] The new law specified that the appearance of military personnel, even if they do not wear uniforms or have designations of their membership in the military of another state, will be considered a form of attack that threatens the territorial integrity and sovereignty of Belarus. The new law also specifies conditions that Minsk will view as a military threat sufficient to introduce martial law. These include the concentration of military forces of another state on the Belarusian border with a clear indication that they are intended for an attack.

Minsk also announced its largest-ever peacetime exercises of military reserves, involving some 15,000 troops.

In one potentially threatening scenario, several neo-Cossack groups in Belarus could be employed to stir unrest or provide an excuse for Russia's military intervention.[104] A number of Cossack groups that emerged in the country are reportedly closely tied with Russia's security services. Some members have attended special military camps organized by Russia's special operations airborne troops.

In December 2014, the Belarusian ambassador to Kyiv, Valentin Velichko, asserted that Minsk would never allow other countries to use Belarus's territory for military intervention in Ukraine: "We support Ukraine as an integral unitarian state along the lines of the acting constitution, which rules out federalization."[105] Lukashenka has, on occasion, reiterated that it was "inadmissible" for any state to violate the territorial integrity of another state. However, in a classic balancing act between Russia and Ukraine, Lukashenka also asserted that Crimea would not be returned to Ukraine and that the Ukrainians had failed to defend the territory. He pointedly stressed that Belarus would fight for every inch of its territory whoever the invader. Russia's attempts to involve Minsk in the economic war against Ukraine also failed and Lukashenka attended President Poroshenko's inauguration, on June 7, 2014.[106] In an indication of concern over the country's vulnerabilities to a Russian assault, Lukashenka has also reached out to NATO. In comments to the country's military leaders on February 19, 2015, he underscored that Belarus was open to a constructive dialogue with NATO.[107]

There have been several indications that Lukashenka was employing Belarusian defensive nationalism as protection against Moscow. To revive Belarusian identity, he has called for schools to devote more hours to Belarusian-language classes. The authorities have encouraged citizens to rediscover their roots by signing up for language courses, holding weddings in an ethnic style, and donning national dress. By highlighting their distinct national characteristics, people were expressing their opposition to Russia's chauvinism.[108]

Nationalist groups have been permitted to become more publicly prominent.[109] For instance, the Belarusian Congress in Defense of the Independence of Belarus was held on December 21, 2014, in Minsk, organized by representatives of the nationalist wing of the opposition.[110] Elena Anisim, head of the organizing committee, stated that the group's goal was to declare that the Belarusian people would not become part of any other country.[111] She also asserted that Lukashenka did not oppose the congress because "today the interests of the nationalists and the authorities coincide." Forum delegates launched a campaign to collect one million signatures in defense of Belarusian independence. Participants also condemned the Eurasian Economic Union as destructive of the Belarusian economy and enabling Moscow's control.

Shortly after the creation of the EEU, Lukashenka warned that if the Union's agreements were not observed, Minsk reserved the right to leave.[112] Throughout 2015, Minsk was increasingly hampered by Russia's fiscal and economic problems, as 40% of its exports were traded with Russia, and much of the rest to countries closely linked to Russia's economy. The Belarusian parliament asserted that it would ratify the EEU agreement with reservations.[113] Lukashenka's value as a political ally for Moscow grew during the Western economic boycott of Russia and new loans could be provided to ensure Lukashenka's re-election in October 2015.[114] Conversely, as a result of economic crisis, Moscow may only possess limited funds to provide assistance to Minsk.[115] This may result in a more pronounced Western tilt by Belarus that would stir conflicts with the Kremlin.

Lukashenka has been outspoken about protecting national sovereignty and territorial integrity given that the country contains a sizable Russian minority. In 2014, it was estimated at 8.3% of the population of 9.6 million, with an even larger share of Belarusians using Russian as their first language.[116] The President is fearful of externally generated internal unrest, as witnessed in Ukraine. His speeches indicate anxiety that Russia might annex parts of Belarus and admits that the threat to independence may emerge due to economic pressures because of the country's dependence on Moscow.[117]

Some Russian nationalists claim that Moscow should take back territory in Belarus that was once part of the Russian Republic in the Soviet Union, similarly to the annexation of Crimea from Ukraine.[118] Moscow could also engineer the creation of "people's republics" in eastern Belarus as it had in eastern Ukraine in order to "federalize" the country. In 1918, Moscow handed over the Donetsk-Krivorog Soviet Republic to Soviet Ukraine. In the 1920s, Moscow also transferred from Russia to Belarus Vitebsk, Mohilev, and Gomel *oblasts*. The new law passed by the Russian *Duma* concerning the "illegality" of the transfer of Crimea to Ukraine in 1954 could be amended or extended to include Russian areas assigned to Belarus during Soviet times.

The Kremlin is opposed to expressions of Belarus's independence and may use its media dominance in the country to portray Lukashenka as a fascist or a Russophobe, similarly to Ukraine's leaders. In response to Russia's propaganda offensives and the potential threat to Belarus, some analysts have raised the prospect of curtailing official Russian television channels if the government considered them as Moscow's fifth column.[119]

The Kremlin may also lend support to pro-Russian organizations that deny the existence of an independent Belarusian nation and language. Some opinion polls indicated that a sizable percentage of the population, especially pensioners, would favor living in a single state with Russia. People may welcome an invasion or a regime change if it were accompanied by a promise to raise salaries and pensions at a time when economic conditions in Belarus continue to deteriorate. On the other hand, there have been indications that an increasing number of young Belarusians were prepared to defend the country against absorption by Russia. A sense of national distinctiveness has reportedly developed in Belarus since Moscow's attack on Ukraine, while Russia's economic decline will ensure that it becomes less attractive for ordinary Belarusians.[120]

Moldova

Moscow has kept the Moldovan government off balance in its aspirations toward EU membership and threatened more intensive pressures if Chisinau signed and ratified the Association and Free Trade agreements with Brussels. Deputy Prime Minister Dmitriy Rogozin, who oversees relations with Moldova, warned that moving closer to the EU would prove costly while incorporation in Russia's Customs Union would be beneficial.[121] Russian officials push the line that Moldova can only preserve its independence if it joins the Eurasian Economic Union, otherwise it will be absorbed by Romania, and the separatist region of Transnistria will become independent. Moscow claims that "Westernizers" in the Moldovan government plan to change the constitution to remove the provision on neutral status, promote NATO membership, and enshrine EU accession aspirations in the document. To prevent such a scenario, Russia deploys four main tools of pressure: informational, political, economic, and territorial.

Since the eruption of war in Ukraine in early 2014, Russian news channels have warned of plans for a concerted attack on Transnistria by Moldovan, Romanian, and Ukrainian forces supported by Washington. Propagandists claim that Kyiv is preparing to forcibly reintegrate Moldova and Transnistria and to assist Romania in absorbing Moldova with American involvement.[122] Anti-Romanian propaganda has been a constant feature of Moscow's line on Moldova, claiming that Bucharest seeks to annex the country as well as pockets of territory in Ukraine, including northern Bukovina, southern Bessarabia, and several islands on the Danube.[123] In this multi-layered game of threats, Moscow plays both Moldova and Transnistria against Romania, claiming at times that Transnistria supports Ukraine in its opposition to Romanian expansionism.

At the same time, officials in Moscow assert that Kyiv is a threat to Transnistrian statehood, thus justifying Russia's military presence in the territory together with a possible link between Transnistria and a future Novorossyia carved out of southern Ukraine, or by enabling Transnistria to forcefully obtain a narrow Black Sea coastline from Ukraine. Moscow has also supported Gagauz separatism in southern Moldova. The Gagauz are an ethnic Turkish, Orthodox Christian, and Russian-speaking population that the Kremlin considers part of the Russian World and which possesses an autonomous region inside Moldova called *Gagauz Yeri* (Gagauzia).

Additionally, Moscow has threatened both Romania and Ukraine with territorial partition by claiming the wider Bessarabian region for an enlarged Moldova and backing the creation of a Budjak Republic in southern Moldova to include Gagauzia, Bulgarian inhabited areas of Moldova, and parts of Odesa *oblast* in Ukraine that contain Moldovan, Gagauz, Russian, and Bulgarian minorities. Alternatively, Moscow may favor the option of splitting Moldova by offering Romania sections of right bank Moldova and Ukraine's Bukovina in exchange for Bucharest recognizing Novorossiya and Budjak hacked out of Ukraine.

The Kremlin prolongs the "frozen conflict" in Transnistria and uses it to maintain Moldova as a split state. Transnistria is perceived in Moscow as part of the Russian World, where approximately 60% of the population of half a million are either Russian or Ukrainian and the majority use Russian as their first language.[124] In a meeting with Moldovan President Igor Voronin in January 2008, Putin proposed a settlement to ensure Moldova's permanent neutrality.[125] This would entail transforming the country into a confederation with Transnistria while prolonging the presence of Russian troops cloaked as peacekeepers until a final settlement was reached in the indefinite future. Although Chisinau rejected the proposal, Moscow has continued to maintain a *de facto* confederation in Moldova by aiding and abetting Transnistrian separatism.

Foreign Minister Lavrov has warned that Transnistria has a right to independently decide on its future if Moldova changes its non-bloc military-political status.[126] He deliberately linked such a prospect with Romania's alleged drive for unification. Transnistrian President Yevgeny Shevchuk has also condemned any initiative to integrate Moldova with Romania.[127] He claimed that he was troubled by the presence of Romanian advisers in Moldova's security services. At the same time, Transnistrian leaders worked closely with separatists in Ukraine's Donbas. For instance, in July 2014 Vladimir Antyufeyev, the state security minister in Transnistria, was appointed deputy prime minister responsible for security issues in the "Donetsk People's Republic."[128]

As Chisinau moves closer to the EU, Transnistria will have to decide whether to join the EU as part of Moldova or to remain an unrecognized region dependent on Russia.[129] Russia invests heavily in Transnistria's economy, supplying free natural gas and paying the budget, pensions, and wages in the public sector. However, because of Russia's declining revenues, subsidies have been lowered for Transnistria, business is leaving, revenues are depleting, welfare benefits and payments are being reduced, and youth and able-bodied citizenry are evacuating the region in increasing numbers.

Transnistrian leaders in the region's capital Tiraspol have claimed that their region is in deep economic crisis.[130] The agreement allowing Transnistria to trade with the EU independently of Moldova expires in 2015, and Chisinau can use this opportunity to tighten the screws on Tiraspol. The population has officially declined since 1990, from 750,000 to 500,000, and unofficially to 300,000. If Transnistria were to be reabsorbed by Moldova, a quarter of a million Russian citizens and an equivalent number of Russian speakers will be left in the country or may seek refuge in Russia or elsewhere. To highlight the urgency of Moscow's intervention, in June 2015 the Transnistrian government called for the prevention of a Maidan-type revolution triggered by growing economic difficulties.[131] According to Tiraspol, agitators have appeared in several cities and villages urging the population to stage protests.

Kyiv has endeavored to shield itself from further instability along its borders and views Transnistria as a potential springboard for further Russian attacks on its territory. Ukraine's Ministry of Interior has reinforced police and military forces in the Odesa region bordering Transnistria and considered housing a National Guard brigade in the area.[132] Restrictions were also imposed, in 2014, on the movement of military-age civilians across the border from Transnistria. Russian officials complained about problems in the rotation of their military contingent in the territory and their logistical support. On June 8, 2015, President Poroshenko terminated the agreement between Kyiv and Moscow on the transit of Russian military units and equipment to Moldova across Ukrainian territory.[133] The move was condemned by Moscow, which warned of imminent retaliation.

If the threat from Transnistria becomes more blatant, Kyiv could close all crossing points, refuse to recognize separatist license plates, and allow Moldovan customs officials to monitor its checkpoints. Coordination between Ukraine and Moldova has been enhanced, particularly in the foreign ministries and intelligence services, with the possibility of fully isolating the secessionist entity. In June 2015, the new Odesa regional administrator, the former President of Georgia Mikheil Saakashvili, asserted that the border with Transnistria would be strengthened to combat smuggling.[134] Such a policy would severely squeeze the separatist economy. Saakashvili claimed that Transnistria was Europe's black hole for smuggling and organized crime with tentacles in Odesa *oblast* and closely linked with the Kremlin.

Some voices in Russia depicted Kyiv's measures as the first step in terminating Transnistrian autonomy and called on the Kremlin to recognize the independence of the entity and sign an agreement on mutual assistance. Officials in Moscow declared that they would not abandon the population of Transnistria or permit a blockade, and could intervene military to unblock it, thus threatening Ukraine with further military assaults. Both Chisinau and Kyiv want Russia's military units in Transnistria replaced with a civilian mission led by Western police officers.[135]

International negotiations over Transnistria remain deadlocked. Moscow asserts that reunification would require its agreement, troop presence, and a special status enabling the region to veto Chisinau's decisions. According to Lavrov, Moldova's foreign policy must reflect its permanent neutrality, and this is incompatible with EU entry. Hence, Moscow has pressed Chisinau not to sign the EU Association Agreement. Transnistrian President Yevgeny Shevchuk favors integration with Russia and was encouraged after the Crimean annexation. He urged Transnistria's residents with Russian citizenship to vote for Putin and supported the Eurasian Economic Union. Additionally, Russia has issued an estimated 150,000 passports to Transnistria's inhabitants.

Moscow has encouraged autonomist movements in other parts of Moldova to unsettle the Europe-oriented government. According to a former deputy Minister of Internal Affairs in Moldova, "little green men" (Russian security service personnel) are present in Moldova recruiting young people and training them in the use of small weapons.[136] According to him, in south Moldova, more than 500 people have been recruited and trained in Transnistria, Rostov, and Moscow.

According to Mihai Balan, director of Moldova's Information and Security Service (SIS), the number of organizations supporting Moscow has been growing in Moldova with the objective of splitting the country.[137] They bring together sportsmen, people with criminal records, and veterans of the Soviet security services. Some operate paramilitary camps training pro-Kremlin fighters or run security forms hiring detachments of armed fighters. For instance, Serghei Perciun, the deputy chairman of the Patriots of Moldova, is a former KGB officer, and he regularly broadcasts xenophobic statements against Romanians. The party calls for a Greater Moldova with the incorporation of territories in Romania and Ukraine, and charges that EU accession would result in Moldova's absorption by Romania.

The autonomous territory of Gagauzia has been exploited by Moscow to gain greater influence over Chisinau. Russian officials backed the unrecognized February 2, 2014, referendum in the region on inclusion in Russia's Customs Union. Reportedly, 98.4% voted for integration with the Customs Union and 97.2% voted against closer EU association.[138] In addition, 98.9% of voters supported Gagauzia's right to declare independence should Moldova surrender its sovereignty by uniting with Romania. Gagauzia has a population of about 155,000 people, mostly ethnic Gagauz. Local activists have campaigned against Moldova signing an EU Association Agreement and a Deep and Comprehensive Free Trade Agreement.

Gagauz parties advocate Moldova's entry to the EEU and threaten to cut off relations with Chisinau because of the country's pro-EU policy. Some have warned about the potential for a "Donbas-2" or a "Transnistria-2" in Gagauzia.[139] To enhance the appeal of Russia's economic alternative, the Kremlin lifted the import embargo on Moldova for Gagauzia's winemakers and its fruit and vegetable producers.[140] Irina Vlah, a staunch supporter of Putin and openly backed by Moscow, was elected the governor (Başkan) of Gagauzia in local elections on March 22, 2015.[141] She received 53.21% of the vote and was endorsed by the pro-Kremlin Socialist Party, by Russian pop artists, and Russian *Duma* deputies. Vlah called for Gagauzia to follow a Eurasian not European direction. Her victory will enable Moscow to exert greater influence in the country and apply pressure on the Moldovan administration.

Some Gagauz activists advocate the incorporation of the predominantly Bulgarian district of Taraclia into Gagauzia in order to increase the region's leverage vis-à-vis Chisinau.[142] Tellingly, since the start of the war in Ukraine, the local authorities in Taraclia have been seeking a "special status" for the district, which has a Bulgarian majority of 65% out of 44,000 people.[143] Chisinau fears that following the example of Gagauzia, Bulgarians from Taraclia may also demand their own police, courts, army, and security services. The local government in Taraclia has warned that they will join the Gagauz autonomous region if their demands are not met.

The chairman of Moldova's Liberal Democratic Party, Vlad Filat, insisted that law-enforcement agencies investigate Russia's interference in the country's domestic affairs, including local elections in Gagauzia.[144] Chisinau was concerned that Gagauz leaders incited by Moscow and encouraged by Transnistria may seek to turn the autonomous unit into a quasi-state with its own legal system and security force.[145] As a result, members of the Moldovan parliament want to restrict Gagauz autonomy to prevent separatism. Mihai Formuzal, the former governor of *Gagauz Yeri* accused the Moldovan authorities of planning to curtail the region's status. [146] Vadim Yanioglo, the deputy governor of Gagauzia, even requested protection from the Turkish Embassy. In 1994 the law on Gagauz autonomy was adopted with the assistance of Turkish President Suleyman Demirel.

The Kremlin has backed selected Moldovan politicians, parties, and social movements that lean in its direction or are susceptible to corruption or manipulation. The vulnerability of Moldova's political structure, legal system, and banking sector to Russia's corrupt influences was revealed in April 2014 when Moldova's Supreme Court of Justice uncovered massive money laundering schemes involving corrupt judges and *Moldinconbank*, which moved over $18.5 billion from Russia into offshore accounts during 2010–2013.

In the parliamentary elections of November 30, 2014, the Party of Socialists led by Putin supporter Igor Dodon gained first place with 20.51% of the vote and 25 parliamentary seats.[147] However, the three pro-European parties, the Liberal Democrats, Democrats, and Liberals, won 45% of the vote and secured a slim parliamentary majority of 55 out of 101 seats to form the new government. Another new formation, styled as Our Party and headed by Renato Usatii, a Russian businessman of Moldovan extraction, also followed a pro-Moscow line but was disqualified before the elections on the grounds of foreign financing.[148] Following the elections, pro-Moscow parties have capitalized on government corruption scandals and staged demonstrations in imitation of previous "colored revolutions," but not with the intent to democratize the state and integrate it with the EU.

To pressure the new administration in Chisinau, Moscow opened two criminal cases against Prime Minister Chiril Gaburici on charges of illegally crossing state borders without valid documents. [149] The minority coalition also faced challenges from pro-Eurasian forces actively backed by Moscow through its television broadcasts in Moldova. Gaburici resigned from office on June 12, 2015, in response to a brewing scandal questioning the authenticity of his school-leaving certificate, asserting that he no longer wanted to participate in political games. His resignation and the appointment of Vladimir Strelets as Prime Minister ignited new political battles over the composition and longevity of the new government and enabled Moscow to reinforce its influence.

The pro-EU parties rebounded in elections for the mayorship of Chisinau on June 28, 2015.[150] Incumbent Dorin Chirtoaca captured almost 54% of the vote, while the pro-Putin candidate, Zinaida Greceanai, garnered under 47%. Chirtoaca's victory boosted the pro-

EU parties holding a slender majority in parliament. At the national level, the four pro-EU parties gained enough seats to form majorities in 22 out of 32 district councils.[151] The ruling Liberal Democratic Party (LDP) won the largest number of votes for councilors in village and district councils. According to local analysts, the results reflected public disappointment with Moscow in failing to provide a market for Moldovan products.

However, the local elections also accelerated the tendency toward political-territorial fragmentation of the main part of Moldova outside of Transnistria and Gagauzia.[152] Voting patterns closely followed ethnic and linguistic lines and the choice between Europe and Eurasia. Pro-Russia parties and politicians funded by Moscow have entrenched themselves in several regions. Renato Usatii won the mayorship of Moldova's second largest city of Balti, and his organization Our Party captured at least six adjoining districts (*raions)* in Moldova's north.

In southern Moldova, the drive toward autonomy in Bulgarian-populated Taraclia district was strengthened by election victories for the Socialist Party and billionaire Vlad Plahotniuc's Democratic Party. And the town of Orhei in central Moldova became a virtual fiefdom of Moscow tycoon Ilan Shor, the newly elected mayor. Such developments seriously challenge the country's unity and pro-EU consensus. Additionally, protest rallies have been held in Chisinau against President Nicolae Timofti and the current cabinet amidst suspicions that Moscow finances and infiltrates movements that can be used against the pro-EU administration, as it stands to benefit from a collapse of the elected government.[153]

Compounding the disarray in the government coalition, in October 2015, Liberal-Democrat Party leader Vlad Filat, one of the most pro-Western officials, resigned over corruption charges and was promptly arrested. Filat's supporter asserted that the case against him was engineered by billionaire Vlad Plahotniuc's Democratic Party and supported by Moldova's pro-Russian organizations, including the Socialist Party.[154] On October 29, 2015, Plahotniuc orchestrated a parliamentary no-confidence vote that forced the resignation of Prime Minister Valeriu Strelet and the collapse of the government. A new administration under Prime Minister Pavel Filip was installed in January 2015 but faced mounting public protests against official corruption that may precipitate an early general election in which pro-Moscow parties stand to benefit.

In response to Russia's state propaganda—which contributes to subverting Moldova's political system, state independence, territorial integrity, and foreign policy—Moldova's Audio Visual Council, or media watchdog, decided to monitor Russian news and analytical programs rebroadcast in Moldova.[155] The Council monitors all programs by Russia's television channels as a reaction to their biased coverage of the conflict in Ukraine and Chisinau's foreign policy goals. As a result, the government suspended the broadcasts of *Rossiya-24* on several occasions, in an attempt to curtail Moscow's persistent disinformation campaigns.[156]

Moscow's economic instruments against Chisinau have included a coercive energy policy through the manipulation of supplies, prices, and debts, as Moldova is almost fully dependent on Russian energy sources. It has also imposed periodic embargoes on Moldovan wine and other vital agricultural exports.[157] Russia's officials complain that the EU Association Agreement poses a danger to the Russian market by flooding it with EU products and that Moscow is obliged to protect its interests by raising customs taxes on Moldovan products and imposing restrictions on labor migrants.[158] Moscow's propaganda portrays Moldova to the Russian public as an example of how the West is deliberately pushing the neighborhood into damaging Russia's interests.

In response to Chisinau signing an Association Agreement with the EU on June 27, 2014, Russia stopped importing Moldovan fruit and vegetables, seeking to worsen the country's economic and social climate. According to Agriculture and Food Industry Minister Vasile Bumacov, Moldova's losses could amount to $150 million per annum if Russia continues to ban all imports of fresh and canned fruits and vegetables.[159] Russia also blatantly violated its agreement on free trade with Moldova by applying customs taxes on Moldovan goods.

According to Moldovan Deputy Prime Minister Andrian Candu, Russia violates both the CIS agreement on free trade and World Trade Organization (WTO) rules. On August 1, 2014, Moscow imposed customs duties on goods imported from Moldova in line with the tariffs of the Customs Union of Russia, Belarus, and Kazakhstan.[160] Moldova is also substantially dependent on financial remittances sent back by over 700,000 migrant laborers in Russia. Although this constitutes another lever of pressure against Chisinau, Moscow is unlikely to expel these workers, as they are potential pro-Moscow voters in Moldovan elections and their removal could alter their voting preferences.[161]

In March 2012, Prime Minister Medvedev appointed the former envoy to NATO, Dmitry Rogozin, as Special Presidential Representative to Transnistria. President Putin also appointed Rogozin as chairman of the Russian side of the Russia-Moldova inter-governmental cooperation commission. The dual appointment was designed to treat the two parts of Moldova separately and contribute to institutionalizing the country's division. Moscow intends to upgrade its peacekeeping forces in Transnistria over the coming years and may also deploy a radar system, establish a military base, and position *Iskander* missiles in an alleged response to US Missile Defense plans and the creation of US bases in Romania. In this way, Moldova can become more closely entwined in Russia's integrationist agenda and its separatist regions could become a direct pretext for more intensive intervention, as Moscow endeavors to control the entire northern Black Sea coastline.

Romania

Romania's political elite has no illusions about or favorable historical memories of Russia's policy. They view Moscow as a traditional rival that has revived its aspirations toward territories along Romania's northern borders, whether in Moldova or Ukraine. While the struggle over Moldova is ever-present, Bucharest also complains that the Black Sea has been turned into a Russian-Turkish condominium increasingly dominated by Moscow. President Traian Basescu in particular resisted Moscow's pressures and energy enticements, while the Kremlin endeavored to appeal to opposition parties to gain a political foothold in the country.

In the aftermath of Russia's offensive against Ukraine, during 2014, Romania intensified its support for Moldova's EU Association Agreement. Basescu also underscored that rationally there was no danger to Romania, but Bucharest must also be prepared for the irrational.[162] The government has campaigned for a greater presence of NATO navy forces in the Black Sea because the major security threats were generated by differences in naval capacities between Russia and NATO members Romania and Bulgaria, Turkey's proximity notwithstanding. Officials believe that the Monroe Treaty, whereby only ships of the riparian countries may station in the Black Sea for more than 21 days, should either be amended or there should be a more frequent rotation of NATO vessels.

Moscow's representative to NATO, Aleksandr Grushko, accused the US of eroding regional security by deploying a missile defense shield in Europe. He warned that Russia would take measures in response to the US army assuming command of a missile defense base in Deveselu, Romania.[163] US naval forces established a Naval Support Facility (NSF) in Deveselu, on October 10, 2014. In the words of Romanian Prime Minister Victor Ponta, the opening of a permanent

NATO military base on Romania's territory represented a "strategic project."[164]

Russia's state propaganda conjures up convoluted schemes to foster disputes between neighbors in the Black Sea region. For instance, it claims that Kyiv is preparing to forcibly merge Moldova and the separatist enclave of Transnistria and will assist Romania in absorbing the whole of Moldova. Simultaneously, it charges that Bucharest seeks to annex pockets of territory in Ukraine, including northern Bukovina and southern Bessarabia. Hence, Moldova, Romania, and Ukraine are all portrayed as threatening each other's integrity and statehood. In addition, by asserting that Kyiv and Bucharest menace Transnistria's autonomy, Putin can justify a land link between Transnistria and a future Novorossiya forcibly sliced away from southern Ukraine.

Moscow may also threaten both Romania and Ukraine with territorial partition by claiming a broad swath of territory for an enlarged Moldova. Alternatively, it may back splitting both Ukraine and Moldova through the creation of a separate Budjak Republic to include Gagauzia, Taraclia, and parts of the Odesa region in Ukraine. Romania can then be offered the rest of Moldova and slivers of Ukraine in exchange for Bucharest's recognition of Novorossiya.

Another avenue to unsettle Romania is the Greater Moldovan question. Seeking to turn the tables on Romanian nationalist aspirations for uniting Romania and Moldova, the Moldova Mare People's Patriotic Alliance was formed in Balti, Moldova, on May 5, 2014, to openly support a Greater Moldova within its "historical borders" with Russia's assistance. This would purportedly include parts of northern Romania.[165] The organizers stated that they were encouraged by Moscow regaining Crimea and claimed to have branches inside Romania. Moldova Mare is considered a separatist group by both Chisinau and Bucharest, and it has links with Gagauz leaders.

On the energy front, Romania was dismissive of the South Stream project, viewing it as a tool to deepen the region's dependence on Russian energy. As an oil and gas producer, Romania has one of the lowest energy dependence rates in Europe. It has also diversified its oil imports, with Kazakhstan supplying twice as much crude oil as Russia.[166] Romania previously imported about a quarter of its natural gas from Russia, but this is decreasing. As new discoveries of gas reserves are registered in the Black Sea shelf, Romania plans to become energy self-sufficient by 2020. In April 2015, Romania stopped buying Russian gas for several months because its domestic gas production exceeded demand. However, its gas consumption is expected to grow again after 2020.[167]

Russian companies have sought to penetrate Romania's energy sector. Oil giant *Lukoil* has operated in the country since 1998 and owns one of the largest Romanian refineries in Ploiesti (*Lukoil Petrotel*). In October 2014, Romanian prosecutors started investigating *Lukoil Petrotel* for tax evasion and money laundering, seizing the company's assets. The investigators estimated that the Romanian state lost about €230 million due to the company's illegal activities. As *Lukoil* threatened to permanently close the refinery, President Basescu asked his government to be ready to take over the Ploiesti refinery.[168] *Lukoil* planned to appeal accusations of money laundering and tax evasion after Romanian prosecutors seized €2 billion ($2.2 billion) worth of its assets.[169]

Russia's energy companies experience greater difficulties in entering Romania than other countries in the region. The most recent attempts to establish a presence have been through proxies, such as Serbia's oil company *Naftna Industrija Srbije* (NIS), in which *Gazpromneft* has a majority stake. NIS has purchased a number of petrol stations in Romania, as Russia's energy companies try to close the circle of supply, production, and trade in Romania, similarly to Bulgaria.[170]

Romanian politicians and activists have claimed that Russia was behind the environmental protests against shale gas exploration by the US company Chevron in 2012–2014. Potential shale gas discoveries in Central and Eastern Europe would shrink *Gazprom's* European markets. Hard evidence of money transfers from Russian sources to Romanian activists is not readily available. However, the accounts of several witnesses point to Moldovan nationals from pro-Russian political parties actively agitating the population in eastern Romania against Chevron operations.[171]

Bulgarian activists, also suspected of being funded by Russia's energy lobby, have likewise contributed to stirring non-governmental organizations in Romania to protest against fracking. On June 5, 2013, scores of Bulgarians crossed the border with Romania to join the protest against drilling for shale gas. Simultaneous rallies took place in Bucharest, Cluj, Sibiu, Mangalia, Iaşi, Sighisoara, and Braşov in Romania, and Sofia, Varna, and Dobrich in Bulgaria.[172]

Anca-Maria Cernea of the conservative Ioan Bărbuş Foundation has noted that "the protesters included groups that usually have nothing to do with one another, like radical socialists, some with ties to the heavily Russian influenced security apparatus in neighboring Moldova, and deeply conservative Orthodox priests." The Russian media was extremely active in mobilizing the anti-fracking movement, with the newly licensed RT news channel in Romania carrying warnings that villagers, along with their crops and animals, would perish from poisoned water.[173] While Chevron was bombarded with demonstrations, *Gazprom's* Serbian subsidiary NIS continued conducting shale gas exploration in western Romania. The company was never subjected to public protests or objections of any kind, and exploration has continued.

In the metals sector, *RusAl*, which accounts for 75% of Russia's aluminum output and 10% of global supplies, purchased *Cemtrade*, a Romanian aluminum refinery. *RusAl* controls an extensive network of production outlets in several countries, including two giant alumina refineries in Ukraine. Russia's efforts to acquire the aluminum industry were viewed with great concern by Romania's intelligence service. They reported that oligarch Oleg Deripaska had attempted to take over the entire industry when three state-owned aluminum enterprises were slated for privatization. Although Deripaska failed to win the tenders, the Russian-Israeli magnate Vitaliy Machitsky, with close ties to *Gazprom,* subsequently acquired two aluminum firms, *Alum Tulcea* and *Alro Slatina.*

Endnotes

[1] Maciej Szymanowski, "Wary of Russia," *Do Rzeczy,* Warsaw, September 8, 2014, pp. 58–59.

[2] Lubosz Palata, "Prague With Vienna And Closer to Moscow" *Gazeta Wyborcza,* Warsaw, February 2, 2015.

[3] Peter G. Feher, "A Pole and a Hungarian, Two Bad Friends?" *Heti Valasz,* Budapest, March 13, 2015.

[4] For a longer analysis see Janusz Bugajski, "Poland and Russia: Strategic Rivalry Deferred," *Limes: Italian Geopolitical Review,* January 2014, http://temi.repubblica.it/limes/anteprima-di-limes-114-polonia-leuropa-senza-euro/56481?photo=14.

[5] Andrzej Talaga, "Little Green Men Polish Style," *Rzeczpospolita,* Warsaw, February 26, 2015.

[6] Wiktor Ferfecki, "Pro-Putin Party in Poland," *Rzeczpospolita,* Warsaw, December 31, 2014.

[7] Interview with Mateusz Piskorski, leader of *Zmiana,* by Andrey Vypolzov, "Poles Are Awakening," *Newsbalt,* Kaliningrad, March 10, 2015, http://www.newsbalt.ru. Piskorski invited Aleksandr Kofman, the self-proclaimed foreign minister of the Donetsk People's Republic, to attend

Zmiana's inaugural convention in March 2015. See Jakub Kowalski, "Little Red Men." *Rzeczpospolita,* Warsaw, March 7–8, 2015.

[8] Marcin Pienkowski, "Anti-Polish Borderland Trust," *Rzeczpospolita,* Warsaw, April 22, 2015. Pawel Kowal from the group Poland Together, pointed out that in fact Russia holds legal accountability for the Soviet Union and any property claims should be lodged with Moscow.

[9] Elisabeth Braw, "The Kremlin's Influence Game," March 10, 2015, *World Affairs,* http://www.worldaffairsjournal.org/blog/elisabeth-braw/kremlin%E2%80%99s-influence-game.

[10] "FM Schetyna: Pro-Russian Propaganda a 'Challenge' for Poland," Warsaw, *thenews.pl,* February 20, 2015, http://www.thenews.pl.

[11] Matthew Czekaj, "Russia's Hybrid War Against Poland," *Eurasia Daily Monitor,* April 29, 2015, Volume 12, Issue 80.

[12] Interview with General Mieczyslaw Gocul, Chief of General Staff of the Polish Armed Forces, in Pawel Wronski: "Poland--Russia: Who Calls the Shots Here," *Gazeta Wyborcza,* Warsaw, December 8, 2014.

[13] "Moscow Expels Our People," *Gazeta Wyborcza,* Warsaw, November 18, 2014.

[14] Wojciech Czuchnowski, "Quiet Departure of Spies From Poland?" *Gazeta Wyborcza,* Warsaw, October 23, 2014, p. 6, http://kontrowersje.net/czy_kto_wie_kim_jest_stanis_aw_szypowski_praw nik_z_polskim_obywatelstwem.

[15] Marek Kozubal, "Poland Sharpens Its Claws," *Rzeczpospolita,* Warsaw, November 26, 2014.

[16] "Polish Security Chief: Poland Should Prepare for a Hybrid War," *thenews.pl,* Warsaw, March 3, 2015, http://www.thenews.pl.

[17] Cezary Bielakowski, "Invitation To Don a Uniform," *Wprost,* Warsaw, February 17, 2015.

Poland has over 80 paramilitary organizations, which formed a federation in March 2015. The Ministry of Defense aims to involve these groups in a military training program with Poland's Armed Forces. Such organizations include *Strzelec* (Rifleman), LOK (National Defense League), and *Obrona Narodowa* (National Defense).

[18] Andrew A. Michta, "Poland Picks US Missile Shield," *The American Interest*, April 21, 2015, http://www.the-american-interest.com/byline/michta/.

[19] Zbigniew Lentowicz, "Polish Weapons for Neighbors," *Rzeczpospolita*, Warsaw, April 15, 2015.

[20] For details on military equipment see Zbigniew Lentowicz, "Billions on Missiles, Ships, and Drones," *Rzeczpospolita*, Warsaw, November 5, 2014, and Pawel Wronski, "Machines for Russian Phobias: Polish Army Wants To Buy Over 30 Attack Helicopters," *Gazeta Wyborcza*, Warsaw, July 17, 2014.

[21] "Poland Urges NATO to Push Ahead With Missile Shield," Warsaw, June 10, 2014, *AFP*, http://www.afp.com/en/home.

[22] Marek Kozubal, "Army To Practice Deployment of NATO Forces to Poland," Warsaw, *rp.pl*, August 19, 2014, http://www.rp.pl.

[23] Jedrzej Bielecki, "Germans Coming to Our Rescue," *Rzeczpospolita*, Warsaw, February 4, 2015.

[24] "Poles More Skeptical of NATO Alliance?" Warsaw, *thenews.pl*, March 3, 2015, www.thenews.pl.

[25] "European Reassurance Initiative and Other US Efforts in Support of NATO Allies and Partners," The White House, Office of the Press Secretary, June 3, 2014, http://www.whitehouse.gov/the-press-office/2014/06/03/fact-sheet-european-reassurance-initiative-and-other-us-efforts-support-.

[26] Jedrzej Bielecki, "NATO Lacks Funds To Defend Poland," *Rzeczpospolita*, Warsaw, December 3, 2014.

[27] "Washington Returns to a Cold War Strategy," January 27, 2015, *Stratfor*, http://www.stratfor.com/sample/geopolitical-diary/washington-returns-cold-war-strategy.

[28] Pawel Wronski, "Waiting for NATO," *Gazeta Wyborcza*, Warsaw, July 28, 2014.

[29] "Joint Military Brigade: Ukraine, Poland, Lithuania Sign Framework Agreement," *Ukraine Today*, July 25, 2015, http://uatoday.tv/politics/joint-military-brigade-ukraine-poland-lithuania-sign-framework-agreement-462648.html.

[30] Pawel Wronski, "Sanctions Against the National Pride," *Gazeta Wyborcza*, Warsaw, January 28, 2015.

[31] "Putin Seems to Have Found Trojan Horse in Central Europe," *CTK*, Prague, September 3, 2014.

[32] As an example, the Institute of Slavonic Strategic Studies (ISSTRAS) operates in the Czech Republic and promotes Moscow's positions on its website. See "Czech ISSTRAS Institute Spreads Russian Propaganda – Press," *Lidove Noviny*, August 10, 2014.

[33] Lubos Palata, "Prague Is Growing Apart From Warsaw and Drifting East," *Gazeta Wyborcza*, Warsaw, January 12, 2015, p. 12.

[34] "Czech President Milos Zeman in War of Words Over Russia," http://www.euro2day.gr/ftcom_en/article-ft-en/1302265/czech-president-milos-zeman-in-war-of-words-over.html. Zeman's comments were in sharp contrast to statements by Prime Minister Bohuslav Sobotka and Defense Minister Martin Stropnicky, who asserted that about 5,000 Russian soldiers were fighting in eastern Ukraine.

[35] "Czech PM Rejects Zeman's Idea of Finlandisation of Ukraine Policy," *CTK*, Prague, December 11, 2014.

[36] "Senators Call on Zeman To Stop Dividing Society," Prague, December 5, 2014, http://www.ctk.eu/.

[37] Moscow, *Interfax,* May 9, 2015, www.interfax.ru.

[38] "Sanctions Harmed Russian Economy, Did Not Change Conduct - Czech PM," September 10, 2014, Prague, *CTK.*

[39] Karel Hrubes, "Spies Pretended To Be Embassy Employees, But BIS Put its Finger on Them," *Mlada Fronta Dnes,* Prague, March 13, 2015.

[40] "Most Czechs Consider Russia Threat to Their Country – Poll," *Ceske Noviny,* Prague, October 24, 2014, http://www.ceskenoviny.cz/news/zpravy/most-czechs-consider-russia-threat-to-their-country-poll/1139147.

[41] "Most Czechs Are Afraid of Russia, Mainly Secret Services – Poll," *CTK,* Prague, May 4, 2015.

[42] "Czech Army Forms New Unit Including Combat Commando, IT Experts," *CTK,* Prague, May 12, 2015.

[43] Grigory Mesezhnikov, "West Should Launch Counterattack In War With Russia," *Charter 97,* July 20, 2015, http://charter97.org/en/news/2015/7/20/160609.

[44] "Fico's Moscow Visit Sent Slovak Foreign Policy Into Chaos – Press," *CTK,* Prague, June 8, 2015.

[45] "Fico: No Reason for Bad Relations With President Kiska," *TASR,* Bratislava, January 25, 2015, http://www.tasr.sk.

[46] "Slovak President for Closer Cooperation of V4 Armed Forces," Bratislava, July 7, 2014, www.ctk.cz.

[47] Milan Suplata, "What Slovakia for NATO?" *Central European Policy Institute,* Bratislava, May 20, 2014.

[48] Jaroslav Nad, Marian Majer and Milan Suplata, "75 Solutions for Slovakia's Defence," *Central European Policy Institute,* Bratislava, October 27, 2014.

[49] Fico's statements have been heralded in Moscow as resistance to American pressure. See "Fico: I Would Say No to NATO Military Base on Slovak Territory," *TASR,* Bratislava, September 7, 2014.

[50] Slobodan Samardzija, "NATO or Warsaw Pact," *Politika Online,* Belgrade, June 23, 2014, www.politika.rs.

[51] "SDKU: Fico Acting Like Russian Agent," *TASR,* Bratislava, June 25, 2014, www.tasr.sk.

[52] "Slovakia Wants to Build Logistics Base for NATO in Poprad," *TASR,* Bratislava, September 5, 2014, www.tasr.sk.

[53] "Fico, Zeman Address People Nostalgic for Communism – Radicova," *CTK,* Bratislava, January 5, 2015, www.ctk.cz.

[54] Michal Pisko, "Slovaks Do Not Approve of Russia's Intervention in Ukraine," *Sme Online,* Bratislava, June 23, 2014.

[55] Charles Gati, "The Mask Is Off," *The American Interest,* August 7, 2014, http://www.the-american-interest.com/articles/2014/08/07/the-mask-is-off/.

[56] Zoltan Simon, "Orban Says He Seeks to End Liberal Democracy in Hungary," *Bloomberg,* July 28, 2014.

[57] "E-PM Turns to Brussels Over Orban Speech," *MTI,* Budapest, July 28, 2014.

[58] Peter G. Feher, "A Pole and a Hungarian, Two Bad Friends?" *Heti Valasz,* Budapest, March 13, 2015.

59 "Hungary's Orban Accuses US of Meddling in Central Europe," *AFP*, Budapest, December 23, 2014, http://www.afp.com/en/home.

60 "Putin Praises Hungary," *Hungary Around the Clock*, Budapest, November 20, 2014, http://www.hatc.hu.

61 "Hungary Seeks EU Alliance to Push Closer Ties With Russia," *AFP*, Budapest, August 25, 2014, http://www.afp.com/en/home.

62 Maksim Samorukov, "How Russia Is Turning Hungary Into an Energy Power," *Slon*, Moscow, August 6, 2014, http://slon.ru.

63 Keith Johnson, "Hungary Is Helping Putin Keep His Chokehold on Europe's Energy," *Foreign Policy*, November 6, 2014, http://foreignpolicy.com/2014/11/06/hungary-is-helping-putin-keep-his-chokehold-on-europes-energy.

64 "Russia To Prefer Hungary in Lifting Ban," *Hungary Around the Clock*, Budapest, January 27, 2015, http://www.hatc.hu.

65 "Ukraine Hungarians Concerned About Mobilisation, Urge Peaceful Resolution," *MTI*, Budapest, July 31, 2014.

66 According to Petro Hetsko, leader of the Rusyn national movement and prime minister of the non-recognized Republic of Subcarpathian Rus, on December 1, 1991, simultaneously with Ukraine's independence referendum, two other referenda were held in Transcarpathia. One was an *oblast*-wide ballot where almost 80% of residents voted for Transcarpathia as a "special self-governing territory within Ukraine." A referendum was also held on the establishment of a cultural and ethnic autonomous entity in Berehivskyy (Berehove) *rayon*, home to a sizable Hungarian community. The results of the vote were declared illegal by Ukraine's government.

67 Svetlana Gomzikova, "March on Kyiv via Budapest; Residents of Transcarpathia Appeal to Hungary To Protect Them Against Genocide," *Svobodnaya Pressa*, August 18, 2014, www.svpressa.ru.

[68] Paul Goble, "Hungary Helping Moscow Destabilize Ukraine from the West. Pozhivanov Says," *Window on Eurasia – New Series,* March 5, 2015, http://windowoneurasia2.blogspot.com/2015/03/hungary-helping-moscow-destabilize.html.

[69] "The Foreign Policy Concept of the Russian Federation," President of Russia, Official Web Portal, July 12, 2008, www.kremlin.ru/eng/text/docs/2008/07/204750.shtml. According to Thomas Graham, a prominent Western apologist for Russia's imperial policies toward neighboring states, the "near abroad" occupies a "special place" in the "Russian psyche," and this "emotional yearning" needs to be "accommodated." See Thomas Graham, "US-Russia Relations: Facing Reality Pragmatically," in *Europe, Russia and the United States: Finding a New Balance,* Center for Strategic and International Studies, Washington, D.C., July 2008, p. 12.

[70] Wolfgang Gerke and P.S. Zolotarev, "Russian-German Relations in the Context of Global Politics," *International Affairs* 53, Issue 3 (2007): 90.

[71] Moscow claims that Russia and its post-Soviet neighbors are "united by centuries of historical, cultural, and economic ties." Check Tanguy de Wilde and Gaelle Pellon, "The Implications of the European Neighbourhood Policy (ENP) on the EU-Russian 'Strategic Partnership,' " *Helsinki Monitor* 17 (2), 127. In reality, Russia and its neighbors are mostly "united" by centuries of conflict, conquest, colonialism, and Russification, with a 20th century veneer of communist totalitarianism and Soviet imperialism. Moscow flexes its neo-imperial muscle through a language campaign promoting Russian as the *lingua franca* throughout the CIS and undermining governments focused on reviving national identity and indigenous languages after years of Russification. Only Belarus currently recognizes Russian as a state language.

[72] Rainer Lindner, "New Realism: The Making of Russia's Foreign Policy in the Post-Soviet World," *The EU-Russia Centre Review,* Issue 8, Russian Foreign Policy, Eurasia Centre, October 2008, p. 30.

[73] James Sherr, "Russia and the 'Near Abroad,' in a Medvedev Presidency," in *Russia After Putin: Implications for Russia's Politics and Neighbors,*

Institute for Security and Development Policy, Policy Paper, March 2008, pp. 28–29.

74 For a summary of official threats to the territorial integrity of neighbors see Vladimir Socor, "Moscow Makes Furious but Empty Threats to Georgia and Ukraine," *Eurasia Daily Monitor*, April 14, 2008, Volume 5, Issue 70.

75 Matthew Schofield, "Russian News Report: Ukraine Invasion Strategy Existed Before Collapse," McClatchy Foreign Staff, February 21, 2015, http://www.novayagazeta.ru/politics/67389.html?print=1 and http://www.mcclatchydc.com/2015/02/21/257386/russian-news-report-ukraine-invasion.html.

76 Vladimir Socor, "Minsk Armistice: Enforced at Ukraine's Expense? *Eurasian Daily Monitor*, July 20, 2015, Volume 12, Issue 135.

77 Index Mundi, "Ukraine Country Profile, 2014," http://www.indexmundi.com/ukraine.

78 For the full text of Minsk II see http://www.unian.info/politics/1043394-minsk-agreement-full-text-in-english.html.

79 Vladimir Socor, "Ukraine Rapidly Dismantling Gazprom's Supply Monopoly," *Eurasia Daily Monitor*, April 8, 2015, Volume 12, Issue 65.

80 Anders Åslund, "Ukraine Is More Important Than Greece," Atlantic Council, July 6, 2015, http://www.atlanticcouncil.org/blogs/new-atlanticist/ukraine-is-more-important-than-greece.

81 Paul Goble, "Moscow Patriarch Says Ukrainian Faithful No Longer Obligated to Obey Kyiv," *Eurasia Daily Monitor*, June 2, 2015, Volume 12, Issue 102.

82 Paul Goble, "The Two Major Non-Moscow Ukrainian Orthodox Churches Move Toward Unity, *Window on Eurasia – New Series*, June 10, 2015, http://windowoneurasia2.blogspot.com/2015/06/the-two-major-non-moscow-ukrainian.html.

[83] Paul Goble, "To Moscow's Making of Republics Inside Ukraine, There is Apparently No End," *Window on Eurasia – New Series*, April 8, 2015, http://windowoneurasia2.blogspot.com/2015/04/to-moscows-making-of-republics-inside.html; and Vladimir Socor, "Ukraine Defuses Pro-Russia Instigations in Odesa Province," *Eurasia Daily Monitor*, April 9, 2015, Volume 12, Issue 66.

[84] Nina Perstneva, "In the Quiet Besssarabian Whirlpool..." *Zerkalo Nedeli Online*, Kyiv, April 10, 2015, http://zn.ua.

[85] Paul Goble, "Ukraine Must Organize to Fight and Win Cyberwar against Russia, Analyst Says," *Window on Eurasia – New Series*, February 22, 2015, http://windowoneurasia2.blogspot.com/2015/02/ukraine-must-organize-to-fight-and-win.html.

[86] "Ukraine Sets Sights on Joining NATO," *Reuters*, Kyiv, April 9, 2015.

[87] Paul Goble, "Two-Thirds of Ukrainians Want to Join NATO and Be Inside 'Borders of Civilized World,' Portnikov Says," *Window on Eurasia – New Series*, August 16, 2015, http://windowoneurasia2.blogspot.com/2015/08/two-thirds-of-ukrainians-want-to-join.html.

[88] "ATO Headquarters: Russia Continues to Concentrate Troops On Border With Ukraine And Donbas," *Unian Information Agency*, June 26, 2015, http://www.unian.info/war/1094127-ato-headquarters-russia-continues-to-concentrate-troops-on-border-with-ukraine-and-donbas.html.

[89] *Interfax*, Kyiv, January 20, 2015, http://www.interfax.com.

[90] Anna Cherevko, "Battle Noise Simulator for Ukraine," *Glavkom*, Kyiv, December 10, 2014, http://glavcom.ua.

[91] "Ukraine Crisis: Deadly Bomb Blast Hits Rally in Kharkiv," *BBC News*, February 22, 2015, http://www.bbc.com/news/world-europe-31575384.

[92] Alyaksandr Klaskowski, "2015 Election: Will Russia Spoil Lukashenka's Mood?" *Belorusskiye Novosti*, Minsk, September 8, 2014, http://naviny.by.

[93] Paul Goble, "Lukashenka Now a 'Lesser Evil' for Belarusians than Putin, Popular Front Party Leader Says," *Window on Eurasia – New Series*, March 9, 2015, http://windowoneurasia2.blogspot.com/2015/03/lukashenka-now-lesser-evil-for.html.

[94] Paul Goble, "Most Belarusian Officers Ready to Take Orders from Moscow, Borodach Says," *Window on Eurasia – New Series*, September 12, 2014, http://windowoneurasia2.blogspot.com/2014/09/window-on-eurasia-most-belarusian.html.

[95] Henadz Kosaraw, "Air Warning: What Is The Threat Posed By The Reinforcement Of Russia's Air Base In Babruysk," *Zawtra Tvayoy Krainy*, Minsk, December 24, 2014, www.zautra.by.

[96] Kaarel Kaas, "Russian Armed Forces in the Baltic Sea Region," *Diplomaatia*, Estonia, August 7, 2014, http://icds.ee/index.php?id=73&L=1&tx_ttnews%5Btt_news%5D=1547&tx_ttnews%5BbackPid%5D=71&cHash=db5c854d31.

[97] Paul Goble, "Putin's Plan for Military Base in Belarus Destabilizing that Country," *Window on Eurasia – New Series*, September 29, 2015, http://windowoneurasia2.blogspot.com/2015/09/putins-plan-for-military-base-in.html.

[98] Interview with Pavel Usov, head of the Center of Political Analysis and Forecast, by Konstantin Amelyushkin, "Analyst: Kremlin Is Capable of Turning Belarus Into Its Bridgehead," Vilnius, *Delfi*, December 25, 2014, http://www.ru.delfi.lt.

[99] Natallya Pravalinskaya and Yelena Vasilyeva, "Is Belarus Prepared For Challenges?" *BelGazeta*, Minsk, June 23, 2014.

[100] Paul Goble, "Belarusian Spy Agencies' Cooperation with Russian Ones in Lithuania Highlights Larger Problem," *Window on Eurasia – New Series*,

March 31, 2015,
http://windowoneurasia2.blogspot.com/2015/03/belarusian-spy-agencies-cooperation.html.

[101] *Belorusskiye Novosti*, Minsk, July 7, 2014, http://naviny.by.

[102] Grigory Ioffe, "Lukashenka's Marathon Press Conference in Minsk," *Eurasia Daily Monitor*, February 5, 2015, Volume 12, Issue 23.

[103] Paul Goble, "Putin's 'Hybrid War' Prompts Belarus to Redefine 'Invasion,'" *Window on Eurasia – New Series*, January 26, 2015, http://windowoneurasia2.blogspot.com/2015/01/food-prices-in-kaliningrad-rising-far.html.

[104] Paul Goble, "Moscow Readying Neo-Cossacks of Belarus for Use Against Lukashenka," *Eurasia Daily Monitor*, May 5, 2015, Vol. 12, Issue 84.

[105] Grigory Ioffe, "Reasserting Belarus's Independent Voice," *Eurasia Daily Monitor*, January 23, 2015, Vol. 12, Issue 14.

[106] A Belarusian-Ukrainian agreement on the adoption of border demarcation regulations was signed in Chernihiv, Ukraine, on July 30, 2014. The agreement will make it possible to speed up the demarcation of the Belarusian-Ukrainian border. See *Belapan*, Minsk, July 30, 2014.

[107] Minsk, *Belapan*, February 19, 2015.

[108] "Ukraine Conflict Fuels Patriotism in Authoritarian Belarus," Minsk, October 22, 2014, *AFP, North European Service*, http://www.afp.com/en/home.

[109] Dzyanis Lawnikevich, "Lukashenka Trying National Costume," *Gazeta.ru,* Moscow, December 21, 2014, http://www.gazeta.ru. A monument to Olgerd, a ruler of the Great Duchy of Lithuania, in which the ancestors of Belarusians played an important role, was unveiled in Vitebsk in June 2014. Vitebsk governor Alyaksandr Kasinets praised the prince's historical mission in the development of Belarusian statehood. Lukashenka surprised everyone with his speeches in Belarusian and warnings over

threats to national unity and independence. See Alyaksandr Yarashevich, "Lukashenka Uses Belarusian Language As Shield Against Russian World," *Belorusskiye Novosti*, July 9, 2014, http://naviny.by.

[110] Leaflets calling for preparations for a guerrilla war against Russia have been disseminated in some cities in Belarus. Exiled Belarusian nationalist leader Zyanon Paznyak claimed that Putin might encroach on Belarus and called on Belarusians to start forming small armed groups and prepare for resistance. See *Belorusskiy Partizan*, Minsk, July 16, 2014. Some Belarusian volunteers also reportedly joined Ukrainian military operations against pro-Moscow separatists in Donbas.

[111] Paul Goble, "Belarusian Nationalism Emerges as a Political Force," *Window on Eurasia – New Series*, December 22, 2014, http://windowoneurasia2.blogspot.com/2014/12/window-on-eurasia-belarusian.html.

[112] Reid Standish, "Russia May Need to Say 'Do Svidaniya' to Belarus," *Foreign Policy*, January 30, 2015, https://foreignpolicy.com/2015/01/30/russia-may-need-to-say-do-svidaniya-to-belarus.

[113] Alyaksandr Klaskouski, "Minsk Congratulated Putin With Surprise Up Its Sleeve," Minsk, *Belorusskiye Novosti*, Minsk, October 9, 2014, http://naviny.by/Parliamentary. Parliament expressed reservations about the removal of barriers in the sale of particular goods and the provision of certain services, particularly in the energy field. Minsk insisted on compensation for future losses that the Belarusian oil industry will suffer in re-exporting oil products.

[114] Tatsyana Kalynowska, "Lukashenka Between Devil and Deep Blue Sea," *Ukrayinska Pravda*, Kyiv, August 26, 2014, www.pravda.com.ua.

[115] Alyaksandr Klaskowski, "Lukashenka and Makey Played Up To Lavrov, But Had Own Things In Mind," *Belorusskiye Novosti*, Minsk, November 19, 2014, http://naviny.by. The Russia sanctions initially benefited Belarus in such areas as transportation, agriculture, and food processing. Belarus's food exports to Russia grew substantially, particularly to Kaliningrad as a

result of Moscow's counter-sanctions on the EU.

[116] Index Mundi, "Belarus Country Profile, 2014,"
http://www.indexmundi.com/belarus.

[117] Alyaksandr Klaskovski, "On The Eve of Putin's Visit, Lukashenka Spoke About Independence in Belarusian," Minsk, *Belorusskiye Novosti*, July 2, 2014, http://naviny.by.

[118] Paul Goble, "Russian Nationalist Calls for Partition of Belarus to Correct Soviet 'Mistakes,'" *Window on Eurasia – New Series*, March 16, 2015, http://windowoneurasia2.blogspot.com/2015/03/russian-nationalist-calls-for-partition.html.

[119] Alyaksandr Yurych, "Klaskowski: Moscow Once May Need Not a Little War, But Anschluss of Belarus," Minsk, *Zawtra Tvayoy Krainy*, June 18, 2014, www.zautra.by.

[120] Paul Goble, "Moscow's Pressure on Belarus Increasingly Counterproductive," *Eurasia Daily Monitor*, Volume 12, Issue 69, April 14, 2015.

[121] Vladimir Solovyev and Yelizaveta Surnacheva, "Moldovan Voices: Chisinau Ahead of Parliamentary Election," *Kommersant*, Moscow, November 24, 2014, http://kommersant.ru.

[122] Sergey Aksenov, "Poroshenko Is Prepared to Fight in Transnistria. Russia Will Apparently Have To Take the Republic's Population Under Its Protection On An Emergency Basis And Recognize The PMR," *Svobodnaya Pressa*, Moscow March 18, 2015, http://www.svpressa.ru.

[123] Andrei Safonov, "Ukraine is Being Played Against Transnistria. Romania Is the Beneficiary!" *Informatsionnyy Portal Andreya Safonova*, December 20, 2014, http://safonovpmr.com.

[124] Index Mundi, "Moldova Country Profile, 2014," http://www.indexmundi.com/moldova/population.html, and

"Demographic History of Transnistria," *Wikipeda,*
https://en.wikipedia.org/wiki/Demographic_history_of_Transnistria.

[125] Vladimir Socor, "Putin-Voronin Farewell: An Anti-Climactic Coda," *Eurasia Daily Monitor,* January 25, 2008, Vol. 5, Issue 15.

[126] *Interfax,* Moscow, October 20, 2014, http://www.interfax.com.

[127] *Interfax,* Moscow, October 2, 2014, http://www.interfax.com.

[128] *Interfax,* Moscow, July 10, 2014, http://www.interfax.com.

[129] Darya Laptiyeva, " 'If Necessary, We Will Go In,' Russia Promises Not To Abandon Transnistria," *Lenta.ru,* Moscow, January 27, 2015, http://lenta.ru.

[130] Paul Goble, "Encouraged By Initial Russian Moves In Ukraine, Transnistria Now Fears For Its Future," *Eurasia Daily Monitor,* January 20, 2015, Volume 12, Issue 11.

[131] *Tiras.ru* June 15, 2015, http://tiras.ru.

[132] *Interfax,* Kyiv, September 12, 2014, http://www.interfax.com.

[133] *Unian,* Kyiv, June 8, 2015, and *Dniester Channel One Television Online,* Tiraspol, May 28, 2015, http://tv.pgtrk.ru.

[134] *Interfax,* Odesa, June 9, 2015, http://www.interfax.com.

[135] "Ukraine Intends To Have Russian Peacekeepers Leave The Dniester Region," *Vzglyad Online,* Moscow, July 22, 2014, www.vzglyad.ru.

[136] *Unian,* Kyiv, September 8, 2014, http://www.unian.net/world/960308-zelenyie-chelovechki-poyavilis-na-territorii-moldovyi-snbo.html.

[137] Mariana Rata, "Hybrid-Soldiers Of Moldova," *Ziarul National Online,* Chisinau, October 3, 2014, www.ziarulnational.md.

[138] "Gagauzia Voters Reject Closer EU Ties For Moldova," *RFE/RL's Moldovan Service* February 3, 2014, http://www.rferl.org/content/moldova-gagauz-referendum-counting/25251251.html.

[139] "Andrievschi Calls Gagauzia's Present State a Potential 'Second Donbas,' " *Gagauzinfo.MD*, Comrat, January 8, 2015, http://gagauzinfo.md.

[140] "Moscow Could Activate 'Gagauz Component' in Moldova Elections," *Gagauz.info*, Comrat, October 9, 2014, http://gagauzinfo.md.

[141] Paul Goble, "Kremlin's Candidate Wins Race in Gagauzia, Pointing to More Trouble Ahead in Moldova," *Window on Eurasia – New Series*, March 23, 2015, http://windowoneurasia2.blogspot.com/2015/03/kremlins-candidate-wins-race-in.html.

[142] For a valuable analysis of autonomist and separatist opportunities exploited by Moscow in south Moldova and south west Ukraine see "A Quarrel In A Far-Away Country: The Rise Of A Budzhak People's Republic?" John R. Haines, *Foreign Policy Research Institute*, April 2015, http://www.fpri.org/articles/2015/04/quarrel-far-away-country-rise-budzhak-peoples-republic.

[143] Nicolae Negru, "Bulgar-Yeri," *Ziarul National Online*, Chisinau, April 6, 2015, http://www.ziarulnational.md.

[144] *Infotag*, Chisinau, March 5, 2015, http://www.infotag.md.

[145] Nicolae Negru, "Between A Compromise And Party Interests," *Ziarul National Online*, Chisinau, July 22, 2014, www.ziarulnational.md.

[146] Svetlana Gamova, "Door to Russia Being Closed to Gagauz. Moldovan Parliament Intends to Curtail Southern Autonomy's Rights," *Nezavisimaya Gazeta Online*, Moscow, August 15, 2014, http://www.ng.ru/.

[147] "Moldovans Choose Europe, Barely," The Economist, Chisinau, December 1, 2014, http://www.economist.com/news/europe/21635339-moldovans-choose-europe-barely.

148 A helpful overview can be found in Vladimir Socor, "Moldova's New Government: Daunting Challenges Ahead," *Eurasia Daily Monitor*, March 6, 2015, Volume 12, Issue 42.

149 *Infotag*, Chisinau, February 18, 2015, http://www.infotag.md.

150 Corneliu Rusnac, "Pro-European candidate leads in Moldova vote," *Associated Press*, June 28, 2015, https://www.yahoo.com/news/moldova-chooses-between-russia-europe-local-elections-051921841.html.

151 *Ziarul National Online*, Chisinau, June 16, 2015, http://www.ziarulnational.md.

152 Vladimir Socor, "Net Setback for Moldova and Its Reforms in the Latest Elections (Part Two)," *Eurasia Daily Monitor*, July 2, 2015, Volume 12, Issue 124.

153 Based on discussions by the authors in Chisinau, Moldova in November 2015.

154 Vladimir Socor, "Moldovan Political Leader Filat Arrested in Intra-Coalition Coup," *Eurasia Daily Monitor*, October 19, 2015, Volume 12, Issue 188.

155 *Infotag*, Chisinau, March 4, 2015, http://www.infotag.md.

156 *Interfax*, Chisinau, May 27, 2015, http://www.interfax.com.

157 Chloe Bruce, "Power Resources: The Political Agenda in Russo-Moldovan Gas Relations," *Problems of Post-Communism*, No. 54, Issue 3, May/June 2007, pp. 29–47.

158 Nicolae Negru, "Ukraineization of the Republic of Moldova," *Ziarul National Online*, Chisinau, July 18, 2014, www.ziarulnational.md.

159 *Infotag*, Chisinau, July 22, 2014, http://www.infotag.md.

160 *Infotag*, Chisinau, September 10, 2014, http://www.infotag.md.

[161] Dumitru Minzarari, "Russia Likely to Review Its Strategy Toward Moldova," *Eurasia Daily Monitor*, July 23, 2014, Volume 11, Issue 134.

[162] "Traian Basescu: Rationally, There Is No Danger To Romania; We Have To Be Prepared For The Irrational," *Agerpres,* Bucharest, August 29, 2014, http://www.agerpres.ro/.

[163] R.C, "Russia Will Take Measures To US Missile Defense Shield Deployment In Romania," *Cotidianul Online,* Bucharest, October 15, 2014, www.cotidianul.ro.

[164] "Ponta: Desire To Have Permanent NATO Military Presence In Romania, A Strategic Project" *Agerpres,* Bucharest, August 25, 2014, http://www.agerpres.ro/.

[165] Alexandru Tocarschi, " 'Secret' Meeting in Balti. Beyond the Prut Pro-Moldavia Organizations Are in a Semi-Clandestine State," *MK Moldova Online*, Chisinau, June 25, 2014, http://mk.kn.md.

[166] Romania imports only 15% of its oil needs—65% from Kazakhstan, 30% from Russia, and smaller quantities from Azerbaijan and Iraq. See Eurostat: Energy Dependency 2013, http://ec.europa.eu/eurostat/en/web/products-datasets/-/TSDCC310; and "In-Depth Study of European Energy Security," European Commission, Brussels, July 2, 2014, http://ec.europa.eu/energy/sites/ener/files/documents/20140528_energy_security_study_0.pdf.

[167] "Economica: Romania Plans to Abandon Russian Gas Imports in April 2015," *Focus News Agency*, March 21, 2015; "Romania No Longer Relies on Russian Gas for First Time in Decades," *Ukraine Today TV*, March 20, 2015, http://uatoday.tv/business/romania-no-longer-relies-on-russian-gas-for-first-time-in-decades-416782.html.

[168] "Romanian President: Government Should be Prepared to Take Over *Lukoil* Refinery if Russians Decide to Shut it Down," *Romania Insider*, October 9, 2014, http://www.romania-insider.com/romanian-president-

government-should-be-prepared-to-take-over-lukoil-refinery-if-russians-decide-to-shut-it-down/133220.

169 "*Lukoil* Set to Fight Romania Money-Laundering Case," *CNBC,* July 10, 2015, http://www.cnbc.com/2015/07/10/lukoil-set-to-fight-romania-money-laundering-case.html.

170 Based on interviews by the authors with Romanian government officials and energy experts in Bucharest, November 2014.

171 Interviews by authors in Bucharest, Romania in November 2014.

172 "Bulgaria, Romania Launch Wave of Anti-Fracking Protests," *Novite.com,* June 5, 2013, http://www.novinite.com/articles/150993/Bulgaria,+Romania+Launch+Wave+of+Anti-Fracking+Protests#sthash.hl5z8tFR.dpuf.

173 Andrew Higgins, "Russian Money Suspected Behind Fracking Protests," *The New York Times,* November 30, 2014, http://www.nytimes.com/2014/12/01/world/russian-money-suspected-behind-fracking-protests.html.

4. South Western Flank: South East Europe

The Balkan Peninsula is viewed by Moscow as Europe's weakest link. The Western Balkans in particular are important to Moscow from a propagandistic vantage point vis-à-vis Washington. The fracturing of Yugoslavia in the 1990s is exploited as evidence of an alleged Western conspiracy to overthrow governments, break up states, and change international borders. Such actions have evidently challenged the international legal order and set precedents for Russia's policies toward its post-Soviet neighbors.

Despite their EU and NATO membership, Greece and Bulgaria are considered potentially pliable states that can, on occasion, favor Russia's interests. However, the Western Balkans are viewed as Europe's "soft underbelly," where the Kremlin can capitalize on local conflicts, democratic deficits, and nationalist surpluses to undermine Western objectives and promote its geopolitical ambitions. The financial crisis in Greece has also generated political radicalism beneficial for Moscow. Both the extreme right and radical left parties in Athens are anti-American and view Russia as a close ally. The election of the ultra-left Syriza movement in January 2015 bolstered Moscow's opportunities for using Greece to undermine EU and NATO unity.

Balkan Front

Since the break-up of Yugoslavia, the Russian government has opportunistically exploited ethno-national grievances and divisions to gain political leverage with favored governments. Given the stuttering progress of most West Balkan states toward EU and NATO accession, the persistence of ethnic tensions, the weakness of national institutions, and the susceptibility of government officials to corruption, the region has grown in importance as a locus of Russia's interest and influence.

Moscow pursues four main channels of entry into the region: nationalism, corruption, business, and propaganda. First, ethno-nationalism is a combustible substance that can be encouraged and exploited by the Kremlin overtly or covertly, whether through diplomatic backing, international campaigning, direct or indirect funding of extremist groups, media exposure, or linkages with Russia's intelligence services and ultra-nationalist formations. Russian propagandists and pro-Kremlin academics seek to drive wedges between Muslims and Christians in the region and incite Islamophobia to stir local nationalisms. Some have claimed that radical Islamists will try to seize Serb-populated territories and conduct terrorist attacks in Serbia, Bosnia-Herzegovina, Macedonia, and other states.[1] They also claim that Albanian Muslims throughout the region are secretly preparing for armed conflicts against Christian populations.

Moscow's support for nationalist groups has been evident with the radical right Ataka movement in Bulgaria and various Serbian nationalist formations in Serbia, Bosnia-Herzegovina, and Montenegro. Although Syriza in Greece is not a nationalist grouping but an ultra-leftist formation, its deep-rooted anti-Americanism and resentment against Germany for imposing tough conditions to secure crucial bailout loans has suited Moscow. Promoting local nationalism or leftist statism can contribute to undermining support for NATO, the US, and the EU, it can raise sympathies for Moscow's international positions, and it may stir regional rivalries that preoccupy Western institutions and empower the Kremlin to inject itself as a mediator.

Second, Moscow encourages political corruption throughout Europe. In the Balkans, where the rule of law remains relatively weak, politicians are especially vulnerable to Moscow's enticements. Various public figures are targeted, including national and local politicians, government ministers, security personnel, businessmen, and media heads. The objectives are both political and economic. Through outright bribery or opaque transactions, Balkan officials may favor Russian business interests and remain neutral or support Moscow in its foreign policy offensives. This can undermine Western unity whether in the NATO or EU contexts.

Political corruption is also evident in funding for NGOs that support positions at odds with EU and US policy. This has been visible in the campaign against shale gas development in Bulgaria, which would reduce Russia's preponderance as an energy supplier. Russian sources have reportedly funded Bulgarian and Romanian environmentalist groups. Similarly, some individuals involved in the protest campaign in Tirana in the fall of 2013 against Washington's request to dismantle chemical weapons agents from Syria inside Albania allegedly maintained contacts with the Russian embassy in Tirana.[2]

A third well-tested method of Russian influence is the fostering of energy dependence. This included tying Balkan countries into South Stream and other energy project led by *Gazprom* and gaining majority shares in local pipelines, refineries, and other energy facilities. Energy dependence can undergird diplomatic and political compliance. Serbia has been the most prone to Moscow's energy inducements, having sold majority shares of its NIS *(Naftna Industrija Srbije)* oil and gas complex to *Gazprom*. Belgrade has favored Russian investment and energy supplies partly as a form of reciprocity for Moscow blocking its former province of Kosova from membership in the United Nations. The Kremlin has also offered aid and investment to the Serb Republic (RS) entity in Bosnia-Herzegovina as a way to court a potential ally.

The Kremlin promotes economic dependence by using energy resources, state loans, and business investments to gain political influence. Since the late 1990s, Russia's energy giants such as *Lukoil* and *Gazprom* have made inroads in Bulgaria, Romania, Serbia, and Bosnia-Herzegovina. Plans to build major energy transportation systems between the Black Sea and the Adriatic Sea and Central Europe placed the Balkans at the center of Russia's South European strategy. Moscow seeks to monopolize the supply of natural gas passing through the region to Western Europe. Contracts and investments provide the Kremlin with significant inroads in a targeted country's economy and substantial influence over its foreign policy. Planned cross-regional pipelines have been calculated to place Serbia and Bulgaria, in particular, at the center of Russia's energy ambitions and prevent the construction of an energy network independent of Russia that would link Central Asia, the South Caucasus, and Europe.

Countries with fewer alternative sources of supply are more vulnerable to energy blackmail, high energy prices, and political interference. The most illustrative examples include Bulgaria, Macedonia, Serbia, and Bosnia-Herzegovina, which have been among the most ardent supporters of Russian energy projects such as South Stream but pay some of the highest prices for Russian natural gas.[3] These countries also have a high proportion of Russian energy asset acquisitions and critical energy contracts. Russian economic penetration is much more restricted in countries that have their own oil and gas reserves, such as Romania and Croatia.

Although dependence on Russian crude oil is generally higher than on gas, the existing alternatives to oil supplies and transportation options make it secondary to gas when used by the Kremlin as a form of pressure. Russia has also focused on expanding the presence of its oil giants *Lukoil*, *Gazprom* Oil, and *Zarubezhneft* on the Balkan market by investing in the oil and petrochemical industry, critical asset acquisitions such as oil refineries (Bulgaria, Romania), gas stations and oil storage facilities throughout the region, and energy distribution companies such as *NIS* and *Beopetrol* in Serbia, *Europe-mil* in Croatia, and *Montenegro Bonus* in Montenegro. Russian oil companies have also engaged in geological exploration and development of oil fields in the Balkan countries and the Black Sea shelf.

The natural gas sector in the Balkans, including Greece, Romania, Croatia, and Slovenia, is small, with annual consumption of 26 billion cubic meters (bcm) of gas per year according to data from 2013, of which more than half is locally produced and only 10 bcm imported from Russia.[4] Nevertheless, the Balkans have become a battleground for several gas pipeline projects, with the now defunct South Stream managing to involve almost all countries in the region. Promising large investments, high transit fees and taxes, and thousands of jobs to the unemployment stricken economies, Moscow succeeded in pitting these countries against the EU as lobbyists to exempt the pipeline from EU laws.

South Stream's main purpose was political. It aimed to bypass Ukraine as a transit country and eliminate the Trans-Balkan pipeline as a major supply line; undermine the Nabucco pipeline as an alternative gas route from the Caspian basin to Central Europe, and divide EU members over Union regulations. The main line for Russian gas to the Balkans is the Trans-Balkan gas pipeline, which traverses Ukraine and Moldova toward Greece and Turkey. Moscow has been trying to close this pipeline since 2006, in order to circumvent Ukraine as a transit country for its gas deliveries to Europe.

However, Kremlin plans to construct South Stream fell apart under legal pressure from Brussels as well as Russia's worsening financial situation due to Western sanctions and falling oil prices. The proposed substitute, Turkish Stream, which is slated to come onshore in Turkey and bypass Bulgaria, will experience even greater financial troubles as Russia has lost its Western investors. *Gazprom's* South Stream partners, the Italian *ENI*, German *Wintershall,* and French *EDF*, recuperated their investments in the cancelled project and seem uninterested in constructing Turkish Stream.

Since the cancelation of South Stream in December 2014, Moscow has been courting Greece, Macedonia, and Serbia to recruit investors and build Turkish Stream. For Skopje, the pipeline is dubbed the Trans-Macedonian pipeline, while for Belgrade it is called Balkan Stream.[5] Nevertheless, the project is not one of the top three priorities for Macedonia. Instead, Skopje announced that it intends to join the Azerbaijan-led Trans-Adriatic Pipeline (TAP) initiative.[6] It would consider joining Turkish Stream only if Brussels and Moscow reach an agreement, which remains a distant prospect. Serbia has expressed a similar position on taking the lead from Brussels rather than Moscow, despite its close relations with Russia.[7] The strategic purpose of Turkish Stream is similar to South Stream: to isolate Ukraine, undermine the strategic importance of the Azerbaijan-led Southern Gas Corridor, and create divisions among EU members. Furthermore, through Turkish Stream, Moscow aims to undermine Azerbaijan's strategic partnership with Turkey, torpedo Baku's budding relations with southeast European capitals, and stall its expanding partnership with the EU.

In the fourth component of its Balkan strategy, the Russian state engages in propaganda offensives through the local media, Internet, and social networks to enhance Moscow's position and undermine Western institutions or to discredit local politicians who favor NATO and the US. For instance, Montenegro's Prime Minister Milo Đukanović has come under intense attack from Russia's officials and media outlets in recent years for openly petitioning for NATO membership.

Strident messages are intended to appeal to anti-globalist, euroskeptic, anti-American, ultra-conservative, and religious orthodox constituencies in which Russia poses as the defender of traditional values and the EU and US are depicted as deviant and immoral. Russia's Orthodox Church also upholds close ties with the Serbian and Bulgarian Orthodox Churches to coordinate their promulgation of ultra-conservatism and anti-liberalism. Additionally, Moscow has supported political leaders who have been criticized by Washington and Brussels for backtracking on democracy. The most prominent recent example is Macedonia's Prime Minister Nikola Gruevski, whom Moscow has defended against allegations of pervasive government abuses, claiming instead that the US seeks to conduct another "color revolution" to install a more loyalist government in Skopje.

A tepid Western reaction to Moscow's attack on Ukraine can encourage separatist aspirations in parts of the Western Balkans, especially if these can gain Moscow's endorsement. The Kremlin has signaled to Milorad Dodik, President of the *Republika Srpska* (RS) quasi-autonomous entity in Bosnia-Herzegovina, that it may back the potential partition of this divided state. At the height of the Crimea crisis in March 2014, Moscow hosted Dodik, whose threats to secede from Bosnia-Herzegovina have periodically escalated tensions in the country. Dodik returned home with €70 million to strengthen his position ahead of national elections.

The government in Serbia will need to tread a fine line between deepening its economic and energy ties with Russia, supporting Bosnia's Serb leaders, and realizing its aspirations to join the EU. If Dodik pushes for a referendum on secession, then Belgrade may be unwittingly drawn into the ensuing dispute. Serbia will be unable to sit on the sidelines if conflicts escalate in Bosnia between Serbs, Bosniaks, and Croats and if Moscow assists its "endangered Slavic brothers" in the RS. In a worst-case scenario, direct conflict could erupt between Bosnia, Serbia, and Croatia over the future of Bosnia-Herzegovina and the position of its constituent nations, thus sabotaging the EU integration project in the region.

If the West fails to prevent Ukraine's division, several radical groups in the Western Balkans may be encouraged to canvas for autonomy or secession. These could include Bosniaks or Albanians in southern Serbia and Albanians in western Macedonia. Such heightened ambitions feeding on social and economic grievances and unresolved territorial disputes would heat up tensions between governments across the region and provide Moscow with further avenues of penetration. Instability in the Western Balkans has three direct implications for EU and US policy. First, it distracts Western attention from the Kremlin's offensive in Ukraine and potentially elsewhere closer to Russia's borders. Renewed disputes ensnare Western diplomacy and peace-making efforts and allow the Kremlin a freer hand to pursue its objectives in the former Soviet Union.

Second, ethno-national conflicts in the Western Balkans help provide a cover and justification for the dismemberment of Ukraine, Moldova, Georgia, and other states that have been earmarked by the Kremlin. Russia's officials can claim in international forums that they are simply acknowledging the will of the majority and the principles of self-determination that are also visible in the West Balkans and which have been supported by Western powers.

And third, by encouraging nationalist disputes and corrupting the political leadership throughout South East Europe, Putin will hope to procure new allies who will be offered diplomatic support, economic assistance, and energy benefits. At the same time, the ultimate objective of Western capitals to include the entire region within the EU and NATO could suffer long-term setbacks.

Bulgaria

Bulgaria has always been considered a good prospect by Moscow for gaining political influence if not outright state capture. Old Socialist networks, a selective historical memory regarding Slavic solidarity and Russian assistance against Ottoman occupation, elite susceptibility to lucrative corruption, and offers of profitable energy contracts have enticed Sofia closer to Moscow. Nonetheless, there is a struggle in Bulgaria over Russia's influence, as some politicians realize that short-term benefits could be followed by long-term costs. This was evident in Russian investments in Montenegro that virtually bankrupted the country's most important Aluminum enterprise. The struggle over South Stream and other energy plans highlighted how Moscow exploits political divisions to weaken NATO and the EU and uses countries such as Bulgaria as pawns in its anti-Western offensive.

On the propaganda, disinformation, and psychological operations (psych-ops) fronts, Bulgarian Defense Minister Nikolay Nenchev stated that a Russian propaganda center operated in Bulgaria, designed to generate tension in the local and international communities over alleged war preparations.[8]Moscow aims to incite protests against Bulgaria's NATO membership, warning that it could lead to a war between Bulgaria and Russia. The goal is to create panic and confusion among the Bulgarian public and to imply that NATO was planning to engage in a military offensive. Nenchev's comments came after Voice of Russia's Bulgarian-language website ran a report citing the TV station of the ultra-right Ataka party, according to which scores of Bulgarian men received call-up orders for the military, a rumor that the government flatly denied.

According to Ataka and the Voice of Russia: "The threats to Bulgaria from its involvement in a dangerous adventure as a satellite of NATO in Eastern Europe, not too far from the borders of Ukraine and Russia, are very realistic." Additional Russian disinformation topics have included the construction of a NATO nuclear base near Varna on the Black Sea, the deployment of a NATO battalion nearby, and a massive influx of US troops.[9] Ataka has claimed that a huge quantity of US combat equipment and servicemen have been unloaded in Bulgaria, together with CIA agents who will foment ethnic and religious strife.[10] This will then be used as a pretext for the arrival of huge numbers of NATO troops as peacekeepers. Such a scenario appears to be a projected replica of Russia's strategies in neighboring states.

Contrary to Russia's disinformation, NATO planned to position a command-and-control center in Bulgaria and establish similar facilities in five other East Central European countries. The Center on Effective Communication, involving Bulgarian armed forces and NATO troops, will be located in the Ministry of Defense. It is intended to improve coordination between Sofia and Brussels and focus on planning and coordination of joint training and exercises, some of which will be held on Bulgarian territory. This in line with the commitments agreed under the Readiness Action Plan adopted at the NATO Wales Summit, in September 2014. NATO will also station a center for the command and management of ships near the Bulgarian Black Sea port of Varna.[11] The command center will be constructed with funds allocated under the NATO Security Investment Program (NSIP).

In a barely veiled threat from the Kremlin conveyed through Vladimir Yevseyev, director of the Center on Military-Political Studies in Moscow, "the deployment of any NATO infrastructure in Bulgaria compels Russia to view those places as a target of a possible strike in the case of an assumed clash." The purpose of this statement was to increase anxiety among the Bulgarian public and heighten pressure on the administration. In February 2015, Prime Minister Boyko Borisov answered Socialist Party questions in parliament regarding plans to deploy a NATO center in Bulgaria.[12] At that time, Sofia had not finalized any commitments regarding the deployment of heavy arms, even though NATO commanders explored the feasibility of storing weapons in Bulgaria, Romania, Poland, Estonia, Lithuania, and Latvia. In the face of a broad disinformation campaign, Bulgaria's Foreign Minister Daniel Mitov felt compelled to reiterate that the country did not face any kind of emergency situation. Rumors about weapons deployments, including nuclear weapons, from other NATO states on Bulgarian territory were purely fabrications.[13]

Socialist Party officials have acted as Moscow's proxies in melodramatically appealing to the government "to prevent dragging Bulgaria into a war with Russia or even enhancing tensions with Russia." Socialist leader Mikhail Mikov visited Moscow in March 2015 and returned complaining about the allegedly servile attitude of the Bulgarian government toward NATO and that sanctions against Russia hurt both Europe and Bulgaria.[14] According to Russia's *Duma* Chairman Sergey Narishkin, the main reason why Bulgarian-Russian relations deteriorated were instructions from Washington and Brussels to downgrade ties with Moscow. Following Russia's attack on Ukraine, Narishkin was placed on the list of individuals financially sanctioned by the West.[15] Ataka party leader Volen Siderov went a step further than the Socialists and echoed the far-right Hungarian Jobbik party by demanding the protection of Bulgarians in Ukraine, who were allegedly recruited forcefully by Kyiv to participate in a "fratricidal war."

Russia has deeply penetrated the Bulgarian economy. Russian business has sought increasing access to the energy sector, including the electric and nuclear industries, and aimed to use Bulgaria as a major transit country for gas supplies. Bulgaria is the most dependent country on Russian energy in Europe's east. It imports three critical energy supplies from Russia: crude oil, natural gas, and nuclear fuel.

Sofia played a central role in the South Stream project, as the pipeline was supposed to come onshore on its territory. The government gave the project the status of "national importance" and intensively lobbied Brussels to bend its rules for *Gazprom*. Bulgaria's energy policy has been historically entwined with the government's foreign policy priorities. Socialist administrations are more likely to accommodate Moscow's interests and hand strategic energy projects to Russian companies, because of their political and personal connections and opaque business interests. By contrast, center-right governments generally try to reduce dependence on Russia and diversify the country's energy supplies.

In January 2008, Bulgarian President Georgi Parvanov, elected on the Socialist ticket, signed with President Putin agreements on building the Burgas–Alexandroupolis oil pipeline, the second Bulgarian nuclear power plant (Belene NPP), and the South Stream gas pipeline. Putin announced that €3.8 billion had been already designated in the Russian budget for prospective work at NPP Belene.[16] However, the opposition viewed the deal as a betrayal of Bulgaria's national interests. One year later, the new center-right Borisov government pledged to review all pending Russian energy contracts signed by the previous Socialist government. In 2012, the Burgas-Alexandroupolis oil pipeline and the Belene NPP projects were cancelled and South Stream was sidelined by Sofia's support for the Nabucco gas plan.[17]

Corruption has seriously affected the energy sector in Bulgaria, as a great number of procurement contracts with significant monetary value are awarded for energy projects. Some of the shady dealings with Russian companies were linked with South Stream and the construction of the second nuclear power plant at Belene. In June 2014, the European Commission started infringement procedures against Bulgaria for setting up the South Stream–Bulgaria joint venture in violation of EU competition laws. The Commission stated that the government was not allowed to award such a large public procurement to a specially established joint entity between *Gazprom* and Bulgaria's Energy Holding without an open tender for other bidders.

South Stream–Bulgaria subsequently awarded a contract for the construction of the Bulgarian part of the pipeline to a consortium led by Russia's *Stroytransgas Holding*. A major shareholder in *Stroytransgaz*, with 63% ownership, is the Volga Group, owned by Gennady Timchenko, who was placed on the US sanctions list on March 20, 2014. Timchenko is a close Putin ally and Russia's sixth richest man, according to Forbes Magazine. His Volga Group and another ten related entities, including *Stroytransgaz Holding*, were also sanctioned by the US Treasury Department on April 28, 2014.[18]

Russian oil and gas companies or their Bulgarian subsidiaries have heavily permeated Bulgaria's energy sector. The largest business in the country is *Lukoil Neftohim Burgas*, a subsidiary of *Lukoil*, which acquired 58% of Bulgaria's main refining company through a privatization deal in 1999. The second largest business is *Lukoil-Bulgaria* EOOD, which owns over 200 service stations, with a market share of about 26% on the retail market.[19] The two companies close a Russian-controlled circle of supply, production and trade, as the refinery on the Black Sea coast processes Russian oil, delivered by tankers across the Black Sea, while the oil products are then distributed and exported by *Lukoil-Bulgaria*. This advantage allows the Russian company to bid successfully for public procurement contracts at national and local level.

Another Russian company, *Overgas*, a subsidiary of *Gazprom*, has played a lucrative intermediary role in all Russian gas supply contracts with Bulgaria for almost two decades. *Overgas* and *Wintershall Erdgas Handelshaus Zug AG*, also a *Gazprom* subsidiary, were finally pushed out as intermediaries from the long-term contract between *Gazprom* and state-owned *Bulgargaz*, signed on November 15, 2012. The Bulgarian government managed to remove the two middleman companies in exchange for signing an agreement on South Stream.[20] Instructively, Alexander Medvedev was serving simultaneously as *Gazprom's* Deputy CEO, Director-General of *Gazprom* Export, and

Chairman of the Board of *Overgas*, thereby practically signing contracts with himself.[21]

Overgas announced in 2010 that it would start buying gas directly from *Gazprom* for its consumers, instead of buying it from *Bulgargaz*. However, the state-owned gas transport entity *Bulgartransgaz* refused to give *Overgas* access to the Trans-Balkan supply pipeline entering from Romania. As a result, *Overgas* filed a complaint with the European Commission, which led to infringement procedures against Bulgarian Energy Holding and its subsidiaries *Bulgargaz* and *Bulgartransgaz* for violating the Third Energy Package.[22] Evidently, *Gazprom* and its subsidiaries such as *Overgas* only respect the EU's energy market regulations when they can benefit from them.

In July 2011, tensions between Sofia and Moscow increased over tax evasion by *Lukoil* Bulgaria. *Lukoil's* license suspension came after the Bulgarian Customs Agency conducted a probe into its refinery, which confirmed gross excise duty violations. The legal saga between *Lukoil* and the Bulgarian state continued for two years, until the Russian oil company was ordered by Bulgaria's Supreme Administrative Court to install measuring devices on its tax warehouse connected to the main pipeline between the Burgas refinery and Sofia. However, the Socialist-led coalition that replaced Borisov in February 2013 dismissed the Customs Agency Director Vanyo Tanov.[23]

Putin's cancelation of South Stream may prove beneficial for Bulgaria, as it can focus on alternative gas supplies from the Caspian and finally escape *Gazprom's* grip. After Moscow abandoned South Stream, Sofia expressed an interest in participating in the Southern Gas Corridor from Azerbaijan.[24] Although only 10 billion cubic meters per year are expected to be delivered to the EU by 2019–2020, Azerbaijan possesses substantial gas reserves and could increase future volumes. The Southern Gas Corridor has the potential to meet up to 20% of the EU's future gas needs, with prospective longer-term supplies from the

Caspian Region, the Middle East, and the East Mediterranean. To counter Sofia's energy reorientation, Russia's ambassador in Bulgaria declared that Moscow would be prepared to consider the possibility of diverting Turkish Stream toward Bulgaria. [25] On the broader economic front, Russia plays a significant role in foreign investment. According to the Bulgarian National Bank, the net inflow of foreign investment between January and October 2014 was €805 million ($974 million).[26] Of that, some €177 million, or about 22%, came from Russia.

During a visit to Sofia on January 15, 2015, as part of Washington's regional reassurance initiative in the aftermath of Russia's attack on Ukraine, US Secretary of State John Kerry warned Russia not to seek retribution against Bulgaria for opposing South Stream.[27] In meetings with President Rosen Plevneliev and Prime Minister Borisov, Kerry underscored that NATO's Article 5 commitment to Bulgaria's defense was "rock solid." Some commentators pointed out that Kerry publicly declared something that no Bulgarian politician had mentioned, that there was a threat of Moscow seeking retribution against Sofia for the termination of South Stream. Kerry also pledged that the US would help Bulgaria reduce its dependence on Russia for energy supplies through investments and assistance in gaining alternative sources.[28] Bulgaria relies on Russia for approximately 85% of its gas usage and 100% of its nuclear fuel. Washington announced plans to work with officials in Sofia and Athens to establish a pipeline to Bulgaria from an LNG terminal in Greece.

Moscow has endeavored to manipulate Bulgaria in the Balkan region by implying that it has irredentist aspirations toward Macedonia. Such accusations are partially punishment for Sofia's stance on supporting EU energy diversity, reducing its dependence on Russian energy, supporting Western sanctions against Moscow, and hosting a NATO command-and-control center. It is also an additional way for Moscow to ingratiate itself with Skopje by concocting conspiracies against the beleaguered Gruevski government. On May 20, 2015, Bulgaria's

Foreign Minister Daniel Mitov condemned as "extremely irresponsible" suggestions by Russia's Foreign Minister Lavrov that a partition of Macedonia between Bulgaria and Albania was being considered.[29]

Bulgarian nationalists are also useful for the Kremlin in its multi-pronged campaign against Ukrainian statehood and territorial integrity. Representatives of the Ataka party attended the launching congress of the People's Council of Bessarabia, formed in Odesa in April 2015 to campaign for the region's national-territorial autonomy in Ukraine.[30] About 150,000 Bulgarians live in the region, and pro-Moscow groups could recruit some of their leaders to further undermine Ukraine's territorial integrity. In addition, former members of Ataka established another nationalist group, the United Bulgaria Movement (UBM), in March 2015, claiming that their goal was for Bulgaria to become a monolithic one-nation state.[31] Its chairman, Georgi Dimitrov, asserted that the movement was pro-Russian and wanted Bulgaria to terminate its NATO membership.

Serbia and Kosova

Diplomatically, Moscow is outspoken in support of Serbia, especially in blocking the membership of its former autonomous region of Kosova from major international institutions, such as the UN and the OSCE. Kosova gained independence from Serbia in February 2008, after NATO intervened in 1999 to prevent the murder and expulsion of the majority Albanian population by Serbian forces. Kosova's statehood has been recognized by the majority of UN members and by all but five EU member states. Serbia remains the Kremlin's most reliable political link in the region, not because of any Slavic-Orthodox fraternity, but as a consequence of dispassionate political calculation. Since the collapse of Yugoslavia in the 1990s, Belgrade has consistently appealed to Russian solidarity, whether over preserving Yugoslavia's integrity, creating a Greater Serbia, or retaining control over Kosova, which gained independence in February 2008 and was recognized by the US and the majority of EU and NATO members. Moscow in turn exploits Serbia's grievances against the US and NATO to demonstrate that Russia remains a major factor in European affairs protecting vulnerable states such as Serbia and resolving intra-European disputes. Such symbiosis has proved beneficial for both governments.

Moscow is pursuing a security foothold in the Balkans that can challenge what it views as growing NATO hegemony. It continues to trumpet the charge that Serbia is a primary victim of US machinations to gain a dominant position in the Balkans. The creation of a Russian security structure in Serbia was the most significant result of then-president Dmitry Medvedev's visit to Belgrade in October 20, 2009.[32] Russia's Emergency Situations Minister Sergei Shoigu signed an agreement with Serbian Deputy Prime Minister Ivica Dacic regarding the establishment of a logistical center for response to natural and technological catastrophes. The center was located near Niš, in southern Serbia, and was opened under an agreement signed in 2011 with plans for development into a larger operation to serve the entire Balkan region for disaster prevention and response. The Niš base is believed to be a cover for Moscow's intelligence gathering operations in the region.

Russia's Emergency Situations Ministry is a fully militarized ministry and the agreement allows for Russian uniformed personnel and dual-purpose supplies to be deployed in Serbia on a long-term basis. Russia and Serbia together ran a military drill in the village of Nikinci, west of Belgrade, on November 14, 2014. Billed as an anti-terrorist exercise and held just thirty miles from Serbia's border with NATO-member Croatia, the activity was an opportunity to demonstrate Russia's reach in the region.[33] In early September 2015, Serbian airborne units also trained with Russian and Belarusian forces near Russia's Black Sea port of Novorossiysk.[34] The exercise dubbed "Slavic Brotherhood" included simulation drills to prevent a "Majdan scenario," in effect a

defense of corrupt and authoritarian governments exemplified by the
Putin administration.

Although Serbia also participates in NATO exercises, it provides little
publicity on its ties with the Alliance and thereby creates the
impression that it is closer to Russia and supports Moscow's
campaigns to dominate its neighbors. Meanwhile, Russian officials
and state media trumpet the notion that Serbia is one of Russia's
closest allies. While training with Russian troops adds little value to
Serbia's military development, Belgrade's involvement in NATO's
Individual Partnership Action Plan (IPAP), considered the highest
level of cooperation with the Alliance for a non-member country,
helps enhance the capabilities of Serbia's armed forces.

The depth of Russian-Serbian relations should not be exaggerated, but
certain politicians try to use Moscow to their advantage and are, in
turn, exploited by Moscow. Serbia's Socialist Party is closer to Russia
than other major Serbian formations. However, they are junior
partners in the current government coalition led by the Progressive
Party. In general, the government pursues a dual track approach in its
foreign policy, with President Tomislav Nikolic displaying a strident
pro-Moscow position while Prime Minister Aleksandar Vucic is
publicly committed to EU integration. However, in the midst of the
escalating confrontation between the West and Russia, the Serbian
government will find it difficult to play the role of non-aligned
Yugoslavia during the Cold War. Either it qualifies for entry into
Western international institutions or Serbia will remain exposed to
diplomatic and political exploitation and anti-Western intrigues
concocted by the Kremlin.

In June 2015, the Democratic Party of Serbia (DSS), originally
founded by former Serbian Prime Minister Vojislav Kostunica, helped
to establish the Patriotic Bloc as a nationalist alternative to the
incumbent government.[35] It advocates "the strongest and closest
possible cooperation with the Russian Federation," is vehemently

anti-NATO and anti-EU, and does not want Serbia to become a "colony of Brussels." Although the Patriotic Bloc has limited prospects for gaining office, it serves a useful purpose for Moscow, as a critic of any pro-Western Serbian government and a supporter of Russia's policies. Several Serbian political parties and movements support Moscow's stance in various policy arenas, including the Serbian Radical Party, the Democratic Party of Serbia, *Dveri*, the Statehood Movement, the Serbian People's Party, *Nasi*, and Third Serbia. There are indications that most of these formations are funded by Moscow.[36]

State-linked organizations in Moscow have been involved in various cultural and political events with their Serbian counterparts. *Nasa Srbija*, an organization that arranges youth activities and promotes Serbian culture, signed a cooperation agreement with the Russian Institute for Strategic Studies (RISS), an analytical center closely linked with the Kremlin's presidential office.[37] Its director, Leonid Reshetnikov, is an ex-Foreign Intelligence Service (FSB) lieutenant general who has also worked in Bulgaria with the leadership of the ultra-nationalist Ataka party and with the leadership of the ultra-leftist ABV party.[38] He claims that RISS provides major analytical inputs for Putin's foreign and domestic policies.[39]

On the media front, some resistance to Russian influence has been evident in government circles in Belgrade. Moscow has been trying for several years to buy a Serbian TV station during the process of media privatization. Although Russian investors wanted to buy TV B92, the station was sold to a Greek investor. Similarly, three Russian companies failed to purchase the popular Studio B, which was sold to a domestic buyer.[40] According to Nikita Bondarov from the Russian Institute of Strategic Studies, Serbian authorities have prevented Russian companies from positioning themselves inside Serbia's media arena. Nonetheless, pro-Kremlin positions are commonplace in the tabloid press and also some high-circulation dailies, such as *Vecernje Novosti* and *Politika*. This helps to shape public opinion, so that when disillusionment with the prospect for EU membership increases, support for an alliance with Russia grows.

On the military front, in October 2014, Russia's Deputy Emergency Situations Minister Vladimir Artamonov opened the Russian-Serbian crisis management center in Niš.[41] Although the avowed purpose of the center is to collect, analyze, and exchange information to deal with national humanitarian emergencies, some analysts view the center as a Russian military base. Airborne troops and special forces from Russia, Serbia, and Belarus were also due to conduct joint exercises close to Novorossiysk in Russia in September 2015.[42] In addition, Serbia maintains observer status in the Moscow-led Collective Security Treaty Organization (CSTO). In April 2015, Milovan Drecun, head of the Serbian parliamentary delegation to the CSTO, announced that Belgrade is seeking to boost its cooperation with the organization.[43]

President Putin visited Belgrade on October 16, 2014, to attend celebrations marking the 70th anniversary of the liberation of Belgrade from Nazi occupation. The event included the largest military parade in Serbia in over 40 years and Serbian President Tomislav Nikolic bestowed Putin with the highest state award, the Medal of the Republic of Serbia, for "outstanding merits in strengthening peaceful cooperation and friendly relations between Serbia and Russia." Nikolic was also one of the few European leaders attending the Victory Day military parade in Moscow on May 9, 2015.[44] Bosnia's Serb Republic President Milorad Dodik also participated.

Prime Minister Vucic claimed that Serbia was not "taking sides" in the Ukrainian crisis and was advocating a diplomatic solution to the conflict. Hence, Belgrade was equating an elected Ukrainian government with a proxy insurgency engineered by Moscow. Russia was not looking for outright support in its neo-imperial policies but the neutrality of European states such as Serbia was sufficient.

Belgrade did not join the EU's limited sanctions regime against Moscow, which ostracized Russia's leaders, businesses, and banks that most directly benefited from the war against Ukraine.

Although not all EU countries have been eager on sanctioning Russia, Brussels seeks consensus on foreign policy principles especially from aspirants such as Serbia. A European Commission report released in October 2014 urged Belgrade to align its foreign policy with Brussels. Serb leaders argued that sanctions would be disastrous, especially as *Gazprom* controls most of the country's energy sector. The Kremlin threatened Belgrade with a loss of preferential trade status if it adopted the EU-US sanctions. Officials also sounded warnings that Russia could drop its opposition to the independence of Kosova in the UN Security Council if Belgrade complied with EU policy toward Moscow.

Russian officials have stated that they would maintain support for Serbia's territorial integrity and described Kosova's independence as reversible. To try and delegitimize Kosova's struggle for independence during the 1990s, Moscow proposed establishing a special court under a UN Security Council mandate to try members of the Kosova Liberation Army (KLA) for war crimes and to depict the group as a terrorist organization. Moscow has also favored the "parallel structures" in northern Kosova's Serb-majority municipalities that challenge Kosova's administrative and territorial integrity. On August 25, 2015, under EU supervision, an agreement was signed between Belgrade and Prishtina to establish an association of Serb majority municipalities in Kosova in order to ensure the full array of minority rights. Some Kosovar officials fear that this arrangement could revive autonomist and separatist aspirations among Serbs or hinder Kosova's institutional development and Western integration, a scenario that Moscow would actively encourage.[45] The Kremlin will also seek to benefit on the propaganda front if Kosova experiences political instability and public unrest as a result of difficult economic conditions, pervasive official corruption, and slow progress toward

EU entry. It will claim that Kosova is a failed state and that NATO and the EU have simply created new instabilities in the region by recognizing its independence. In October 2015, Prishtina witnessed opposition protests inside parliament against Kosova's agreement with Belgrade on establishing a Serbian municipalities association between minority regions in the new state. There were fears that continuing protests could ignite broader resistance to the government.

In terms of conflict prolongation, Russia's blockage of Kosova's entry into the United Nations enabled Moscow to portray itself as the defender of international legality and the promoter of state sovereignty and territorial integrity. Concurrently, it condemned the US and NATO for allegedly partitioning Yugoslavia and Serbia and promulgated the thesis of a pan-Albanian Islamic fundamentalist menace in attempts to forge pan-Slavic Orthodox unity under Russia's patronage. Russia's Patriarch Kirill visited Serbia in November 2014 to express inter-Church solidarity and accused Europe of abandoning Christian values, thereby reinforcing the Kremlin's propaganda offensive against the West.[46]

Some analysts contend that Moscow's influence in the western Balkans weakened after the EU initiative to establish dialogue between Belgrade and Prishtina culminated in the signing of the Brussels agreement on April 19, 2013 under the mediation of the EU's High Representative for Foreign Policy, Baroness Catherine Ashton. Nonetheless, Moscow continues to foment ethnic rivalries and espouses essentially anti-Albanian positions in order to pose as the protector of Serbia and Macedonia. For instance, the firefight in Kumanovo on May 9–10, 2015, between Macedonian police and a group of gunmen believed to be from Kosovo, brought dividends to the Kremlin, which accused the allegedly pan-Albanian government in Kosova of seeking to destabilize Macedonia and the broader region.

Belgrade obtained EU candidate status in March 2012, but talks on membership could not be formally opened until the April 2013 Brussels agreement was fully implemented. In one important move, on February 10, 2015, the Prime Ministers of Kosova and Serbia signed an accord on integrating law courts in four northern municipalities of Kosova where Serbs form a majority into the Kosova judicial system and agreeing on their ethnic composition. [47] Nonetheless, the planned creation of an Association of Serbian Municipalities with autonomous powers, as stipulated in the initial agreement, had still not been fully resolved and could again raise tensions between Prishtina and Belgrade. In the long term, Serbia appeared determined to move toward EU accession regardless of Russia's objectives. It was willing to withdraw support from the parallel structures in northern Kosova and undercut any prospects for Serbian secession. Some Russian official criticized Belgrade for surrendering too much to the EU and failing to defend the country's national interests.

Moscow has used financial loans, strategic acquisitions, trade agreements, energy projects, and direct business investments to strengthen its presence in Serbia. According to the National Bank of Serbia, during 2013 net foreign direct investment totaled around €769 million. Of that, €45 million, or 9.7%, came from Russia. In April 2013, Belgrade signed an agreement with Moscow to borrow $500 million to support the Serbian budget and to help modernize the country's infrastructure. In July 2013, $300 million was transferred, but Belgrade would have to wait for the remaining $200 million until it signed an arrangement with the IMF. [48] The remainder of this deal fell through when Belgrade failed to negotiate an arrangement with the IMF. Negative growth in 2015 and a weakened currency in Russia may inhibit the Kremlin's ability to compete with the EU in allocating resources and extending its influence in Serbia. [49]

The crumbling of the Russian ruble, which lost almost one-half of its value in 2014, also slowed down the export of Serbian goods to the

Russian market, causing substantial losses for domestic exporters. Belgrade has a free trade agreement with Moscow, with about 7% of its exports destined for Russia. A weak currency and high interest rates will undermine Russian investments, including the operations of subsidiaries in Serbia. In addition, there has been a diminishing demand for Serbian goods; in effect sanctions imposed on Russia by the West harmed Serbia's exports.[50] After a four-year average growth of 33%, in 2014 total exports to Russia were down by 3%.

On the energy front, Serbia has experienced intensified Russian influence.[51] Belgrade was a major supporter of South Stream before its cancelation, but became careful in voicing support for Turkish Stream in the light of the EU's strained relations with Russia. In 2014, 40% of the natural gas Serbia consumed (1.14 bcm of a total of 2.827 bcm) was imported from Russia.[52] Serbian natural gas imports from Russia are handled by *Gazprom* subsidiary *JugoRosGas*. In addition, in 2003 *Lukoil* gained 80% of Serbia's oil trade and product retailer *Beopetrol*. *Lukoil* failed to buy oil companies in Croatia, the Czech Republic, Greece, Lithuania, Montenegro, and Poland.[53]

On January 25, 2008, Russia and Serbia signed an energy pact, adding Serbia to South Stream and allowing *Gazpromneft* to buy the controlling share in Serbia's national oil and gas monopoly *Naftna Industrija Srbije* (NIS) for €400 million and €550 million in investments until 2012. The agreements secured *Gazpromneft* a 51% stake in NIS for an undisclosed price. *Gazpromneft* later obtained another 5.15% of the company's shares, bringing its ownership to 56.15%.[54] NIS dominates Serbia's market with a monopoly on oil refining and a network of almost 500 petrol stations across the country. Estimates of its market value vary between €1.0 billion and €2.0 billion.[55] *Gazpromneft* modernized the Pancevo refinery and turned it into an exporter to Balkan markets.[56]

NIS is currently the main proxy vehicle for Russian energy penetration in southeastern Europe, with the company acquiring a number of fuel stations in Bulgaria, Romania, and Bosnia-Herzegovina. However, *NIS* was reportedly sold at a fraction of its market value and spurred protests among the political opposition. In 2009 *Srbijagas* and *Gazprom* signed a 25-year agreement to complete the construction of an underground gas storage facility in Banatski Dvor in Serbia's northern province of Vojvodina. The deal guaranteed *Gazprom* 51% of the shares. The Banatski Dvor facility possesses the capacity to distribute up to five million cubic meters per day. Although Moscow promised to make Serbia an energy hub in the Balkans following the construction of South Stream, it became clear that its political appetite outmatched its economic capabilities.[57]

Bosnia-Herzegovina

Moscow is especially active in countries that have no immediate prospect of Western institutional integration. Such "frozen states" enable the Kremlin to penetrate the region and to delay or derail plans for EU and NATO expansion. Officials have focused on Bosnia-Herzegovina by supporting the leaders of *Republika Srpska* (RS), one of the two autonomous entities established under the Dayton Accords of November 1995. Moscow has backed Banja Luka, the RS capital, in its resistance to streamlining the state and providing greater powers to the central government in Sarajevo. Officials pledged that they would reject any "imposed solutions" by the US and EU and encouraged the RS to pursue more extensive autonomy. This would further disqualify Bosnia from potential EU and NATO accession.

Having recognized the independence of two separatist regions in Georgia (Abkhazia and South Ossetia), Russia retains the option of recognizing Bosnia's RS as an independent state. In acknowledging Putin's support, Dodik opposed Western sanctions against Russia for its attack on Ukraine and visited Moscow on the eve of Bosnia's general elections in October 2014 to reportedly receive a donation for his election campaign. Prior to that, in March 2014, he also received an award of the International Fund for the Unity of Orthodox Nations, presented in Moscow by Russian Orthodox Patriarch Kirill.[58] However, Russian officials have indicated that they are not tied exclusively to Dodik and remain mindful of not restricting support to specific individuals who may be replaced through elections.

On April 25, 2015, the congress of the ruling party in the RS, the Alliance of Independent Social Democrats (AISD), adopted a new statute and a resolution that underscored a free and independent RS as the ultimate goal. It recommended that the RS National Assembly make a decision on independence. Dodik, the AISD chairman, asserted that a referendum on the entity's secession would be held in 2018 unless the powers taken away from the RS by international agencies were returned to the entity by 2017 and institutions not specified under the Dayton accords, such as the High Judicial and Prosecutorial Council, were liquidated.[59] After the referendum, the RS will supposedly offer the other Bosnian entity, the Bosnia-Herzegovina Federation, a proposal for peaceful separation and mutual recognition.

Dodik's critics in the RS, led by Mladen Ivanic, leader of the Party of Democratic Progress, charged that the AISD manipulates citizens with promises of a referendum as a way of maintaining power. Growing discontent with economic conditions encourages the entity government to turn to nationalism and pledges of statehood to shift attention away from escalating social and economic problems. Following a deadly terrorist attack on an RS police station in Zvornik in April 2015, Dodik threatened that the entity could withdraw from Bosnian state security structures.[60] He condemned the work of the state intelligence agencies for failing to prevent the incident. In practice, the establishment of parallel security agencies would signify a concrete step toward Bosnia's dissolution.

In a prescient step designed to weaken the authority of the central government in Sarajevo, on July 15, 2015, the RS National Assembly adopted a decision to hold a referendum on the authority of the state-level judiciary and the Prosecutor's Office. [61] The move was condemned by Western governments as threatening Bosnian statehood but was defended by the Russian embassy, which claimed that international actors should not interfere in Bosnia's internal disputes by pressurizing Banja Luka to cancel the plebiscite.[62] Moscow has also engaged in various diplomatic moves to block Bosnia's progress toward the EU and NATO. For instance, at a UN Security Council session in November 2014, it opposed the extension of the European Union Force (EUFOR) peacekeeping mission, claiming that Bosnia was being pushed in the direction of the EU regardless of the will of the people. Although it abstained from vetoing the UN decision, the incident served as a warning that Russia could block future extensions of EUFOR mandates.

Russian authorities contribute to prolonging disputes and uncertainties within Bosnia-Herzegovina. The calculation is that shortcomings in inter-ethnic reconciliation and state-building will slow down or terminate the region's integration into NATO and the EU. Such prospects will also justify Kremlin contentions that NATO cannot guarantee European security and a new structure is needed in which Russia would play a major role. Moscow prefers a weak and divided Bosnia and not a country that successfully integrates with the West. During a potential escalation of conflict with the US and NATO, it reserves the option of supporting the outright secession of the RS.

In its ploy to impede inter-ethnic reconciliation in Bosnia, Moscow has consistently supported the RS in preventing the passage of a UN Security Council resolution on the genocide perpetrated by Bosnian Serb troops against unarmed Bosniak Muslim civilians in Srebrenica in July 1995, when approximately 8,000 men and boys were exterminated. Russia's Foreign Ministry has downplayed the role of

Bosnian Serb forces in murdering and expelling Bosniak civilians throughout the 1992–1995 war. It attempts to equalize responsibility for the massacres even though all evidence demonstrates that the primary victims were Muslims.

In a further indication of close ties between Moscow and Banja Luka, on January 9, 2015, the official RS Day, Dodik presented Russia's General Abrekovich Valiev with the Order of the Flag of *Republika Srpska* with a Silver Wreath.[63] Dodik also received an endorsement from indicted Serbian war criminal and Radical Party leader Vojislav Seselj who favors a strong pro-Moscow policy by Serbia.[64] Close relations are maintained between Dodik and Russia's ambassador to Bosnia-Herzegovina.[65] Mladen Ivanic, the Serb chairman in the Presidency of Bosnia-Herzegovina, leader of the Party of Democratic Progress, and a staunch opponent of Dodik, claims that the Russian embassy wants to lead the RS into isolation and "Asiatic integration" with Russia.

Dodik has consistently backed the creation of a third entity in Bosnia-Herzegovina for the Croatian population. By ingratiating himself with Croat leaders and confirming their claims about discrimination and marginalization by Bosniak Muslims, the RS leader seeks to weaken the central government and potentially split the Bosniak-Croat Federation.[66] According to Dodik, without an "equal position of the Croats as a political nation it is impossible to maintain a multiethnic community. The desire of the Bosniaks for absolute domination over the Croats and Serbs is notorious." He has also supported the Bosnian government in its border dispute with Montenegro over a small stretch of territory along the Sutorina River that would give Bosnia and the RS an outlet to the Adriatic Sea. Such disputes can be heated up with Russia's encouragement to place pressure on the Montenegrin government and disqualify that country from entering NATO.

On the economic front, RS leaders view Russia as a source of financial assistance and investment and have been seeking loans to prevent a liquidity crisis in the entity. The prolonged political stalemate and lack of legislative work in Bosnia during 2015 halted foreign investments and blocked financial support from the IMF, the World Bank, and the EU. Reports indicated that Moscow would be willing to provide a loan of up to $794 million but with commercial interest rates and collateral guarantees, most probably in the form of control over the RS power company. Some local officials expressed concern that the Russian loan would place the Kremlin in a position to effectively control the RS government.[67]

On the energy front, Bosnia-Herzegovina is dependent on expensive natural gas from Russia, although its annual consumption only reaches 0.24 bcm. For example, it paid $515 per thousand cubic meters in 2014, constituting 73% of its annual consumption.[68] An agreement providing for a direct supply of gas by Moscow to the RS at a reduced price was signed on February 27, 2015. In 2007, the RS government sold a package of majority stakes in *Bosanski Brod* oil refinery and the *Modrica* and *Petrol* fuel retailers to Russia's state-owned oil company *Zarubezhneft* for $1.4 billion through its subsidiary *Neftegazinkor*. *Zarubezhneft* eventually owned 80% of *Brod*, 75.65% of *Modrica*, and 80% of *Petrol*. Dodik expanded the entity's links with Russia by signing a series of economic and cultural agreements in St. Petersburg in September 2007.[69] Since then, high-level Russian delegations periodically visit the RS, including finance and economy ministers interested in purchasing energy and other assets slated for privatization.

Moscow has enticed the RS with the prospect of lucrative business deals. It exploited the possibility of building a branch of South Stream to RS, a project that would have led to conflicts with EU energy regulations, thus endangering Sarajevo's bid for EU candidacy.[70] The Bosnian Federation entity expressed support for the Trans-Adriatic Pipeline (TAP) and the Ionian Adriatic Pipeline (IAP) projects, while the RS mistakenly banked on South Stream.[71] However, since December 2014, when Moscow scrapped South Stream and asserted that it would build a gas hub via the Black Sea to Turkey, both the Federation and RS have expressed support for the Azerbaijani-sponsored TAP/IAP network.[72]

Despite the financial unfeasibility of Moscow's Turkish Stream plans, Dodik claimed that he had received promises in Moscow that the RS would be connected to the new gas pipeline.[73] According to Dusko Perovic, head of the RS representative office in Moscow, the interconnector will be completed by 2018 to cover the entity's gas needs.[74] In the context of Kremlin pledges, Dodik declared that a law on natural gas imports at Bosnia's state level was unacceptable because it implied a transfer of powers to Sarajevo. He claimed that the central government had no jurisdiction over energy, while alleging that the EU wanted to make the RS fully dependent on Croatia for gas supplies. Uncertain energy deals with Russia thereby contribute to undermining Bosnia's state integrity.

Croatia and Slovenia

Moscow aspires to open up Croatia for its energy penetration in the Adriatic region. One third of all Croatia's energy imports, including crude oil and natural gas, originate in Russia, and nearly all of its gas imports are purchased from *Gazprom*.[75] However, unlike Russia's other regional customers, Croatia has been able to negotiate its purchases under conditions of spot prices rather than being locked into long-term contracts with *Gazprom*.[76] Moscow has endeavored to engage Zagreb in several politically charged energy deals. *Gazprom* attempted to acquire the controlling share of the Croatian energy champion *Industrija Nafte* (INA) in 2014, which demonstrated the symbiosis between energy, foreign policy, and official corruption. The Russian firm tried to buy the stake of Hungary's MOL oil and gas company in INA and acquire another 5% stake on the Croatian stock exchange. Washington reportedly stepped in to discourage the MOL sale to *Gazprom,* but US influence over the Hungarian government has its limitations.[77] Such a transaction would have given Moscow decisive energy leverage over both Hungary and Croatia.[78]

The INA consortium represents an attractive target for Russian energy firms, considering the experience of the Croatian energy company in offshore and onshore operations and production in the Adriatic Sea and the Pannonian basin, respectively.[79] MOL's share in INA is just under 50%, while the Croatian government holds nearly 45%. The Hungarian company acquired management rights in INA in 2009, in a non-transparent deal that eventually resulted in the imprisonment of Croatia's Prime Minister Ivo Sanader. In 2012, Sanader was found guilty of corruption, accused of taking a bribe from MOL to ensure the Hungarian company obtained management rights in INA. However, in July 2015, Croatia's constitutional court revoked the verdict because of procedural errors and ordered a retrial.[80] Given Moscow's intervention in Ukraine and the Western sanctions on Russia, a potential deal with *Gazprom* would create problems for Croatia as an EU member forging long-term strategic cooperation with a Russian company.[81]

Croatia has the potential of developing into a strategically important energy transit corridor to Central Europe, especially if the proposed Liquefied Natural Gas (LNG) terminal on the Adriatic island of Krk is built. This terminal would be linked with the existing Croatia–Hungary interconnector and continue to the Hungary-Slovakia border. The pipeline could also link with the planned Poland–Slovakia interconnector and with the existing Hungary–Romania interconnector. Such a project would complete an EU-backed Baltic Sea–Adriatic Sea–Black Sea network that would significantly reduce dependence on Russian gas by providing avenues of entry for diverse gas imports.[82]

During Soviet time, Moscow constructed an energy network in Europe's east that was deliberately intended to stifle regional integration and maintain dependence on the Kremlin. It has attempted to repeat this pattern under Putin's rule. However, a major European energy project such as the projected North-South Corridor between Poland's Baltic coast and Croatia's Adriatic coast would prevent Moscow from using Croatia for its energy penetration throughout the region.

The Kremlin seeks to attract Croatia into its energy sphere in order to obstruct EU plans to construct an energy corridor across the Balkans or the North-South Corridor through Central Europe. In addition, Croatia possesses promising offshore energy reserves that Russia would like to exploit. Several Russian energy companies have offered investments to develop domestic pipelines to connect the planned LNG facilities in Krk and explore oil fields in the Adriatic. For instance, *Rosneft* has shown interest in the acquisition of Croatia's INA and Slovenia's *Petrol*, which would support Russian expansion in the region.

GazpromNeft has offered lucrative deals to Zagreb to enable it to use the *Adria* oil pipeline (JANAF) (connecting Croatia, Serbia, and Hungary) in reverse for Russian oil exports, instead of oil from the Middle East and other sources flowing into Central Europe through Croatia. [83] Such a reversal would cut Central Europe's access to international oil markets, leaving the region more dependent on Russian oil from the *Druzhba* pipeline that crosses Ukraine and Belarus into the EU. By offering a pipeline extension from the South Stream project to Croatia, *Gazprom* also intended to block the Adria LNG terminal project on Krk, to prevent it undercutting *Gazprom's* monopolistic ambitions. *Rosneft, Lukoil,* and *Sibneft* have also expressed strong interests in acquiring stakes in INA. Despite Moscow's efforts, in July 2015, the Croatian government announced that it would construct an LNG terminal on Krk as a strategic investment that will contribute to the EU's Energy Security Strategy.

Slovenia remains highly dependent on Russia's gas imports, but its gas market is among the smallest in Europe, with an annual consumption of around 865 million cubic meters.[84] Gas constitutes only 10% of the country's primary energy supply, although Ljubljana pays one of the highest rates for Russian gas supplies: $486 per thousand cubic meters in 2013.[85]

Croatia's Social Democrat–led government has focused on generating business with Russia regardless of the latter's international censure. In a display of Moscow's economic enticements, over 100 Croatian companies attended the Russian-Croatian Economic Forum and Business Conference in Moscow on February 17, 2015, while the Croatian Chamber of Commerce (HGK) and the Moscow Association of Entrepreneurs signed a cooperation agreement.[86] The Croatian delegation was headed by Economy Minister Ivan Vrdoljak to explore prospects in the chemical industry, construction, shipbuilding, tourism, and the car industry. US Ambassador to Croatia Kenneth Merten criticized the business forum, held at a time when the EU and the US were intensifying sanctions against Moscow for its attack on Ukraine.[87]

Leaders of the opposition Croatian Democratic Union (CDU) asserted that the large business delegation sent the wrong message to the Kremlin that EU unity on Russian sanctions was brittle and that Croatia could be influenced by Moscow against Western solidarity. The forum took place one day after the EU broadened its sanctions against Russia to include an additional 19 individuals and 9 more companies.[88] The list subsequently included 151 individuals and 37 companies. Under the sanctions, their EU-based assets were frozen and their entry to EU territory was prohibited.

On the propaganda front, Moscow applies pressure on various states from where volunteers have reportedly enlisted to fight Kremlin-sponsored separatists in Ukraine. Despite the presence of Russian officers, soldiers, and mercenaries on the side of rebels in Donbas, Moscow perversely protests the participation of volunteers from countries such as Croatia on the side of the legally elected Ukrainian government. [89] Officials vehemently protested a statement from Croatia's Minister of Foreign Affairs Vesna Pusic confirming that a few Croatian volunteers were involved in combat operations on the side of the Ukrainian army.

Montenegro

Russia's administration has viewed Montenegro as a useful target along the Adriatic coast, where it can profit from the country's eagerness for foreign investment and thereby implant its political influences. While it has cultivated ties with the government, Moscow's closest links are with some sectors of the Serbian political opposition. Suspicions also persist that Russian sources fund the Movement for Neutrality, an essentially anti-NATO grouping opposed to Montenegrin accession to the Alliance.[90]

The Kremlin was dismayed when the Montenegrin government petitioned for NATO membership and its officials have spent the past two years discouraging such a move. According to Russia's Ambassador to Podgorica Andrey Nesterenko, Montenegro will be forced to adhere to "corporate discipline" in case it joins NATO and will have to deploy on its territory weapons, which will pose a threat to Russia's security interests, including a missile defense shield.[91] In seeking to alarm the Montenegrin public, he claimed that preparations for a confrontation with Russia were behind the Alliance's expansion. Nesterenko predicted that Montenegro's entry into NATO would not bring progress or peace to the country.[92]

Russia's Foreign Minister Lavrov went a step further by asserting that Montenegro's planned accession into NATO and that of Macedonia and Bosnia-Herzegovina was a direct provocation against Russia.[93] And according to Russia's Permanent Representative to NATO, Alexander Grushko, Montenegro's inclusion in NATO will have a negative impact on European security and on Russia's relations with

Podgorica.[94] Despite such threats, by the close of 2014 Montenegrin officials claimed that almost half of the population supported NATO accession. Parties endorsing NATO entry held about two-thirds of parliamentary seats. Nonetheless, anti-government and anti-NATO demonstrations have been staged in Podgorica with the evident backing of Moscow in a Russian version of a "colored revolution."

Prime Minister Đukanović accused Moscow of supporting Serbian nationalists in a bid to force a regime change.[95] Russia's Foreign Ministry claimed in an online statement that Montenegro's "Euro-Atlantic integration" would lead to "the exacerbation of socio-economic problems." In October 2015, organizers from the oppositionist Democratic Front assembled several hundred people in Podgorica and provoked clashes with the police. Suspicions grew that they received funding from the Russian embassy and from nationalist groups in Serbia in order to unseat the government, destabilize the country, and disqualify Montenegro from NATO entry.[96]

On the cultural front, Nesterenko stressed that Moscow was devoting significant attention to educating Montenegrin citizens at Russian universities, and the number of state scholarships for students from Montenegro had increased significantly. According to the Russian Embassy, there were between 10,000 to 20,000 Russians in Montenegro by 2014, among an indigenous population of some 620,000, and some of these were real estate owners dissatisfied with their residence status. Under the Law on Foreigners, which came into force on April 1, 2015, a foreigner who owns real estate is not entitled to temporary residence, whereas prior Montenegrin legislation allowed for such a status and attracted Russian buyers.

Russian companies gained a major position in the Montenegrin economy during the 2000s. In 2005, Kremlin-linked oligarch Oleg Deripaska and his *En Plus* group working through Russia's aluminum giant *RusAl* purchased the *Kombinat Aluminijuma Podgorica* (KAP) aluminum factory that produced one-fifth of Montenegro's GDP and generated almost 80% of its exports at that time. During 2007, parliament blocked the sale to Deripaska of the Thermal Power Plant in Pljevlja, which produces one-third of Montenegro's electricity, as well as the *Rudnik* coal mine.[97] If *En Plus* had gained these facilities it would in effect have controlled about 25% of Montenegro's GDP and key parts of the economy.

By the late 2000s, Montenegro reportedly received more foreign investment per capita than any other country in Europe and the bulk originated in Russia.[98] Russians bought-up hotels, real estate, and extensive stretches of the Montenegrin coastline. Among the major purchasers was former Moscow mayor Yuriy Luzhkov. The European Commission repeatedly warned Podgorica that Russian-linked money laundering was a critical problem, which had to be tackled if Montenegro was to qualify for EU entry. In a report issued in 2007, the Commission complained that there was no proper monitoring of financial transactions, especially in real estate and "considerable room for corruption in land-use planning, construction and privatization."[99]

The Montenegrin government eventually realized that large-scale Russian investments were an impediment to EU membership, that they came attached by political strings regarding Montenegro's national security choices, and that they ultimately damaged the country's economic development and business climate. As a result, restrictions were placed on further large-scale Russian investments. In June 2014, the Podgorica Aluminum Plant, KAP, was taken over by local businessman Veselin Pejovic amid charges that Deripaska's management team ran it into the ground and racked up more than $470 million in debt. Deripaska's mismanagement threatened KAP with bankruptcy and closure.[100]

Montenegro also joined EU sanctions against Russia after its attack on Ukraine in early 2014. The authorities were committed to EU membership and wanted to display their harmonization in foreign policy. Officials in Moscow criticized Podgorica's stance and issued the customary warnings about serious economic repercussions. In seeking to discredit the Đukanović government, Kremlin-connected sources claimed that Podgorica was planning to push Russian companies out of the country and appropriate their property as one of the requirements for NATO entry.[101] An estimated 7,000 Russian nationals are permanent residents in Montenegro, and by 2015 Russians still owned about 40% of the country's Adriatic Sea coast tourist attractions. However, the numbers are likely to diminish given the projected decline in Russia's economy that will affect many of the new rich and members of the middle class who travel or vacation in Europe.

Macedonia

Over the past few years, Macedonia has increasingly resembled a "frozen state," paralyzed from entry into either NATO or the EU because of Greek government objections to the country's name. Athens maintains veto power in both international organizations and asserts that Macedonia has claims on Greek territory, history, and identity. The charges are clearly exaggerated to appeal to Greek nationalism, but they prolong inter-state disputes and undermine regional stability. Simultaneously, the government led by the Internal Macedonian Revolutionary Organization (IMRO) has also aggravated relations by claiming the ancient Macedonian heritage for the new state.

While Macedonia, the EU, NATO, and the US all lose through the Greek-Macedonian dispute, there is one power that gains from this paralysis—Putin's Russia.[102] Moscow has played both sides of the Greek-Macedonian dispute. By blocking further NATO enlargement in the Balkans, Athens has assisted Moscow's ambitions; and the Kremlin was elated by the victory of the ultra-left Syriza party in the Greek general elections on January 25, 2015, because of its anti-NATO and anti-American positions.

At the same time, Moscow has pursued closer ties with Macedonian Prime Minister Nikola Gruevski, following government charges against Social Democrat opposition leader Zoran Zaev for alleged blackmail, espionage, undermining the constitutional order, and planning a *coup d'état*.[103] The authorities in Skopje raised suspicions that Greek secret services sought to destabilize Macedonia by providing Zaev with evidence of the government's alleged mismanagement, abuse of office, extensive corruption, and surveillance of opponents. Zaev's charges against the government precipitated the official clampdown.

Putin is hoping that Gruevski can become another Viktor Orban, the Hungarian Prime Minister ostracized by the EU and US for avowedly backtracking on democracy. Concurrently, the charges against Gruevski will also strengthen those in the EU who argue against Macedonia's membership in either NATO or the EU. This will assist Moscow's objectives even while it acts as Skopje's supporter and protector on the international arena.

To ingratiate itself with the Macedonian government, Russia's officials publicly validated Skopje's allegations of coup preparations by the opposition and called for a detailed investigation.[104] They were playing the Macedonia card to demonstrate Kremlin support for the legal order of all states and opposition to clandestine US support for political coups. Paradoxically, Moscow charged that Washington wanted to destabilize the Macedonian administration, even though Kremlin support for successive Greek governments contributed to blocking Macedonia from entering NATO and the EU and tested regional stability. When the Macedonian opposition organized anti-government protests in April 2015 and increased pressure on Gruevski to resign, Russia's Ministry of Foreign Affairs declared its support for the government, accusing the opposition and "Western-inspired" NGOs of destabilizing the country through an attempted "color revolution."[105]

On the religious front, Moscow has encouraged the Russian Orthodox Church to become more active in Macedonia, similarly to other majority–Orthodox Slavic states. A Russian Orthodox church was constructed in 2015 in the Skopje municipality of Aerodrom, funded by Sergei Samsonenko, a rich Russian businessman who owns Macedonian handball and soccer teams.[106] Archbishop Stefan, the head of the Macedonian Orthodox Church, blessed the site of the new Holy Trinity church. However, officials in Skopje have expressed concern that Russia may try to use the Orthodox Church to advance its interests in Macedonia.

On the ethnic front, a clash between police and an unidentified armed group in Kumanovo, northern Macedonia, on May 9, 2015, resulted in 22 deaths. The gunfight precipitated assertions by Russia's Foreign Minister Lavrov on a visit to Belgrade on May 15, 2015, that the region faced instability from Islamic extremism, pointing the finger at Albanians and Bosniaks.[107] He expressed concerns over "manifestations of Greater Albania pretensions" and linked them with various terrorist attacks in the region, thereby highlighting Russia as an ally against international terrorism.

On May 15, 2015, Lavrov added that the Kumanovo "terrorist attack" was connected with Macedonia's objections to anti-Russian sanctions and participation in the planned Turkish Stream gas pipeline.[108] Expanding on Lavrov's statement, Russia's Foreign Ministry accused the West of masterminding the violence in Macedonia and supporting the opposition to oust the Gruevski government[109] Russia's propaganda offensive against the West, picked up by the local Macedonian media, was intended to sway the public against NATO and EU membership. Ali Ahmeti, leader of the Democratic Union for Integration (DUI), the Albanian coalition partner of the IMRO administration, expressed concern with the increasingly frequent comments from Moscow that spread conspiracy theories about Macedonia in order to expand its influence with the administration.[110]

Ethnic tensions lurk beneath the surface in Macedonia and they can be fueled by an assortment of radicals hoping to provoke a police crackdown that would precipitate inter-ethnic clashes. In the midst of a political crisis with blocked NATO and EU integration because of the Greek veto over the country's name, simmering grievances can be exploited to deepen ethnic and religious divisions and raise recruits for militant causes.

According to Finance Minister Zoran Stavreski, Russia remains an important economic partner for Macedonia.[111] Putin has observed that Russian companies are prepared to invest substantially in the country.[112] *Lukoil* has built several dozen filling stations and three oil storage bases. *Itera* and the Macedonian government have also signed agreements on investment projects in energy infrastructure. *Itera* and Macedonia's *Toplifikacija* established a joint venture in 2004 to construct a gas thermal power plant that would generate one fifth of the country's annual electricity output.

Macedonia and Bulgaria are the most vulnerable European states to Russian gas supply interruptions, not only because of their dependence on a single gas supplier, but also for the limited alternatives they possess in case of another gas crisis caused by Russian supply disruptions in the Balkans. The completion of reverse-flow gas interconnectors between neighboring states has been delayed numerous times, and gas storage facilities are insufficient. In fact, Macedonia lacks any gas storage facilities.[113] Macedonia's gas market is very small, but the country pays the highest prices for Russian gas—$564 per thousand cubic meters in 2013.[114] Skopje was also among the South Stream project supporters, hoping that the country would be supplied with natural gas through a spur from the Russian pipeline. Currently, all gas supplies to Macedonia are delivered through Bulgaria via the Trans-Balkan pipeline, making the country as dependent on Russian gas as its neighbor.

Prime Minister Gruevski has developed a special relationship with the Kremlin. He personally lobbied Putin for Macedonia's inclusion in South Stream. The initial route did not include Macedonia, but after Gruevski's visit, *Gazprom* decided to build a spur to Skopje. Since the cancelation of South Stream in December 2014, Moscow has been courting Greece, Macedonia, and Serbia to recruit investors and build a new pipeline for gas transiting through Turkey. Playing on the national sensitivities of the Macedonian public, the official Russian media has promoted the pipeline as a Trans-Macedonian pipeline, while for the Serbian public the line is called Balkan Stream.[115]

The value of Russian investments in Macedonia was estimated at $400 million in 2014, and growing. *Lukoil* is the largest investor with $32 million and owning a number of petrol stations. The Russian *Sintez* Group has invested $100 million in the gas-fired thermal power station TE-TO. Another Russian company, Power Machines, has invested $56 million in the reconstruction and modernization of the thermal power station in Bitola.[116] In February 2015, Russian company *Stroytransgaz* launched the construction of a national gas pipeline between the towns of Klecovce and Stip. According to Zoran Stavrevski, Macedonia's Deputy Finance Minister, this investment is expected to motivate other Russian companies.[117] The same company had been contracted to build the Macedonian spur to South Stream. However, *Stroytransgaz* and its owner Gennady Timchenko were placed on the US sanctions list in 2014. Macedonia refused to join the EU-US measures against Russian officials and companies. By disregarding EU policy despite its candidate status for Union entry, Skopje has become one of Moscow's preferred partners in the Balkans.

After Bulgaria stopped South Stream construction in June 2014, largely because of its non-compliance with EU laws, Russia has been courting non-EU states Macedonia and Serbia, troubled EU member Greece in desperate need of revenues, and Hungary, which remains highly dependent on Russia for gas supplies. Although *Gazprom* announced, on May 7, 2015, that gas deliveries through Turkish

Stream would start in December 2016, it remains unclear which route the pipeline will take from Greece to the rest of Europe.[118] Macedonia and Serbia are the logical choice, if *Gazprom* wants to reach the Serbian hub at Banatski Dvor and then continue to Hungary and Austria.

The Kremlin seeks to entice non-EU states such as Macedonia with favorable agreements, including lowered customs rates for exports, free trade accords, and investments in various economic sectors. To increase its influence in the region, Moscow has proposed establishing a free trade zone with Macedonia and Serbia.[119] Given the economic difficulties faced by both states, such an arrangement may appear beneficial even though it would create obstacles to EU integration. The Kremlin has also offered to provide Macedonia with lucrative energy transit to Serbia from Greece and Turkey while bypassing EU member Bulgaria, which has grown more suspicious over the repercussions of Russian investments. If Turkish Stream is constructed, it is likely to traverse Macedonia, but prospects for the pipeline remain highly uncertain.[120] In a potential setback for Russia, according to comments by Prime Minister Gruevski in May 2015, Macedonia would only join Turkish Stream if the European Commission and Moscow reach agreement on its construction.[121]

Greece and Cyprus

Greece has traditionally maintained cordial relations with Russia regardless of the political coloration of its government. A Gallup poll published in February 2015 reported that 35% of Greeks approved of Russia's political leadership compared to just 23% support for EU leaders.[122] For President Putin's reinvigorated offensive against NATO and EU interests in the Balkans, the victory of the Syriza movement in the Greek general elections on January 25, 2015, was especially advantageous. The leftist government could potentially generate two negative consequences for European security. First, it encourages radical leftist parties across Europe to believe their moment in the political limelight had arrived. This may pose a direct challenge to the principles of liberalism and a free market and give greater opportunities for Moscow's penetration. And second, the Syriza government, re-elected in a snap parliamentary ballot on September 20, 2015, may contribute to further undermining coherence in EU foreign policy by opposing policies that irritate Moscow.

The first meeting of Prime Minister Alexis Tsipras with a foreign ambassador was with the newly installed Russian Ambassador Andrey Maslov. Tsipras also visited Moscow at Putin's invitation for the annual Victory Day parade on May 9, 2015. [123] Nikos Kotzias, foreign minister of the Syriza government, was a former Communist Party official who defended General Wojciech Jaruzelski's imposition of martial law in Poland in 1981 in his book *Poland and We: Observations and Prospects*. [124] Kotzias is accused of having ties to Putin's close advisor and Eurasian ideologist, Alexander Dugin, who also communicates with leaders of the Greek neo-fascist Golden Dawn movement. Kotzias has been outspoken that Greece must move away from a European Atlanticist perspective by opening up to the other major states, particularly Russia.

Tsipras indicated that he may seek loans and other contributions from Moscow to alleviate growing hardships in Greece's cash-strapped economy. [125] Russia's Finance Minister Anton Siluanov stated that if Greece asked for aid, then Russia would definitely consider it. Tsipras was also sending a message to EU leaders negotiating over Greece's monumental debt and bail out funds that Athens had alternatives in Russia despite the fact that in 2015 the Russian economy was sinking and the government in Moscow was running out of money. In a comment that was either based on naiveté, bravado, or ignorance, Tsipras added that Cyprus and Greece should be a "bridge of peace and co-operation between Europe and Russia."

Although Russia has long since rejected any form of communism, it is still viewed among ultra-leftist and nationalist circles in Greece and other EU states as an anti-imperialist and anti-American older brother that can help undermine Europe's neo-liberal system.[126] And for the Kremlin, Syriza's anti-capitalist agenda corresponds with its own objectives to divide the EU and isolate Germany. Greece and Russia can also act in tandem to sabotage Trans-Atlanticism, especially if Athens begins to question its NATO commitments. Moscow would then exploit Greece to accelerate its Greater Russia project in Europe's East.

Russia's state media relishes the prospect of Greece exiting the Eurozone currency bloc and even the EU. Some commentaries assert that this would be the beginning of Europe's unraveling, with Portugal, Ireland, Spain, and Italy to follow.[127] Some Russian analysts are even urging Greece to abandon NATO and join the Moscow-led Customs Union and the Eurasian Economic Union. At the very least, Moscow expects that a Greek exit from the Eurozone in the midst of severe economic decline will discourage several of Russia's neighbors from petitioning for EU entry. Although Athens negotiated a third bailout package with the EU in August 2015 worth $95 billion, there are serious doubts whether the country will conduct essential structural reforms and it could be faced with an even messier financial collapse when the funds expire in 2018. This will provide the Kremlin with various avenues of subterfuge.

While Syriza may view Moscow as a bargaining chip with EU creditors, some analysts believe that Athens is moving away from the West toward the Russian sphere hoping to obtain financial loans regardless of conditions.[128] Greece also seeks cheaper energy supplies and increased Russian investment and tourism. In return, Moscow would supposedly gain an ally with veto powers inside the EU. Greece could also paralyze NATO by vetoing any future military action against Moscow or in defense of new member states vulnerable to Russia's subversion. Such prospects could accelerate if Greece ejects itself from the Eurozone by defaulting on its massive debts to the EU and the IMF. This could exacerbate anti-EU, anti-NATO, and pro-Moscow sentiments among the Greek population and contribute to regional instability.

On April 27, 2015, *Gazprom* and Greece signed a natural gas pipeline deal to extend the planned Turkish Stream, in which Russia would reportedly pay $5.4 billion in advance payment for future gas transit fees. However, there is broad skepticism about the alleged Russian offer, as well as the feasibility of the pipeline itself, which is not expected to come into service until 2019 while Ankara and Moscow struggle to reach an agreement. Under the Syriza administration, the Greek-Russian Joint Interministerial Committee (JIC) was reactivated to tighten bilateral relations. Athens could also play the Russian card in a snub to the EU by favoring Russian rather than European investment in state railways, the port of Thessaloniki, and other major state assets.

In an added bonus for the Kremlin, Syriza and its successor government is unlikely to resolve the name dispute with Macedonia that would allow that country to enter NATO and the EU. Parties of all political stripes in Greece are unwilling to reach any compromises with Macedonia, as this could undermine their patriotic credentials at a time of economic crisis and fiscal austerity. Greece is thereby viewed in some quarters as Putin's Trojan Horse inside the EU and NATO and may enable him to increase his influence in European politics.

Soon after it was elected in January 2015, the Syriza government resisted an agreement on new sanctions against Russia by objecting to language in the EU Declaration concerning the Ukraine crisis. Syriza's members in the European Parliament also voted against the EU-Ukraine Association Agreement. The open opposition of Athens to sanctions partially subsided during the crucial bailout negotiations with Eurogroup creditors in June 2015, evidently in order to placate Berlin and Brussels for more beneficial terms. On June 22, 2015, EU foreign ministers prolonged the sanctions against Russia until January 31, 2016. The Kremlin is seeking partners that can veto decisions in the EU and NATO that affect sanctions or other actions that punish Moscow.[129] It tries to achieve this through governments that either sympathize with Russia's position or are economically dependent on Moscow. Greece is also deeply susceptible to corruption, and the higher the vulnerability the stronger is Moscow's influence.

Anti-Ukrainian rallies have been held at Greek universities, where attendees flew flags of the Donetsk People's Republic, and anyone who supports Ukraine has been labeled a fascist.[130] According to the Pew Research Center in early 2015, while support for Russia has dropped across the world, 61% percent of Greeks hold positive views toward Moscow. The prevailing view in Greece is that Ukraine's EuroMaidan Revolution was the result of Western intervention. There is also evidence of active engagement between RISS, a Russian think tank that provides "information support" to the Russian government, and both Syriza and the nationalist Independent Greeks party in the months preceding their election victory.

On the security front, in early 2015, Moscow reportedly requested that Greece allocate land for the construction of military base on its territory.[131] Russian interest in acquiring naval bases in Greece and Cyprus is longstanding.[132] Moscow has sought a base at Paphos in western Cyprus since at least 2012, as well as a naval base on the Adriatic at Bar in Montenegro. So far, Moscow has not reached host-country agreements for any of these Mediterranean locations. Russia's base plans are an important component of its attempts to increase influence throughout southeast Europe. To help coordinate military ties with Moscow, Tsipras appointed as Minister of Defense Panos Kammenos, leader of the Independent Greeks, which seeks closer ties with Russia. [133] Kammenos attended an international defense conference in Moscow on April 16–17, 2015.

On the economic front, Greece has a strategic interest in upholding cordial ties with Russia, especially as it is dependent on Russian natural gas and pricing is always a sensitive question. Greek shipping magnates also depend on Russia to maintain their quasi-monopoly on Black Sea trade. If Greece is forced out of the eurozone, the *drachma* would rapidly devalue, making energy imports more expensive. Consolidating energy ties with Russia could then become indispensable. In 2013, 54% of 3.86 bcm of Greek gas needs were imported from Russia, with Athens paying $478 per thousand cubic meters.[134] However, natural gas represents only 13.9% in Greece's total primary energy supply, while oil has been the dominant source of energy, accounting for 45.9% in 2012, and coal makes up over 30%.[135]

Potential energy projects in Greece are of considerable interest to Russia. Since December 2014, Putin has tried to lure Greece into Turkish Stream. There are two reasons for this project: to bypass Bulgaria as an EU member that refused to bend the rules for South Stream, and to undermine the EU-backed and Azerbaijan-led Southern Gas Corridor as an alternative gas supply vehicle for the Balkans.[136] Athens is desperate to benefit from Turkish Stream, and in April 2015 it signed a deal with *Gazprom* to connect Turkish Stream with existing Greek pipelines.[137] If it is ever built, the pipeline is projected to have an annual capacity of 63 bcm. Around 14 billion bcm will be supplied to Turkey. The rest would be pumped to a receiving hub on the Turkish-Greek border for European customers.

Moscow has also tried to obstruct the planned Trans-Anatolian Gas Pipeline (TANAP) and its connection to the Trans-Adriatic Pipeline (TAP) that would pump natural gas from Azerbaijan to Italy through Greece and Albania and is slated for completion by 2018. Baku's attempts to buy a majority stake in the Greek gas grid operator DESFA has been countered by Moscow, which seeks to purchase a number of gas distribution networks in Europe. Overall Russian investment in Greece has picked up in recent years, rising from $33 million in 2007 to $98 million in 2013. Officials in Moscow also planned to exempt Greek fruits from a Russian food import ban imposed on the EU in retaliation against Western sanctions in the summer of 2014. Additionally, Russia wants to participate in the potential privatization of the Thessaloniki Port Authority and national rail and bus service providers, *Trainose* and *Esssty*.

Cyprus, another EU member, is also prone to Russia's influences. The Cypriot economy is closely linked to Greece and would be severely affected by Athens' potential exit from the euro. This will also impact on Russia, as Cyprus is one of the major destinations for Russian money. A banking crisis in Greece and abandonment of the Euro currency could undermine Cyprus as an offshore destination for Russian businesses.

In February 2015, the President of Cyprus Nicos Anastasiades visited Moscow to promote bilateral ties. The two countries signed a range of agreements, including intensified military cooperation that gives the Russian navy access to Cypriot ports and a memorandum of understanding between Russian and Cypriot investment agencies. European and Western experts criticized the military agreement as a political document. According to General Chuck Wald, deputy commander of United States European Command, the new agreement "is part of the bigger picture of regaining the old spheres of influence."[138] It gives Moscow access to a Mediterranean port and an intelligence presence to observe the British Royal Air Force base at Akrotiri, which has been crucial in refueling allied jets participating in air strikes against the Islamic State (ISIS) *jihadist* insurgency in Iraq and Syria.

Endnotes

[1] For instance, see R.Z. Markovic, "Islamists To Attack Serbia in August?!" Belgrade, *Nase Novine*, July 9, 2015.

[2] Based on conversations by the authors with analysts in Tirana, Albania, in October and November 2013.

[3] "Больше всех в Европе «Газпрому» платят македонцы и поляки," (Macedonians and Poles Pay The Highest Prices to *Gazprom*), *Izvestiya*, February 1, 2013, http://izvestia.ru/news/544100.

[4] Jonathan Stern, Simon Pirani and Katja Yafimava, "Does The Cancellation of South Stream Signal a Fundamental Reorientation of Russian Gas Export Policy?" The Oxford Institute for Energy Studies, January 2015, http://www.oxfordenergy.org/wpcms/wp-content/uploads/2015/01/Does-cancellation-of-South-Stream-signal-a-fundamental-reorientation-of-Russian-gas-export-policy-GPC-5.pdf.

[5] Sergey Strokan and Andrew Korybko, "South Stream: Life After Death?" *Sputnik International*, March 20, 2015, http://sptnkne.ws/aru.

[6] "Macedonia Has Azerbaijani Gas In Its Sight," *Trend News Agency*, May 28, 2015, https://www.oilandgaseurasia.com/en/news/macedonia-has-azerbaijani-gas-its-sight.

[7] "Serbia 'Will Not Get Gas From Turkish Stream'," *B92*, May 8, 2015, http://www.b92.net/eng/news/business.php?yyyy=2015&mm=05&dd=08&nav_id=94049.

[8] Georgi Papakochev, "No One Wants To Fight a War Against Russia," Sofia, *novinite.com*, February 3, 2015, www.novinite.com and *DW.de*, February 11, 2015, www.dw.de.

[9] Panayot Angarev, "Characteristics Of Russian Information War Fishing," *Sega Online*, Sofia, March 24, 2015, http://www.segabg.com.

[10] "Overdosing: Siderov Has Revealed That the CIA and the Pentagon Are Planning Ethnic Clashes in Bulgaria," *Dnevnik Online*, Sofia, April 8, 2015, www.dnevnik.bg.

[11] "NATO To Station Ship Command Centre Near Bulgaria's Varna," *Novinite*, Sofia, February 27, 2015,

http://www.novinite.com/newsletter/print.php?id=166878#sthash.x7mTW9t6.dpuf.

[12] "Borisov Justifies Deployment of NATO Logistics Staff in Bulgaria," *Mediapool.bg*, Sofia, February 5, 2015.

[13] Interview with Bulgarian Foreign Minister Daniel Mitov by Tsvetanka Rizova, "Daniel Mitov: There Is No Danger of Entering War Against Anyone," *Focus Online*, Sofia February 2, 2015, www.focus-news.net.

[14] "The Bulgarian Government Behaves in a Servile Manner," *Duma Online*, Sofia, March 20, 2015, http://www.duma.bg.

[15] *Novinite.com*, March 17, 2015, http://www.novinite.com.

[16] "We Achieved a Grand Slam, Parvanov Announced," *News.bg*, January 18, 2008, http://news.ibox.bg/news/id_443771292.

[17] "Nabucco Pipeline Secures Bulgarian Environmental Permit," *The Sofia Globe*, May 8, 2013, http://sofiaglobe.com/2013/05/08/nabucco-pipeline-secures-bulgarian-environmental-permit.

[18] Margarita Assenova, "Bulgaria Suspends South Stream as the Ruling Coalition Falls Apart," *Eurasia Daily Monitor*, Volume: 11 Issue: 103, June 9, 2014, Washington, The Jamestown Foundation, http://www.jamestown.org/single/?tx_ttnews%5Btt_news%5D=42475&no_cache=1.

[19] "Bulgaria Energy Report," *Enerdata*, May 2014, https://estore.enerdata.net/energy-market/bulgaria-energy-report-and-data.html.

[20] "Газова Прегръдка" (Gas Embrace), November 16, 2012, *Capital Weekly*, http://www.capital.bg/politika_i_ikonomika/bulgaria/2012/11/16/1949092_gazova_pregrudka/.

[21] Roman Kupchinsky, "Bulgaria's *Overgas,* a Russian Spy in Canada, and *Gazprom,*" *Eurasia Daily Monitor,* Volume 6, Issue 30, February 13, 2009, http://www.jamestown.org/single/?no_cache=1&tx_ttnews%5Btt_news%5D=34511.

[22] "Брюксел обвини БЕХ в злоупотреба с господстващо положение на газовия пазар" (Brussels Accused BEH of Abusing its Dominant Position in the Gas Market), March 25, 2015, *Capital Weekly,* http://www.capital.bg/politika_i_ikonomika/bulgaria/2015/03/23/2498171_brjuksel_obvini_beh_v_zloupotreba_s_gospodstvashto/; "*Overgas* Snubs State-Owned *Bulgargaz* in Contract Negotiations," *Sofia News Agency,* May 27, 2010, http://www.novinite.com/view_news.php?id=116613.

[23] "Bulgarian PM Backs *Lukoil* License Suspension, Says Ministers Should Secure Fuel," *Sofia News Agency,* July 29, 2011, http://www.novinite.com/articles/130684/Bulgarian+PM+Backs+Lukoil+License+Suspension%2C+Says+Ministers+Should+Secure+Fuel; "*Lukoil* Bulgaria Suffers Setback in Court," *Sofia News Agency,* August 23, 2013, http://www.novinite.com/articles/153083/Lukoil+Bulgaria+Suffers+Setback+in+Court.

[24] "Sefcovic Gives His Blessing To Southern Gas Corridor," *EurActiv.com,* February 13, 2015, Brussels, http://www.euractiv.com.

[25] Interview with Russian ambassador Yuriy Isakov by Evelina Branimirova on February 27, 2015, "Blood of Soldiers Killed in Russian-Turkish War Is Substance That Connects Bulgarians And Russians," *Focus Online,* Sofia, March 3, 2015, http://www.focus-news.net.

[26] "Russia Is Losing Ground in the Balkans," *Stratfor,* January 4, 2015, http://www.stratfor.com/sample/analysis/russia-losing-ground-balkans.

[27] Ivo Indzhev, "In Sofia, the United States Warned Russia Not to Seek Retribution on Bulgaria" *e-vestnik.bg,* Sofia, January 15, 2015, http://e-vestnik.bg/.

[28] Michael R. Gordon, "US to Help Bulgaria Depend Less on Russians," *The New York Times,* January 15, 2015,

http://www.nytimes.com/2015/01/16/world/europe/us-vows-to-help-bulgaria-reduce-energy-dependency-on-russia.html?smprod=nytcore-ipad&smid=nytcore-ipad-share&_r=0.

[29] *Novinite.com*, Sofia, May 20, 2015, http://www.novinite.com.

[30] Svetlana Gamova, "A Bessarabian Autonomy Could Emerge In Ukraine. The National Minorities of Odesa Oblast Have Formed Their Own People's Rada," *Nezavisimaya Gazeta Online*, Moscow, April 8, 2015, http://www.ng.ru.

[31] *BTA Online*, Sofia, June 2, 2015, http://www.bta.bg.

[32] Vladimir Socor, "Medvedev Exploits Past-Oriented Nationalism in Belgrade," *Eurasia Daily Monitor*, Volume 6, Issue 197, October 27, 2009, http://www.jamestown.org/programs/edm/single/?tx_ttnews[tt_news]=356 54&tx_ttnews[backPid]=485&no_cache=1#.VXiDsab9p5g.

[33] "Russia And Serbia Conducted A Spectacular Military Drill Today, Just Miles From NATO Ground," *Business Insider*, November 15, 2014, http://www.businessinsider.com/russia-and-serbia-conduct-military-drill-2014-11#ixzz3JAdB6Mey.

[34] "'Slavic Brotherhood Exercises Aimed at Crushing Potential Maidan Scenario," *Sputnik International*, September 3, 2015, http://sputniknews.com/military/20150903/1026549545/slavic-brotherhood-russia-serbia-belarus.html#ixzz3kgd9UzBA.

[35] Z.R, "Patriotic Bloc Calls for Strongest Possible Cooperation With Russia," *Danas*, Belgrade, June 18, 2015, http://www.danas.rs.

[36] "Russia's Soft Power Expands," Helsinki Bulletin, No. 120, October 2015, p. 5, http://www.helsinki.org.rs.

[37] Elisabeth Brew, "The Kremlin's Influence Game," *World Affairs*, March 10, 2015, http://www.worldaffairsjournal.org/blog/elisabeth-braw/kremlin%E2%80%99s-influence-game.

[38] *B92 Online*, Belgrade, February 20, 2015, www.b92.net.

[39] Paul Goble, "Reshetnikov Details How RISI Helps Putin Make Decisions," *Window on Eurasia – New Series*, March 30, 2015, http://windowoneurasia2.blogspot.com/2015/03/reshetnikov-details-how-risi-helps.html.

[40] "Russia's Soft Power Expands," Helsinki Bulletin, No .120, October 2015, p. 4, http://www.helsinki.org.rs.

[41] "Russian-Serbian Crisis Management Center Working in Nis," *Interfax*, Belgrade, October 16, 2014, www.interfax.com/newsinf.asp?id=544333.

[42] "Russian Airborne Troops Will Be Conducting Joint Exercises With Belarusian and Serbian Paratroops," *Lenta*, Moscow, June 25, 2015, http://lenta.ru.

[43] *B92 Online*, Belgrade, April 7, 2015, www.b92.net.

[44] Lena Gedosevic and Irena Hadziomerovic, "Nikolic Going to Putin, EU and United States Boycotting Him," *Blic Online*, Belgrade, March 20, 2015, http://www.blic.rs.

[45] For an analysis of the destabilizing threats facing the Western Balkans, consult Janusz Bugajski, *Return of the Balkans: Challenges to European Integration and U.S. Disengagement*, Strategic Studies Institute, U.S. Army War College, 2013.

[46] "Patriarch Kirill Urges Europe To Return to Christian Values, Warns Against 'Rewriting History,'" *RT News*, November 14, 2014, http://rt.com/news/205671-orthodox-patriarch-kirill-serbia.

[47] Una Hajdari and Gordana Andric, "Kosovo And Serbia Reach Key Deal On Judiciary," *Balkan Insight*, February 10, 2015, http://www.balkaninsight.com/en/article/belgrade-pristina-reach-deal-on-judiciary.

[48] Gordana Bulatovic, "Nothing Without the IMF; Russian $200 Million Loan Falls Through," *Blic Online*, Belgrade, February 6, 2015, http://www.blic.rs.

[49] "Russia Is Losing Ground in the Balkans," *Stratfor*, January 4, 2015, http://www.stratfor.com/sample/analysis/russia-losing-ground-balkans.

[50] Aleksandar Mikavica, "European Sanctions Against Russia Hurting Us, Too," *Politika Online*, Belgrade, February 1, 2015, www.politika.rs.

[51] Ebi Spahiu, "In the Balkans, Putin's Winning Ticket Is Kosovo," *Eurasia Daily Monitor*, Volume 11, Issue 225, The Jamestown Foundation, December 17, 2014, http://www.jamestown.org/single/?tx_ttnews[tt_news]=43211&no_cache=1#.VKMF_f-oAc.

[52] "*Gazprom's* Grip," *RFE/RL*, December 19, 2014; "Serbia," *CIA World Factbook*, June 20, 2014, https://www.cia.gov/library/publications/the-world-factbook/geos/ri.html; "Delivery Statistics," *Gazprom Export*, http://www.gazpromexport.ru/en/statistics.

[53] Vladimir Todres and Marta Srnic, "*Lukoil* Wins Bid for Serbian Fuel Retailer," *The Moscow Times*, August 26, 2003, http://www.themoscowtimes.com/business/article/lukoil-wins-bid-for-serbian-fuel-retailer/236308.html.

[54] *Gazpromneft* official website, March 18, 2011, http://www.gazprom-neft.com/press-center/news/3914/.

[55] "Energetski Sporazum na Granici Ključanja: Sergej Šojgu Dolazi kod Tadića" (The Energy Agreement at Boiling Point: Sergey Shoygu Meets Tadić), Belgrade, *Ekonomist*, No. 429, August 11, 2008; "Serbia Could Be Left Out Of South Stream," *RBC Daily*, August 12, 2008, http://www.focus-fen.net.

[56] "Russian Investment in Serbian Oil Business," *Voice of Russia*, December 18, 2013, http://sputniknews.com/voiceofrussia/2013_12_18/Russian-investment-in-Serbian-oil-business-8361/.

[57] Vladimir Socor, "*Gazprom, Gazpromneft,* in Serbia's Oil and Gas Sector," *Eurasia Daily Monitor,* Volume 6, Issue 198, October 28, 2009.

[58] "RS President Receives Award In Moscow," *B92,* March 12, 2014, http://www.b92.net/eng/news/region.php?yyyy=2014&mm=03&dd=12&nav_id=89607.

[59] G. Katana-E. Godinjak, "Political Manipulation and Desire for Power,"*Oslobodjenje,* Sarajevo, April 27, 2015.

[60] Srecko Latal, "Bosnian Serbs Raise Stakes After Zvornik Terror Attack," *Balkan Insight.com,* Sarajevo, April 28, 2015, http://www.balkaninsight.com/en/article/bosnian-serbs-may-withdraw-from-state-security-system-over-terrorist-attack.

[61] "Bosnian Serb Entity Parliament's Referendum Vote Elicits Dramatic Warnings," Zagreb, *Hina,* July 16, 2015.

[62] "Russian Embassy: Complicated Issues Should Be Resolved Through Mutual Respect and Dialogue," Sarajevo, *Fena,* July 14, 2015.

[63] "Dodik: Srpska - True Aspiration For Freedom," *SRNA,* Bijeljina, January 8, 2015, http://www.srna.rs.

[64] M. Osmovic, "What Does Seselj Have in Plan for B-H in Spring?" *Dnevni List Online,* Mostar, http://www.dnevni-list.ba.

[65] Omer Karabeg, "Dodik – Russia's Faithful Ally," *Radio Free Europe,* September 29, 2014, http://www.slobodnaevropa.org/content/dodik-russias-faithfullally/26611368.html.

[66] Interview with Serb Republic President Milorad Dodik, by Mirjana R.Milenkovic, "I Support Creation Of Third Entity In B-H," *Danas.rs,* Belgrade, January 27, 2015, http://www.danas.rs.

[67] Katarina Panic, Srecko Latal, "Bosnian Serb Leader Puts Hopes in Russian Loan," Sarajevo, *Balkan Insight,* June 22, 2015, http://www.balkaninsight.com/en/article/bosnian-serb-leader-places-last-hope-in-russian-loan.

[68] "*Gazprom's* Grip," *RFE/RL*, December 19, 2014, http://www.rferl.org/contentinfographics/gazprom-russia-gas-leverage-europe/25441983.html.

[69] Radio Free Europe/ Radio Liberty, *Newsline*, Vol. 11, No. 174, Part II, September 19, 2007.

[70] Margarita Assenova, "South Stream Not Bankable After Fresh US Sanctions," *Eurasia Daily Monitor*, Volume 11, Issue 130, July 17, 2014, http://www.jamestown.org/single/?tx_ttnews[swords]=8fd5893941d69d0be3f378576261ae3e&tx_ttnews[any_of_the_words]=republika%20srbska&tx_ttnews[tt_news]=42634&tx_ttnews[backPid]=7&cHash=12cf90cb5bf597ad5b8a32ab1d3a3211#.VKRrFntSKHg.

[71] The central government in Bosnia-Herzegovina signed on to the Ionian Adriatic Gas Pipeline (IAP) project, which will enable countries in the region to connect to the Southern Gas Corridor supplying Europe with gas from Azerbaijan through the Trans-Adriatic Pipeline (TAP). See *Business Magazine*, May 13, Sarajevo, 2014, http://www.seebiz.net.

[72] Darya Korsunskaya, "Putin Drops South Stream Gas Pipeline to EU, Courts Turkey," Ankara, *Reuters*, December 1, 2014.

[73] Ivana Frank, "Bosnian Serbs Sign Direct Gas Supply Deal With Russia's Gazprom," *RTRS Radio Online*, Banja Luka, February 19, 2015, http://rtrs.tv.

[74] *RTRS Radio Online*, Banja Luka, April 3, 2015, http://rtrs.tv.

[75] "How Much Europe Depends on Russian Energy," *The New York Times*, September 2, 2014, http://www.nytimes.com/interactive/2014/03/21/world/europe/how-much-europe-depends-on-russian-energy.html, and Guy Chazan, "Europe Seeks

Alternative Gas Supplies," *The Financial Times*, April 27, 2014, http://www.ft.com/intl/cms/s/0/b943b2c4-b8ed-11e3-98c5-00144feabdc0.html#axzz3NhPi6axw.

[76] Marta Szpala, "Russia in Serbia – Soft Power and Hard Interests," *OSW Commentary*, Centre for Eastern Studies, October 29, 2014, http://www.osw.waw.pl/en/publikacje/osw-commentary/2014-10-29/russia-serbia-soft-power-and-hard-interests#_ftn2.

[77] "US Worried It Could 'Lose' Hungary to Russia Over MOL Gas Deal," *The Moscow Times*, November 3, 2014, http://www.themoscowtimes.com/business/article/u-s-worried-it-could-lose-hungary-to-russia-over-mol-gas-deal/510566.html.

[78] Stephen Blank, "Russia's New Greek Project: The Balkans in Russian Policy," in Margarita Assenova and Zaur Shiriyev (Editors), *Azerbaijan and the New Energy Geopolitics in Southeastern Europe*, Washington DC: The Jamestown Foundation, June 2015.

[79] Joseph Orovic, "Russia's *Rosneft* said looking to buy INA and Petrol in the Balkans," *Business New Europe*, February 26, 2014, http://www.bne.eu/content/russias-rosneft-said-looking-buy-ina-and-petrol-balkans; "*Zarubezhneft* Mulls $1.27 Billion Projects in Croatia," *Reuters*, January 17, 2012, http://de.reuters.com/article/idUKL6E8CH4CD20120117.

[80] Sven Milekic, "Croatia Court Orders Retrial for Ex-PM Sanader," *Balkan Insight*, July 27, 2015, http://www.balkaninsight.com/en/article/croatian-constitution-court-revokes-former-pm-s-corruption-verdics.

[81] "Russia's *Gazprom* Eyes INA Stake of Hungarian MOL," July 15, 2014, http://www.energynomics.ro/en/russias-gazprom-eyes-ina-stake-of-hungarian-mol.

[82] "South Stream Demise Leads Croatia to Revive Gas Terminal Project," *EurActiv*, December 10, 2014, http://www.euractiv.com/sections/energy/south-stream-demise-leads-croatia-revive-gas-terminal-project-310727.

83 Vladimir Socor, "*Gazprom* Wooing Croatia Ahead of Putin-Kosor Meeting," *Eurasia Daily Monitor*, Volume 7, Issue 9, January 14, 2010.

84 Geoplin, "Natural Gas in Slovenia," http://www.geoplin.si/en/natural-gas/slovenian-market.

85 "*Gazprom's* Grip," *RFE/RL*, December 19, 2014, http://www.rferl.org/contentinfographics/gazprom-russia-gas-leverage-europe/25441983.html.

86 "Over 350 Russian And Croatian Companies Attend Moscow Forum," *Hina*, Zagreb, February 17, 2015.

87 *Hina*, Zagreb, February 13, 2015, http://www.tportal.hr/vijesti/hrvatska/369782/Karamarko-uz-Mertena-Hrvatska-se-mora-znati-ponasati.html.

88 Sven Milekic, "Croatia-Russia Trade Forum Opens in Moscow," *Balkan Insight*, February 17, 2015, http://www.balkaninsight.com/en/article/high-croatian-representation-in-moscow-despite-eu-sanctions.

89 Official website of the Russian Ministry of Foreign Affairs, Moscow, February 12, 2015, http://www.mid.ru.

90 Based on conversations by the authors with analysts in Podgorica, Montenegro, during several visits in 2013 and 2014.

91 V. R, "Nesterenko: I Would Not Provoke Moscow if I Were You," *Dan Online*, Podgorica, January 8, 2015, http://www.dan.co.me.

92 "Nesterenko: No Sense in NATO Expansion," *MINA*, Podgorica, March 16, 2015, www.securities.com.

93 "NATO's Planned Balkan Expansion a 'Provocation,' Russia's Lavrov," *Reuters*, September 29, 2014, http://www.reuters.com/article/2014/09/29/us-nato-balkans-russia-idUSKCN0HO11W20140929.

[94] "Moscow Opposed To Possible Entry of Montenegro Into NATO (Part 2)," *Interfax*, Moscow, Jun 30, 2015, http://www.interfax.com/.

[95] "Montenegro Says Russia Trying to Force Regime Change," *The Moscow Times*, October 26, 2015 http://www.themoscowtimes.com/news/article/montenegro-says-russia-trying-to-force-regime-change/540359.html.

[96] Based on the authors discussions with political analysts in Podgorica in October 2015.

[97] Radio Free Europe/Radio Liberty, *Newsline*, Vol. 11, No. 108, Part II, June 13, 2007.

[98] Estimated at over $1000 for each of Montenegro's 650,000 citizens. See Oana Lungescu, "Russians Prompt Boom in Montenegro," *BBC News*, February 21, 2008, Podgorica, http://news.bbc.co.uk/go/pr/fr/-/2/hi/europe/7255240.stm.

[99] *Montenegro 2007 Progress Report*, Commission of the European Communities, SEC 1434, Brussels, 2007, p. 42.

[100] For a summary of the KAP dispute see "Deripaska's CEAC Sues Montenegro Over Aluminum Plant Bankruptcy," *Reuters*, December 3, 2013, http://www.reuters.com/article/2013/12/03/montenegro-ceac-idUSL5N0JI2WH20131203.

[101] Srdjan Jankovic and Robert Coalson, "As NATO Membership Gets Closer, Montenegro Feels the Heat From Russia," *Radio Free Europe/ Radio Liberty*, June 12, 2014, http://www.rferl.org/content/montenegro-nato-russia-pressure/25419459.html.

[102] Janusz Bugajski, "Moscow Applauds Greece-Macedonia Drama," *Europe's Edge*, CEPA, February 17, 2015, http://cepa.org/content/moscow-applauds.

[103] For background see Sinisa Jakov Marusic, "Macedonian 'Coup' Charges

Alarm US, EU," *Eurasia Review,* February 2, 2015,
http://www.eurasiareview.com/02022015-macedonian-coup-charges-alarm-us-eu/.

[104] "Moscow Expects Thorough Investigation of Reported Coup Attempt in Macedonia," *Sputnik,* Moscow, February 1, 2015,
http://sputniknews.com/europe/20150201/1017615163.html.

[105] Sinisa Jakov Marusic, "Macedonia Declares Mourning For Police Killed In Gunbattles," *Balkan Insight,* Skopje, May 10, 2015,
http://www.balkaninsight.com/en/article/macedonia-mourns-for-killed-policemen-while-shootout-continues.

[106] Elisabeth Braw, "Mixed Feelings In Macedonia As A Russian Orthodox Church Rises," *Radio Free Europe/Radio Liberty,* June 25, 2015,
http://www.rferl.org/content/macedonia-russian-orthodox-church-skopje/27093507.html.

[107] Shoaib-ur-Rehman Siddiqu, "Russia Worried Over Deadly Macedonian Incidents: Lavrov," *Business Recorder,* May 15, 2015,
http://www.brecorder.com/top-news/108-pakistan-top-news/242402-russsia-worried-over-deadly-macedonian-incidents-lavrov.html.

[108] "Macedonia Terrorist Raid May Be Linked to Country's Support of Russia – Lavrov," *Russia Today,* May 16, 2015, http://rt.com/news/259245-machedonia-shooting-russia-support/.

[109] *Ibid.*

[110] "There is No Reason for Renewed Hostilities in Macedonia, Ahmeti Tells *Die Presse,*" *MIA,* Skopje, May 20, 2015.

[111] "Stavreski: Russia is One of Macedonia's Leading Economic and Political Partners," *MIA,* Skopje, March 25, 2015.

[112] Radio Free Europe/Radio Liberty, *Newsline,* Vol. 11, No. 118, Part II, June 27, 2007.

[113] Jack Sharples and Andy Judge, "Russian Gas Supplies to Europe: the Likelihood, and Potential Impact, of an Interruption in Gas Transit via Ukraine," The European Geopolitical Forum, March 24, 2014, http://gpf-europe.com/forum/?page=post&blog=energy&id=157.

[114] "*Gazprom's* Grip," *RFE/RL*, December 19, 2014; and "Delivery Statistics," *Gazprom Export*.

[115] Sergey Strokan and Andrew Korybko, "South Stream: Life after Death?" *Sputnik International*, March 20, 2015, http://sptnkne.ws/aru.

[116] "Руските инвестиции земаат залет" (Russian Investments Kick Up a Gear), *Business*, August 30, 2013, https://archive.is/WaoAV.

[117] "Macedonian Finance Minister: Russia Remains One of Most Significant Economic and Political Partners," *Independent.mk*, March 25, 2015, http://www.independent.mk/articles/15742/Macedonian+Finance+Minister+Russia+Remains+One+of+Most+Significant+Economic+and+Political+Partners.

[118] "Gas to Start Flowing Through Turkish Stream in December 2016 – Gazprom," *novinite.com*, May 7, 2015, http://www.novinite.com/articles/168380/Gas+to+Start+Flowing+Through+Turkish+Stream+in+Dec+2016+-+Gazprom.

[119] Petrit Haliti, "Project for Russia-Serbia-Macedonia Bloc," *Gazeta Shqiptare*, Tirana, December 14, 2014, http://www.spiegel.de/international/europe/germany-worried-about-russian-influence-in-the-balkans-a-1003427.html.

[120] Dejan Azeski, "New Russian Gas Pipeline To Make Macedonia Choose Between East, West," *Kapital*, Skopje, February 27, 2015 - March 6, 2015.

[121] *Novinite*, Sofia, May 27, 2015, http://www.novinite.com.

[122] Andrew Rettman, "Greece Equivocates On Russia Bailout Option," Brussels, *euobserver.com*, February 3, 2015, www.euobserver.com.

[123] "Greek Prime Minister Set To Visit Russia In May," _AFP (North European Service)_, Paris, February 5, 2015, http://www.afp.com/en/home.

[124] Angelos Al. Athanasopoulos, "Nikos Kotzias: Theoretician of Party Leaders With Machiavelli as His 'Weapon,' " _To Vima_, Athens, February 1, 2015.

[125] Andrew Rettman, "Greece Equivocates On Russia Bailout Option," _euobserver.com_, Brussels, February 3, 2015, www.euobserver.com.

[126] Janusz Bugajski, "Athens-Moscow Axis Endangers Europe," _Europe's Edge_, Center for European Policy Analysis, July 2, 2015, http://www.cepa.org/content/athens-moscow-axis-endangers-europe-0.

[127] Timothy Heritage, "Russia Waits In Wings As Greek Debt Crisis Deepens," _Reuters_, July 3, 2015, http://news.yahoo.com/russia-waits-wings-greek-debt-crisis-deepens-095531257--business.html.

[128] Giorgos Christides, "Could Europe Lose Greece To Russia?" _BBC News_, March 11, 2015, http://www.bbc.com/news/world-europe-31837660.

[129] Egle Samoskaite, "Just Several Putin's Targeted Maneuvers Could Ruin The West," _Delfi_, Vilnius, February 2, 2015, www.delfi.lt.

[130] David Patrikarakos, "Is Greece Becoming A New Russian Satellite State?" _The Daily Beast_, February 27, 2015, http://www.thedailybeast.com/articles/2015/02/27/is-greece-becoming-a-new-russian-satellite-state.html.

[131] "Russia Wants To Build A Military Base In Greece," _ZN,UA_, Kyiv, February 3, 2015, http://mw.ua/WORLD/russia-wants-to-build-a-military-base-in-greece-1093_.html.

[132] Steve Blank, "Russia's Quest For Balkan Influence And Bases," _Eurasia Daily Monitor_, February 25, 2015, Volume 12, Issue 35.

[133] "Greece Uses Russia To Strengthen Its Position," _Stratfor_, January 31, 2015,

https://www.stratfor.com/analysis/greece-uses-russia-strengthen-its-position.

[134] "*Gazprom's* Grip: Russia's Leverage Over Europe," *RFE/RL*, December 19, 2014, http://www.rferl.org/contentinfographics/gazprom-russia-gas-leverage-europe/25441983.html.

[135] "Energy Supply Security 2014: Greece," International Energy Agency, https://www.iea.org/media/freepublications/security/EnergySupplySecurity 2014_Greece.pdf.

[136] Orhan Gafarli, "Russian Energy Proposals for Turkey Could Undermine Southern Gas Corridor," *Eurasia Daily Monitor*, Volume 11, Issue 225, December 17, 2014, http://www.jamestown.org/single/?tx_ttnews[tt_news]=43210&no_cache=1 #.VKRgcntSKHg.

[137] Kenneth Rapoza, "Washington Muscles In On Russia's Oil Deal With Greece," *Forbes*, April 29, 2015, http://www.forbes.com/sites/kenrapoza/2015/04/29/washington-muscles-in-on-russias-oil-deal-with-greece/.

[138] Damien Sharkov, "Cyprus Agrees Deal To Let Russian Navy Use Ports," *Reuters*, February 26, 2015, http://www.newsweek.com/cyprus-agrees-deal-let-russian-navy-use-ports-309759.

5. Southern Flank: South Caucasus

The strategic location of the South Caucasus makes it simultaneously a "land bridge" between the Black Sea and the energy rich Caspian Sea, a crossroads of major trade and security corridors, and an arena for competition between the regional powers of Russia, Turkey and Iran. By exporting energy resources westward and serving as Europe's gateway to the landlocked Central Asia, the region is also critically important for the European Union and the United States. However, the geopolitical rivalry over the Middle East between the US, EU and Turkey on the one side, and Russia and Iran on the other, along with Russia's expansionism in its flanks, require assigning the South Caucasus a much higher place among Western strategic priorities than it currently holds.

Through the South Caucasus, Western influence and ideas are able to reach over half of the former Soviet republics—most of them with predominantly Muslim populations. In fact, six out of the eight countries in the South Caucasus and Central Asia have moderate Muslim majorities (Shia in Azerbaijan and Sunni in Central Asia) and determinedly secular governments, which are seeking closer cooperation with the West.

For the past two decades, Western interests in the region have been dominated by energy and security with the main emphasis on 1) channeling Caspian oil and natural gas westward to boost European energy independence; and 2) ensuring a safe transportation corridor for the international military forces in Afghanistan. Since early 1990s,

US policy toward the South Caucasus has also promoted resolution of the conflict between Armenia and Azerbaijan over the Nagorno-Karabakh region, and finding solutions to the conflicts in Georgia's breakaway provinces of South Ossetia and Abkhazia, torn by civil war in the early 1990s and subsequently occupied by Russia since 2008. An essential part of Western priorities in the South Caucasus has been supporting the emerging new democracies, a sphere viewed by Russia as a direct threat to its stranglehold over the region.

For Russia, the South Caucasus has always been a critical outpost where Moscow has either pursued outright colonization or, after the Soviet Union dissolved, sought to achieve a level of significant control in order to keep the region within its sphere of influence. The fact that Moscow became involved in or manipulated several conflicts in the region as soon as the Soviet empire collapsed demonstrates how important it has been for Russia to retain domination over its southern flank.

Three of the four wars of the early 1990s that raged in the former Soviet Union and ultimately resulted in "frozen conflicts" took place in the South Caucasus: in Nagorno-Karabakh, Abkhazia and South Ossetia.[1] Subsequently, Moscow has used them to play the countries and the peoples in the region against each other, weaken the newly independent states, pull them away from the West, and limit the development of strong institutions and democratic societies. For over 25 years, Russia has maintained a constant level of security threat in the South Caucasus by direct occupation, incitement of hostilities, support for one or the other side of a conflict while arming both and, at the same time, positioning itself as an arbiter or indispensable peacemaker—all with the purpose of holding the region in its tight grip. Russia has expanded its military presence in the region by turning the conflict zones into its strongholds that any rival power would need to take account of. The partitioning of the South Caucasus has served a number of the Kremlin's goals, with the main one being keeping the young independent states as far away from NATO and the European Union as possible.

As a result, the South Caucasus today is increasingly perceived as a region only geographically. Politically, it is divided, with each country having different security priorities and relying on diverse sources of security. Economically, the region is staggeringly imbalanced: while oil and natural gas have helped Azerbaijan's economy thrive for a long time, isolated Armenia relies on Russian subsidies to survive, and Georgia is striving to develop a modern economy with limited natural resources and perpetual threats of Russian trade embargos. The government systems of the three countries are also divergent, ranging from a fledging democracy in Georgia, to a quasi-autocracy in Azerbaijan, and a political system that is nominally democratic, but heavily influenced by the Kremlin, in Armenia.

Of the three states in the South Caucasus, only Armenia is a member of the Russia-led Collective Security Treaty Organization (CSTO). Although Azerbaijan and Georgia initially signed the Collective Security Treaty in 1993, they refused to extend it five years later, along with Uzbekistan. Azerbaijan claims it would not participate in any military alliance in which Armenia takes part, while Georgia has pursued NATO membership, inciting Moscow's wrath. For Russia, the South Caucasus is not only the "near abroad," it is also a buffer zone to the south and a critical part of the north-south corridors connecting it with Iran and Turkey. Furthermore, Moscow treats these countries as a neocolonialist—it considers them inferior, views them as not fully sovereign, and believes in its right to dictate their foreign and security policies.

As Moscow advances an expansionist agenda in its periphery, the divided South Caucasus has become an extremely vulnerable region. The little common ground between the three South Caucasus states prevents them from formulating a united regional approach to push back against an encroaching Russia. Furthermore, following the war in Ukraine, all three governments have become more cautious in their rhetoric and diplomatic relations with Moscow and sometimes appear to be appeasing the Kremlin, although resentments against Russia's policies run deep in all three capitals.

Their fears are not without reason: being on the receiving end of Moscow's instruments of subversion for decades and witnessing the latest Western failure to stop Russia's aggression in Ukraine, the governments in the South Caucasus have reasonably concluded that the West would not rush to help them should they become the Kremlin's next target. After all, the West did not militarily defend Georgia when Russian forces invaded the country in 2008—despite the fact that Georgia's military contingent in Iraq was at the time the third-largest in the coalition, after the US and Britain.[2]

The dangers of Russian intervention in the South Caucasus are greater than perceived by most policymakers in the US and the EU. Russia is likely to take advantage of every available tool to disrupt and subvert the region. In its attempts to undercut the region's Western connections, Moscow could reignite conflict between Armenia and Azerbaijan over Nagorno-Karabakh or split Georgia by creating a military corridor across the country to link Russia with its military bases in Armenia. This could push Tbilisi and Baku into an enforced Russian orbit and embroil Turkey in a conflict close to its borders, especially if tensions between Armenia and Azerbaijan are heightened or a renewed war erupts.

Moscow's offensive would also sever energy pipeline connections between the Caspian and Europe, undermine Europe's goals of greater energy diversity, and curtail Western connections with Central Asia. In fact, disrupting the Southern Gas Corridor from Azerbaijan to Europe may become a major means for Moscow's retaliation against Ankara after Turkey downed a Russian bomber that had encroached into Turkish airspace near the Syrian border in November 2015.[3]

With fighting around Nagorno-Karabakh intensifying throughout 2015, threatening to ignite another war, Moscow could use the opportunity to deploy Russian peacekeeping forces in the disputed territory, just as it did in South Ossetia and Abkhazia in the 1990s. Russia's policy of "borderization"—aiming to separate the occupied provinces of Abkhazia and South Ossetia from Georgia combined with the ongoing "creeping" annexation of additional Georgian territories around these two provinces—along with Moscow's plans to restore the railway from Russia through Abkhazia and on to Armenia and also build a new parallel highway, all indicate that preparations for opening a potential Russian military corridor through Georgia are already under way.

Another serious threat is a possible attempt by Moscow to turn the region into a corridor for its military operations in Syria. In fact, Russian bombers have been flying over the Caspian Sea on their way to Syria, just 50 miles from Azerbaijan's territorial waters, barely skirting the region, while the Russian Navy has launched cruise missiles to Syrian targets from warships in the Caspian Sea.[4] Moscow might also decide to use its military base at Gyumri in Armenia as a "lily pad" facility to support its Syrian campaign. Located in northwestern Armenia, not far from the Turkish border, Gyumri is the closest Russian military base to the Syrian front. Yerevan fears that Armenia, as Russia's strategic ally and a member of the Moscow-led Collective Security Treaty Organization (CSTO), may also be asked to contribute to the war effort.[5]

Continuous Russian operations in Syria to back Bashar al-Assad's Alawite-dominated regime could result in increased support for the Islamist militant group Islamic State (IS) by the Sunni Muslim youth in the North Caucasus, northern Azerbaijan and some regions in Georgia, particularly the Pankisi Gorge.[6] In fact, IS is evidently targeting Azerbaijan not only to destabilize the strategically located country and recruit fighters among its Sunni minority, but also as a way to put pressure on Shiite Iran from the north and reach the North

Caucasus and particularly Dagestan from the south.[7]

These developments could lead to the involuntary involvement of Azerbaijan, Georgia and Armenia in the complicated military environment in Syria and Iraq, where Russia is trying to regain international standing and protect its military bases in Latakia and Tartus by bombing the opponents of Bashar al-Assad instead of IS militants.[8] In fact, the Moscow-Ankara standoff after the Turkish air force downed a Russian Su-24 bomber in November 2015, is taking a heavy toll on the South Caucasus by creating further divisions within the region, which is pressed hard to choose sides.[9]

While Armenia has unequivocally supported Russia, having a perpetual dispute with Turkey over the claimed Armenian genocide in 1915 and over the conflict in Nagorno-Karabakh, Azerbaijan is caught between a rock and a hard place, having to make the impossible choice between its valued strategic partner Turkey and its feared neighbor Russia. In the worsening economic situation, Azerbaijan cannot afford to endanger its relations with Turkey and the West on behalf of a declining Russia. However, Russia's economic downturn may prove to be even more perilous for its neighbors, at least in the short run. Georgia on the other hand is split internally in its reaction—a public that cheers Turkey for teaching Russia a lesson and a government that carefully treads around Moscow, fearful of retribution. However, rather than retribution against any of the South Caucasus governments, Moscow may issue threats in order to extract more concessions from neighbors who refuse to condemn Turkey.

South Caucasus Front

Several important developments in the South Caucasus in the early 2000s raised Western attention to the region, but also brought it higher on the list of strategic priorities of President Vladimir Putin since he was initially emplaced in power in 1999. First, following the

1999 OSCE Istanbul Summit, Russia agreed to close down its remaining military bases in Georgia, while Azerbaijan proceeded to dispense with all but one Moscow-maintained military facility at Gabala, which was subsequently terminated in 2012.

Second, the "Contract of the Century" for the construction of the Baku–Tbilisi–Ceyhan oil pipeline was signed in 1994. The oil pipeline and an associated gas pipeline became operational in 2006, bringing Caspian energy resources westward for the first time. Meanwhile, plans to build a major new gas pipeline from the Caspian basin to Europe were progressing—what started as the Nabucco natural gas pipeline to Central Europe eventually became the Southern Gas Corridor, crossing Turkey and the Balkans to Italy.

Third, NATO increased its ties with the countries in the region following the 9/11 terrorist attacks on the US and the subsequent military interventions in Afghanistan and Iraq. The South Caucasus countries not only became a part of the Northern Distribution Network, but they also contributed large numbers of troops to combat and support missions, particularly Georgia.

Lastly, but probably most importantly, Georgia's "Rose Revolution" in November 2003 brought to power a pro-Western government with a democratic agenda in Tbilisi. Both of these characteristics—pro-Western and democratic—were perceived by Moscow as threats to its strategic interests in the region. These drawbacks required a new strategy, and the new Russian President wasted no time to pursue it.

The new strategy included restructuring Russia's military power in the region by boosting its military bases in Armenia and increasing Russian peacekeeping forces in Abkhazia and South Ossetia before the 2008 invasion of Georgia—which ultimately served Moscow well during the Russia-Georgia war. After occupying the two provinces and proclaiming them independent, Russia permanently stationed two army brigades and border troops there. In addition, it deployed a part of its Black Sea fleet to the port of Ochamchira in Abkhazia. In November 2015, Moscow announced plans to expand the port of Ochamchira and make it an integral part of the planned transport corridor from the North Caucasus to Abkhazia, a resurrection of the Sukhumi Military Road, as it was known before 1946. Analysts argue that the road has little chance to be completed given Russia's financial troubles, but Moscow is using the project to enlist the elites in the North Caucasus in convincing Abkhazia to join the Russian Federation.[10] If built, however, this corridor could be extended through Georgia to Armenia and used not only for trade and transportation, but also for military purposes.

In another development, in trying to maintain the military balance in the South Caucasus, Russia started selling more weapons to Azerbaijan, while donating military equipment to Armenia, or selling it at preferential prices. Moscow has also increased its Navy Fleet capacity in the Caspian Sea by deploying more than a hundred ships with various dimensions and functions, including amphibious aircraft, anti-submarine helicopters, missile ships, and 20,000 soldiers.[11] Russia did not miss the opportunity to demonstrate its military power to the world, and particularly to neighboring Azerbaijan and Turkmenistan, by firing missiles at targets in Syria from its warships in the Caspian Sea. However, Russia's navy buildup, along with Iran's opposition to dividing the sea into national sectors, has prompted Kazakhstan, Azerbaijan and Turkmenistan to establish their own maritime forces to protect their offshore natural resources, leading to further militarization of the Caspian Sea. At the same time, Moscow pushed in 2014 for a declaration by the five littoral states denying any foreign military forces presence in the Caspian Sea, thus effectively ruling out future possible deployment of NATO forces in the basin.[12]

On the economic front, Russia's goal is to become the primary trade and economic partner of the countries in the South Caucasus, but success has been achieved only in Armenia. However, while Russia remains the biggest investor in Armenia, Yerevan's largest trade partner for years has been the EU—a relationship Moscow is trying to change by enlisting the country in the Eurasian Economic Union. Azerbaijan's principal trade partner is also the European Union and Georgia's has been Turkey, with Russia taking third place after Azerbaijan.[13] Moscow's trade embargo against Georgia between 2006 and 2013, although initially hurting the country's economy, has prompted Tbilisi to seek other CIS and European markets for its wine and mineral water.

Russia opened its market to Georgian products again after the Georgian Dream coalition replaced the United National Movement (UNM) government in 2012 and launched trade negotiations with Moscow. However, Moscow periodically announces new embargo threats or warnings about the quality of Georgian production, every time Tbilisi undertakes closer cooperation with NATO and the EU. A new warning was issued in August 2015, immediately after Georgia's defense ministry acquired the latest anti-aircraft systems, including radars and medium-range missiles, from France and NATO opened a joint military training center in Tbilisi. Previously, the Russian government announced the imminent suspension of the Free Trade Regime between the Russian Federation and Georgia in July 2014 after the latter country signed an association agreement with the EU.[14]

In terms of energy security and export, it became critical for Russia to prevent Azerbaijan from channeling its oil and gas westward, and particularly from reaching Europe. Putin's political pet project, the South Stream natural gas pipeline across the Black Sea, was conceived in 2006, with three major purposes, one of which was to compete with and render insignificant the Nabucco pipeline project from the Caspian basin to Europe, which later became the Southern Gas Corridor. The other two goals were to bypass Ukraine and undermine the EU's legal framework and unity by enticing EU member states with energy deals. When the project failed, Moscow substituted it with a modification called the Turkish Stream project. In addition to the goals pursued with South Stream, Turkish Stream was also intended to undermine Azerbaijan's strategic partnership with Turkey, particularly on the joint Trans-Anatolian Natural Gas Pipeline (TANAP), a critical part of the Southern Gas Corridor.[15]

Turkish Stream also failed when Russia and Turkey clashed over the downed Russian military plane in November 2015, although from the very start there had been indications that the project was unlikely to be completed. Russia's next steps on the energy front will involve expanding Gazprom's reach in the South Caucasus, taking control of the electricity export lines, buying energy infrastructure, and obtaining major management and operation contracts.

Politically, Moscow is using a variety of tools to influence decision-making in the three capitals. Forcing Yerevan to give up its plans for association with the EU and to instead join the Russian-led Customs Union was a glaring demonstration of the level of the Kremlin's influence over the Armenian government. The decision undercut Yerevan's prospects for breaking out of its isolation and strengthening vital economic relations with Europe.

In Georgia, Moscow uses political agents of influence such as former Prime Minister Bidzina Ivanishvili, a Russian-made billionaire of Georgian origin and the founder of the ruling Georgian Dream coalition. Ivanishvili, who is still considered the man behind all of the government's decisions, seems to exercise undue influence on Georgia's executive power. One of the tasks of Russia's political agents of influence is to pacify the Western-minded Georgian public regarding the Kremlin's intentions in the country and make it more sympathetic toward Russia, even while Moscow deploys new weaponry in South Ossetia, tries to annex the strategically critical Abkhazia, grabs additional Georgian territory, or threatens vital energy export routes.

In Azerbaijan, as well as in Armenia, Russia uses the Nagorno-Karabakh conflict to achieve political concessions. As a member of the OSCE's Minsk Group, Moscow has immense power in the negotiations; but unlike the other members, it has no interest to resolve the conflict. For as long as Nagorno-Karabakh is unresolved, Russia will have significant clout over the region.

As a relatively new strategic tool, Moscow is also using its soft power in the South Caucasus, including Russian-funded non-governmental organizations, politicians with Russian citizenship or businessmen who made their fortunes in Russia, the clergy of the Orthodox Church, sympathetic or bribed media organizations for propaganda purposes, or individual agents of public influence.

President Putin has vowed that Russia would never leave the "Trans-Caucasus" region, using the Tsarist and Soviet terminology for the South Caucasus. In a speech before the Russian-Armenian Interregional Forum held in Gyumri, Armenia, in December 2013, he declared: "On the contrary, we will make our place here even stronger. We will strengthen our position here, drawing on the best of what our forebears left us and with the support of good relations with all countries in the region, including Armenia."[16] As Russia is using a number of instruments to strengthen its positions in the region, its good relations with the countries in the South Caucasus are clearly an illusion promoted by a neo-colonialist power.

Along Russia's southern flank, it is imperative that Washington pay attention to the security of the South Caucasus corridor through Georgia and Azerbaijan, which is crucial for energy supplies between the Caspian Basin and Europe. Baku is particularly worried about the security of its gas transportation through Georgia to Turkey, which is currently being expanded to become the Southern Gas Corridor. Without control over the South Caucasus corridor, Russia will find it more difficult to secure the Caspian Sea and Central Asia. Moreover, both the land and air corridor through Georgia and Azerbaijan have proved vital for the NATO war effort in Afghanistan.

US President Barak Obama's "reset" policy with Moscow had a negative impact in the region as relations between Washington and Baku and Tbilisi deteriorated, while enabling greater scope for Russian coercion to distance the region from the West. The Kremlin pressed Armenia not to sign the Association Agreement with the EU in November 2013 and cajoled Yerevan to join the Customs Union and later the Eurasian Economic Union (EEU) with Russia, Belarus and Kazakhstan. Moscow is also pressing Azerbaijan to join the EEU, using promises about resolving the Nagorno-Karabakh conflict and returning to Azerbaijan the Armenian-occupied districts around the disputed region.[17]

In the midst of the Ukrainian crisis, the Kremlin appointed a high-ranking hardliner as its envoy for cooperation with Azerbaijan—Dmitriy Rogozin, Russia's deputy prime minister in charge of defense and space industry, who is one of seven persons named in the first US sanctions list for his role in Russia's annexation of Crimea. The move was a clear attempt to tighten control over Azerbaijan and send a warning to Baku and the West to curtail their cooperation. Following the annexation of Crimea, the Azerbaijani government started actively seeking defense arrangements and security guarantees from NATO, pointing to the fact that its troops were serving in the ISAF mission in Afghanistan.[18]

Azerbaijan is threatened by Russia from at least three sides: the presence of about 5,000 Russian troops at two military bases in Armenia, a build-up of Russian forces in the captured Georgian provinces of Abkhazia and South Ossetia after the 2008 war, and Russia's substantial naval presence in the Caspian Sea, which has been also used as a platform for military operations in Syria. In addition, both Azerbaijan and Georgia are threatened by approximately 88,000 troops Moscow has stationed in the North Caucasus.[19] Concurrently,

Baku's relations with Washington and Brussels significantly deteriorated in 2015 over concerns for human rights in Azerbaijan. This development was beneficial for the Kremlin, which increased its attention toward Azerbaijan, trying to portray it as a Russian ally.

Neighboring Georgia continues to pursue its aspirations toward NATO membership, contrary to the Kremlin's expectations after Ivanishvili's Georgian Dream party won the elections in October 2012. These efforts are supported by Azerbaijan, although Baku has never expressed its desire to join the Alliance. Despite the disappointment brought about by President Obama's statement at the start of the Ukrainian conflict that neither Georgia nor Ukraine are on the path toward NATO membership, Tbilisi is defiant in its intent to eventually join the Alliance.[20]

However, notwithstanding enhanced relations between NATO and Georgia, following the Alliance's Wales summit in September 2014, Georgia was not considered for a Membership Action Plan (MAP) at the NATO meeting of Foreign Ministers on December 1–2, 2015. In a positive development, the EU recommended granting Georgian citizens a visa-free regime starting in mid-2016, a development that raised hopes that residents of Abkhazia and South Ossetia may apply to obtain Georgian passports and even seek reintegration. As Georgian Prime Minister Irakli Garibashvili commented, "This is the path to Georgia's unification. Only by building a modern European state can we be attractive to our Abkhazian and Ossetian brothers and sisters."[21]

Although Armenia remains loyal to Russia—mainly to enlist Moscow's military protection against Azerbaijan and Turkey—Yerevan's overwhelming dependence on Russian subsidies and the domineering position of Russian businesses in the country has created resentment among both the political elite and the public. Public protests in the summer of 2015 against an electricity price hike by the Russian monopolist Inter RAO UES, which controls Armenia's electricity grid, were as much a political manifestation of this resentment as they were an expression of economic concerns.

With Armenia's major infrastructure, including a pipeline to Iran, owned by Russian companies, with essentially all of its military equipment provided by Russia, and with major political decisions dictated by Moscow, Armenia has turned into a Russian hostage in the middle of a strategically important region. The ongoing conflict with Azerbaijan over Nagorno-Karabakh and other occupied Azerbaijani territories, along with Yerevan's strained relations with Ankara, have caused Armenia's isolation in the region.[22] Although Yerevan has maintained traditionally good relations with Tehran, Moscow has tried to preclude the development of critical joint projects between Armenia and Iran, after the nuclear agreement brokered by the West in mid-2015. Gazprom was quick to acquire ownership of the pipeline connecting Armenia with Iran, while Gazprom-Armenia obtained management rights over the prospective high-voltage electricity lines to be used for export to Iran. In sum, Moscow is acquiring controlling positions for future deals with Iran in both the electricity and gas sectors.

Moscow can intensify its pressures in the South Caucasus to undercut the region's Western connections, including the vital relationship of Azerbaijan and Georgia with Turkey. Benefiting from its substantial military presence in Armenia, Moscow could reignite the conflict with Azerbaijan over Nagorno-Karabakh. It can also split Georgia territorially by creating a military corridor across the country to link Russia with Armenia. Such moves would have a lasting impact on the stability of governments in Azerbaijan and Georgia, and without Western support it could push these countries into an enforced Russian orbit.

Moscow's offensive in the South Caucasus and intensifying regional turmoil could either sever the energy pipeline connections between the Caspian and Europe or place these under Moscow's control. Either scenario would set back Europe's attempts to pursue energy diversity and would be particularly harmful to the Southeast European states that are most dependent on Russian supplies. Additionally, a more prominent Russian role in the South Caucasus would contribute to curtailing US and EU connections with Central Asia.

Armenia

There was no surprise when Yerevan backed Moscow after the Turkish air forces downed a Russian fighter jet in Syria in November 2015—Armenia is a staunch ally of Russia and has had a strained relationship with Turkey for decades. For many, it was also not surprising that Armenia voted with Russia against the UN resolution affirming the territorial integrity of Ukraine and rendering the Crimea referendum invalid. Indeed, Yerevan has regularly championed the principle of self-determination and the right to secession in its unresolved dispute with Azerbaijan over Nagorno-Karabakh. However, that support for the Kremlin contradicted some of Armenia's past positions on territorial integrity: Yerevan refused to recognize the independence of Kosovo, and has not even recognized Nagorno-Karabakh as an independent state, despite fighting a war over this separatist Azerbaijani region. The logical conclusion for this legal inconsistency is that Yerevan's backing of Russia on the Anschluss of Crimea may have been driven by Armenia's deep desire to annex Nagorno-Karabakh, after first forcing Azerbaijan to give it up. In any event, the conflict in Nagorno-Karabakh is the most important factor in contemporary Armenian politics, both domestic and foreign policy related.

Armenia is Russia's most loyal ally among all former Soviet states, but this alliance is born out of Yerevan's necessity for security protection from both Azerbaijan and its strategic partner, Turkey. For Russia, providing security to Armenia means continuing its military presence in the South Caucasus. Armenia's loyalty—rooted in Moscow's support for Yerevan during the war over Nagorno-Karabakh—has gradually transformed into a complex relationship of dependency and resentment. As Russia demands more concessions in return for security protection and weapons deliveries, Armenia is becoming more isolated from the world while its younger generation is growing more aggravated.

Although Armenia *de facto* controls Nagorno-Karabakh as well as seven Azerbaijani districts bordering the separatist territory, the country may have become the biggest casualty of this conflict—it essentially lost its political and economic sovereignty to Russia, became isolated from its neighbors Azerbaijan and Turkey, sank into international isolation for supporting the separatists in Nagorno-Karabakh, and poisoned international discussions about the future of the South Caucasus due to continuing hostilities with Azerbaijan.

The heavy dependence on Moscow prevents Yerevan from exercising an independent foreign policy. Russia is Armenia's largest investor, energy supplier and donor, and second largest trade partner, although the two countries do not even share borders. Yerevan depends on Georgia for transportation of goods and energy; however, Russia's occupation of two Georgian regions presents a constant threat to the security of trade routes, and also impedes supply lines to the Russian military base in Gyumri and the air base at Erebuni Airport. Meanwhile, Armenia's traditionally friendly southern neighbor, Iran, was under an international embargo for decades, and trade relations with Tehran were essentially barter deals—swapping electricity for gas, for example. Furthermore, Moscow is interfering in Yerevan's prospects for deepening economic relations with Tehran in the wake of the nuclear agreement signed between the West and Iran in July 2015.

The Kremlin is aware of Armenia's dire predicament, its growing resentment and desperate need to break out of isolation; this is why it has tried to prevent any attempt for association with Western institutions. Under pressure from the Kremlin, Yerevan decided, in September 2013, to suspend its European integration process and not sign the long-negotiated Association Agreement with the EU, which was to include a Deep and Comprehensive Free Trade Area (AA/DCFTA)—despite the trade boost it urgently needed. Instead, Armenia joined the Russian-led Customs Union, which became the Eurasian Economic Union (EEU) in January 2015, an organization fraught with problems and heavily affected by the declining Russian economy and a depreciating ruble.

Armenian President Serzh Sargsyan stunned the EU and his own public when he unexpectedly ceased negotiations with the EU after talks in Moscow with President Putin in early September 2013. According to EU diplomats, Moscow had been placing pressure on all candidates for association with the EU (Georgia, Moldova, Ukraine and Armenia), achieving success first with Armenia and then with Ukraine, on the eve of the Vilnius Summit.[23] Apparently, Armenia's security concerns and obvious Russian threats to withdraw support for Yerevan and potentially back Baku on the Nagorno-Karabakh dispute played a decisive role in Sargsyan's historic decision, which committed his country to continuous isolation.

Charles Tannok, a British member of the European Parliament noted: "I know that Putin has been to Baku and has offered to sell up-to-date arms to Azerbaijan. So I can see what it is all about—it is about putting pressure on Yerevan to do Moscow's bidding and, sadly, it succeeded."[24] Armenia's participation in the Eurasian Economic Union is a critical factor for Moscow, because no other South Caucasus country is likely to join this union.

The decision to join the EEU was met with protests in Armenia, albeit not very large, but giving rise to a more distinct anti-Russian sentiment. This reaction exploded in the summer of 2015, when a wave of rallies engulfed Yerevan and other cities. Ostensibly, the public demonstrations, called in social media #ElectricYerevan, were against increasing electricity prices by the Russian state-controlled company Inter RAO UES, which fully owned the electricity network of Armenia at the time. Nonetheless, as the protests ramped up, calls for abolishing the country's dependence on Russia and ending Russian corrupt schemes, perceived to be supported by the government, became common.

Former Armenian Minister of National Security David Shahnazaryan pointed out that "Armenia's government authorities, with their actions, supported the interests of the Russian corrupt system in Armenia. A considerable part of our state's economy is owned by Russian state-owned companies, for whom the business interests are not the number one priority, but the political presence and corrupt interests, and now, their main task is to squeeze Armenia financially, thereby increasing emigration."[25]

The *#ElectricYerevan* protests in Yerevan evidently worried Moscow that another "colored revolution" might be under way and that it could lose its only faithful ally in the South Caucasus. Russian state-owned TV claimed the protests had the same origin as previous public protests leading to regime change in Georgia and Ukraine and accused US-funded non-governmental organizations of provoking the unrest. Political analyst Sergey Markov, known for his close Kremlin connections, alleged that the protests were not spontaneous and that the opposition would attempt to seize power by means of a "colored revolution." He claimed that the attack on Yerevan was expected as a reaction to the country's decision not to sign a "semi-colonial" agreement for association with the EU and joining the Eurasian Economic Union instead.[26]

Moscow acted swiftly to pacify the Armenian public and protect the Sargsyan government, which already felt threatened by the recently formed alliance between four main opposition parties in the country. As a result, the Kremlin reached for the carrots. Firstly, Russia offered Armenia a $200 million loan for new modern weapons. The Russian and Armenian media immediately spread the rumor that Moscow would provide Yerevan with the coveted *Iskander-M* missile system, which would give the country an unmatched advantage over Azerbaijan. Secondly, Russian *Gazprom* swiftly concluded the prolonged negotiations on gas prices, further cutting rates for Armenia from $189 to $165 per thousand cubic meters, effective January 2016.[27] The price reduction was based on an earlier agreement on lowering the cost of Russian gas from January 2015, after Armenia joined the Eurasian Economic Union, but the negotiations had dragged on for months.[28]

Finally, in an exceptional kind of concession, Moscow agreed to transfer Russian serviceman Valery Permyakov to the custody of Armenian law enforcement to be tried by an Armenian court for the January 2015 murder of an Armenian family of seven, including a six-month old boy, in Gyumri. The murders caused national outrage directed at the Russian military.[29]

The *#ElectricYerevan* protests gradually subsided after the government promised to subsidize electricity prices. In September 2015, it was announced that Russian state-owned electricity company Inter RAO UES sold the utility company Electric Networks of Armenia (ENA) to Tashir Group, a Russian real estate holding owned by Armenian-born billionaire Samvel Karapetyan, who is ranked by Forbes as the 26th richest person in Russia with an estimated wealth of $4.4 billion.[30] The new owner said his company would share the burden of price increases with the government of Armenia, which has supported the deal, eager to reduce anti-Russia sentiment over the proposed electricity price rises in the summer.[31]

However, it transpired that Inter RAO UES sold only 25% of its shares in both ENA and the new modern gas-fired Hrazdan thermal power plant for $8.25 million, not 100% as it was initially reported.[32] Such developments are consistent with Russian policy aiming to acquire and control as much of the existing energy assets in the region as possible. By advertising the sale, but not actually selling the control package, Moscow is deceiving the Armenian public and continuing its energy domination in Armenia. Inter RAO UES explained to the Armenian media that its assets would be sold to Tashir Group on a stage-by-stage basis, but this explanation does not seem credible. The sale price of $8.25 million also raises questions about the extent of ENA's debt, considering that Inter RAO UES invested $300 million in the state-of-the-art Hrazdan thermal power plant. ENA is believed to have more than $220 million in outstanding debts to Armenian power-generating plants and commercial banks, with the public convinced that corrupt management and embezzlement played the main role in financial losses.[33]

Nevertheless, Russian tactics regarding Armenian protests were generally successful, as Moscow offered incentives instead of firm support for the government's initial use of police force against the demonstrators, which could have alienated the public and strengthened anti-Russia sentiments. However, Armenia's social problems are deepening with the decline of the Russian economy and subsequent reduction of the flow of remittances from Armenians working in Russia. The value of remittances in January–October 2015 decreased by 38%, while exports to Russia fell by 29.4%.[34] In 2014, remittances decreased by 56% due to ruble depreciation and a slowdown in the Russian market.[35]

According to the World Bank, 32% of Armenians live under the poverty line, 18% of the state budget comes from remittances, and the unemployment is over 17%.[36] Yerevan can expect more social protests, which could eventually become political and demand policy changes or a change of government. Moscow apparently realizes this possibility, as well as the new opportunity before Yerevan to conclude a modified association agreement with the EU, offered by the European Commission at the end of 2015. Therefore, the Kremlin is preparing various proxies to enter Armenian politics in the future. Among them are Russian-grown businessmen of Armenian origin such as Samvel Karapetyan, Ruben Vardanyan, and Ara Abrahamyan, who is also the president of the Union of Armenians in Russia. Abrahamian announced he would establish a political party to participate in the 2017 parliamentary election.[37]

Despite the setback with the EU Association Agreement, Armenia and the European Union have continued their political and trade dialogue in areas where this is compatible with Armenia's new obligations to the EEU. They launched negotiations on a future legally binding and overarching agreement compatible with Armenia's new international obligations on December 7, 2015. The new agreement will replace the current EU-Armenia Partnership and Cooperation agreement.[38]

On the military front, Russia's military presence in Armenia has been a major element of the country's defense doctrine. Yerevan claims it needs Russian troops primarily for precluding Turkey's direct military intervention on Azerbaijan's side in case of another war over Nagorno-Karabakh. Not surprisingly, the September 2014 drills of Russian and Armenian troops were based on a scenario of Turkish intervention in Armenia and codenamed "Ottomania."[39]

Russia maintains in Armenia its only legally recognized military bases in the South Caucasus—the 102nd military base in Gyumri and the 3,624th Air Base in Erebuni Airport near Yerevan—as the deployments in the Georgia's breakaway provinces are considered occupation forces by international institutions. A successor of the Soviet military installations in the South Caucasus, the current Russian facilities in Armenia are the only remaining components of the previous extensive defense infrastructure in the region. This infrastructure comprised of a range of airfields connected with different divisions and installations based in Georgia, Azerbaijan and Armenia. Azerbaijan and Georgia gradually eliminated all Russian military bases on their territories. Some analysts argue that, left alone in the region, the Gyumri base lacks the capability to effectively guarantee the security of Armenia. However, its presence and potential hostile actions against Georgia can upset the delicate balance in relations between Armenia and Georgia and raise more tensions between Russia and NATO.[40]

Although the Russian military presence serves as a deterrent to Azerbaijan in case it decides to retake Nagorno-Karabakh by force, Moscow only has the responsibility to ensure the security of Armenia, not that of Nagorno-Karabakh, which is legally part of Azerbaijan. According to the Armenian media, the bilateral agreement on the Russian military base states: "When deployed in the territory of Armenia, the Russian military base, in addition to protection functions of the interests of Russia, together with the Armed Forces of Armenia, shall ensure the security of Armenia."[41] In addition, Russia's Federal Security Service Border Guard Directorate is responsible for guarding Armenia's boarders with Turkey and Iran.

The Russian-Armenian agreement establishing the Gyumri military base and airfield near Yerevan was initially signed in 1995, soon after the end of the Nagorno-Karabakh war. Its renewal in 2010 extended that presence until 2044 and upgraded the 102nd military base to 4,000–5,000 soldiers with heavy weaponry. Russia has also stationed an aviation unit at the Erebuni military airfield, numbering more than three dozen MiG-29 fighter jets and Mi-24 combat helicopters. Moscow deployed the helicopters in 2014 as part of a broader reinforcement of its military presence in Armenia and also modernized the MiG-29 jets stationed there.[42] In December 2015, Erebuni was reinforced with additional six modern attack Mi-24P and transport Mi-8MT helicopters.[43]

Among other provisions, the 2010 agreement committed Moscow to helping Yerevan obtain "modern and compatible weaponry and special military hardware." In June 2013, media reports claimed that Russia had deployed in Armenia several *Iskander-M* ballistic missiles systems, supposedly stationed at the Russian military base.[44] The information was not confirmed, but in July 2015, in the midst of anti-

Russian protests in Yerevan, reports resurfaced that Moscow was poised to sign a contract with the Armenian military to provide *Iskander-M* short-range ballistic missiles. However, the Russian company KBM, which builds the *Iskander-M* missile, said the systems would not be ready until 2016 at the earliest.[45]

Regarded as one of the most advanced missile systems of its kind in the world, the *Iskander-M*, with an operational range of at least 400 kilometers, can overcome existing missile-defense systems, according to Russian military officials and experts.[46] If the Armenian army obtains such a cutting-edge missile system, it will change the military balance in the region, as Yerevan will be able to reach targets as far as Azerbaijan's Caspian Sea coast. According to Russian military expert Igor Korotcheko: "The existence of such rockets in Armenia and their absence in Azerbaijan may introduce into the conflict elements of a provocative nature, and nobody needs that."[47] At the same time, Armenian Major General Arkady Ter-Tadevosyan asserted that while Armenia needs the missile system to maintain the military balance with Azerbaijan, the country simply cannot afford to buy it. He stated that any *Iskander-M* operative tactical missile systems being sent to Armenia, would certainly end up solely on the territory of the 102nd Russian military base, as Russia keeps expanding its military presence in the country.[48]

After the annexation of Crimea caused tensions between Russia and the West, Russian military activities in Armenia have increased steadily, including periodic exercises and checks of combat readiness of the Russian 102nd military base as well as frequent joint drills within the Collective Security Treaty Organization (CSTO)—of which Armenia is the South Caucasus region's sole member. Armenian analysts believe that Russia is using Armenia to demonstrate its military capability to NATO. One of the "sudden inspections" of combat readiness took place as the *#ElectricYerevan* protests were still going on and NATO was preparing a joint drill in Georgia. The deputy commander of the Southern Military District, Lieutenant-General

Igor Turchenyuk, personally inspected ground troops at Gyumri and warplanes and combat helicopters in Yerevan. The units were put on high alert and told to conduct unplanned exercises at two shooting ranges in central Armenia.[49]

Russia was clearly irritated by NATO's "Agile Spirit 2015" drill, conducted at the Georgian Vaziani base with the participation of Georgia, the US, Bulgaria, Lithuania, Romania, and Latvia. The exercise was a part of the "Substantial Package" framework offered to Tbilisi during the Wales Summit in 2014 in order to advance Georgia's preparations toward membership in the Alliance.[50]

In November 2015, President Vladimir Putin instructed his government to sign an agreement with Armenia on the creation of a joint regional missile defense system in the Caucasus.[51] The defense ministers of the two countries signed the agreement in Moscow a month later. Russia and Armenia already have a joint integrated air defense system that was given a "regional" status by the CSTO in 2007. It was not immediately clear how the new regional system would differ from the old one and whether it would operate within the framework of the CSTO. Russia is building similar systems with Belarus and Kazakhstan and planning to sign agreements with Kyrgyzstan and Tajikistan.[52]

Armenia also cooperates with NATO, including sending a small contingent to the ISAF mission in Afghanistan. Yerevan has signed an Individual Partnership Action Plan (IPAP) with NATO and has completed a Strategic Defense Review in 2011.[53] However, close defense ties with Russia are impeding more substantial involvement with NATO and preventing Armenia from seeking sources of security elsewhere.

On the economic and energy fronts, by joining the Customs Union under Kremlin pressure, Yerevan surrendered its hopes for economic independence from Russia. As political analyst Vladimir Socor noted, the model of operation of the Russian-led Customs Union (which became the Eurasian Economic Union in 2015) replicates that of the defunct Comecon and Warsaw Pact, as well as that of the existing CSTO. By placing itself in a privileged position, Russia is conducting "vertical" relations with each member state, while the other members are not engaged in "horizontal" relations with each other.[54] Such a model limits the economic opportunities for EEU member states, except for Russia, and distinctly separates the EEU from the principles and structure of the EU, regardless of how much Russian President Vladimir Putin tries to promote it as an equal counterpart to the European Union.

Armenia's president defended his decision to join the Eurasian Economic Union as pragmatic, since Russia sells natural gas to landlocked, energy-poor Armenia "at quite a good price." In addition, Armenia exports to the CIS one-third of its production, including agricultural products, on which the rural areas depend. [55] However, official statistics indicate that trade with the EU has been surpassing not only trade with the four other EEU members (Russia, Kazakhstan, Belarus, Kyrgyzstan) but also with all CIS countries—and this has been the case since 1999.[56] Exports to the EU in 2014 were over $437.4 million, while those to CIS countries—$365.5 million. In 2015, the EU continued to be Armenia's biggest export and import market, with a respective 39.4% and 26.5% share of total Armenian exports and imports.[57]

During his visit to Yerevan on December 2, 2013, Russian President Vladimir Putin dispersed a number of gifts to Armenia and obtained in return more assets and contracts that further cemented Russia's dominant position in the country's economy. They included reducing natural gas prices to $189 per thousand cubic meters (at the time Russia was selling gas to Eastern Europe for over $500); abolishing the export tax on oil and petroleum products by 30–35% as a good will gesture to Armenia; modernizing the country's Metsamor Nuclear Power Plant; upgrading Armenia's railroads, which are under Russian concession and trust management for 30 years; and opening the Hrazdan Thermal Power Plant, in which Russian Inter RAO invested $300 million.[58]

In return, *Gazprom* increased ownership in the *ArmRosGaz* supply and distribution company to 100%, with the Armenian government losing its last 20% stake in the formally joint company. *Rosatom* and *Russian Railways* state companies received lucrative contracts for big reconstruction and modernization projects. Moscow also ensured that it would remain Armenia's largest trade partner and biggest investor.

As a result, Armenia's energy sector is now almost entirely controlled by Russia. Russian state-controlled Inter RAO UES owns the country's electricity network, and *Gazprom* has a monopoly over Armenia's natural gas network for the next thirty years, according to the deal signed in 2013. But Moscow did not stop here. In June 2015, *Gazprom* also purchased the pipeline supplying natural gas from Iran—Armenia's only alternative gas supplier—giving Moscow full control of the natural gas delivery routes to Armenia. [59] In a subsequent development, in August 2015, *Gazprom Armenia* was given the rights to operate the high-voltage transmission lines, which are under construction and will be used for export of electricity to Iran and Georgia in the future.[60]

On a positive note, in addition to starting new negotiations with the EU on an Association Agreement, which will not include trade clauses since Armenia joined the EEU, Yerevan managed to conclude a Trade and Investment Framework Agreement (TIFA) with Washington, in May 2015. The agreement is expected to provide favorable conditions for investments and trade between the two countries. In October 2015, the American *Contour Global* Company acquired the *Vorotan* hydropower complex, registering one of the largest single investments in Armenia. The American company will invest $50 million in *Vorotan* Hydro Cascade during the next five years.[61]

Armenia's dependency on Russia does not exempt the country from Moscow's "soft power" tactics of penetrating its educational institutions, cultural environment, non-governmental sector, or politics. Organizations such as RosSotrudnichestvo (Russian Partnership) under the auspices of the Russian Ministry of Foreign Affairs, the Russian International Affairs Council (RIAC), the Public Diplomacy Fund Gorchakov, the Russian World Foundation, and others are particularly active in Armenia, as they are in the rest of the South Caucasus. They promote the Russian language and culture, sponsor conferences and seminars, and uphold a positive image of Russia abroad.

The Armenian Institute for Strategic Development, headed by Andranik Nikoghosyan, has launched since 2012 over 100 centers of Russian language and culture in Armenia, where more than 300 Russian-language teachers provide free-of-charge instruction. The Union of Russian Armenians, led by Ara Abrahamyan, organizes Russian cultural events throughout the country. More significantly, Abrahamyan apparently is not limited to cultural activities only—he plans to establish a political party and run for parliament in 2017.[62]

In addition, Moscow is active in establishing branches of its universities in Armenia. In 2015, a branch of the Moscow State University was opened in Yerevan, despite the fact that the Russian-Armenian Slavonic University and branches of seven other Russian universities with 3,500 students are already operating in the country.[63]

Armenian analysts observe a noticeable increase in public diplomacy activities as well—from visits of Russian governors to individual political and cultural figures—apparently tasked to strengthen Russian-Armenian ties within the political elites and civil society. Similar efforts are undertaken to promote the Eurasian Economic Union through the Eurasian Information League, Russian Partnership, and Russian World Foundation. They work to raise public support for the EEU and promote "Eurasian values," while also preaching anti-liberalism, anti-globalism, and anti-Western sentiments, and try to evoke nostalgia for the Soviet Union.

Armenia is also not exempt from the global informational war waged by the Kremlin, with a number of Russian digital TV channels broadcasting in the country. In addition, individuals connected to the Kremlin have established numerous websites, bombarding the local public with Russian propaganda. They serve to promote a positive image of Russia and the EEU, spread anti-Western attitudes, as well as discredit Western-minded politicians and civil society activists.[64]

Moscow is evidently backing Russia-based loyalists and wealthy businessmen such Ara Abrahamyan, Ruben Vardanyan and Samvel Karapetyan to enter politics and serve as its proxies, in case Yerevan seeks to escape Russia's control and enhance its cooperation with the US, EU, Georgia, or Iran, and especially if President Sargsyan decides to undertake steps vis-à-vis Azerbaijan that are not sanctioned by the Kremlin. Armenian commentators see this change as the next stage of "strengthening" Armenian-Russian relations, a kind of reformatting or recalculating of Russia's presence in the country. In other words, Moscow wants to transition to a "mediated" presence in Armenia, shedding responsibility for economic problems and avoiding future waves of protests, while still controlling Yerevan.[65]

But this recalculation of policy has another purpose as well—managing the Nagorno-Karabakh conflict in a way that suits Moscow. The Kremlin needs the right conditions to achieve its long-pursued goal of dispatching Russian peacekeeping troops to Nagorno-Karabakh and making it a Russian-controlled territory, as it did in Abkhazia and South Ossetia in the 1990s. Russia was never able to send its own peacekeepers to Nagorno-Karabakh, as neither Armenia's nor Azerbaijan's governments allowed this to happen after the end of the war. Now Russia sees an opportunity to impose its military presence on what is legally Azerbaijani territory and, at the same time, cement its political positions in Yerevan, while presenting itself as an indispensable peacemaker, against the background of the Ukrainian debacle.

Moscow calculates that the only way to obtain Baku's consent to Russian peacekeeping forces is by convincing Armenia to return the seven occupied regions to Azerbaijan as the first condition, and promise to start talks on a certain level of autonomy for Nagorno-Karabakh within Azerbaijan. Yerevan claims it cannot protect Nagorno-Karabakh without the seven surrounding regions, if it is returned to Azerbaijan.

The three Russian-made Armenian tycoons, Abrahamyan, Vardanyan, and Karapetyan, are said to have significant interests in Nagorno-Karabakh, where they are implementing large-scale projects. They would gladly support the deployment of Russian troops to Nagorno-Karabakh to protect their investments, if the seven surrounding regions are indeed returned to Azerbaijan. As Putin's loyalists, they are expected to lobby Yerevan for Moscow's interests and push the government to agree to Kremlin plans.[66]

However, as the "frozen" conflict has ignited several times since 2014, all sides are concerned that it could accidentally turn into a full-scale war. Armenian sources claim that Moscow has been trying to incite intensified clashes along the line of contact since the war in Ukraine began in 2014, in order to justify the deployment of a Russian peacekeeping mission.[67] The Azerbaijani press also reported that Russia is interested in increased tensions at the contact line between Armenian and Azerbaijani troops in order to divert attention away from Ukraine and undertake the leading role in conflict mediation. Since Germany expressed a desire in January 2015 to be more active in the negotiation process and even become an OSCE Minsk Group co-chair, Moscow has been trying to highlight its own importance and political weight and show that it is not realistic for the conflict to be resolved without its help.[68]

Azerbaijan

The unresolved conflict in Nagorno-Karabakh has been front and center of Azerbaijan's foreign and security policy as well as the reason for its staggering military spending. Armenia's defense budget is just of fraction of what Azerbaijan has been spending on arms in the past ten years—Azerbaijan's 2014 military budget was $3.8 billion, up from $3.6 billion in 2013; in comparison, Armenia's 2013 defense budget was $447 million.[69] This pushes Yerevan to take more loans from Moscow for military supplies in order to maintain the arms balance between the two hostile countries, and consequently makes Armenia more dependent on Russia.

Since 2010, Azerbaijan's defense budget has equaled 4.7–4.8% of its GDP, reaching a number that is higher than Armenia's annual state budget of $2.9 billion in 2015. However, Armenia's military spending has also remained high at around 4% of GDP.[70] The Global Militarization Index places Armenia and Azerbaijan among the ten most militarized countries in the world (third and eighth positions, respectively), concluding that it is a sign of a protracted arms race in the South Caucasus. Against the background of the ongoing Nagorno-Karabakh conflict, both countries are still investing their resources to an inordinate degree in expanding and modernizing their armed forces, while health expenditures remains at relatively modest levels.[71]

Azerbaijani officials say that the most important task facing the country's foreign policy is to settle the Nagorno-Karabakh conflict and end the Armenian occupation of around 20 percent of Azerbaijani territory in order to ensure the sovereignty of Azerbaijani territory within the internationally recognized borders.[72] However, the conflict has intensified since August 2014, despite international diplomatic efforts to negotiate a solution. Baku said that in 2015 alone, 143 Armenian servicemen were killed and over 100 were wounded, while 19 Azerbaijani servicemen were killed in skirmishes with

Armenians. During that year, the air defense troops of the Azerbaijani air forces were reported to have hit and destroyed 11 Armenian drones by precise strikes.[73]

Since the early 1990s, Azerbaijan has maintained a multi-vector foreign policy, with emphasis on developing strong ties with the United States and Europe, hoping that the West would help resolve the Nagorno-Karabakh conflict with Armenia. Located between an expansionist Russia and an assertive Iran, and locked in disputes with Armenia, Azerbaijan needs Western allies as a counterbalance and security guarantee. This is the reasoning behind Baku's Western-oriented energy export strategy and cooperation with the EU and NATO, including serving as a logistic center for the transit of cargo to Afghanistan. To that end, Azerbaijan's western neighbor Turkey, a member of NATO and close in terms of language and culture, has been its most valuable strategic partner.

However, Baku's relations with Washington and Brussels, which were already strained because of Azerbaijan's human rights record, rapidly deteriorated during 2015 due to the imprisonment of several activists and journalists by the authorities in Baku. These developments led to a delay in negotiating an agreement on a strategic partnership between Azerbaijan and the EU, after the European Parliament passed a motion criticizing Baku for human rights violations.[74]

The proposed Strategic Modernization Partnership agreement between Baku and Brussels will be significant from a geopolitical and geostrategic standpoint, as Azerbaijan's role as an energy supplier grows in Europe.[75] Relations with Washington were damaged to the extent that the Helsinki Commission Chairman Congressman Chris Smith proposed legislation that would deny US visas to senior members of the Azerbaijani government and their associates and potentially impose financial sanctions on them.[76] These developments and Baku's cautious approach to Moscow have placed Azerbaijan involuntarily closer to Russia, which has become more assertive after the annexation of Crimea. As a former high-ranking Azerbaijani diplomat pointed out, "Azerbaijan feels quite lonely, not supported much by the West or even by its neighbors."[77]

Although Baku has not publically stated its choice to definitely align itself with either the EU or Russia, an alliance with Russia within the EEU is highly unlikely as Azerbaijan's main concern is preserving its independence and controlling its foreign and economic policies.[78] When Russia and the West clashed over Ukraine, Azerbaijan was able to tone down its European ambitions in order not to irritate Russia, but it was faced with a stark choice between standing with its strategic partner Turkey or pacifying Russia when the two countries clashed over the downed Russian plane. Azerbaijan depends on Turkey for its European energy projects as well as on Ankara's support for its territorial integrity in the Nagorno-Karabakh conflict.

Baku's relations with Moscow have been a balancing act, with intricacies that are often difficult to understand from the outside. On the one hand, Azerbaijan is the only country in the South Caucasus that successfully rid itself of Russia's military presence and closed down all Russian military bases on its territory remaining after the unraveling of the Soviet Union. On the other hand, Baku is among the top buyers of Russian arms and military equipment, with military cooperation worth $4 billion and growing.[79] Trade relations amounted to $4 billion in 2014, although this number declined by over 23% in 2015, due to economic difficulties caused by low oil prices.[80]

However, the two countries have differences on several critical matters, first and foremost regarding Russia's military cooperation with Armenia and its evident reluctance to resolve the Nagorno-Karabakh conflict. Other differences appeared after the Russia-Georgia war, as Moscow's aggression against an independent neighboring state shocked the Azerbaijani public and changed the perception of Russia from that of a pragmatic economic partner to one of an aggressor. The war generated new sources of instability, which, together with the unresolved conflict in Nagorno-Karabakh and the significant new leverage by Moscow in the region, would have long-lasting negative implications for the integration of Azerbaijan and Georgia into Euro-Atlantic institutions.

Azerbaijan, similarly to other former Soviet states, has had to reevaluate its foreign policy. Baku became more cautious with its ambitions for membership in either NATO or the EU. As Azerbaijani political scientist Anar Valiyev wrote, "Some might describe Azerbaijan's policy as a kind of Finlandization, akin to the Finnish pursuit of neutrality after World War Two in the face of a hostile Soviet Union."[81]

Although Azerbaijan contributes to NATO projects and works on making its army compatible with NATO standards, it has expressed a more reserved approach to becoming a member of the Alliance. In May 2011, soon after Russia's invasion of Georgia, Baku officially joined the Non-Aligned Movement (NAM), binding itself to the goal of non-participation in any military blocs.

Russia was particularly concerned with the South Caucasus countries' pending Association Agreement (AA) and Deep and Comprehensive Free Trade Area (DCFTA) deals with the EU at the close of 2013. At that time, Moscow was enlisting prospective members for its own creation, the Eurasian Economic Union. Armenia and Georgia were ready to initial agreements at the EU Vilnius Summit in November 2013, while Azerbaijan was making progress in negotiations for an Association Agreement with the EU, with the prospect to start negotiations on a DCFTA, following its accession to the World Trade Organization (WTO).[82]

In August 2013, just three months before the EU Vilnius Summit, President Putin made an ostentatious visit to Baku, which included the presence of ships from Russia's Caspian Sea Flotilla. The high level of the delegation suggested the importance of this diplomatic effort to boost Moscow's influence after strains in the relationship with Baku over the Gabala radar station the previous year. Putin brought to Baku his Foreign Minister Sergei Lavrov, Defense Minister Sergei Shoigu, and Energy Minister Alexander Novak, as well as the heads of *Rosneft* and *Lukoil,* Igor Sechin and Vagit Alekperov. He hailed Azerbaijan as "one of Russia's long-standing, traditional and loyal partners" and as Russia's "strategic partner"—although Baku is reluctant to proclaim this relationship as strategic until the Nagorno-Karabakh conflict is resolved.[83]

Presidents Aliyev and Putin signed a substantive agreement on military cooperation, allowing for the transfer of Russian weapons and hardware worth $4 billion, providing technical assistance to modernize Azerbaijan's defense industry facilities, and permitting Russian defense industry companies to repair and upgrade Azerbaijani military hardware and weapons. Azerbaijani military expert Casur Sumarinli warned that the agreement could create serious threats to Azerbaijan's national security interests. "Azerbaijan will, in effect, have to halt its already weak cooperation with NATO. This will mean for Azerbaijan the loss of independent state policies, and military and political priorities," Sumarinli told the opposition *Yeni Musafat* newspaper in Baku.[84]

Moscow's demonstration of support for Azerbaijan and particularly the expansion of arms sales to Baku was not only aimed to lure the South Caucasus republic into Russia's camp and discourage it from pursuing cooperation with NATO and the EU association, it was also supposed to serve as a warning to Yerevan, which had pursued its own integration with the EU during the previous three years. In this respect, although Putin was unable to secure an energy deal that would place *Rosneft* and *Lukoil* in a competitive position vis-à-vis Western companies such as BP, Statoil and Exxon Mobil in Azerbaijan, the visit delivered the targeted result. Three weeks later, Armenian President Sargsyan caved in and suspended his country's

EU integration plans by declaring that Armenia would be joining the Russian-dominated Customs Union instead.

The annexation of Crimea revealed that Russia would continue its expansionist agenda toward the former Soviet states and raised new fears in Baku. Rejecting separatism and the revision of national borders by an occupying power, Azerbaijan, similarly to Georgia and Moldova, declined to recognize the referendum in Crimea organized by Russia's special forces. Azerbaijani President Ilam Aliyev stated that, "a country's territorial integrity cannot be changed without its agreement." A week later, Azerbaijani representative Tofig Musayev voted in favor of the UN resolution affirming Baku's commitment to Ukraine's sovereignty, political independence, unity and territorial integrity within its internationally recognized borders and rejecting the validity of the referendum held in Crimea on March 16, 2014. He reiterated Azerbaijan's adherence to the fundamental principles of sovereignty, territorial integrity and inviolability of internationally recognized borders, saying they constituted the basic foundation of international relations and the international legal order.[85]

Two weeks later, Russian Prime Minister Dmitry Medvedev appointed Dmitry Rogozin, deputy prime minister for the defense and space industry and a former Russian ambassador to NATO, as chairman of the Russian part of the inter-governmental commission on economic cooperation with Azerbaijan. As a member of Putin's inner circle, Rogozin was included on the US sanctions list on March 17, 2014, following the controversial referendum in Crimea that served as a pretext for Russian annexation. The new Russian envoy's high-level government position was interpreted as a warning to both Azerbaijan and the West as tensions in eastern Ukraine continued.[86]

The appointment was also a reminder that military cooperation is a key element of Russian-Azerbaijani relations. In the period 2010—2014, Azerbaijan has imported about $3.35 billion in arms, of which 80% has come from Russia, including two S-300 missile systems, 94

T-90S tanks, 20 Mi-35M helicopters, and 100 BMP-3 armored vehicles. In addition, Azerbaijan has purchased 25 Su-25 planes and 93 T-72M1 tanks from Belarus.[87] The purchase of Russian weapons is mainly a tactical tool for Baku, which aims to stay on Russia's good side while keeping Armenia worried about its military power.

The annexation of Crimea prompted NATO to strengthen ties with partners in Central-Eastern Europe and the South Caucasus. On April 1, 2014, NATO's Ministerial Council decided to increase cooperation with and expand its presence in Armenia, Azerbaijan and Moldova. The enhanced cooperation, taking place within the framework of existing partnerships, outlines several areas related to the changing security environment in Ukraine and Afghanistan: security, energy security, terrorism, and information technologies. As the conflict in Ukraine and Western sanctions against Russia threaten both Europe's energy supplies from Russia via Ukraine and NATO's transportation routes to Afghanistan via Russia, Azerbaijan's cooperation with NATO is important in light of the withdrawal of troops from Afghanistan, according to Sorin Ducaru, Assistant Secretary General for Emerging Security Challenges.[88]

Despite active collaboration with NATO within the Partnership for Peace program and recent plans to expand it, the mood in Baku remained pessimistic about possible protection by the West in case of Russian intervention in the region. The experience from the Russia-Georgia war in August 2008, and the muted Western reaction to Russia's invasion of Crimea in March 2014, indicated that the South Caucasus countries might not be able to depend on help from the outside. Russia is treating the South Caucasus as a military polygon, with about 5,000 Russian troops stationed at its Gyumri base in Armenia, thousands of occupation troops and border guards in Abkhazia and South Ossetia, and a substantial military presence in the Caspian Sea, in addition to Russia's domestic contingent in the North Caucasus.

President Obama's remarks in Brussels, on March 26, 2014, that neither Ukraine nor Georgia were currently on the path to NATO membership and there were no immediate plans for expansion resonated negatively not only in Georgia, but also in Baku, although Azerbaijan does not have plans to join the Alliance and has maintained a balanced relationship with Russia and the West. Nevertheless, Baku is concerned about the unresolved conflict with Armenia over Nagorno-Karabakh and the threat of deterioration if Russia attempts to destabilize Azerbaijan.

President Ilham Aliyev has pointed out that the West is applying double standards when reacting to the occupation of Crimea: it has enforced sanctions against Moscow, but has never considered sanctions against Armenia for the occupation of Nagorno-Karabakh and seven other Azerbaijani districts. His voice was joined by the Conservative member of the British parliament David Davies, who said in a statement that "despite global recognition, Azerbaijan's position in Nagorno-Karabakh is not supported enough by the Western states."[89] The statement also reflected the fact that the British company BP is the largest investor in Azerbaijan and has much to lose in case of a resumption of the conflict.

Azerbaijan is strategically important for European energy security as a nearby supplier of oil and prospective supplier of natural gas through Georgia and Turkey to Southern Europe. Azerbaijan became the first Caspian littoral state to export oil to European markets via the Baku–Tbilisi–Ceyhan oil pipeline. Its State Oil Company (SOCAR) is currently expanding the natural gas corridor from the Caspian Sea through Georgia to Turkey and building the Trans-Anatolian natural gas pipeline (TANAP), which will connect with the prospective Trans-Adriatic pipeline (TAP) on EU territory. When deliveries of Azerbaijani gas start, in early 2019, this will be the first Caspian gas reaching European markets. Although the quantities will be relatively small—from 10 billion cubic meters (bcm) a year at the beginning, to 31 bcm later—they will be an important diversification factor on the European market, which currently depends on Russia for up to 25 percent of its gas consumption.

Baku is also working with the government in Ashgabat to ensure a transfer to Europe of much larger quantities of natural gas from Turkmenistan—at least 40 bcm a year. "The Azerbaijani side is always ready to offer its transit opportunities in the case of implementation of the Trans-Caspian gas pipeline project," claimed SOCAR's President Rovnag Abdullayev.[90] Turkmenistan and the EU have been negotiating the Trans-Caspian gas pipeline project—a 300-kilometer (186-mile) pipeline along the Caspian Sea bed from Turkmenistan to Azerbaijan—but Russia objects to the initiative as it will fully bypass Russian territory.

Soon after the annexation of Crimea, former presidential foreign policy adviser Vafa Guluzade claimed that Russian military representatives demanded that Azerbaijan stop its cooperation with NATO. "They warn Azerbaijan that if gas and communication grids are directed to the West and if it [Azerbaijan] cooperates with NATO, then there may be a threat to our country," Guluzade said. He added that NATO must provide guarantees for Azerbaijan's security if it wishes to cooperate with Baku. He also advocated closer military ties with Turkey, such as signing a military agreement between Ankara and Baku and creating a Turkish military base in the country.[91]

After the annexation of Crimea, and particularly when the war in eastern Ukraine erupted, Baku focused on limiting Russian attempts to place pressure on Azerbaijan by avoiding any actions that would irritate Moscow. It was a decision made out of necessity and consideration of the geopolitical realities. Squeezed between Russia and Iran, with 2,000 km of coastline in the Caspian open to Russian aggression and almost 20% of its territory occupied by Armenia, Azerbaijan had to remain careful, despite its economic independence.[92]

Russia's maximum objective for the countries in its southern flank is: 1) for them to join the Collective Security Treaty Organization and 2) the Eurasian Economic Union; 3) the establishment of Russian military bases; and 4) the protection of the rights of Russian minorities, including promotion of the Russian language and culture. At a minimum, Moscow aims to prevent each country from joining NATO, develop extensive trade relations, as well as collaborate in counter-terrorism and various forms of military cooperation.[93]

While Kremlin's optimum plan is in place in Belarus, Armenia, Kazakhstan, and Kyrgyzstan, Azerbaijan is trying to fit into Russia's minimum plan. Baku refused to join the CSTO because Armenia is a member, but it also gave up potential NATO membership by joining the Non-Aligned Movement in 2011—a decision provoked mainly by the 2008 Russia-Georgia war, as Georgia's NATO inspirations were blamed for Moscow's invasion.

At the same time, Azerbaijan skillfully forced Russia to close down its last military installation in the country, the Gabala radar station, in 2012. Although Azerbaijan still depends on Moscow for military equipment and technology, importing 85% of military equipment from Russia, Baku is pursuing contracts for arms and military equipment with Turkey and Israel as well.[94] In 2012, Azerbaijan signed contracts valued at $1.6 billion to buy advanced weapons from Israel, such as drones as well as anti-aircraft and missile defense systems and also started joint production of drones in Baku.[95] In addition, Azerbaijan is planning to acquire new Mbombe six-wheel-drive armored fighting vehicles from Kazakhstan, built on the know-how of the South African Paramount Group.[96] However, Azerbaijan's defense budget, which was projected at $4.8 billion in 2015, is expected to dramatically decrease by 40% in 2016 as a result of low oil prices and the devaluation of the local currency, the manat.[97]

According to the 2009 census, there are about 120,000 ethnic Russians in Azerbaijan, or only 1.3% of the total population. Yet, Russian-language instruction has been preserved at all educational levels. Not only Russians and Russian-speakers can earn university degrees in Russian, but many ethnic Azerbaijanis also choose to receive instruction in Russian at domestic higher education institutions. Reportedly, around 9,000 students are currently enrolled in the "Russian sector" of Azerbaijani universities.[98] Having done the work to establish the Azerbaijani language as the official language of the country in early 1990s, including limiting Russian broadcasting to Azerbaijan, Baku is now willing to make cultural compromises to Russia. Such a gesture was the memorandum of understanding on establishing an Association of Universities of Azerbaijan and Russia, signed by the two countries' ministers of education in Baku, in November 2015.[99]

As Russia remains an important trade partner for Azerbaijan, Baku has developed its most significant trade partnership with the EU. Considering its options after Moscow's attack on Ukraine, and particularly after the EU Eastern Partnership Summit, in Riga, in May 2015, when Russia was openly hostile and the EU appeared unable to confront it, Azerbaijan decided not to pursue an Association Agreement or a DCFTA with Brussels. However, it also declined to join the Eurasian Economic Union. Azerbaijan's total non-oil exports amount to $1.6 billion, of which less than 30% goes to CIS countries. Baku believes that these trade agreements can de decided on a bilateral basis, which makes it unnecessary to join a collective structure such as the EEU.[100]

On the military front, while Baku continues military cooperation with Moscow, Russia's military presence in Azerbaijan ended in December 2012, when Baku demanded 40-times-higher lease payments from Moscow to host the Gabala radar station and Russia decided to close it instead. In 1993, Azerbaijan was the first former Soviet state to compel Russian troops to withdraw, except for the radar site. The Daryal-type radar station was built by the Soviet Union, in 1985, to monitor missile launches throughout the Middle East. Since 2002,

Russia had been paying Azerbaijan $7 million a year plus operational costs for the radar. But at the end of the ten-year contract, Baku reportedly demanded $300 million a year for rent and other costs to continue hosting the station. In addition, Baku insisted that the majority of the 1,500 service personnel at the radar station to be Azerbaijani (1,000 of them were Russian) and demanded assistance from Moscow to eliminate the environmental damage from the operation of the radar. Negotiations continued for over a year, until Moscow gave up and announced it was shutting down the station.[101]

Although the radar station was outdated and no longer had significant military value for Russia, it was politically critical for the Kremlin to maintain some kind of military presence on Azerbaijani territory. Compared to the Russian military bases in Armenia and the occupied Georgian territories of Abkhazia and South Ossetia, Azerbaijan is currently the only country in the South Caucasus where Russian soldiers are not present. In addition, Gabala served as an instrument for Russia in negotiating with other key players, such as the US and Iran. In 2007, President Putin offered US President Obama to jointly use the Gabala radar station as part of the planned US missile defense system, instead of basing components in Poland and the Czech Republic.[102]

Some analysts argued that by kicking out the remaining Russian military presence, Azerbaijan also lost a tool to pressure the Kremlin for resolution of the Nagorno-Karabakh conflict.[103] Others asserted that it has been actually the other way around—Moscow hasd been using the conflict in Nagorno-Karabakh in negotiations with Baku as leverage to extract concessions and receive beneficial contractual terms.[104]

The Gabala case was indicative of Azerbaijan's ability to stand its ground with Russia and achieve its goals—on this occasion denying Moscow military presence in the country. After the annexation of Crimea and the war in Ukraine, however, Baku seems less willing to oppose Russia. For its part, Russia appears more determined to reverse its loss and is reportedly planning to build another military base in Azerbaijan—this time a Voronezh-DM early warning radar station. Russia's Ministry of Defense broadcast channel, *Zvezda-TV*, reported on August 18, 2015, that the construction of the Voronezh-DM radar will start at Azerbaijan's Gabala military complex in 2017 and will be completed during 2019. The new radar station was to be fully under Russian control.[105]

The Azerbaijani opposition was unhappy with the news, but also noted the lack of immediate response from the government in Baku, while the Armenian Speaker of Parliament speculated that a Russian military base in Azerbaijan is likely to be a missile-tracking radar station serving solely Russian interests, not those of the Azerbaijani Armed Forces.[106] However, Moscow is hardly in a position to spare billions of dollars on another radar installation, given its financial difficulties since oil prices began their sharp descent in 2014. This rumor seems to be part of the Russian disinformation machine, following the announcement of Azerbaijan's defense ministry in July that it is ready to continue military cooperation with the Pentagon and NATO and fully restore confidence between the two countries' defense agencies after a period of cold relations. The message was delivered to the US defense attaché by the highest-ranking military commander, the Army Chief of Staff Colonell General Najmaddin Sadikov.[107]

In the Caspian Sea, Russia's joint naval exercises with Iran in August and October 2015 demonstrated a blatant disregard for the other three Caspian littoral states of Azerbaijan, Kazakhstan and Turkmenistan. Moscow not only excludes them from such joint exercises, but it even fails to consult with them when war ships of the two countries cross the Caspian Sea. Apparently, Russia has decided to divide control over the Caspian Sea with Iran, similarly to the division during Soviet times.[108]

This time, however, Russia's contempt for its neighbors backfired. Irritated by the launching of cruise missiles from Russia's squadron in the Caspian Sea against targets in Syria, and determined to develop their own naval forces, Azerbaijan and Kazakhstan concluded, on November 4, 2015, a bilateral defense cooperation agreement focused on joint naval exercises. This agreement clearly outlined the current divisions in the Caspian basin—with Russia and Iran pursuing their agenda in the Middle East, and the rest of the littoral states increasingly trying to avoid the risks of such cooperation. The rift between these two groups became even clearer when Turkey shot down a Russian jet on November 24, 2015, after which, Azerbaijan, Kazakhstan and Turkmenistan have continued to maintain strong relations with Turkey.[109]

At the same time, Moscow opposes its Caspian neighbors' joint initiatives, such as the proposed Trans-Caspian gas pipeline between Turkmenistan and Azerbaijan to be built under the Caspian Sea. The Russian foreign ministry views the energy project as a foreign intervention in the Caspian Sea, recalling the five littoral states' decision to bar foreign militaries from the Caspian. By equating foreign military presence with energy projects involving foreign companies, Moscow clearly shows its uneasiness with any foreign presence in its backyard.[110]

Georgia

Georgia's "Rose Revolution" in 2003 was the first in a series of public upheavals in the former Soviet Union that led to a regime change in several post-Soviet countries, including Ukraine in 2004 and Kyrgyzstan in 2005. As the pro-Western government of President Mikheil Saakashvili took power in 2003, Moscow became worried about the possibility of losing influence in its southern neighborhood. The new government's determination to bring Georgia closer to the EU and join NATO, develop a robust relationship with Washington, eliminate corruption, and conduct swift reforms, especially in the security forces, meant that Russia would lose its dominant position in the country. That position had been nurtured for years through its energy monopoly, economic supremacy, trade relations, and military presence in the form of "peacekeeping" forces in Abkhazia and South Ossetia, along with four military bases, some of which were only closed down in 2007.

Although Moscow's priority has been to influence the military-strategic sphere in the region, it often used economic means and other instruments of pressure to coerce Tbilisi to change its pro-Western direction. For example, in 2007, Russia started expelling Georgian labor migrants from Russia, causing many families to lose their income from remittances. A year earlier, Moscow instituted a trade embargo against Georgia, closing the Russian market to Georgian wines, the country's most exported commodity, and inflicting losses not only on agricultural workers and wine-makers, but also on the state budget. At the time, Georgia was sending as much as 89% of its wine exports to Russia.[111] This measure, however, failed to undermine Saakashvili's government: Tbilisi re-oriented its exports to Europe and, with the help of the EU, managed to not only overcome the hardship, but also gain positions in the lucrative Western market. As a result, Moscow's policies only reinforced Georgia's pro-Western aspirations.

However, Russia was determined to put an end to Georgia's Western aspirations, particularly its application for a NATO membership. In his last speech before the United Nation's General Assembly on September 26, 2013, President Saakashvili stated that: "The Georgian experience of successful reforms and the creation of a functioning state was therefore considered to be a virus—a virus that could and would contaminate the whole post-Soviet region; we became the least corrupt country in Europe, the world's number one reformer according to the World Bank, one of the top places to do business; the least criminalized country in Europe after being one of the most criminalized ones; and that was the virus that should have been eliminated, by every means possible. This is why the Georgian nation has suffered an embargo, a war, an invasion, and an occupation—all since 2006."[112]

In August 2008, as Georgia was advancing its EU and NATO agenda, Russia invaded Georgia and established a substantial military presence in Abkhazia and South Ossetia, deploying two army brigades at new military bases in those separatist regions. As of early 2015, Russia had 7,000 troops on Georgian territory based at Gudauta in Abkhazia and Djava-Tskhinvali in South Ossetia. [113] Moscow recognized the two Georgian regions as independent states, while only Russia, Venezuela, Nicaragua and few Pacific Island nations have established diplomatic relations with the two entities.

In the early 1990s, Russia had lent support and armed all sides in the secessionist conflicts, the Georgian government and the breakaway regions, thus fueling a civil war that resulted in hundreds of thousands of deaths, brutal atrocities, ethnic cleansing, and prolonged political and economic crises. Following the wars, Moscow established a peacekeeping presence in the two provinces and prevented international organizations from effectively conducting peacekeeping activities in the regions. The UN had a small monitoring mission and the OSCE's functions were essentially taken over by Russian peacekeepers. In reality, Russia's peacekeepers served their government, which was entrenching itself deeper into the political and economic life of Abkhazia and South Ossetia, pulling the regions further away from Georgia and even giving Russian passports to as many as 80 percent of their residents.[114]

After the August 2008 war with Georgia, Russia blocked the ability of the OSCE to function in South Ossetia and other parts of Georgia. Using the consensus principle of the organization, Moscow blocked OSCE deployments, holding the organization hostage to its determination to gain international recognition for the independence of Abkhazia and South Ossetia.[115] The OSCE had to leave when its previous mandate expired on December 31, 2008 The model was repeated with regard to the UN mission in Abkhazia six months later.[116] Thus, taking advantage of the democratic principles on which two of the largest international organizations are based, Moscow has essentially evicted them from Georgia's conflict zones and prevented the internationalization of the conflict.[117]

In addition to the two Russian military brigades based in Abkhazia and South Ossetia after 2008, Moscow dispatched Russian border troops along the administrative lines with Georgia and built trenches, fences and minefields—actions described by Tbilisi as "borderization" within Georgia. Units of Russia's Black Sea Fleet were also deployed to the port of Ochamchira in Abkhazia.

Since the annexation of Crimea, Russia has increased the process of integration of Abkhazia and South Ossetia into its economic, political and security system. Following the signing of a treaty with Abkhazia in November 2014, Russia signed a treaty on "alliance and integration" with South Ossetia in March 2015. A month earlier, it signed a border agreement with South Ossetia. These agreements have virtually frozen the normalization talks with Georgia. While the treaty with Abkhazia was not ratified a year after its signing, the parliament of South Ossetia approved the alliance and integration treaty with Russia in April 2015 and the ratification was signed by the Russian President on June 30, 2015.[118]

The treaty effectively transferred responsibility for South Ossetia's security and defense to the Russian Federation, including protection of its borders. South Ossetia's armed forces and security agencies became part of the Russian army and security services (FSB), respectively. The customs regime of South Ossetia is to be integrated with that of the Russian Federation through legislation of the Customs Union and the Russian Federation. This provision opened the way for integration with the Russian-led Eurasian Economic Union, a move

328 | EURASIAN DISUNION

that the Georgian government strongly opposed. In addition, the treaty stated that the procedure for obtaining Russian citizenship by South Ossetians would be simplified and the requirement for giving up the original citizenship was waved for them. Furthermore, South Ossetia will adopt Russian regulations on education, school curricula, educational qualifications and health insurance. In all areas subject to this agreement, Russian legislation will be effective on the territory of South Ossetia.[119]

Calls for unification with the Russian Federation have increased in South Ossetia, as it is becoming clear that Tskhinvali has failed to develop the basic attributes of an independent state. Local economists admit that the region has completed only 20–30% of necessary work to build a viable state, despite substantial Russian subsidies. There is no real program for strategic development or even a comprehensive analysis of the local economy. Also absent are fundamental documents such as a foreign policy strategy and a military doctrine. Pointing to these failures and the new geopolitical developments affecting the region, mainly Russia's involvement in Syria and the outreach of Islamist movements into the Caucasus, both local and Russian experts are advocating the unification of South Ossetia with Russia and possible merger with North Ossetia as its best defense strategy. They claim that Moscow would be far better positioned to defend South Ossetia if it were a part of the Russian Federation than if it remained outside its borders.[120]

Taking into account the demographic disaster facing South Ossetia, local political analyst Kosta Dzugaev warned in Tskhinvali in late 2015 that "our only way out is to join Russia. 'Russia or death'—that is our bitter reality." As US political analyst Paul Goble concludes, it seems that support for unification with South Ossetia is growing in Russia as well, since the Russian media dedicated a lengthy publication on the matter. Moreover, the local branch of the Russian Orthodox Church of the Moscow Patriarchate is openly serving as a major force pushing for unity. Its clergy are warning people of the dangers surrounding the region and thus helping to convince the South Ossetians that their only prospects for survival are within the borders of the Russian Federation.[121]

The leadership of South Ossetia has advocated formal incorporation into Russia since before the war in 2008. In fact, campaigns for joining the Republic of North Ossetia within the Russian Federation had mounted even before the dissolution of the Soviet Union. In October 2015, the President of South Ossetia Leonid Tibilov announced plans to hold a referendum on joining Russia.[122] He claimed that the result of such a referendum would be strongly in favor of inclusion in Russia. The announcement coincided with the visit of Vladislav Surkov, President Putin's adviser who reportedly played a critical role in coordinating the annexation of Crimea. However, Moscow's official reaction was far from enthusiastic. Kremlin spokesman Dmitry Peskov stressed that the holding of a referendum on joining Russia was not discussed at the meeting between Tibilov and Surkov in Tskhinvali.[123]

South Ossetia's leaders can undoubtedly see the benefits of accession to Russia: they not only want Moscow to guarantee the security of the breakaway region, but they also hope that the Kremlin will continue to subsidize the region. Pressured by low oil prices and international sanctions, the Kremlin has been reducing subsidies for breakaway regions outside of its territory, causing a series of protests in Transnistria and dissatisfaction in Abkhazia. Moreover, the potential annexation of South Ossetia would provoke a strong international reaction and could result in more sanctions against Moscow. As the Deputy chairman of the *Duma's* foreign affairs committee, Leonid Kalashnikov, commented, "The pros of accession to the Russian Federation are quite obvious for South Ossetia. But there are not so many [pros] for Russia; there are too many cons for Russia of a diplomatic and international nature."[124]

Despite Tskhinvali's frequent calls for joining Russia, Moscow is unlikely to endorse a referendum and accept the region as part of the Russian Federation. The benefits to Russia would be negligible, if any, compared to the financial cost and risk of further international ostracism. South Ossetia is important to Russia mostly as a method of destabilizing Georgia, and not as territory to be added to the Federation. It cannot offer the benefits of Crimea and Sevastopol, which brought a large section of the Black Sea, allowing Russia significant control over its navigation, economic zones and gas reserves in addition to the critical navy base at Sevastopol and expanded military power over the Black Sea countries. In this respect, Abkhazia, which is located at a critical part of the Black Sea coast, could offer Russia more substantial benefits than South Ossetia, should it want to enter the Russian Federation. But the idea of such a union is politically toxic among the independence-minded Abkhaz.

More importantly, the Kremlin has no interest in resolving the conflict in South Ossetia by either annexing the territory or returning it to Georgia. In fact, South Ossetia's potential accession to Russia would deprive Moscow of a major instrument of influence vis-a-vis Georgia and the wider region. By holding part of Georgia occupied, Moscow maintains a level of instability and, at the same time, uses the conflict to create loyalties or instill fear. It manipulates the South Ossetians by neither confirming nor denying their potential accession into Russia, while hinting to Tbilisi that it may compromise on the two regions and eventually return them to Georgia. More often, it uses the conflicts to threaten Georgia with further aggression if the country pursues NATO membership.

With regard to Abkhazia, relations between Russia and Abkhazia deteriorated during 2015, after Moscow sharply reduced funding for the breakaway region. When the agreement with Sukhumi was signed in November 2014, President Putin promised that Moscow would allocate 5 billion rubles (approximately $111.5 million at the time) for the Abkhaz government in 2015. Putin also said that Russia had long-term plans for Abkhazia that would be backed with generous funding. He claimed that Moscow planned a new "investment program" for the period 2015–2017, with annual funding of over 4 billion rubles (about $89.2 million). The Russian President thereby promised that funding would double to 9.2–9.3 billion rubles (about $205–207 million).[125]

But the promises soon evaporated as Russian oil sales declined in monetary value, reducing the Federation's budget dramatically. The decrease for Abkhazia involved a dramatic 28-fold drop in subsidies. Instead of the promised 3.7 billion rubles ($56 million), Sukhumi was to receive 127 million rubles (approximately $2 million). Reportedly, Russia has effectively ceased financing joint social and economic programs in Abkhazia.[126] The Abkhazian authorities were planning to use the promised subsidy of $56 million to repay the credits they obtained from Russia in 2010 for the reconstruction of the railroad— the same railroad used by Russian troops deploying into Georgia in August 2008. Sukhumi needs this railroad to deliver trade goods to Russia.

The disappointment with Moscow is gradually transforming into anti-Russian sentiment. Although Russia has no available money to attract Abkhazia, it is also putting pressure on Sukhumi to ratify the strategic treaty signed in November 2014. Reportedly, the Abkhazian parliament refuses to ratify the treaty, because this would mean giving up Abkhazia's independence. The Russian *Duma* has already ratified the treaty in January 2015. Some members of Abkhazia's parliament are proposing to raise money for the budget by collecting rent from the Russian military base in Abkhazia.

On the energy front, Moscow's use of its energy monopoly as an instrument of political subversion prompted Georgia to restructure and develop its energy sector, allowing the country to become almost self-sufficient in electricity production, mostly from hydropower. Tbilisi also diversified oil supplies and switched gas deliveries from Russia to Azerbaijan as the east-west gas corridor started shaping up.

The Kremlin, however, has not ceased its attempts to acquire energy assets in Georgia in the oil, natural gas and electricity sectors. In fact, the Russian state-controlled company Inter RAO manages or owns almost half of Georgia's electricity generation plants, has a 50% share in the critical high-voltage transmission line used for exports, and holds a significant interest in Georgia's electricity distribution.[127]

Georgia's past dependence on Russian oil and gas supplies had made it vulnerable to political blackmail by the Kremlin. Capitalizing on its energy monopoly, Russia was employing tools such as gas price manipulation and supply interruption, particularly after the November 2003 "Rose Revolution," in order to pressure Saakashvili's pro-Western government. In January 2006, for example, after a dramatic gas price spike, three unexplained simultaneous explosions damaged both tubes of a gas pipeline on Russian territory near the border with Georgia and destroyed an electrical pylon, interrupting gas deliveries for days during a particularly cold winter. President Saakashvili called the blasts "outrageous blackmail" and "a serious act of sabotage on the part of Russia on Georgia's energy system."[128]

By the time of the pipeline explosions, Georgia had seen Russian gas prices increase by almost 500%, from $50 to $235 per thousand cubic meters. While Russia portrayed this enormous increase as designed to bring the price paid by Georgia closer to world market prices, it was clear that Georgia was being punished for being a pro-Western state, while the "friendly states" of Belarus and Armenia were treated to a much lower gas price. The purpose was to undermine the Saakashvili government by forcing it to raise gas prices for domestic consumers. This would have also affected consumer prices for all goods and caused public unrest, or placed enormous pressure on the state budget to subsidize gas prices. Fearing public protests, Tbilisi paid out $300 million to *Gazprom*, which amounted to about 10% of the state budget.[129]

The argument that Russia used gas price hikes to sanction Georgia, in the same way it punished Ukraine and Moldova later, is true in all three cases. However, one would not understand the complexity of Moscow's utilization of gas price increases as an instrument of subversion unless one compares this to similar cases in other states, some of them friendly toward Russia. For example, countries such as Bulgaria and Macedonia have been paying the highest prices to *Gazprom*, regardless of traditionally cordial relations with Russia. The reason is that Moscow uses gas prices not only to punish or reward, but also to demonstrate its might, underline how much a country depends on Russian energy resources, and portray itself as an indispensable supplier and partner.

By projecting power, Moscow aims to extract various concessions: a refinery purchase, a new international pipeline agreement, a hydropower plant acquisition, controlling stakes in electricity networks or major infrastructure. In the end, even friendly governments end up paying high prices for Russian gas and giving away major infrastructure deals without competitive bidding. Furthermore, corrupt politics and mafia-type alliances with Russia's oligarchic structures help the Kremlin achieve its goal of subverting and controlling regions it has depicted as its "near-abroad" (Russia's flanks) as well as ones that it used to consider its "near abroad" before the end of the Cold War (Central- Eastern Europe).

Moscow's attempts to expand influence in Georgia's energy sector started before the "Rose Revolution," when Russian power monopoly United Energy System, through its international arm Inter RAO UES, took control of 75% of Tbilisi's electricity distribution company *Telasi* in the summer of 2003. Georgia's biggest gas-fired thermal power plant *Mtkvari* was also sold to Inter RAO in 2003.[130]

The pursuit of energy assets continued after Eduard Shevardnadze was ousted from power in November 2003. In addition to obtaining management rights of two hydro power plants—Khrami I and

Khrami II—Inter RAO also operates the Enguri-Vardnili hydropower cascade, which produces around 40% of Georgia's electricity. Located partially in Abkhazia, this massive hydro energy complex presents another energy security risk. Its water dam and reservoir are under the control of the central Georgian authorities but the turbines and generation equipment are located on Abkhazian territory, and *de facto* controlled by Russia.

The Enguri hydropower plant has become another target of Russian strategic interest. Russia allegedly intends to register Georgia's most powerful hydroelectric station in Abkhazia. In December 2014, Abkhazia's *de facto* leader Raul Khajimba claimed "what is located on our territory should be owned by the Abkhaz people." But since Abkhazia has secured quite favorable terms to receive 40% of the Enguri-produced electricity for free, under an informal agreement with Tbilisi, analysts believe that the question raised over the plant's ownership comes from Moscow rather than Sukhumi.[131]

Inter RAO UES has 50% ownership of the critical 500 kV transmission line running across Georgia from west to east, which is used for exports of electricity to Turkey. Although electricity transmission is a natural monopoly protected by many countries, Georgia has opened most of its energy assets to privatization, of which Russian companies have gained the most. But Czech, Lithuanian, Swiss, British, Azerbaijani, Kazakhstani and Turkish companies have also taken a smaller part in the privatization of Georgian energy assets. At the same time, critical infrastructure was built and repaired by the Georgian government through the support of donors or international financial institutions, rather than solely through foreign direct investments.[132]

The natural gas pipeline that connects Russia with Armenia through Georgian territory was one of the most desirable acquisitions for *Gazprom*, but the Georgian government dropped negotiations in 2006, under US advisement, as the White House supported the east-west energy corridor from the Caspian basin to Europe. US Special Envoy for Eurasian Energy, Steven Mann, stressed that privatization of the pipeline "would mean that our chance to assure independent and alternative energy resources would be lost." He also added that selling the pipeline "would impede gas development for the Shah Deniz project." Georgian politicians such as former economy minister Vladimer Papava, have also warned that "*Gazprom* is a state company and, therefore, if it purchases the pipeline, that would mean that a foreign state company has bought Georgia's strategic property." Moscow punished Georgia almost immediately, banning the import of Georgian wines and mineral waters, both of which are key export goods.[133]

Georgia owes its escape from heavy natural gas dependence on Russia largely to Azerbaijan's national strategy centered on developing viable ties with the West, mainly through the export of oil and natural gas to Europe, and thus limiting Russian economic and political influence in the South Caucasus. Since the signing of the "Contract of the Century" in 1994, Azerbaijan has included Georgia as a transit country for its oil and gas exports. The critical Baku–Tbilisi–Ceyhan oil pipeline transports Azerbaijani oil directly westward, instead of transiting through Russia. In addition, another important oil pipeline, Baku–Supsa, was built to the Georgian Black Sea coast for delivering Caspian oil to Central-Eastern Europe. The Baku–Tbilisi–Erzurum natural gas pipeline, which supplies gas to Georgia and Turkey, is currently being expanded to become a part of the Southern Gas Corridor from Azerbaijan to Southern Europe.

These energy routes have raised the international profile and geopolitical importance of Georgia. They have also secured alternative oil and gas supply sources and limited Russian influence on the country's energy sector. Georgia's authorities, political parties of different orientation and the majority of the public often connect the country's future with the development of the Caspian energy reserves and their transportation via Georgian territory. Being a part of the

Trans-Caucasus energy corridor is considered a guarantee for the country's economic development, foreign direct investments, creation of new jobs and increased budgetary revenues.

Moscow is aware of the impact these major energy corridors have on boosting Georgia's independence, and therefore tries to undermine investor confidence by creating additional security concerns. The Baku–Supsa pipeline, which skirts South Ossetia and was temporarily shut down during the August 2008 war, has now been affected by the creeping Russian annexation of Georgian territory, pursued by Russian occupation troops and border guards stationed in the breakaway region.

In July 2015, Tbilisi reported that the administrative border of South Ossetia had been marked as a "state border" and moved south by 300 m (980 ft), leaving a 1.6 km (1-mile) segment of the BP-operated Baku–Supsa pipeline under Russia's effective control, thus threatening the interests of both Georgia and Azerbaijan. The action was particularly brazen because the barbwire installations left only a 500 m (0.3-mile) distance to the main Georgian highway linking the Black Sea and Azerbaijan. Georgian Foreign Minister Tamar Beruchashvili condemned the border move as a continuation of "creeping Russian annexation."[134] Such acts of political blackmail and potential sabotage of energy installations in Georgia, such as electricity lines and pipelines, can shake trust in Georgia as a reliable energy transit country.

After Armenia made its historic choice to abandon EU integration and join the Eurasian Economic Union, Russia intensified its campaign to regain a monopoly position in Georgia's energy sector. Moscow needs to secure energy supply and transportation corridors to Armenia, but it is also using this opportunity to tighten its grip on Georgia's economy, particularly since the Georgian Dream government seems to be more accommodating than that of Saakashvili's. Russia is mainly targeting oil and gas transit routes, but also hydropower plants, electricity networks and transportation infrastructure.

In December 2014, Russia's state oil company *Rosneft* acquired a 49% stake in the Georgian company *Petrocas* Energy International Ltd., which owns a strategically important oil terminal at Georgia's Black Sea port of Poti, with a capacity of 1.9 million tons per year, and the most extensive network of 140 gas stations branded Gulf. The offshore company *Petrocas* is owned by an influential Russian businessman of Georgian origin, David Iakobachvili and operates from Limassol, Tbilisi and Moscow. The acquisition would allow *Rosneft* to considerably expand its presence in the region, diversify supply routes and solidify positions in the oil products markets of Central Asia and the South Caucasus, two regions with a high growth potential.[135]

Georgia's opposition parties responded to the deal with criticism, and economists claimed that it jeopardized national security. They insisted that the government should annul the acquisition for several reasons. First, *Rosneft* is developing offshore oil and gas fields along Abkhazia's Black Sea coast under a 2009 agreement with Sukhumi, which violates Georgia's Law on Occupied Territories. The law adopted in October 2008 forbids foreign companies from operating in the breakaway regions of Abkhazia and South Ossetia without authorization from the Georgian government. [136] However, the reaction of Georgian Foreign Minister Tamar Beruchashvili was surprising: he told reporters that since *Rosneft* does not conduct direct financial and other operations in the occupied territories, the deal does not fall foul of Georgian legislation. In March 2014, Georgian Finance Minister Nodar Khaduri stated that he saw nothing wrong with *Rosneft's* interest in acquiring Poti as part of Russia's efforts to secure gasoline deliveries to Armenia.[137]

Second, the purchase of strategic infrastructure by a Russian state-owned company presents a national security risk for Georgia. The Kremlin can use the presence of Russian state-owned companies in a foreign country to justify the protection of its assets by either staging a military intervention and annexing territory or inventing a cause to serve as a "mediator" in any future conflict to "ensure peace and stability in the region."[138] In other words, Georgia faces the possibility of another war or territorial expropriation should Moscow determine that it needs the port of Poti for its strategic corridor from the North Caucasus to Armenia and further to Iran. Such a scenario would undermine Tbilisi's relations with Azerbaijan and Turkey as well as with Western companies such as BP, which rely on Georgia as a critical transit route for oil and gas.

Third, *Rosneft* is under international sanctions for Russia's annexation of Crimea and the war in eastern Ukraine. The inaction of the Georgian government has undermined Western sanctions against Moscow, sanctions that were put in place to protect vulnerable countries such as Ukraine and Georgia. Tbilisi clearly lacks a legal mechanism to restrict private companies from divesting their stakes in entities of national strategic importance, or the Georgian Dream government has no desire to prevent such acquisitions. By allowing *Rosneft* to obtain a 49% stake of a strategically important oil terminal and with the prospect of a potential controlling package as Russian media have claimed, Tbilisi has permitted a Russian state-owned company, specifically included among sanctioned Russian entities, to evade those sanctions.

Georgia has not joined all European sanctions against Russia, which puts it at odds with the EU and US. In 2014, the EU introduced 15 sets of sanctions against Russia in connection to its actions in Ukraine and Crimea. Fearing a strong backlash by Moscow, Georgia decided to join only one of them, banning imports from Crimea and Sevastopol. Nevertheless, Russian Prime Minister Dmitry Medvedev was quick to threaten Tbilisi with "response measures" when the EU extended its sanctions in 2015.[139]

Most recently, *Gazprom* has also resumed attempts to secure a share of the Georgian natural gas market. Tbilisi no longer imports gas from Russia, except for 0.3 bcm per year received as compensation for the transit of gas to Armenia. In September 2015, it emerged that Tbilisi was in talks with *Gazprom* for future natural gas purchases. According to Energy Minister Kakha Kaladze, Georgia's commercial gas consumption is expected to increase by 27% in 2015 compared to 2012. Kaladze claimed there was no possibility to import additional volumes from Azerbaijan, which is Georgia's main gas supplier. The Energy Ministry asserted that the country may face a gap until the second phase of the Shah Deniz project becomes operational in 2019. However, Azerbaijan's state oil company SOCAR refuted this claim by announcing that production in 2015 might double that of previous years and reach 10 billion cubic meters. During his visit to Tbilisi in November 2015, Azerbaijan's President Ilham Aliyev also stressed that his country has huge natural gas reserves—enough not only for domestic consumption, but also for supplying its neighbors and Europe for the next hundred years.[140]

Talks with *Gazprom* continued toward the end of 2015, and it will not be a surprise if Tbilisi caves in to *Gazprom* pressure. Former prime minister and founder of the ruling Georgian Dream party, Bidzina Ivanishvili, publicly supported gas supply diversification through purchases from *Gazprom* (and Iran, although there is no pipeline for deliveries from Iran.) Although retired from politics, Ivanishvili is believed to still make all major government decisions. The Russian-made billionaire who defeated Saakashvili's party in 2012, was and maybe still is the largest private shareholder of *Gazprom*, with a 1% stake in the Russian energy giant.[141]

In terms of soft power, Georgia's own traumatic experience with the Russian occupation and with a strong pro-Western public have made traditional Russian propaganda tools largely inapplicable. Therefore, the Kremlin's "politechnologists" have designed a tailored approach to Georgia by choosing a more subtle way of influencing society.

Instead of seeking public support for Russia's actions in Donbas through anti-Ukrainian propaganda and outright lies to justify the war as protection of Russian-speakers, the Kremlin's strategy is to increase anti-Western rhetoric among opinion-influencers in Georgian society and instill anti-Western sentiment. This strategy is additionally tailored to large urban centers and rural areas.

In big cities, where the population is more eager to see Georgia associated with the EU and NATO, carriers of Moscow's propaganda (usually Russian-funded NGOs or individual agents) point to the "unreliability" of the West, stressing that NATO and the EU do not really care about Georgia. If they did, Tbilisi would have already received a roadmap to NATO membership and the Allies would have helped Georgia restore its authority in Abkhazia and South Ossetia. They also claim that if Georgia joins NATO, the country will lose the chance to ever regain control over Abkhazia and South Ossetia. The other propaganda line is that Georgia needs to decide whether to continue insisting on joining NATO and risk Russian aggression, or give up such aspirations to pacify an expanding Russia.

In rural areas, the propaganda message is that the EU and NATO would not accept Georgia, because they look down on the poor and underdeveloped state, considering it to be a Third World country. Such a message acts as an insult by playing on the emotions of people living in poor rural areas. Georgia has a 47% rural population, but agricultural production contributes only 9% of the gross domestic product.[142] However, the rural population, which is much poorer than the rest, makes up the critical mass deciding every election in the country. Having the advantage of knowing the South Caucasus well, Russia is using demographics, income levels, education, culture and social problems when targeting specific groups to engineer their attitudes.[143]

Georgian observers comment that if public support for the West is eroded, Georgia could fall into Russia's hands. They also say that the

Georgian government's message concerning its policy toward Moscow is not consolidated; it is often contradictory and confusing to the public, which makes Russia's strategy more effective.[144]

Opinion polls conducted by the Washington-based National Democratic Institute (NDI) in August 2015 suggest that, although 61% of Georgians support the country's goal to join the EU, a part of the Georgian public (31%) is not averse to the idea of joining the Eurasian Economic Union. Those Georgians approving Eurasian Union membership primarily cite perceived economic benefits (71%), not political or governance improvements. It is apparent that, in the midst of economic stagnation and insufficient government initiative to develop the economy, the message that Georgia would be better off economically if it were closer to its northern neighbor is finding some resonance. However, only 6% of the public believes that Russia should have high political influence in Georgia, and 13% think that this influence should be moderate. Nevertheless, current Russian influence is perceived as high: 70–80% of citizens are convinced that Russia has influence over Georgia, and the majority assesses this influence as negative.[145]

Russia's propaganda agents in Georgia are usually Moscow-funded NGOs, Russian oligarchs of Georgian origin, Georgian citizens residing in Russia with ties to the Kremlin's security apparatus, some of the Georgian Orthodox Church clergy or paid individual agents. Unlike in the Baltic states and Ukraine, where the Kremlin's strategy has been to use Russian speakers and the Russian-language media for propaganda purposes, in Georgia the agents of influence are invariably Georgian-language speakers using Georgian-language media outlets, as there is virtually no possibility to influence the Georgian public through Russian sources.

A widely used propaganda tool in Georgia is the claim that the Western decay of family values and its protection of gay rights is threatening to destroy the centuries-old traditions of Georgian society—a fundamental premise on which Putin has built his strategy to counter the West. And similarly to Russia, members of the Georgian Orthodox clergy in particular are pushing the line of social conservatism: the often irrational but powerful message resonates widely with Georgian society, partly because the Church is the most respected institution in the country, with Patriarch Ilia II enjoying the highest approval rating of 87%.[146]

Georgian activists, whose anti-homophobia rally in 2013 was attacked by dozens of priests armed with sticks and crucifixes, believe that Moscow is using the Church to spread anti-Western messages in Georgia. Although the Georgian Orthodox Church denies being an instrument of Russia, local priests admit that visiting Russian clergy have been organizing annual religious "boot camps" in Georgia for the last three years, where they have claimed that "pedophile parties are taking over Europe."[147]

The xenophobic and homophobic narratives of Russian propaganda, depicting the West as destructive of traditional Georgian family values and faith, aim not only to undermine Georgia's pro-Western attitudes. They also aim to change the public perception of Russia from an enemy and occupier of two Georgian regions to a protector of Georgian traditions and a mighty defender of Orthodox Christianity. But this effort is unlikely to produce the desired result, according to Georgian Defense Minister Tinatin Khidasheli, because the Georgians are reminded of the Russian occupation every day; they can see the Russian tanks on their territory from the country's main highway.[148]

Nevertheless, Kremlin ideologists are relentless in inventing ways to get in through the window when they are shown the door. A Georgian civil society group conducted an extensive investigation of Russian use of "soft power" to influence Georgian society and undermine Georgia's independence. The report "Russian Influence on Georgian Non-Governmental Organizations and the Media" lists numerous pro-Russian NGOs, founded in Georgia mostly after the Georgian Dream (GD) ruling coalition's ascent to power in 2012. It also presents a detailed analysis of their makeup and *modus operandi*.[149]

According to the report, pro-Russian propaganda in Georgia's civil sector stems from two key organizations: the Eurasian Institute and Eurasian Choice, which have further spawned several other organizations and platforms. They depict the West as Georgia's enemy and emphasize the potential benefits of normalizing Russian-Georgian relations and restoring their "friendship," or alternatively they stress the importance of Georgia's neutrality. Interestingly, along with anti-Western propaganda, they are also attempting to create anti-Turkish sentiment in Georgia. Turkey is Georgia's main trade partners and a critical actor, along with Azerbaijan, in turning the country into a strategically important energy corridor to Europe. Characteristically, these organizations are also using xenophobic and homophobic rhetoric.[150]

The two main organizations have branched out to form other groups and forge partnerships serving the same purpose. The Eurasian Institute has founded the Young Political Scientists Club and the People's Movement of Georgian-Russian Dialogue and Cooperation. It is also a partner of the non-commercial organization Historical Legacy and the information portals *Sakinformi* and *Iverioni*, with connections to Russian media organizations and former Kremlin functionaries or Georgian oligarchs based in Russia. *Sakinformi*'s partner in Russia is Information Agency Rex with editor Modest Kolerov, who was the main ideologist of the Kremlin's policy in the CIS when serving in the Regional and Cultural Relations Department of Russia's Presidential Administration until 2007. According to the report's authors, Kolerov is banned from entering Georgia and considered *persona non-grata* in Latvia and Estonia. The organization Historical Legacy, in turn, founded the online portal *Georgia and the World* (Geworld.ge). According to research on anti-Western propaganda carried out by the Georgian Media Development

Foundation, Geworld.ge is among the websites most frequently circulating anti-Western sentiments as well as homophobic and xenophobic writings.[151] The Eurasian Institute closely cooperates with various Russian organizations, including the Caucasian Scientific Society.

Eurasian Choice serves as an umbrella for pro-Russian organizations such as Erekle II Society and the Internet television channel *Patriot TV*, which popularize the idea of the Eurasian Union in Georgia. Eurasian Choice partners with the International Eurasian Movement, led by prominent ideologist of the Kremlin's expansionist policy, Alexander Dugin[152] Another prominent partner of Eurasian Choice is the Gorchakov Fund, established in 2010 by then-President of Russia Dmitry Medvedev with the purpose of "exerting influence in the international space by using [Russian] cultural, historic and political values." Members of its board of trustees include Russia's Foreign Minister Sergei Lavrov as well as *Lukoil* shareholder Vatig Alegperov, the sixth-richest Russian according to *Forbes'* 2015 rating.[153]

Despite the flurry of activities, pro-Kremlin NGOs can only have an impact on Georgian society if economic conditions continue to deteriorate and Georgia's Euro-Atlantic integration stalls. Therefore, the July 2016 NATO summit in Warsaw will be critical for Georgia and the South Caucasus. The issuing of a NATO Membership Action Plan (MAP) for Tbilisi would not only re-energize pro-Western attitudes in Georgia and support the government's Euro-Atlantic direction, it would also repair the trust toward the West that has eroded throughout the region.

Furthermore, this would send a strong message to President Putin that the former Soviet countries will not be left alone in their efforts to uphold their sovereignty. In the opposite scenario, NATO's failure to provide Georgia with a roadmap for NATO accession will increase skepticism toward the West, strengthen the influence of Russia in the South Caucasus, and even contribute to bringing pro-Russian political parties for the first time into Georgia's parliament. It will also allow Russia to expand its military presence in the occupied regions, potentially annex South Ossetia, and incorporate Abkhazia as a bridge between the Russian North Caucasus and Armenia.

Turkey and Iran

Turkey's potential to play a major role in the South Caucasus and Central Asia has only been partially fulfilled, despite the high expectations in the early 1990s. The country's relationship with the South Caucasus has been determined mainly by its partnership with Azerbaijan, which officially became "strategic" in 2010. It expanded to Georgia when the three countries started implementing large energy and transportation projects such as the Baku–Tbilisi–Ceyhan oil pipeline, the Southern Gas Corridor, and the Baku–Tbilisi–Akhalkalaki–Kars railway. Ankara's energy and economic cooperation with Baku and Tbilisi underscored and deepened Armenia's regional isolation, as its borders with Turkey have remained closed since 1993.

Turkey, Azerbaijan, and Georgia formed an informal alliance in the South Caucasus, which for a while existed simultaneously with the Russia-Armenia-Iran axis. Both Turkey and Azerbaijan have had a difficult relationship with Iran, although for completely different reasons. The Sunni-Shia divisions that play a role in relations between Ankara and Tehran, are not a factor in Baku-Tehran relations, as the majority of Azerbaijan's population is Shia. However, the fact that Tehran backed Armenia in the war over Nagorno-Karabakh is not forgotten. Iran's support for Armenia was mostly born out of fears that Baku would sponsor secessionism among the large Azerbaijani minority in Iran. Subsequently, Baku's military cooperation with Israel fueled concerns in Tehran that its northern neighbor could be used as a launch pad for attacks against Iran. Relations improved after

2012–2013, when prospects for regional projects emerged as Iran was negotiating a nuclear deal with West.[154]

Although for a while these two groupings of countries were able to focus on the economic aspects of their partnerships, Moscow's expansionist behavior challenged Turkey and threatened its important economic cooperation with Russia, particularly as a critical energy supplier. Judging by its weak reaction to Russia's invasion of Georgia in 2008, as well as to Crimea's annexation in 2014, it was clear that Turkey was not willing to risk its business interests by confronting Russia.

However, as Moscow's involvement in the war in eastern Ukraine was continuing and Russia was becoming exceedingly assertive in the South Caucasus, Ankara undertook more intensive military cooperation with both Azerbaijan and Georgia. In June 2015, Turkish, Georgian and Azerbaijani military forces held a series of exercises codenamed "Caucasian Eagle" in eastern Turkey. Earlier, Baku hosted tactical drills by the armed forces of Azerbaijan and Turkey. [155] Although some analysts claimed that Moscow began strengthening its military bases in Armenia, Abkhazia, and South Ossetia as a response to the military encirclement of an isolated Armenia by Turkey, Azerbaijan, and Georgia, it is more likely to be the other way round. It is Russia's neighbors that are becoming increasingly concerned with its expansionist actions that have threatened Azerbaijani, Georgian, and Turkish energy and transportation interests along the oil and gas pipelines and railways from the Caspian to Turkey.

The geopolitical alliances in the South Caucasus have changed as a result of the Russian-Turkish confrontation over the shooting down of a Russian fighter jet in November 2015. Both Russia and Turkey took their struggle to the neighbors, and the resonance was heard from the Balkans to the Caspian. Azerbaijan, in particular, found itself in a very difficult position, pressed to choose between Russia and Turkey by both sides. In the days after the Russian Su-24 was downed,

Turkish Foreign Minister Mevlüt Çavuşoğlu traveled to Baku, followed by the visit of Prime Minister Ahmet Davutoğlu, who declared that Ankara would "do everything possible to free the occupied territories of Nagorno-Karabakh." But Baku's response was cautious; it officially expressed regret about the conflict between its "two friends and neighbors," but only offered to mediate between Moscow and Ankara, avoiding a clear stand on the incident.[156] Faced with an economic and financial crisis as a result of low oil prices, Azerbaijan cannot afford to alienate either of its two big neighbors.

Reportedly, energy issues dominated the Turkish officials' visit more than seeking vocal support. Anticipating Russian gas supply interruptions and eager to diversify energy sources, Ankara is urging Azerbaijan to speed up the expansion of the South Caucasus pipeline to Turkey and start delivering natural gas earlier than planned, possibly in 2018.[157] Despite the Kremlin's pressure, Azerbaijan did not join Russia's sanctions against Turkey, unlike the Georgian breakaway region of Abkhazia, which accepted Moscow's demand, regardless of the losses to its fragile economy.[158]

The nuclear program agreement between Tehran and the P5+1 (the United States, the United Kingdom, France, Russia, China and Germany), signed in July 2015, opened new economic opportunities for the South Caucasus, but also exposed geopolitical difficulties and regional rivalries. If north-south trade and energy corridors predominate over current east-west connections, Russia and Iran will become the dominant players in the South Caucasus, diminishing the influence of Turkey and the US. This, in turn, may delay indefinitely the resolution of the Nagorno-Karabakh conflict between Armenia and Azerbaijan and prolong the occupation of South Ossetia and Abkhazia.

Azerbaijan and Armenia are competing for transportation corridors linking them to Iran. The prospective railway project connecting Azerbaijan and Iran seems more feasible than the one that would link

Armenia to Iran for both technical reasons and available financing. Official Tehran has stated that cooperation with its neighbors is its first priority, with Azerbaijan taking first place. Iranian President Hassan Rouhani also stated in August 2015 that for Iran, Azerbaijan is "the gate to the Caucasus" and for Azerbaijan, Iran "can become Baku's path to the Persian Gulf."[159]

Russia will benefit directly from the railway connection between Azerbaijan and Iran as its goods could reach the Indian Ocean instead of seeking Western routes, while collecting revenues from the transit of Iranian goods to Russia and further to Europe. Iran also hopes to use the Baku–Tbilisi–Akhalkalaki–Kars railway for moving cargo westward. Connecting to Armenia would be a chance to bring the country out of regional transportation isolation. Although the Armenian route does not offer Russia direct benefits, unless a railway through Georgia is constructed and Yerevan's relationship with Turkey improves, it will bring significant geopolitical advantages. Consequently, Moscow and Tehran are likely to press for the construction of north-south railway links because they will increase dramatically the role of Russia and Iran and reduce the influence of Turkey, Georgia and the United States.[160] Russia's goal is to redirect trade traffic from the east-west lines to the north-south corridors in order to position itself as the dominant player in the South Caucasus, even if it has to share influence with Iran, or rather to use Iran to achieve dominance.

An agreement on electricity exchanges between Russia, Georgia, Armenia, and Iran signed in Yerevan in December 2015 demonstrates that Moscow is seeking control of the region's energy sector as well. According to the Armenian Ministry of Energy and Natural Resources, a 400/500-kilovolt (kV) power transmission line between Armenia and Georgia, and a 400 kV power transmission line between Armenia and Iran will start operating in 2018.[161] Tellingly, the high-voltage export lines in both Armenia and Georgia are managed by Russian companies—*Gazprom* Armenia and Inter RAO, respectively.

In August 2015, just a few weeks after the Iranian nuclear deal was signed, *Gazprom* Armenia was granted the right to operate the high-voltage transmission lines that will be used to export electricity to Iran and Georgia.[162] In addition, a 2013 deal between Armenia and Russia has given *Gazprom* a monopoly over Armenia's gas network for 30 years. Furthermore, *Gazprom* also bought a critical gas pipeline delivering gas from Iran, leaving Moscow in full control of natural gas supply routes to Armenia.[163]

While the South Caucasus can benefit substantially from the expected abolishment of sanctions against Iran, Moscow is carefully calculating how much influence it would allow Iran to have in the region. Evidently, the Kremlin is using the Islamic Republic to achieve several goals: undermine the east-west trade and energy routes, channel the three countries' trade relations toward the Russian Federation and tie them to the Russian economy, impede diversification of energy supply, and expand *Gazprom* and other Russian companies' market share, all the while restricting Iran's outreach to its neighbors and particularly to European energy markets.

Endnotes

[1] The fourth conflict was over Moldova's province of Transnistria.

[2] "Iraq: As Third-Largest Contingent, Georgia Hopes to Show its Worth," *RFE/RL*, September 10, 2007, http://www.rferl.org/content/article/1078614.html.

[3] John Roberts, "Russia & Turkey - Aerial Combat and Energy Security," *Natural Gas Europe*, November 25, 2015, http://www.naturalgaseurope.com/russia-and-turkey-aerial-combat-and-energy-security-26694.

[4] "The Russian Military Build up Continues as Six Su-34 Fullback Attack Planes Arrive in Syria," *TheAviationist.com*, September 29, 2015,

http://theaviationist.com/2015/09/29/su-34-have-arrived-in-syria/; "Russia launches missiles towards Syria from the Caspian Sea – video," *Reuters*, October 7, 2015, Available at: http://www.theguardian.com/world/video/2015/oct/07/russia-launches-missiles-on-isis-from-caspian-sea-video.

5 Giorgi Lomsadze, "Turkey-Russia Conflict Divides South Caucasus," *EurasiaNet.org*, December 2, 2015, http://www.eurasianet.org/node/76376.

6 Mairbek Vatchagaev, "Like Russia, Chechnya is Being Increasingly Drawn into Syrian Conflict," *Eurasia Daily Monitor*, Volume 12, Issue 182, October 8, 2015, http://www.jamestown.org/programs/edm/single/?tx_ttnews%5Btt_news%5D=44467&cHash=760602bbff179e2cb5f467154705ab59#.VkCwuq6rSis; Vasili Rukhadze, "More of Georgia's Muslims Try to Join Islamic State," *Eurasia Daily Monitor*, Volume 12, Issue 71, April 16, 2015, http://www.jamestown.org/programs/edm/single/?tx_ttnews%5Btt_news%5D=43802&cHash=1d7874f8b6ff2e14ba9d0a71c16c2023#.VltuQd-rSis.

7 Paul Goble, "ISIS Fighters Returning to Azerbaijan Seen Creating Serious Problems for Baku," *Window on Eurasia*, November 7, 2015, http://windowoneurasia2.blogspot.com/2015/11/isis-fighters-returning-to-azerbaijan.html.

8 Syria is Russia's main partner in the Middle East. For years, Russia has maintained a naval facility in Tartus and a Russian Air Forces deployment at the Bassel Al-Assad International Airport in Latakia, with an estimated 2,000 military personnel in the country before the start of the air strikes on September 30, 2015. Russia's military force in Syria has grown to 4,000 personnel and is expected to expand further (*Reuters*, November 8, 2015, http://www.reuters.com/article/2015/11/08/us-mideast-crisis-syria-russia-idUSKCN0SX0H820151108.

9 Giorgi Lomsadze, "Turkey-Russia Conflict Divides South Caucasus," *EurasiaNet.org*, December 2, 2015, http://www.eurasianet.org/node/76376.

10 Valery Dzutsati, "Moscow Tries to Seduce the Circassians and Abkhaz With Plans for New Highway," *Eurasia Daily Monitor*, Volume 12, Issue

215, December 2, 2015,
http://www.jamestown.org/regions/thecaucasus/single/?tx_ttnews%5Btt_ne
ws%5D=44853&tx_ttnews%5BbackPid%5D=54&cHash=b73946b863f1e33
9a50da006391624f4#.VpJL2ZMrJmA.

[11] Huseyn Aliyev and Emil A. Souleimanov, "Russia's Missile Launches and
the Militarization of the Caspian Sea," *CACI Analyst*, November 23, 2015,
http://www.cacianalyst.org/publications/analytical-articles/item/13305-
russias-missile-launches-and-the-militarization-of-the-caspian-sea.html.

[12] Jacopo Dettoni, "Russia and Iran lock NATO out of Caspian Sea," *The
Diplomat*, October 1, 2014, http://thediplomat.com/2014/10/russia-and-
iran-lock-nato-out-of-caspian-sea/.

[13] "Georgia's 2014 Foreign Trade," Civil Georgia, January 22, 2015,
http://civil.ge/eng/article.php?id=27984; European Commission, Trade by
Countries and Regions, http://ec.europa.eu/trade/policy/countries-and-
regions/.

[14] See: "О контроле за алкогольной продукцией из Грузии" (About the
control of alcohol production from Georgia), Federal Consumer Protection
Agency, August 4, 2015,
http://rospotrebnadzor.ru/about/info/news/news_details.php?ELEMENT_I
D=3983&sphrase_id=418252; "PM: Suspending Free Trade Agreement by
Russia 'Not a Tragedy,' " *Civil Georgia*, July 31, 2014,
http://www.civil.ge/eng/article.php?id=27542.

[15] Margarita Assenova and Zaur Shiriyev (eds.), *Azerbaijan and the New
Energy Geopolitics of Southeastern Europe*, Washington, DC: The
Jamestown Foundation, 2015.

[16] "Speech at meeting of the Russian-Armenian Interregional Forum",
Kremlin.ru, December 2, 2013, http://eng.kremlin.ru/transcripts/6355.

[17] Author's interviews in Baku, July 2015.

[18] Margarita Assenova, "Ukrainian Crisis Sparks Worries in the South
Caucasus," *Eurasia Daily Monitor*, April 25, 2014, Volume 11, Issue 77,

http://www.jamestown.org/single/?tx_ttnews%5Btt_news%5D=42268&no_cache=1#.Vf9tm51VhBc.

[19] Jim Nichol, "Armenia, Azerbaijan, and Georgia: Political Developments and Implications for U.S. Interests," *Congressional Research Service*, April 2, 2015, https://www.fas.org/sgp/crs/row/RL33453.pdf.

[20] Kirit Radia, "Can Obama Reassure Putin on NATO?" *ABC News*, March 26, 2014, http://abcnews.go.com/blogs/headlines/2014/03/can-obama-reassure-putin-on-nato/.

[21] "Will Abkhazians and Ossetians Benefit from the EU Visa Liberalization?" *Agenda.ge*, December 19, 2015, http://agenda.ge/news/48700/eng.

[22] Armenia's Relations with Turkey are impeded mostly because of Ankara's support for Baku over Nagorno-Karabakh, but also over contradictory positions on the Armenian genocide.

[23] Robert Coalson, "News Analysis: Armenia's Choice Stirs Competition Between Moscow, EU," *RFE/RL*, September 3, 2013, http://www.rferl.org/content/armenia-russia-customs-union-eu-analysys/25095948.html.

[24] *Ibid.*

[25] Emma Gabrielyan, «David Shahnazaryan. "The RA government authorities defended the interests of the Russian corrupted system,"*Aravot*, June 24, 2015, http://en.aravot.am/2015/06/24/170765/.

[26] "Сергей Марков: в Ереване «наверняка среди демонстрантов много боевиков из Украины»!" (Sergey Markov: Probably there are many fighters from Ukraine among the Demonstrators in Yerevan), *First Armenia Information Channel*, June 24, 2015, http://ru.1in.am/1101656.html.

[27] Gazprom reduced energy prices for Armenia by 30–35% in 2013 after the country joined the Customs Union—natural gas prices dropped from the

already low $270 to $189 per thousand cubic meters. Prices in Belarus in 2013 were $166 and some Eastern European countries were paying over $500 of Russian gas at the time. See: "Gazprom's Grip," *RFE/RL*, http://www.rferl.org/contentinfographics/gazprom-russia-gas-leverage-europe/25441983.html.

[28] "Russia and Armenia negotiate possible cut on natural gas price, minister says," *Arka News Agency*, March 30, 2015, http://arka.am/en/news/economy/russia_and_armenia_negotiate_possible_cut_on_natural_gas_price_minister_says/; "Russia cuts gas price for Armenia by $24 to $165," *Armenian Public Radio*, September 7, 2015, http://www.armradio.am/en/2015/09/07/russia-cuts-gas-price-for-armenia-by-24-to-165/.

[29] "Russian Serviceman Permyakov to Be Tried by Armenian Court for Gyumri Killings," *The Armenian Weekly*, June 30, 2015, http://armenianweekly.com/2015/06/30/permyakov-to-be-tried-by-an-armenian-court/.

[30] The World's Billionaires, 2015 Ranking, *Forbes.com*, http://www.forbes.com/profile/samvel-karapetyan/.

[31] Inter RAO UES press release, September 30, 2015, http://www.interrao.ru/en/news/company/?ELEMENT_ID=5238; "Russia's Inter RAO sells Armenia's electricity network," *The Conway Bulletin*, September 30, 2015, http://newsdesk.theconwaybulletin.com/russias-inter-rao-sells-armenias-electricity-network/.

[32] "Интер РАО продала активы в Армении за $8,25 млн," (Inter RAO sold assets in Armenia for $8.25 million), *Rambler News Service*, November 27, 2015, https://rns.online/energy/Inter-RaO-prodala-25-dolyu-v-armyanskih-dochkah-za-825-mln-news-2015-11-27/.

[33] "Inter RAO's assets in Armenia to be sold on a step-by-step basis," *Verelq.com*, December 2, 2015, http://www.verelq.am/en/node/4927; "Russian CEO of Electric Networks of Armenia dismissed," *Arka News Agency*, October 16, 2015,

http://arka.am/en/news/business/russian_ceo_of_electric_networks_of_ar
menia_dismissed/;
Matthew Czekaj, "Russia's Bankrupting Empire," *Eurasia Daily Monitor*,
Volume 12, Issue 121, June 29, 2015,
http://www.jamestown.org/regions/thecaucasus/single/?tx_ttnews%5Bpoint
er%5D=4&tx_ttnews%5Btt_news%5D=44093&tx_ttnews%5BbackPid%5D
=54&cHash=1a4fd5fcb2565332e4c1c3b2dd7c0331#.Vdo1tNNViko.

[34] "Economy in 2015: EEU membership, U.S.-Armenia Trade Agreement,
power grid sale," *ArmeniaNow.com*, December 28, 2015,
https://www.armenianow.com/economy/69038/armenia_economy_year_2
015.

[35] Natalia Konarzewska, "Armenia's Economic Woes," *CACI Analyst*,
September 15, 2015, http://www.cacianalyst.org/publications/analytical-
articles/item/13277-armenias-economic-woes.html.

[36] The World Bank, http://data.worldbank.org.

[37] "Russia Tightens Its Hold on Armenia," *Stratfor*, November 2, 2015,
https://www.stratfor.com/analysis/russia-tightens-its-hold-armenia; "When
Is Next Shock and When Will Ara Abrahamyan's Party Be Dissolved?"
Lragir.com, October 19, 2015,
http://www.lragir.am/index/eng/0/comments/view/34789#sthash.EOPUP8
7g.dpuf.

[38] European Union External Policy Website,
http://eeas.europa.eu/armenia/index_en.htm.

[39] "Russian-Armenian Military Drill Targets 'Ottomania'," *Asbarez.com*,
September 5, 2014, http://asbarez.com/126676/russian-armenian-military-
drill-targets-ottomania/.

[40] Author's interviews in Yerevan, July 2015.

[41] Emma Gabrielyan, "Do Putin and Aliyev clear new heights?" *Aravot*,
August 24, 2015, http://en.aravot.am/2015/08/24/171670/.

[42] "Russian Troops In Armenia Inspected," *Azatutyun*, July 2015, http://www.azatutyun.mobi/a/27115077.html?utm_source=dlvr.it&utm_medium=facebook.

[43] "Russia Reinforces Base in Armenia With Attack, Transport Helicopters," *Sputnik International*, December 21, 2015, http://sputniknews.com/military/20151221/1032081119/russia-military-base-armenia-helicopters.html#ixzz3xTb3nucr.

[44] Sargis Harutyunyan, "Advanced Russian Missiles 'Deployed In Armenia'," *RFE/RL*, June 3, 2013, http://www.azatutyun.am/content/article/25005647.html.

[45] Christopher Harress, "Russia In Talks To Supply Armenia With Iskander-M Missiles As Battle Lines Drawn Across Europe," *International Business Times*, July 2, 2015, http://www.ibtimes.com/russia-talks-supply-armenia-iskander-m-missiles-battle-lines-drawn-across-europe-1994731.

[46] Sargis Harutyunyan, "Advanced Russian Missiles 'Deployed in Armenia'," *RFE/RL*, June 3, 2013, http://www.azatutyun.am/content/article/25005647.html.

[47] "Russia Won't Sell Iskander to Everyone But Will it Sell It to Azerbaijan?" *Lragir.am*, August 10, 2015, http://www.lragir.am/index/eng/0/politics/view/34506#sthash.Ku3pXEGL.dpuf.

[48] David Stepanyan, "Major General Arkady-Ter-Tadevosyan: Iskander Systems Will Appear in Armenia… but in Territory of 102nd Russian Military Base," ArmInfo, July 13, 2015, http://www.arminfo.info/index.cfm?objectid=DA34EF70-2921-11E5-BC5B0EB7C0D21663.

[49] "Russia Checks Combat Readiness of Troops in Armenia," *AFP*, July 7, 2015, http://www.defensenews.com/story/defense/international/europe/2015/07/07/russia-checks-combat-readiness-troops-armenia/29827321/.

[50] NATO Website,
http://www.nato.int/cps/en/natohq/official_texts_112964.htm.

[51] "Russia and Armenia will establish a unified air-defense system in the Caucasus," *Sputnik International*, November 11, 2015, more: http://sputniknews.com/military/20151111/1029906462/putin-russia-armenia-air-defense.html#ixzz3yexVBg9H.

[52] Emil Danielyan, "Russia, Armenia Upgrade Joint Air Defense," *Azatutyun*, December 23, 2015, http://www.azatutyun.am/content/article/27445236.html.

[53] *The Military Balance*, Vol. 115, Issue 1, 2015, International Institute for Strategic Studies, http://www.iiss.org/en/publications/military-s-balance.

[54] Vladimir Socor, "Armenia's Economic Dependence on Russia Insurmountable by the European Union," *Eurasia Daily Monitor*, Volume 10, Issue 221, December 10, 2013, http://www.jamestown.org/regions/russia/single/?tx_ttnews%5Btt_news%5D=41740&tx_ttnews%5BbackPid%5D=48&cHash=408a5840473a1f08b45f64b8178116ba#.Vpf2T5MrLfY.

[55] Fred Hiatt, "Why Armenia turned to Russia instead of the West," *The Washington Post*, May 7, 2015, https://www.washingtonpost.com/blogs/post-partisan/wp/2015/05/07/why-armenia-turned-to-russia-instead-of-the-west/.

[56] Grigor Hayrapetyan and Viktoriya Hayrapetyan, *Regional and International Trade of Armenia: Perspectives and Potentials*, Kyiv: Economics Education and Research Consortium, 2011, http://www.aea.am/files/papers/w1103.pdf.

[57] Marianna Grigoryan, "Armenia: Trying to Break Free of Economic Dependence on Russia?" *EurasiaNet.org*, May 18, 2015, http://www.eurasianet.org/node/73486; European Commission, http://ec.europa.eu/trade/policy/countries-and-regions/countries/armenia/.

[58] Vladimir Socor, "Armenia's Economic Dependence on Russia Insurmountable by the European Union," *Eurasia Daily Monitor*, Volume 10, Issue 221, December 10, 2013, http://www.jamestown.org/single/?tx_ttnews[tt_news]=41740&no_cache=1#.VtdpC-bYHiQ.

[59] "Armenia to sell Iran gas pipeline to Gazprom," *Press TV*, June 5, 2015, http://217.218.67.231/Detail/2015/06/05/414428/Iran-gas-armenia-pipeline-gazprom.

[60] Armen Grigoryan, "Armenia's Regional Energy and Transport Cooperation Squeezed by Russia," *Eurasia Daily Monitor*, Volume 12, Issue 156, September 1, 2015, http://www.jamestown.org/programs/edm/single/?tx_ttnews%5Btt_news%5D=44319&tx_ttnews%5BbackPid%5D=786&no_cache=1#.VpG_G5MrJmC.

[61] "Economy in 2015: EEU membership, U.S.-Armenia Trade Agreement, power grid sale," *ArmeniaNow.com*, December 28, 2015, https://www.armenianow.com/economy/69038/armenia_economy_year_2015.

[62] Armen Vardanyan, "Russian Policy in Armenia and its Impact Tools," *Aravot*, November 19, 2015, http://en.aravot.am/2015/11/19/173046/.

[63] *Ibid.*

[64] Author's interviews in Yerevan in July 2015.

[65] "When Is Next Shock and When Will Ara Abrahamyan's Party Be Dissolved?" *Lragiar.com*, October 19, 2015, http://www.lragir.am/index/eng/0/comments/view/34789#sthash.EOPUP87g.dpuf.

[66] *Ibid.*; Authors interviews in Yerevan, July 2015.

[67] Author's interviews in Yerevan, July 2015.

[68] Teymur Hasanli, "Azerbaijan on the verge of a new 'mini-war': commentary and details," *Yeni Musavat*, January 24, 2015, http://musavat.com/.

[69] Zulfugar Agayev, "Azeris to Boost Defense Spending Amid Risk of Armenia War," *Bloomberg*, November 19, 2014, http://www.bloomberg.com/news/articles/2014-11-19/azeris-to-boost-defense-spending-amid-risk-of-armenia-war.

[70] The World Bank, Military Expenditure, http://data.worldbank.org/indicator/MS.MIL.XPND.GD.ZS/countries/all?display=graph.

[71] Global Militarization Index 2015, Bonn International Center for Conversion, https://www.bicc.de/press/press-releases/press/news/global-militarisation-index-2015-465/.

[72] Victoria Panfilov, "Azerbaijan is committed to peace," *Nezavisimaya Gazeta*, June 2, 2015, available at: http://vestnikkavkaza.net/analysis/politics/71962.html.

[73] "Baku says 143 Armenian, 19 Azeri soldiers killed in 2015," *APA*, January 5, 2016, http://az.apa.az/.

[74] "Azerbaijan furious over EU criticism, wants to 'revise' relations," *EUbusiness*, September 11, 2015, http://www.eubusiness.com/news-eu/azerbaijan-rights.14a2/.

[75] Gulshan Pashayeva, "The EU-Azerbaijan Relationship: Current Status and Future Outlook," *Eurasia Daily Monitor*, Volume 12, Issue 207, November 13, 2015, Washington DC: The Jamestown Foundation, http://www.jamestown.org/single/?tx_ttnews%5Btt_news%5D=44598&tx_ttnews%5BbackPid%5D=7#.Vp4wl1MrLfY.

[76] US Helsinki Commission press release, December 16, 2015, http://csce.gov/index.cfm?FuseAction=ContentRecords.ViewDetail&ContentRecord_id=1228&ContentType=P&ContentRecordType=P.

[77] Author's interviews in Baku, July 2015.

[78] Amanda Paul, "Azerbaijan and the Two EUs", *EU Observer*, July 6, 2014, http://blogs.euobserver.com/paul/2014/07/06/azerbaijanand-the-two-eus/.

[79] "Russia-Azerbaijan Arms Trade Worth $4Bln – Aliyev," *Sputnik International*, August 13, 2013, http://sputniknews.com/russia/20130813/182748495/Russia-Azerbaijan-Arms-Trade-Worth-4Bln--Aliyev.html.

[80] Orkhan Yolchuyev, "Relations with Azerbaijan meet Russia's strategic interests," *Trend News Agency*, October 9, 2015, http://en.trend.az/business/economy/2442213.html.

[81] Anar Valiyev, "Azerbaijan-Russia Relations after the Five-Day War: Friendship, Enmity, or Pragmatism?" *Turkish Policy Quarterly*, Vol. 10 No. 3, FALL 2011, http://turkishpolicy.com/issue/39/natos-future-in-turkeys-neighborhood.

[82] Azerbaijan started negotiations with the WTO in July 1997. The negotiations were accelerated in 2015, but it is not clear when they will conclude.
See:
https://www.wto.org/english/news_e/news15_e/acc_aze_06mar15_e.htm.

[83] Jim Nichol, "Armenia, Azerbaijan, and Georgia: Political Developments and Implications for U.S. Interests," *Congressional Research Service*, April 2, 2015, https://www.fas.org/sgp/crs/row/RL33453.pdf; Donald N. Jensen, "Putin Brings Disappointment Back from Baku," Institute for Modern Russia, August 23, 2013, http://imrussia.org/en/politics/538-putin-brings-disappointment-back-from-baku.

[84] "Azeri military expert anxious about reported defense deals with Russia," *Yeni Musavat*, August 15, 2013.

[85] "General Assembly Adopts Resolution Calling upon States Not to Recognize Changes in Status of Crimea Region," United Nations, March 27, 2014, http://www.un.org/press/en/2014/ga11493.doc.htm; "Mixed Regional

Response to Crimea Annexation," *Economist Intelligence Unit*, March 27, 2014, http://www.eiu.com.

86 "Rogozin put in charge of Russia's relations with Azerbaijan," *CommonSpace.eu*, April 14, 2014, http://commonspace.eu/eng/news/6/id2974.

87 Anar Valiyev, "Azerbaijan's Balancing Act in the Ukraine Crisis," *PONARS Eurasia*, September 2014, http://www.ponarseurasia.org/memo/azerbaijans-balancing-act-ukraine-crisis.

88 Saba Aghayeva, "NATO Appreciates Azerbaijan's contribution to international security," *Trend News Agency*, April 11, 2014, http://en.trend.az/.

89 "The West pursues double standard policy towards Azerbaijan, British MP," *News.az*, April 19, 2014, http://news.az/articles/politics/87869.

90 "Azerbaijan reaffirms readiness to transit gas from east coast of Caspian Sea," *Trend News Agency*, April 23, 2014, http://en.trend.az/business/energy/2266389.html.

91 "NATO Official Says Ties with Azerbaijan to Develop," *BBC Monitoring Trans Caucasus Unit*, April 15, 2014, http://www.bbc.co.uk/monitoring.

92 Author's conversation with Rasim Musabekov, member of Azerbaijan's parliament, in Baku, July 2015.

93 Author's interviews in Baku, July 2015.

94 SIPRI Arms Transfers Database, http://www.sipri.org/research/armaments/transfers/databases/armstransfers.

95 "Israel Signs $1.6 Billion Arms Deal With Azerbaijan," *Associated Press*, February 26, 2012, Available at: http://www.haaretz.com/israel-news/israel-signs-1-6-billion-arms-deal-with-azerbaijan-1.414916; Zulfugar Agayev,

"Israel's Top Oil Supplier Endures Gaza as Azeri Ties Grow," *Bloomberg*, September 28, 2014, http://www.bloomberg.com/news/articles/2014-09-28/israel-s-top-oil-supplier-endures-gaza-as-azeri-ties-grow.

[96] Jaroslaw Adamowski, "Azerbaijan To Acquire Military Vehicles From Kazakhstan," *Defense News*, August 21, 2015, http://www.defensenews.com/story/defense/land/vehicles/2015/08/21/azerbaijan-acquire-military-vehicles-kazakhstan/32088317/.

[97] Craig Caffrey, "Azerbaijan to Cut Defense Spending by 40%," *IHS Jane's Defence Industry*, January 26, 2016, http://www.janes.com/article/57500/azerbaijan-to-cut-defence-spending-by-40; John C. K. Daly, "Azerbaijan's Defense Spending Hits $4.8 Billion," *SilkRoadReporters.com*, November 25, 2014, http://www.silkroadreporters.com/2014/11/25/azerbaijan-defense-spending-hits-4-8-billion/.

[98] Population of Azerbaijan 2015, State Statistical Committee of Azerbaijan, http://www.stat.gov.az/source/demoqraphy/ap/indexen.php.

[99] Nigar Orujova, "Azerbaijan, Russia establish Association of Universities," *AzerNews.com*, November 20, 2015, http://www.azernews.az/azerbaijan/90009.html.

[100] Author's interviews in Baku, July 2015; "Azerbaijan's access to Eurasian Economic Union not on agenda — foreign minister," *TASS*, December 25, 2014, http://tass.ru/en/economy/769271; Microeconomic Indicators 2015, The State Statistical Commission of the Republic of Azerbaijan, http://www.stat.gov.az/macroeconomy/indexen.php.

[101] David M. Herszenhorn, "Russia to Close Radar Station in Azerbaijan," *New York Times*, December 11, 2012, http://www.nytimes.com/2012/12/12/world/europe/russia-to-shut-down-radar-station-in-azerbaijan.html; "Russia stops lease of 'outdated' Gabala radar," *RT*, December 11, 2012, http://www.rt.com/politics/gabala-radar-station-agreement-804.

[102] Richard Rousseau, "Azerbaijan Using Gabala Negotiations to Change Russia's Policy," *Eurasia Daily Monitor*, Volume 9, Issue 133, July 13, 2012, http://www.jamestown.org/single/?tx_ttnews%5Bswords%5D=8fd5893941d 69d0be3f378576261ae3e&tx_ttnews%5Bany_of_the_words%5D=Gabala&t x_ttnews%5Btt_news%5D=39625&tx_ttnews%5BbackPid%5D=7&cHash= 8b7001c2225bf7c84c60ed0fd105d39b#.VeOsMNNVhBc.

[103] Arzu Geybullayeva, "Azerbaijan: Striking a Balance between Russia and the West," in Anahit Shirinyan and Louisa Slavkova, Eds., *Unrewarding Crossroads? The Black Sea Region amidst the European Union and Russia*, Sofia: Sofia Platform, June 2015, http://sofiaplatform.org/wp-content/uploads/2015/06/Azerbaijan_Striking_a_Balance_between_Russia_and_the_West.pdf.

[104] Anar Valiyev, "Azerbaijan-Russia: Friendship or Else," *Turkish Policy*, Volume 10, No.3, 2011, http://www.turkishpolicy.com/pdf/vol_10-no_3-valiyev.pdf.

[105] "Russia to Build New Radar Stations in Azerbaijan, Near Arctic Circle," *RFE/RL*, August 18, 2015, http://www.rferl.org/content/russia-radar-stations-azerbaijan-arctic-circle/27195189.html.

[106] "Armenian Speaker dispels concerns over future Russian radar in Azerbaijan," *News.am*, August 20, 2015, http://news.am/rus/.

[107] "The Ministry of Defense of the Republic of Azerbaijan Restores Relations with Pentagon," Ministry of Defense of Azerbaijan, July 14, 2015, http://mod.gov.az/index2.php?content=news/2015/14_07_melumat_pentaq on.

[108] Paul Goble, "Russia and Iran to Conduct Joint Naval Exercises on the Caspian Sea," *Window on Eurasia*, October 19, 2015, http://www.interpretermag.com/russia-and-iran-to-conduct-joint-naval-exercises-on-the-caspian-sea/.

[109] "A New Military Order in the Caspian Sea?" *Stratfor*, November 24, 2015, https://www.stratfor.com/analysis/new-military-order-caspian-sea; Evan Gotessman, "The Caspian States in Russia's Military Bind," *The Diplomat*,

November 27, 2015, http://thediplomat.com/2015/11/turkey-russia-tensions-put-caspian-states-in-a-bind/.

[110] Ministry of Foreign Affairs of the Russian Federation, June 9, 2015, http://www.mid.ru;
John C. K. Daly, "Russia Convinces 'Caspian Five' to Bar Foreign Militaries From the Caspian," *Eurasia Daily Monitor*, Volume 11, Issue 83, May 5, 2014, http://www.jamestown.org/single/?tx_ttnews%5Btt_news%5D=42316&no_cache=1#.Vdte2dNViko.

[111] Russia simultaneously suspended imports of Moldovan wines citing health and sanitation grounds, but observers believed it was another attempt by Russia to punish ex-Soviet states for severing ties with Moscow. "Russian wine move draws protests," *BBC*, March 30, 2006, http://news.bbc.co.uk/2/hi/europe/4860454.stm.

[112] "Saakashvili's Speech at the UN General Assembly – 2013," *Civil Georgia*, September 26, 2013, http://www.civil.ge/eng/article.php?id=26491.

[113] The Military Balance, Vol. 115, Issue 1, 2015, *International Institute for Strategic Studies*, http://www.iiss.org/en/publications/military-s-balance.

[114] Jim Nichol, "Armenia, Azerbaijan, and Georgia: Political Developments and Implications for U.S. Interests," *Congressional Research Service*, April 2, 2015, https://www.fas.org/sgp/crs/row/RL33453.pdf.

[115] Vladimir Socor, "Moscow Wants the OSCE to Negotiate Directly With South Ossetia," *Eurasia Daily Monitor*, December 11, 2008, http://www.jamestown.org/single/?tx_ttnews%5Btt_news%5D=34252&no_cache=1#.Vp6Q_lMrLfY.

[116] Georgi Lomsadze, "Georgia: United Nations To Leave Abkhazia," *EurasiaNet.org*, June 17, 2009, http://www.eurasianet.org/departments/insightb/articles/eav061609c.shtml.

[117] Socor, *Eurasia Daily Monitor*, December 11, 2008.

118 "Договор между Российской Федерацией и Республикой Южная Осетия о союзничестве и интеграции" (Treaty between the Russian Federation and South Ossetia on Alliance and Integration), *Kavkazkiy Uzel*, June 30, 2015, http://www.kavkaz-uzel.ru/articles/259096/.

119 Kremlin Official Website, March 18, 2015, http://kremlin.ru/supplement/4819.

120 Yana Amelina, "Russia or Death," *Russian Planet*, December 4, 2015, http://rusplt.ru/society/rossiya-ili-smert-20078.html.

121 *Ibid.*; Paul Goble, "Is Putin about to Annex South Osetia," *Window on Eurasia*, December 6, 2015, http://windowoneurasia2.blogspot.com/2015/12/is-putin-about-to-annex-south-osetia.html.

122 "Pursuant to today's political realities, we should make our historic choice, join our brotherly Russia and guarantee security and prosperity for our republic for centuries," Tibilov was quoted by his press office; see "Kremlin Denies Its Aide Discussed Referendum on Joining Russia with S.Ossetia," *Civil Georgia*, October 20, 2015, http://www.civil.ge/eng/article.php?id=28673.

123 *Ibid*; "South Ossetian Leader Calls for Referendum on Joining Russia," *Economist Intelligence Unit*, October 21, 2015, http://country.eiu.com.proxyau.wrlc.org/article.aspx?articleid=1773612161.

124 "Kremlin Denies Its Aide Discussed Referendum on Joining Russia with S. Ossetia," *Civil Georgia*, October 20, 2015, http://www.civil.ge/eng/article.php?id=28673.

125 "After Signing New Treaty, Moscow Pledges over $200m for Abkhazia in 2015," *Civil Georgia*, November 24, 2014, http://www.civil.ge/eng/article.php?id=27846.

126 Shorena Marsagishvili: "Russia Refuses to Continue Financing Abkhazia,"*Akhali Taoba* in Georgian, August 12, 2015.

[127] Courtney Doggart, "Russian Investments in Georgia's Electricity Sector: Causes and Consequences," *International Association for Energy Economics*, 1st Quarter 2011, http://www.iaee.org/en/publications/fullnewsletter.aspx?id=17.

[128] Nick Patton Walsh, "Georgian leader attacks Russia after gas blasts," *The Guardian*, January 2006, http://www.theguardian.com/world/2006/jan/23/russia.georgia.

[129] On Russia's use of sanctions to undermine Saakashvili's government see Randall E. Newnham, "Georgia on my mind? Russian sanctions and the end of the 'Rose Revolution'," *Journal of Eurasian Studies*, Volume 6, Issue 2, July 2015, Pages 161–170, http://www.sciencedirect.com/science/article/pii/S187936651500010X.

[130] Inter RAO UES purchased Telasi and Mtkvari from the US company AES Corporation after the company's Tbilisi office received numerous threats and AES-Telasi's CFO Niko Lominadze was found murdered in his apartment. At the time, Inter RAO was 40% owned by the Russian nuclear energy giant *Rosatom*. Inter RAO is now controlled by the state-owned *Rosneftgaz*, the Russian Federal Grid Company, Norilsk Nickel Group (the world's largest producer of nickel and palladium), the Russian Foreign Economic Bank, and the state-controlled RusHydro (Russia's largest power-generating company).

[131] Eka Janashia, "Russia Increases Presence in Georgia's Energy and Transportation Markets," *CACI Analyst*, January 22, 2014, http://www.cacianalyst.org/publications/field-reports/item/13125-russia-increases-presence-in-georgias-energy-and-transportation-markets.html.

[132] Ariela Shapiro, "The Challenges to Georgia's Energy Sector," *CACI Analyst*, May 27, 2015, http://www.cacianalyst.org/publications/analytical-articles/item/13215-the-challenges-to-georgias-energy-sector.html.

[133] Vladimer Papava, Russia's illiberal "Liberal Empire," *Project Syndicate*, February 28, 2007, http://www.project-syndicate.org/commentary/russia-s-illiberal--liberal-empire#xoimRtK1GCTdIlA9.99; Diana Petriashvili,

"Georgia: No Gas Pipeline Sale For Now," *EurasiaNet.org*, March 8, 2005, http://www.eurasianet.org/departments/business/articles/eav030905.shtml.

134 "EU warning over Russia 'land grab' in South Ossetia border row," *BBC*, July 16, 2015, http://www.bbc.com/news/world-europe-33549462.

135 Rosneft Press Release, December 29, 2014, http://www.rosneft.com/news/pressrelease/29122014.html.

136 The Law on Occupied Territories, October 23, 2008, http://www.ilo.org/dyn/natlex/docs/SERIAL/81268/88220/F1630879580/G EO81268.pdf.

137 Joseph Alexander Smith, "Rosneft takes control of Georgia's Black Sea oil Terminal," *Commonspace.eu*, January 12, 2014, http://commonspace.eu/eng/news/6/id3157.

138 Thomas Kapp and Will Cathcart, "Monopolies do not stop at 49 percent - Rosneft Deal Jeopardizes Georgia's Strategic Energy Transit Corridor," *Georgia Journal*, February 5, 2015, http://www.georgianjournal.ge/business/29552-monopolies-do-not-stop-at-49-percent-rosneft-deal-jeopardizes-georgias-strategic-energy-transit-corridor.html.

139 Giorgi Menabde, "Russia Threatens Georgia With Renewed Trade War," *Eurasia Daily Monitor*, Volume 12, Issue 154, August 14, 2015, http://www.jamestown.org/single/?tx_ttnews%5Bswords%5D=8fd5893941d69d0be3f378576261ae3e&tx_ttnews%5Bany_of_the_words%5D=Net%20assessment&tx_ttnews%5Btt_news%5D=44289&tx_ttnews%5BbackPid%5D=7&cHash=42c882af6feeeaaf76e0365e345e6f5f#.VdoUr9NViko.

140 "Azerbaijani, Georgian Presidents Pledge Strategic Partnership," *Civil Georgia*, November 5, 2015, http://www.civil.ge/eng/article.php?id=28746; "По Оценке SOCAR Объем Добычи Газа в Азербайджане в 2015 г Удвоится," *Neftegaz.ru*, October 29, 2015, http://neftegaz.ru/news/view/142844.

[141] Authors interviews in Tbilisi, July 2015; Tornike Sharashenidze, "Georgia Gazprom Mistery," *Wider Europe Forum*, European Council on Foreign Relations, December 22, 2015, http://www.ecfr.eu/article/commentary_Georgias_Gazprom_mystery5061.

[142] World Bank Open Data for 2014, http://data.worldbank.org/indicator/SP.RUR.TOTL.ZS.

[143] Author's interviews in Tbilisi, July 2015.

[144] *Ibid.*

[145] NDI Opinion Poll, August 2015, https://www.ndi.org/August-2015-Public-Opinion-Poll-Georgia.

[146] NDI Opinion Poll, April 2015, https://www.ndi.org/files/NDI%20Georgia_April%202015%20Poll_Public%20Political_ENG.pdf.

[147] Natalia Antelava, "Georgia: Orthodoxy in the Classroom," *BBC*, May 7, 2015, http://www.bbc.com/news/world-europe-32595514.

[148] CSIS, Statesman's Forum, December 7, 2015, http://csis.org/multimedia/video-statesmens-forum-he-tinatin-khidasheli-defense-minister-georgia.

[149] Nata Dzvelishvili and Tazo Kupreishvili, "Russian influence on the Georgian non-governmental organizations and the media," *Damoukidebloba.com*, June 2015, https://idfi.ge/public/upload/russanimpactongeorgianmediadaNGO.pdf; Eka Janashia, "Russia Enhances Soft Power in Georgia through Local NGOs," *CACI Analyst*, June 24, 2015, http://www.cacianalyst.org/publications/field-reports/item/13243-rujssia-enchances-soft-power-georgia-local-ngos.html.

[150] Dzvelishvili and Kupreishvili, *Damoukidebloba.com*, June 2015.

[151] "Anti-Western Propaganda in Georgia," MDF, in Georgian, http://mdfgeorgia.ge/uploads/Antidasavluri-GEO-web.pdf.

[152] Eka Janashia, "Russia Enhances Soft Power in Georgia through Local NGOs," *CACI Analyst*, June 24, 2015; International Eurasian Movement website, http://www.evrazia.info/article/4672.

[153] Dzvelishvili and Kupreishvili, *Damoukidebloba.com*, June 2015.

[154] Alex Vatantka, "Trangle in the Caucasus: Iran and Israel Fight for Influence in Azerbaijan," *Foreign Affairs*, January 15, 2013, https://www.foreignaffairs.com/articles/united-states/2013-01-15/tangle-caucasus.

[155] "Turkish Military Cooperation Prompts Russian Military Moves in the Caucasus," *Stratfor*, July 11, 2015, https://www.stratfor.com/sample/analysis/turkish-military-cooperation-prompts-russian-military-moves-caucasus.

[156] Eldar Mamedov, "Turkish-Russian Tension Creates Quandary for Azerbaijan," *EurasiaNet.org*, November 30, 2015, http://www.eurasianet.org/node/76331.

[157] Aynur Karimova, "Davutoglu's Baku Visit Sets Important Messages," *AzerNews.az*, December 8, 2015, http://www.azernews.az/analysis/90579.html.

[158] "Breakaway Abkhazia Joins Russia's Anti-Turkish Sanctions," *Agenda.ge*, January 12, 2016, http://agenda.ge/news/50161/eng.

[159] Sohbet Mamedov, "Азербайджан и Иран Объединяют Железные Дороги" (Azerbaijan and Iran Connect Railways), *Nezavisimaya Gazeta*, August 19, 2015, http://www.ng.ru/cis/2015-08-19/1_azerbaijan.html.

[160] Paul Goble, "North-South Railroad Competitions Reordering Geopolitics of the Caucasus," *Eurasia Daily Monitor*, Issue 156, September 1, 2015,

http://www.jamestown.org/programs/edm/single/?tx_ttnews%5Btt_news%5D=44318&tx_ttnews%5BbackPid%5D=786&no_cache=1#.VfCglJ1VhBd.

[161] Armen Grigoryan, "Armenia, Georgia, Iran and Russia Plan to Expand Energy Cooperation," *Eurasia Daily Monitor*, Volume 13, Issue 1, January 4, 2016,
http://www.jamestown.org/regions/thecaucasus/single/?tx_ttnews%5Btt_news%5D=44939&tx_ttnews%5BbackPid%5D=54&cHash=ba8e62cb9c562ed3ee50948da0d33b4c#.VpGiZJMrJmA.

[162] Armen Grigoryan, "Armenia's Regional Energy and Transport Cooperation Squeezed by Russia," *Eurasia Daily Monitor*, Volume 12, Issue 156, September 1, 2015,
http://www.jamestown.org/programs/edm/single/?tx_ttnews%5Btt_news%5D=44319&tx_ttnews%5BbackPid%5D=786&no_cache=1#.VpG_G5MrJmC.

[163] "Armenia to sell Iran gas pipeline to Gazprom," *Press TV*, June 5, 2015, http://217.218.67.231/Detail/2015/06/05/414428/Iran-gas-armenia-pipeline-gazprom.

6. South Eastern Flank: Central Asia

Russia's annexation of Crimea reverberated throughout the five Central Asian states, raising fears of potential similar aggression on their territories. The national governments received a frightening reminder of their own vulnerabilities when Russian President Vladimir Putin justified the "Crimean Anschluss" with the need to protect the rights and interests of the Russian and Russian-speaking populations on the peninsula. Furthermore, Putin rejected accusations of violation of international law by stating that "Russia's Armed Forces never entered Crimea; they were there already in line with an international agreement."[1] These statements sent a chilling message to the Central Asian states, which are vulnerable on both counts: firstly, Russian minorities are still sizeable in the area, despite considerable emigration since the dissolution of the Soviet Union; and secondly, the region hosts Russian military bases with thousands of soldiers, making the parallel with Crimea even more unsettling.[2]

The Central Asian leaders clearly understood that the Kremlin seized Crimea and Sevastopol because of the strategic military and economic advantage Russia would gain in the Black Sea vis-à-vis its neighbors and NATO. By expanding control over the northern coast of the Black Sea, from Crimea through the Russian-occupied Georgian region of Abkhazia, Moscow wants to turn this body of water into a Russian-controlled strategic zone. Similar strategic targets are located in Central Asia—from the Caspian Sea, with the vast energy resources of Kazakhstan and Turkmenistan; to the largest space launch facility in the world, the Baikonur Cosmodrome, in Kazakhstan, which Moscow now is leasing from Astana; to some of the world's most abundant uranium deposits in the world; as well as the strategic roads crossing the region from China to Europe and the Middle East. Each of these strategic resources could become another target of Russian aggression, legitimized by the excuse of protecting the interests of the Russian minorities in Central Asia. Moscow is also well positioned to use Russian military bases located in the region in addition to its navy in the Caspian Sea as occupation forces, just as it did in Crimea and Abkhazia.

Central Asia is a vital part of the *Heartland* that Russia lost after the dissolution of the Soviet Union, but has relentlessly tried to retain control of since then, claiming it as a "zone of privileged interests." Although the 19th century "Great Game" is over and the *Heartland* has changed, it is still an arena of competition between the regional powers of Russia and China as well as Europe and the United States. The vast economic wealth of the landlocked region "with no available waterways to the ocean," as Sir Halford Mackinder once wrote, is now connected to the global world not only by railways, but also by planes and satellites. [3] Moscow understands the strategic importance of Central Asia today. Russia's leaders have always perceived the region as their backyard and used it as a bulwark against a potential invasion from the south. But in the last several years, Moscow has tried to turn it into a stronghold of Russian neo-imperialism, with the Eurasian Union being the heart of this grand political project.

For neighboring China, however, Central Asia is far from a backyard; it is a gateway to Europe, offering land transportation corridors to deliver Chinese goods to European markets much faster than maritime transportation routes. With current trade volumes between China and the EU worth over one billion euros a day, Beijing is interested in rapidly building alternative railways and highways throughout Central Asia. [4]

Consequently, Beijing's policy in the region is dramatically different from that of Moscow. While Moscow attempts to dominate Central Asia—particularly its energy sector and the strategic/military sphere—by playing on the divisions between the five states and taking advantage of their economic weaknesses, Beijing wants to build an economic belt of stability and security that will help integrate Central Asia and connect China with global markets.[5] Thus, by developing Central Asia, Beijing will benefit in both trade and security, while tapping into the region's massive energy resources. China's leaders view a stable and prosperous Central Asia as a security factor to stabilize or insulate their own restless Xinjiang province, which hosts a sizeable Turkic-Muslim minority, the Uyghurs. In parallel with this domestic objective, China's diplomacy and rigorous investment strategy in Central Asia aims to build regional alliances and enlist new international partners in order to offset both Russian and American influence in the region and thus secure Beijing's geopolitical advantage vis-à-vis Moscow and Washington.[6] Nevertheless, "China's march westward" is largely driven by economic factors, not least its need for diversified transport corridors to Europe so that it does not depend on Russia alone. After almost two decades of pursuing this policy on a bilateral basis with each of the Central Asian states, in September 2013, Chinese President Xi Jinping unveiled the Silk Road Economic Belt initiative for the region, which forms part of the *One Belt, One Road* transportation and development strategy of his country.[7]

Central Asia has also been an important region for the security of Europe and the United States. Since the terrorist attacks on the US in 2001, American interests have revolved largely around three questions: the security situation in Afghanistan, stability in the wider region hosting supply lines to Afghanistan, and European energy security. Before NATO troops started withdrawing from Afghanistan in 2015, US interests in regional stability have been guided primarily by the military operation in Afghanistan. Subsequently, the US administration made a half-hearted attempt to remain engaged in the region by promoting the New Silk Road vision. But this remained a paper initiative, lacking funding and political commitment. China eclipsed this idea and developed plans for not one Silk Road, but two—one through the landmass of Central Asia and another one through the Indian Ocean.[8] However, unlike the US concept, Beijing's main purpose does not revolve around linking Afghanistan with the rest of the region through a network of roads and railways.

Europe's primary interests in Central Asia are vested in the enormous mineral resources of the Caspian basin that can provide an alternative to Russian oil and gas supplies. Trafficking of narcotics from Afghanistan via Central Asia and Russia to Europe is also a major concern for the European Union—as are the export of terrorism from the region to Europe and the recruitment of fighters for the Islamic State in Syria. Despite its important interests in Central Asia, EU engagement has lacked focus and sufficient funding.

Since returning to the Russian presidency in 2012, Vladimir Putin has undertaken the establishment of the Eurasian Economic Union (EEU) as a counterbalance to the European Union and NATO on the one hand, and as a barrier to China's expansion in Central Asia, on the other. He succeeded in enlisting Kazakhstan as a founding member, not least because the original idea of a Eurasian Union belongs to Kazakhstan's President Nursultan Nazarbayev. But other factors played a more significant role in Astana's decision to join the Customs Union, which preceded the EEU, such as the harsh financial and economic crises in 2008–2009, long negotiations on Kazakhstan's accession to the World Trade Organization (WTO) that virtually stopped between 2008 and 2012, and the country's extensive trade and economic ties with Russia. Ironically, Kazakhstan's membership in the Customs Union and subsequently in the EEU further complicated its WTO accession.[9]

Kyrgyzstan joined the EEU in August 2015, and with that, the expansion of the Union seems to have reached its limit in Central

Asia. Tajikistan appears unwilling to join the trade bloc, while Turkmenistan and Uzbekistan never considered the possibility. Ashgabat maintains official neutrality and refrains from participating in regional organizations, while Tashkent has been historically distrustful of Moscow.

Nevertheless, Moscow managed to achieve its minimum goal, namely to economically seal most of the borders between China and Central Asia and place all trade through them under Russian control. This small victory was supposed to be the beginning of Russia's economic pushback against China in Central Asia, but instead it might turn out to be Moscow's only achievement. The EEU began to decline shortly after the annexation of Crimea, as Western sanctions against Russia affected all of its members and the economic crisis caused by plummeting oil prices incapacitated Moscow's expansion to Central Asia. As a result, by the end of 2015, Russia began visibly withdrawing from Central Asia both economically and militarily: it scrapped major water projects in Kyrgyzstan, downgraded its military base in Tajikistan, and witnessed trade declining with all Central Asian states.[10]

The Central Asian states were hesitant to openly oppose Russia for the annexation of Crimea and subsequent military intervention in eastern Ukraine. In fact, none of them supported the UN resolution affirming the territorial integrity of Ukraine and rendering the Crimean referendum on joining Russia invalid. Kazakhstan and Uzbekistan abstained (along with China), while the representatives of Kyrgyzstan, Tajikistan and Turkmenistan were absent from the UN General Assembly session.[11] The main reason for the lack of pushback against Moscow's aggressive behavior in its flanks is Central Asia's economic dependence on Russia. However, precisely the strong economic ties with Russia became the region's main liability and the source of significant economic distress. As the war in Ukraine continued through 2015, the Central Asian economies contracted, their currencies plummeted, while remittances coming from Russia drastically declined and forced many labor migrants to return home—all of these factors contributed to increased social discontent across Central Asia.

Another critical reason for the Central Asian capitals' adherence to Moscow has been the rising threat of extremism to the stability of the region, stemming from the deteriorating situation in Afghanistan. As the US and its allies withdraw their troops from Afghanistan, attacks by the Taliban are intensifying and the Islamic State (IS) is gaining more supporters. The United Nations has estimated that the IS has a presence in 25 out of Afghanistan's 34 provinces, while US intelligence sources claim that there are between 1,000 and 3,000 IS fighters in the country, many of them recruited from the ranks of the Taliban.[12]

According to the US Director of National Intelligence James Clapper, Russia is likely to use the threat of instability in Afghanistan to increase its involvement in Central Asian security affairs.[13] However, Moscow is resorting to dangerous tactics in an attempt to prevent the spread of IS influence in the North Caucasus—in 2015, it began backing the Taliban, presumed to be a rival of the IS. The Kremlin has reportedly reached out to elements of the Taliban and provided them with training, weapons and support. In the process, Russia has involved neighboring Tajikistan. This assistance made possible the September 2015 invasion of the city of Kunduz in northern Afghanistan, near the Tajik border—a multi-ethnic province where the Taliban has not been traditionally present. On the contrary, the province is home to the long-time opposition of the Taliban, the Northern Alliance. The invasion threatened the security of Tajikistan and the many Central Asian minorities living in that area of Afghanistan—Tajiks, Uzbeks and Turkmens.[14] Russia's security gambling is more likely to exacerbate the security problems of the Central Asian states than help resolve them.

Central Asian Front

Along Russia's central-eastern flank, the Central Asian states are increasingly wary of Kremlin policy and fear escalating political interference. They are also concerned about the impact of closer economic integration through the EEU, where the cost already outweighs the benefits to their own economies. If coupled with an undercutting of state sovereignty and calls to "protect" Russian ethnics in Kazakhstan and elsewhere, this could raise nationalist voices in Kazakhstan and Uzbekistan in particular and precipitate more direct conflict with Moscow in opposition to the latter's integrationist agenda.

Kazakhstan is the most vulnerable state, where Russian nationalists claim territory or view unification with Russia as a potentially viable solution. The government in Astana is unenthusiastic about Moscow's annexation of Ukrainian territory for fear that it will set a precedent for the fracturing of Kazakhstan. Nevertheless, under Kremlin pressure Astana recognized the March 16, 2014 referendum in Crimea as the expression of the "will of the people," and articulated its understanding for Moscow's concerns about the rights of Russian nationals in Ukraine. In reality, by underscoring its state policy of tolerance and peaceful coexistence toward various ethnic minorities, Astana was trying to obtain assurances from Moscow that the position of the Russian minority will not be a trigger for aggression against Kazakhstan.

Furthermore, the Kremlin may call upon Kazakhstan to provide "brotherly assistance" to a Greater Russia, possibly within the framework of the Moscow-dominated Collective Security Treaty Organization (CSTO), or threaten political repercussions. In the most far-reaching scenario, if state integrity comes under increasing question, some Central Asian states may break with Russia and appeal for international protection.

Uzbekistan has maintained substantial independence from Russia and has so far resisted overtures to join Russian-led organizations. By maneuvering in and out of the CSTO, rejecting the Customs Union, and seeking other regional arrangements, Tashkent has remained a wild card for Russia in Central Asia. However, after NATO's departure from the region, Uzbekistan could be threatened by the expected return of militant Islamist groups currently operating in Afghanistan and Pakistan, as well as Syria and Iraq. Moscow can use various methods to destabilize Uzbekistan, including by undermining the delicate ethnic balance in the Ferghana Valley, where the densely populated territories of Uzbekistan, Tajikistan, and Kyrgyzstan come together in a complicated mesh. In addition, Moscow could encourage separatism in the autonomous republic of Karakalpakstan, in Uzbekistan's northwest. Notably, calls for joining Kazakhstan or Russia were made by local nationalists there shortly after the annexation of Crimea. Furthermore, the Kremlin could incite local political grievances against the authoritarian system of governance and inspire increased penetration of more radical forms of Islam. The potential destabilization of Uzbekistan would have much wider resonance on regional stability.

Kyrgyzstan and Tajikistan, the weakest states in the region, are also the most dependent on Russia. With Russian military bases stationed in both countries and the US Manas air base in Kyrgyzstan closed down under pressure from the Kremlin, their independence is effectively challenged by Moscow. Furthermore, Russia's military installations are also a threat to Kazakhstan and Uzbekistan. The Kremlin has been courting Kyrgyzstan and Tajikistan to join the EEU by applying a combination of defense assistance and economic pressure, including threats to change its immigration policies and make them less favorable for Kyrgyz and Tajik labor migrants in Russia. The tactic was successful in the case of Kyrgyzstan, which joined the EEU in August 2015, but several months later, Bishkek realized that the economic crisis in Russia and Kazakhstan has spread to Kyrgyzstan and trade with other CIS members has actually declined.[15] Russia has also backed Tajikistan and Kyrgyzstan against Uzbekistan and Kazakhstan in contentious disputes over regional water supplies. As a non-allied country, Turkmenistan has avoided pressure to join the Customs Union, the EEU or the CSTO and has been able to develop more intense relations with China. However, Turkmenistan still depends on Russia for the prospective Trans-Caspian natural gas pipeline that will transport Turkmen gas to Europe.

Potential scenarios in Central Asia may include Kazakhstan leaving the EEU if the arrangement becomes a threat to its sovereignty; particularly since Western sanctions against Russia have heavily affected its economy. Kazakhstan may also accelerate its relocations of ethnic Kazakhs to northern Kazakhstan in an effort to thwart a potential Crimean Anschluss. In such a scenario, Russia may stage a Shadow War in Northern Kazakhstan to destabilize the country and seize territories.

The events in Ukraine, coupled with the US military withdrawal from Central Asia, may have a profound impact on the geostrategic orientation of the five republics. Their multi-vector foreign policy was challenged and tested by the Crimean precedent. While Kyrgyzstan and Tajikistan seem to be firmly in Moscow's grip (although Beijing is competing for influence in Kyrgyzstan), Kazakhstan, Uzbekistan, and Turkmenistan are increasing their cooperation with China on a bilateral basis and through the Shanghai Cooperation Organization (SCO). Moreover, this cooperation is no longer limited to the economic sphere, but also encompasses military security. This will have profound implications for the US, as containing China's ambitions may become more difficult once Beijing establishes a bridgehead in Eurasia.[16]

After 9/11, Central Asia became a strategic arena for NATO's military operations in Afghanistan, offering overflight passages for NATO airplanes, hosting military bases, and securing land routes for supplies to NATO troops. Three of the Central Asian republics border Afghanistan (Tajikistan, Turkmenistan, and Uzbekistan); the other two (Kazakhstan and Kyrgyzstan) have been instrumental in providing transportation routes to Afghanistan. Kyrgyzstan and Uzbekistan also hosted US military bases for several years. On the other hand, the region has benefited from the US military presence, which provided short-term security and economic gains from transport fees, supply of commodities, and rent for military bases. However, the US withdrawal from Afghanistan changed the region's strategic position vis-à-vis Washington and, with the dramatic developments in the Middle East, it essentially dropped from the list of strategic priorities for the US administration under President Obama.

The New Silk Road vision for regional stabilization and development, promoted by the US administration in 2011, remained largely a paper initiative with little financial backing or political commitment. At its core was the development of transport infrastructure and encouraging international trade in the wider Central Asian region, including connecting Afghanistan with the rest of Central Asia and reviving the old Silk Roads running through Afghanistan. These Afghanistan-centered long-term plans, however, had a very short window of opportunity to make groundbreaking progress while NATO troops were still providing security in Afghanistan. The window was missed, despite the promise of then–Secretary of State Hilary Clinton that "the United States would continue shifting its development efforts from short-term stabilization projects, largely as part of the military strategy, to longer-term sustainable development that focuses on spurring growth, creating jobs, invigorating the private sector, and integrating Afghanistan into the South and Central Asia economy."[17] While the US administration continues to issue official statements about the New Silk Road strategy, China has actually started building the roads and railways that will make it a reality. Yet, Afghanistan is not taking a central place in the transport network envisioned by Beijing's Central Asia strategy, an omission that could have a negative impact on efforts to stabilize the country and ensure regional security.

After the dissolution of the Soviet Union, Russia has implemented a neo-imperial strategy of dominance over the Central Asian states using diplomatic, political, security, and economic means, treating the region as a zone of its "privileged interests." Moscow has also used the Russian minorities in Central Asia as a tool of influence, pressure, and leverage in domestic and regional politics. Russia's goal is to remain the main security actor and military equipment supplier in the region, continue to be a transit country for oil exports to Europe, preserve (or install) pro-Moscow political regimes in the five Central Asian capitals, and closely coordinate their foreign and security policies.

By involving Central Asian states in administrative, security and economic alliances such as the CIS, the CSTO, the Eurasian Economic Community (Eurasec), the Customs Union, and, most recently, the EEU, Russia has positioned itself as the main pole of power and influence in the region. However, with the economic rise of China and the establishment of the SCO, as a largely Chinese initiative, Moscow's position in the region has been challenged. In fact, Moscow is gradually losing ground in Central Asia and reluctantly ceding control to Beijing, particularly in the economic arena.

Although the SCO was created in 2001 as an economic and security body including Russia, China, and the four of the Central Asian states (Kyrgyzstan, Kazakhstan, Tajikistan, and Uzbekistan), Moscow wants to make sure that the CSTO, in which China does not participate, remains the key Central Asian security network.[18] A Memorandum of Understanding signed between the CSTO and SCO, in 2007, enabled Moscow to present itself as the chief security coordinator in Central Asia.[19] China has restrained its sales of arms to Central Asian militaries and limited the SCO's defense activities to fighting terrorism and other unconventional security threats through intelligence-sharing and law enforcement partnerships.[20] However, the competition between Russia and China in the security domain is likely to continue, particularly as China has become the main economic power in the region.

China sees Central Asia as a critical frontier for its military defense, energy security, trade expansion, and ethnic stability.[21] Beijing has been investing billions of dollars in the region's new energy infrastructure, transportation routes, and major economic enterprises. Its economic expansion is embracing all five Central Asian republics in a regional economic integration mechanism, which was conducted quietly and mostly on a bilateral basis until President Xi Jinping announced in the fall of 2013 the Silk Road Economic Belt development plan for Central Asia, which forms part of the grand Chinese development strategy *One Belt, One Road*.[22]

These economic bonds are changing the region's geopolitics, although China has been careful not to provoke conflict with Russia by openly exhibiting its military or political ambitions, given Moscow's determination to pose as the leading power in Central Asia. Beijing's cultural outreach, however, is intensifying, not least with the opening of numerous Confucius Institutes to teach Mandarin throughout the region. China is also providing aid to the region, including regular technical military assistance and training to all five governments, among them a police training grant to Ashgabat, television receivers for the residents of the Batken Oblast in Kyrgyzstan, and 52 busses along with musical instruments to the Kyrgyz military. China has reportedly allocated $4.4 million for large-scale scanning equipment at customs posts in Uzbekistan.[23]

Central Asian leaders resent Russia's desire for political domination, while they both welcome and fear China's economic might. As the region desperately needs foreign investment to boost economic growth, locate new markets, and curb dependence on Russia, it is also anxious about the political price of economic dependence from an expansive neighbor. Kazakhstani citizens, for example, staged protests in 2009 against their President's intent to rent some of the country's arable land to China, because of fears that large Chinese labor migration to the scarcely populated Kazakhstan would change the country's demographic makeup.[24]

China's massive investments in Central Asia have undermined Russia's influence, forcing the Kremlin to invent new economic and political schemes to retain its positions in the region, with the latest being the EEU, initiated by Putin in October 2011. Worried that the US was leaving Afghanistan and may no longer be an influential factor in the region, the Central Asian governments are forced to play a careful balancing act—they are backing Russian-led integration plans while accepting cash from China. The two international players, however, are becoming increasingly uneven, with China taking the position of economic dominance vis-à-vis Russia.

The global economic crisis did not visibly impact the Chinese economy, which continued to grow by 8.7% in 2009 and 10.3% in 2010, while the Russian economy contracted by a record 7.8% in 2009, and only managed to recover to a modest 4% growth in 2010. After the annexation of Crimea in 2014, Western sanctions, combined with a sharp decline in oil prices, have put the Russian economy in a long-term inferior position in relation to the Chinese economy. The slowdown of the Chinese economy is not projected to impact Beijing nearly as sharply as the plummeting oil prices affected Moscow. China's gross domestic product (GDP) was forecast to grow by 6.8% in 2015, while Russia's economy was expected to shrink by 3.8%, according to the International Monetary Fund (IMF).[25]

Since the economies of the Central Asian republics were developed as an integral part of the Soviet economic system, they remained heavily dependent on Russia for most of the last two decades. Oil and gas from the region has been flowing north to Russia, with Moscow dictating the energy prices. Russia has effectively used the Soviet infrastructure to take advantage of Caspian basin resources and retain its monopoly in providing energy to Europe. However, with rapid Chinese investments in Central Asia's energy sector and particularly in building new pipelines leading east and south to Chinese provinces, Russia's privileged access to energy sources has been curtailed. Russia used to buy fossil fuels at low prices from the Caspian basin and resell them at much higher prices in Europe. The growing competition for energy in Central Asia ensured that Moscow has had to buy energy commodities at much higher prices, which reduced the margin of profit from resale significantly. As a result, *Gazprom* and *Rosneft* have focused on developing Russia's own energy resources in the Arctic region and the Okhotsk Sea, but these plans are not going without problems. At the end of 2014, the US and the EU applied a new round of sanctions specifically targeting Russia's Arctic energy sector by banning EU exports of sensitive technologies to Russia related to deep sea drilling, Arctic exploration, and shale oil extraction.[26]

At the same time, China's ability to gain leverage internationally is growing. Using its immense financial reserves, Beijing purchases state-owned energy companies or invests in natural resources abroad to ensure its energy security and gain political leverage over host countries.[27] Pipelines have been built between China and Central Asia—a gas pipeline from Turkmenistan, an oil pipeline from Kazakhstan, and a spur of the East Siberia–East Pacific Ocean oil pipeline from Russia.

The Central Asia–China pipeline begins in the gas fields in Turkmenistan, transits through Uzbekistan and southern Kazakhstan, and reaches China's Xinjiang province where it connects with China's second west–east gas pipeline. The second line starts from the Xinjiang Uygur autonomous region and ends in Hong Kong, with a total length of 8,704 kilometers (km). The two pipelines allow Central Asian gas from Turkmenistan and Uzbekistan to reach the South China Sea.

The new Central Asia–China gas pipeline has broken Russia's monopoly over gas transport in the region. In 2011, China and

Turkmenistan signed a deal that will allow Turkmenistan to supply China with 65 bcm of natural gas per year, or over 50% more than the initially agreed 30 bcm per annum in 2007.[28] The deal challenged Russia's position as the main buyer of Turkmen gas at the time and subsequently pushed out Russia from Turkmenistan's gas market. China's imports of Turkmen gas were boosted to 40 bcm/a in 2015, as high as the volume previously bought by *Gazprom*.[29] In 2015, Russia ceased buying Turkmen gas due to price disputes, Gazprom's non-payment of received volumes, and the decreased gas demand in Europe. With this, Moscow's influence in Ashgabat further diminished. [30]

China's energy specialists estimate that by the year 2020, China's annual consumption will reach 300 bcm and the country will need to import 80–120 bcm/a of gas. However, due to weakening economic growth in China, the growth of gas consumption has also dropped from 17.4% in 2013 to 8.9% in 2014. In 2015, the growth rate dipped to 3.7% over an 11-month period, as reported by the National Development and Reform Commission (NDRC).[31]

Nevertheless, gas supplies from Central Asia are essential for China's economy, which tries to replace polluting coal usage with clean gas, particularly since energy cooperation between China and Russia has not lived up to its potential.[32] In 2006, *Gazprom* and *China National Petroleum Corporation (CNPC)* agreed to build two gas pipelines from Siberia to China—one connecting Altai with China's Central Asia pipeline, and the other from Sakhalin Island to the northeast of China—but both remained on paper until early 2011. *Gazprom* and *CNPC* subsequently agreed to make the western pipeline commercially operational by 2015, but postponed the eastern line until after 2015. China is concerned whether Russia will be able to deliver the agreed 68 bcm per year through these two pipelines, because *Gazprom's* production in West Siberia is declining while the exploration in the Russian Far East and East Siberia requires enormous infrastructure investments that *Gazprom* has difficulties undertaking. [33]

Although, in 2014, China and Russia finally signed a $400-billion deal for delivering 38 bcm of Russian gas to China for 30 years via the eastern line, the prospective *Power of Siberia* pipeline, Gazprom wants to postpone the $55-billion pipeline project, preferring to pump gas from existing fields through a shorter pipeline to Xinjiang instead.[34] Financial pressures on Russia further delayed work on the pipeline, and by the end of 2015, only 50 miles out of the 2,465-mile-long pipeline were constructed.[35]

In 2009, China provided the SCO with a $10 billion loan to shore up members affected by the economic downturn. Chinese President Hu Jintao offered the same amount of loans again in 2012.[36] Additionally, it provided Kazakhstan with $10 billion in financing to overcome its banking crisis in 2009—partly in loans and partly through the acquisition of the majority of shares in Kazakhstan's fourth-largest state oil company *MangistauMunaiGaz*.[37] The existence of the oil pipeline connecting the two countries and enabling the transport of oil by land makes the acquisition of extraction assets in Kazakhstan particularly important and strategic for Beijing, given China's reliance on maritime oil supplies from the Middle East via the Strait of Malacca.

Subsequently, China proposed the establishment of the SCO Development Bank, whereby the bank's authorized capital would be formed from proportional contributions by each participating country. This will ultimately mean that China would dominate the bank, since its economy is almost five times larger than Russia's. Moscow, however, insists that the SCO bank is based on the Eurasian Development Bank, which already operates within the EEU and is controlled by Russia. [38]

Russia stepped up efforts to secure its economic and political dominance in Central Asia after the US withdrew most of its combat forces from Afghanistan. Putin proclaimed his grand idea of a new Eurasian Union in early October 2011 shortly after announcing his intention to return to the presidency for a third mandate. In an article in the Russian newspaper *Izvestia*, Putin called for the creation of a Eurasian Union as "a powerful supranational union, capable of becoming one of the poles in the modern world and playing the role of an effective link between Europe and the dynamic Asia-Pacific region." [39] Putin denied any intent to recreate the Soviet Union, claiming "it would be naïve to try to restore or copy something that belongs to the past." Instead, he stated "pragmatic" reasons for regional integration based on economic interests, market protection, and free trade. Putin insisted that only by acting together could the CIS countries be included among the global economic leaders participating in the decision-making process. He compared his proposed union to "other key players and regional structures," such as the EU, the US, China, and the Asia-Pacific Economic Cooperation organization.

The EEU is developed on the foundation of the Customs Union of Belarus, Kazakhstan and Russia, which became operational in 2010, and the three countries' Single Economic Space launched at the start of 2012. Putin wrote that the next stage would involve closer coordination of economic and currency policy, thus the establishment of an economic union. In November 2011, the three countries formally agreed to establish the EEU by 2015 that would become open to all former Soviet countries. The Eurasian Union remains one of Putin's key priorities. There are four reasons to launch yet another post-Soviet integration project after failed attempts to revive the CIS and make Eurasec an effective multinational regulatory body:

- First, the extraordinary rise of China and its rapid economic expansion into Central Asia threatens to oust Russia in both the economic and security fields. A Eurasian Union can serve as a defense of Russia's strategic interests by providing a platform for economic and political control over the Central Asian states, not least through a common currency. The logical defense component of the union is the Russian-led CSTO.

- Second, Moscow seeks to reinforce its positions vis-à-vis the EU and NATO, hoping that a Eurasian Union would provide it with increased negotiating powers. Before annexing Crimea and inciting the war in eastern Ukraine, Russia aimed to achieve a special status toward NATO, influence the alliance's decisions, and become its partner with designated responsibilities for Central Asia. It also attempted to establish a free trade regime with the EU, and specifically obtain a visa-free status for Russian citizens to travel to Europe. These plans were squashed by Moscow's aggression in Ukraine, following the refusal of the new government in Kyiv to join the Eurasian Union and instead associate with the EU.

- Third, the Kremlin is determined to keep the West, and particularly the US, out of Central Asia. By assuming responsibility for the region, Russia is positioning itself to handle any regional security problems without interference from Western institutions. In particular, this was a response to the New Silk Road strategy of the US administration, which could have created conditions for regional integration in Central Asia, including Afghanistan, and the development of continental trade between Asia and Europe through Central Asia. While Russia certainly welcomes peace and security in Afghanistan, it sees Western-led economic development and investment effort in Central Asia as a direct threat to its strategic interests.

- Fourth, by pressing ahead with the EEU, Putin is consolidating his control over nationalist constituencies in Russia. Well before the seizure of Crimea, the Russian public was becoming increasingly nationalistic and neo-imperial. A 2011 study by the Pew Research Center unveiled that roughly half of Russians (48%) believe it natural for their country to have an empire, while only

33% disagreed. By contrast, during the final months of the USSR, only 37% considered a Russian empire to be natural. Half of Russians in 2011 also agreed with the statement "it is a great misfortune that the Soviet Union no longer exists." [40] After Crimea's annexation, nationalist tendencies further increased in Russia.

The realization of the EEU project seemed unlikely at the time it was announced.[41] The legacy of the Russian Tsarist empire and the Soviet Union left bitter memories and resentment toward any kind of political domination by Moscow in most of the newly independent post-Soviet states. Although Putin stated that the EEU would be built on the principles of economic cooperation, its governing institutions are based in Moscow. The Customs Union commission is also located in Moscow, and most of its employees are Russian citizens. Kazakhstan's President Nursultan Nazarbayev was the only Central Asian leader endorsing Putin's proposal. He has promoted the idea of a Eurasian Union since the 1990s, but the Kazakhstani president has never envisioned a union dominated by Russia or used by Moscow to advance its own foreign policy and security agendas. Tensions between the founding members of the Customs Union and Eurasian Economic Union were obvious from the beginning.[42]

Cooperation has proven difficult within other regional formats, none of which includes all the former Soviet republics. The newly independent states have different foreign policy priorities, some preferring to develop cooperative relations with Europe and NATO, while others trade more with the East than with each other. The EU has also strengthened its eastward outreach and could offer considerable economic incentives to the former Soviet republics. For example, the current EU energy policy would benefit Turkmenistan both economically and politically, allowing for alternative export routes for Turkmen gas and furthering independence from Russian exports.

Most importantly, for the EEU to be successful, Moscow needs significant resources, which it is not in a position to provide. The structure of its rent-seeking economy, which relies essentially on high prices of energy supplies, cannot sustain an integration effort of the magnitude of the EU, particularly when the energy prices collapse. Moreover, a Russia-led grand regional integration project seems doomed if juxtaposed against the ongoing disintegration processes within the Russian Federation itself.

Militarily, until the fall of 2015, Russia was planning to strengthen its military positions in Central Asia, particularly boosting its military presence in Kyrgyzstan and Tajikistan.[43] In September 2011, Moscow achieved consent from Dushanbe to extend the agreement on hosting its military base in Tajikistan by 49 years.[44] The Russian base in Tajikistan was established in 2005 as the successor to the former 201st Motorized Rifle Division from the Soviet period. The country hosts the second-largest foreign Russian military base (5,000–7,000 troops.) At the CIS summit in October 2015, Russia announced plans to increase its troops in Tajikistan to 9,000. Surprisingly however, two months later Moscow announced that it was planning to downgrade its military base in Tajikistan to a brigade. Analysts explain the decision with Russia's troubled economy and tensions between Russian troops and the local population.[45]

Moscow wanted to install Russian border guards on the Tajikistan–Afghanistan border, but the Tajik government turned down the offer. Russia has criticized Tajikistan for its incapacity to control drug smuggling from Afghanistan. Reportedly, roughly 95 metric tons of heroin pass through Central Asia from Afghanistan annually and only 5 metric tons are intercepted.[46] Russia is concerned about the import of drugs to its own territory, as most of them are sold on the Russian market. It is the second largest drug consumer in the world, with estimated annual consumption of 70 metric tons of heroin and 58 metric tons of opium in 2008. Demand in the Russian Federation has not changed since then, although opium production in Afghanistan has increased in 2014, while seized quantities in Central Asia have decreased. [47]

The Kremlin pressed Kyrgyzstan to sign a 49-year lease on the Kant airbase. Moscow also proposed to merge its five military facilities in Kyrgyzstan into a single base to be deployed on gratis terms for 49 years with the possibility of a 25-year extension. Kyrgyz President Almazbek Atambayev agreed in exchange for a $30 million loan from Russia and a $256 million loan from the Eurasec anti-crisis fund, as well as $180 million in loan forgiveness from Russia. In 2011, Kyrgyzstan canceled any lease payments on the airbase in exchange for lower cost fuel imports from Russia. With the help of Eurasec money, Russia also obtained other lucrative deals. *Gazprom* gained control over Kyrgyzstan's state gas company; a Gazprom-controlled joint venture was supplying 50% of the fuel needed by the US airbase in Manas, and Russia was given 49% of the Dastan torpedo plant. [48]

Russia's plans to renew by 2016 the fleet of its airbase at Kant, Kyrgyzstan, may also be put off for financial reasons, although Moscow has already sent a dozen new and modified Su-25 fighter jets to replace older planes and has been upgrading other equipment at the bases—trucks, armored personnel carriers, and drones. [49]

Russia's biggest demand was the closure of the US Transit Center at Manas International airport, the last large US Air Force base in Central Asia. Manas served as a key transit point for American troops and military supplies to Afghanistan. Immediately after his election on October 30, 2011, Atambayev declared that the US base needed to close by 2014, the deadline for the US troop withdrawal from Afghanistan. He claimed that its presence on Kyrgyz soil placed the country at risk of retaliatory strikes from those in conflict with Washington. Kyrgyz Deputy Prime Minister Omurbek Babanov added that further decisions on the future of the American base would only be made while taking into account the interests of CSTO partners. A Russian government source told *Kommersant* newspaper that Atambayev started fulfilling his pre-election promises to Moscow after the Kremlin helped him win the presidency.[50]

Both the CSTO and the SCO have been gearing up for more intensive involvement in Central Asia after NATO leaves Afghanistan. Notably, the CSTO military drills "Tsentr 2011" held in Tajikistan on September 19–27, 2011, focused not only on counter-terrorism, but also on the prevention of possible uprisings similar to those in the Middle East and North Africa. The Russian Chief of the General Staff Nikolai Makarov admitted that the exercises were designed to respond to mass unrest and instability similar to that seen in Libya and Syria, and to a potential spillover from Afghanistan.[51] The Kremlin has been propping up authoritarian regimes in Central Asia, mostly because limited democratization contributes to isolating these countries from the West and keeps them in a tighter orbit around Russia. In the aftermath of the Arab Spring and earlier colored revolutions, and particularly after the Euro Maidan in Kyiv, Russia is making every effort to stall any possibility for democratic changes in the region.

The relationship between the CSTO and the SCO is complicated since the security interests of their leading countries differ on several key points and often compete. Russia uses both security alliances to achieve two principle objectives in strengthening its strategic presence in Central Asia: keep the US out of the region and limit China's growing power. The Kremlin sees the SCO as a loose military alliance designed to combat any penetration of the area by Western powers, especially the US. Furthermore, Russia uses the SCO as a platform to counter NATO's eastward expansion and block US plans for anti-ballistic missile systems in Europe and Asia.

China's security concerns remain focused on its restive western province of Xinjiang, US policy toward Taiwan, and energy security. China is also interested in limiting US influence in the region for fear of intervention in internal separatist conflicts. However, China's primary concern during the last decade has been related to energy demands for its growing economy. As Beijing worries about the possible disruption of its maritime energy imports from the Middle East, it has intensified efforts to secure access to Central Asia's hydrocarbon resources. By positioning the SCO as an economic cooperation organization and focusing on trade and investment, China has used it as an instrument for economic expansion. As a result, Beijing has managed to achieve its major energy security objective and simultaneously increase its influence in the region.

From the outside, it seems that China and Russia are balancing each other within the SCO since China is stronger economically, while Russia has greater political resources. But the rivalry for influence between them is escalating while disagreements have taken place on more than one issue.

Even before the annexation of Crimea, the Russian invasion of Georgia and subsequent recognition of the independence of the separatist territories of Abkhazia and South Ossetia was a major dividing point in Russia's relations with all SCO members, but particularly with China. Respect for national sovereignty and non-interference in internal affairs of other states are two of the SCO principles that China firmly supports, mostly because of internal secessionist movements. Russia's military intervention in support of the two Georgian breakaway regions was unacceptable to Beijing as is Moscow's continuing military intervention in Ukraine.[52] In addition, Moscow has supported India for full SCO membership as a means of countering growing Chinese influence, while Beijing has encouraged its closest South Asian partner, Pakistan, to apply to join the group. Apart from animosities between India and Pakistan and the risks associated with having them both in the same organization, China also views India as its rival and competitor in Central Asia. Both countries were eventually admitted to the organization in 2015.

The Russian diaspora is a critical factor in Moscow's neo-imperial ambitions, as evidenced in Crimea and Donbas. However, Russia is rapidly losing ground in the demographic make-up of Central Asia: the Russian minority has steeply declined since the collapse of the Soviet Union and continues to shrink. The Russian population in the five Central Asian countries is estimated to have dropped from 9.5 million in 1989 to 4.7–4.8 million in 2015. Although the largest wave of migration to Russia took place in the first decade of independence, when an estimated 3.3 million Russians left Central Asia, the flow of emigrants has not ceased. For example, in the period 2009–2015, an average of 20,000 Russians have left Kazakhstan each year and about 10,000 left Kyrgyzstan. Moreover, the remaining Russian communities consist overwhelmingly of aging population groups with much higher death rates than those of the titular populations. As a result, Russians in Tajikistan and Turkmenistan are likely to be extinct in the next generation.[53]

The exodus of Russians from Central Asia is shrinking the Russian ethnic and linguistic space in the region, directly threatening Putin's "Russian world" project. Population data indicates that the Russian minorities are currently very small in Tajikistan and Turkmenistan and proportionately insignificant in Uzbekistan. However, more than three quarters of the region's Russians (3.7 million) live in Kazakhstan, making them an important demographic, economic and political factor in that country.

Although public attitudes toward Russians in Central Asia are generally friendly, the Russian minorities are completely excluded from the local clan-based patronage networks that are crucial for access to resources and political power.[54] In addition, legal provisions for greater political representation of large national minorities are rarely made, while knowledge of the majority language is often required for access to government jobs. The unwillingness of many Russians to learn the state languages limits their competiveness for public sector employment. Moscow can exploit minority grievances resulting from both factors—the Russian diaspora's exclusion from patronage networks and its limited access to government jobs.

In fact, Moscow's propaganda about the Ukrainian events is already sowing fears among the Russians in Central Asia. Both the Russian media and diplomatic missions are portraying the new government in Kyiv as nationalistic and discriminatory against minorities. Not surprisingly, the annexation of Crimea gave rise to anti-Russian sentiment in a number of Central Asian countries. Uncertain about political transitions in Kazakhstan and Uzbekistan, the local Russians are beginning to worry about their lives if more nationalistic leaders replace the current ones.

Kazakhstan

Three critical factors make the largest Central Asian country, Kazakhstan, acutely vulnerable to Russian pressure: the sizable Russian minority representing one fifth of Kazakhstan's population and concentrated mostly in the northern and eastern provinces; the long border with Russia stretching 7,644 kilometers (4,749 miles); and the extensive economic connections between the two countries, including through the Eurasian Customs Union (ECU) and the Eurasian Economic Union (EEU).

However, there are also a number of elements that prevent Moscow from exercising decisive influence on Astana: among them, Kazakhstan's enormous size and vast energy resources; extensive Western investments in the energy sector and other industries; the country's multi-vector foreign policy and rising international profile; its strong relations with Turkey and the Islamic world; its liberal policy on minorities and minority languages, including Russian; and the ability of Kazakhstan's President Nursultan Nazarbayev to keep Moscow at bay for the last 25 years.

There are many unknowns about the future political succession in Kazakhstan and whether the next leader will be able to balance internal and external pressures to preserve the country's sovereignty. Some Russian nationalists have speculated that a period of political transition and uncertainty would present a chance for Russia to seize territories in northern Kazakhstan. [55] Nevertheless, the main deterrence to potential aggression by Moscow remains China, which is expanding its economic power to Central Asia through Kazakhstan. Beijing needs a stable and secure Central Asia to stabilize its own restless Xinjiang province, which borders the region, and boost trade with Europe. This is why some suggestions that Beijing could be drawn into a potential Moscow plot to partition Kazakhstan between Russia and China are illogical and ungrounded. [56] On the contrary, one can argue that China will seek to avoid another resentful Muslim population in a territory next to Xinjiang. Unlike Russia, which has used military intervention in Ukraine and Georgia in an attempt to change their political direction, China has been pursuing influence in Central Asia primarily through economic means.

The Kazakhstan–China border crossing point of Khorgos has become the grand entrance to Central Asia of China's Silk Road Economic Belt. This 7th-century stop for Silk Road merchants, called "the pearl" on the Silk Road Economic Belt, is hosting one of the largest free economic zones in the region. As China rapidly develops its side of the free economic zone, Kazakhstan is planning to catch up in 2016. Astana hurries to diversify trade relations with countries outside the EEU, including China, as heavy dependence on sanctions-hit Russia has proven economically devastating. [57]

By annexing Crimea and staging a covert military intervention in eastern Ukraine, the Kremlin set a precedent by violating the 1994 Budapest Memorandum. This memorandum concerned not only Ukraine, but also Kazakhstan and Belarus. In 1994, Russia, the US and the UK provided security assurances for the territorial integrity and political independence of all three countries in exchange for surrendering their Soviet-era nuclear stockpiles. When the Soviet Union collapsed in December 1991, Kazakhstan found itself as the fourth-largest nuclear arsenal country in the world after Russia, the US and Ukraine. It inherited 1,410 nuclear warheads and the Semipalatinsk nuclear weapons test site. By April 1995, Kazakhstan sent its nuclear warhead inventory to Russia, and by 2000, it destroyed the nuclear testing infrastructure at Semipalatinsk.[58] Approximately 600 kg (1,322 pounds) of weapons-grade highly enriched uranium (HEU) was removed to the US from the Ulba Metallurgy Plant in 1994 under a joint US-Kazakh operation known as Project Sapphire.[59] The country has prided itself for not only getting rid of its nuclear weapons, but also starting an international campaign to end nuclear testing around the world.[60]

Russia's attack on Ukraine in March 2014 sent shock waves throughout Kazakhstan, stirring a discussion among the public and in the media whether the country is next on Russia's hit list.[61] The initial official reaction was restrained out of concern that Russia could replicate the Crimean scenario in Kazakhstan, but it also exposed Astana's hesitation to oppose its powerful northern neighbor. Official statements were confusing, revealing distress and indicating possible pressure by Kremlin. For example, in a telephone conversation on March 10, 2014, with US President Barak Obama, President Nazarbayev "agreed on the importance of upholding principles of sovereignty and territorial integrity."[62] But in a subsequent phone call with Russian President Putin on the same day, Nazarbayev expressed "understanding of Russia's position on protecting the rights of national minorities in Ukraine, as well as its own security."[63]

At the Nuclear Security Summit on March 25, 2014, in The Hague, Nazarbayev insisted that both the West and Russia should tone down the confrontational rhetoric, take the threat of sanctions off the table, and try to find a peaceful solution to the crisis. His remarks were perceived as strong support for Russia, as he essentially blamed the new leadership in Kyiv for triggering the crisis. His statements that "a constitutional coup d'état" had taken place in Kyiv and there had been "discrimination against minority rights" in Ukraine were perceived as justification for Moscow's actions in Crimea and immediately protested by Kyiv.[64] A week earlier, the Ukrainian government protested the official statement of Kazakhstan's Ministry of Foreign Affairs, which also stated: "The referendum held in Crimea is seen in Kazakhstan as a free expression of [the] will of the Autonomous Republic's population while the decision of the Russian Federation under the existing circumstances is regarded with understanding."[65] Subsequently, Kazakhstan abstained from voting on the UN resolution that rendered the Crimean referendum invalid on March 28, 2014.

Despite the impression of staunch loyalty to Moscow, Astana's reaction was wrongly interpreted as an endorsement of Russia's aggression in Ukraine. As Almaty-based analyst Aidos Sarym pointed out, Kazakhstan's position was "dictated not so much by creed as by fear… Events in Crimea are a possible scenario for Kazakhstan too."[66] The country has the largest Russian minority in the region, estimated at 3.68 million in 2014, or 21.5% of the total population.[67] This figure is calculated to be over three quarters of the total Russian population remaining in the five Central Asian states. If Russia has political leverage through its diaspora in any Central Asian country, this is undoubtedly Kazakhstan.

The fear of repetition of the Crimean events was reinforced by an earlier appeal of Russian nationalist politician Vladimir Zhirinovsky for the creation of a "Central Asian Federal Region" within the Russian Federation, with its capital in "Vernyi," the Tsarist Russian name of Almaty. The statement was made at a public meeting in Moscow, on February 23, 2014, just as Russian troops started appearing in Crimea. A few days earlier, controversial Russian writer and leader of the banned National Bolshevik Party, Eduard Limonov, also suggested that Russia should annex regions in eastern Ukraine and northern Kazakhstan: "I hope Russia will get hold of some part of Ukraine if we don't waste time. And will get hold of northern regions of Kazakhstan as well," Limonov wrote on his Facebook page, provoking a diplomatic note of protest from Astana.[68]

Occasional calls by Russian nationalists for secession of the northern regions of Kazakhstan are not new. In 1990, former Soviet dissident Aleksandr Solzhenitsyn, who became a fervent Russian nationalist after the Soviet collapse, called for the transfer of northern Kazakhstan to Russia. Almaty-born Vladimir Zhirinovsky was banned from entering Kazakhstan for making similar statements in 2005. There was also an alleged attempt by Russian separatists to seize an area in Kazakhstan in late 1999 and early 2000, which ended with a lengthy prison sentence for the main instigator, Moscow resident Victor Kazimirchuk. His small group called "Rus" is believed to have planned to take over the administration of Kazakhstan's northeastern city of Oskemen in the East Kazakhstan region, bordering Russia, declare it Russian territory, and appeal to Moscow to incorporate the area into the Russian Federation. Kazimirchuk claimed that he had support from both the Russian population in Kazakhstan and from the Russian government. Among the 22 individuals arrested and tried for the plot, 12 were Russian citizens.[69]

The Russian minority in Kazakhstan was the only one in Central Asia that managed to organize itself after independence. The local branch of the Russian nationalist organization "Yedinstvo" was established in 1989 when the Kazakh language, native to only 40% of the population at the time, was proclaimed the state language: "the language for state management, legislation, legal proceedings and office work, functioning in all spheres of social relations in the entire territory of the state."[70] Although the Russian language, spoken by more than half of the population at the time, was relegated to a secondary status, the 1995 constitution stipulated that it should be officially used on an equal footing with Kazakh.[71] Considered the language of international and intercultural communication, Russian still has a special status in the country, where the state is obliged to promote conditions for the study and development of the languages of the people of Kazakhstan.[72]

The language laws also require proficiency in Kazakh for all public sector jobs and university admissions. Candidates for elected positions are mandated to pass a Kazakh-language proficiency test before running in an election. The Russian population reacted negatively to losing its privileged status maintained under the Soviets, feeling that the new language policies would threaten the preservation of their culture and they would be gradually assimilated. In response to the language law, "Yedinstvo" campaigned for the annexation of Kazakhstan's northern regions by the Russian Federation. When ethnic Russians started relocating to Russia *en mass*, another organization, the Association of Slavic Movements of Kazakhstan (LAD), urged them not to leave Kazakhstan, because the Russian minority would lose political relevance. [73]

The Cossacks in Kazakhstan, who consider themselves a distinct ethnic group, also organized and demanded territorial secession of Kazakhstan's northern regions in the early 1990s, saying they did not recognize the border between Russia and Kazakhstan. [74] The Cossacks have been angered by the fact that Kazakhstan's government considers them a sociopolitical grouping, denying their claim to separate cultural identity and national self-determination. Their status in Kazakhstan is unlike that of their brethren in Russia, where the state has supported a cultural revival of Cossack communities. [75]

However, while Russian Cossacks have taken part in most armed conflicts in Eurasia, including the wars in Transnistria, Abkhazia, South Ossetia, Chechnya and eastern Ukraine, Kazakhstan's Cossacks have evidently refused to fight on the side of the separatists in eastern Ukraine. They adamantly refuted Russian propaganda claims that Cossacks from eastern Kazakhstan had volunteered to join the "defenders" of Russian-speakers in the Donbas. The Kazakh media also harshly criticized Russian entities, such as the Eurasian Youth Movement, for involvement in Kazakhstan's domestic affairs. [76]

Astana's policy of supporting peaceful inter-ethnic co-existence during the past 20 years has proven effective in integrating the Cossacks in the current political system through the Assembly of People of Kazakhstan, a consultative body chaired by President Nazarbayev. The assembly is a platform for inter-ethnic dialogue and cooperation, which also elects nine representatives of minorities to serve as members of Kazakhstan's parliament, the Majilis. In May 2013, the Astana-based World Union of Cossack Atamans, whose aim is "the recognition of the genocide against the Cossacks in revolutionary Russia," even suggested Nazarbayev as a candidate for the Nobel Peace Prize. Nazarbayev has been pronounced the Honorary Supreme Ataman of Kazakhstan's Cossacks.[77]

The large Russian population has been a concern for Kazakhstan's leadership, which had to balance the interests of the minorities with its strategy of promoting the Kazakh language and culture to reclaim Kazakh national identity after two centuries under Russian and Soviet rule. The task was extremely challenging, given that the Kazakhs were not a majority in their own country at the time. President Nazarbayev had to tread cautiously on the domestic arena while pacifying Moscow when problems occurred. But he did not hesitate to strongly react in 1993 over remarks by Russian Foreign Minister Kozyrev that Moscow would act tough if necessary to protect the rights of Russians in former Soviet republics. "When someone talks about the protection of Russians not in Russia but in Kazakhstan, I recall the times of Hitler, who started with protecting the Sudeten Germans," he famously said in an interview with Interfax.[78]

From the start, Nazarbayev rejected two options: federalization of the country to provide for more minority autonomy and double citizenship. Both would have proven risky, especially when assessing these options in the light of Crimea and Donbas. Eventually, the Russian question did not lead to a security crisis or devastating destabilization of the country, despite the low starting point of inter-ethnic relations back in the 1990s. The government's inter-ethnic policies promoting tolerance and coexistence helped protect the cultural and language rights not only of the Russian population, but also those of the remaining 130 ethnic groups in Kazakhstan.

Furthermore, demographic numbers changed dramatically in the years after independence, due to Russian emigration, repatriation of almost one million Oralmans (ethnic Kazakhs from neighboring countries), and relocation of ethnic Kazakhs to the northern part of the country, as well as high birth rates among Kazakhs. The exodus of mostly urban and better-educated Russians contributed to the relative demobilization of the Russian community and a gradual de-politicization of the "Russian question." Moreover, Moscow preferred not to risk upsetting its relations with Astana by adopting a more active position in protecting its diaspora. [79] Among the factors for upholding Kazakhstan's statehood in the northern parts of the country was also the critical political decision of President Nazarbayev to move the state capital from the southern city of Almaty to Akmola (now Astana) in the north.

Russians and Russian speakers have historically populated Kazakhstan's northern and eastern provinces. In 2014, Russians alone accounted for 49.9% of the population in North Kazakhstan, 42.1% in Kostanay, 34.5% in Akmola, 37.2% in Pavlodar, and 38% in East Kazakhstan. [80] Remarkably, however, Russians are no longer a majority in any of Kazakhstan's provinces and their numbers have dramatically declined nationwide.

While in 1989, the ethnic Kazakhs were almost equal in numbers to ethnic Russians, now the Kazakh population is three times larger. The share of the Russian minority has dropped nationwide from 38% in 1989 to 21.5% in 2014. The share of Kazakhs, on the other hand, has increased dramatically to 65.5%. These demographic changes are not only caused by emigration of many Russians to the Russian Federation, they are also due to significantly higher birth rates and much lower death rates among the Kazakh population. The 2009 census showed that the birth rate of the Russian population was 12.7 per 1,000, while that of the Kazakh population was more than double, at 27 per 1,000. Furthermore, the death rates of the Russian minority were considerably higher than those of the ethnic Kazakhs—15.3 and 6.6 per 1,000, respectively—indicating that the Russian population is also aging.[81]

In the long run, these demographic tendencies, combined with the dwindling political aspirations of the remaining Russians, make a Crimean or Donbas scenario less likely in Kazakhstan. The short-term prospects, however, are uncertain, as the Russian minority is still very large, at 3.7 million. A minority of 20% or more requires comprehensive provisions for securing adequate political representation, which are not as extensive in Kazakhstan as the laws on protecting language and culture. [82] Although Kazakhstan's Russians generally recognize and appreciate the central government's efforts to preserve inter-ethnic peace, many are still unhappy with their limited political representation due to the Kazakh-language proficiency requirement for access to government jobs and universities. The unwillingness of Russians to learn the Kazakh language has been attributed as the main reason for inter-ethnic tensions since the adoption of the language laws, but it has not been perceived as a serious threat to inter-ethnic peace.

The annexation of Crimea changed the inter-ethnic discourse in the country. The events in Ukraine altered the mood among Kazakhs, giving rise to nationalist and anti-Russian sentiments. At the same time, the Russian minority became nervous over Russian state-media coverage of the conflict in Ukraine, which portrayed the new government in Kyiv as nationalist and even fascist. Russian state propaganda readily claims that bloodthirsty nationalists intent on killing ethnic Russians have taken over in Ukraine. Although after Crimea, Kazakhstan adopted stricter laws to curb nationalism of any kind and introduced harsher punishment for expressing separatist sentiment, the Russian minority feels uneasy about its future, particularly when power is transferred from the current president to another leader. They are unsure whether under a different leadership Astana would continue its close relations with Moscow and uphold its current tolerant policies toward Russians. Some Russian communities in Kazakhstan have already turned to the Kremlin to provide assistance in support of Russian language and culture. [83]

Yet, even at this stage, inter-ethnic relations are unlikely to cause major turmoil unless Moscow stirs trouble within the Russian communities. Nonetheless, ethnic grievances tend to become politicized when economic and social conditions worsen or a major political breakdown occurs. In this respect, Kazakhstan is in a very risky position, as the country is going through major economic and financial crises due largely to a sharp decline in oil prices and Western sanctions against Russia. On the one hand, Kazakhstan's economy is overwhelmingly dependent on the export of oil and other raw commodities; most of those prices plummeted in 2014–2015. On the other hand, its non-oil export market is heavily dependent on Russia and the Customs Union/Eurasian Economic Union, whose purchasing ability was steeply diminished in the last two years.

The third risk factor is potential political instability in the country as a result of economic and social problems, particularly as many Kazakhstani citizens lost their savings to currency devaluation, mainly caused by the crash of the Russian ruble. Although President Nazarbayev was reelected in 2015 and the ruling party won the general elections in 2016, the question of succession of the aging president will only become more acute with every passing year. Putin's controversial remarks before the 2014 Seliger Youth Forum struck a sensitive cord in Kazakhstan. Answering a question about growing Kazakh nationalism and whether to expect a Ukrainian scenario in Kazakhstan if Nazarbayev leaves office, Putin said that Nazarbayev "created a state on a territory where no state had ever existed. The Kazakhs had never had statehood—he created it. In this sense, he is a unique person for the former Soviet space and for Kazakhstan too."[84]

The statement was perceived as condescending of Kazakhstan's heritage, which has been a critical tool for nation building in the past two decades. Furthermore, the remarks signaled that Kazakhstan's sovereignty could be challenged once Nazarbayev leaves office, as he has been the main factor in containing Kazakh nationalism. In response, Kazakhstan launched in 2015 a nationwide campaign to celebrate its 550 years of statehood, marking the creation of the first Kazakh khanate by the khans Kerey and Zhanibek.[85]

Russia's actions in Ukraine chilled the traditionally warm relations between Moscow and Astana, bringing them to their lowest point in the summer and fall of 2014. Emboldened by its annexation of Crimea, Moscow became more assertive in dictating the terms of the impending Eurasian Economic Union. President Nazarbayev, who invented the idea of a Eurasian Union in 1995, has always opposed Russian proposals to make this union political as well as financial (including a common currency and bank system), fearing the loss of sovereignty for his country. During the Minsk Summit in October 2013, he sharply criticized "unjustified proposals to increase the European Economic Commission's mandate to form a common financial market and create new supra-national structures."[86] A few months before the EEU came into effect, Nazarbayev reminded Russia that Kazakhstan could pull out of the union if its sovereignty is threatened. "Kazakhstan will not be part of organizations that pose a threat to our independence. Our independence is our dearest treasure, which our grandfathers fought for. First of all, we will never surrender it to someone, and secondly, we will do our best to protect it," he said in an interview for Khabar TV.[87] This was also a message intended to calm down Kazakh nationalists who have taken an anti-EEU position, particularly in the wake of Russia's aggression in Ukraine and the following sharp contraction of the Russian economy.

While for Russia the EEU is mainly a geopolitical project, Kazakhstan seeks a purely economic merger that does not preclude alternative political alliances. Kazakhstani officials succeeded in including in the operating principles of the EEU that the union will operate without interfering with the political systems of its member states. [88] This was a major victory for Astana, along with the make-up of the Eurasian Economic Commission that has now an equal number of representatives from each country and operates on a consensus principle.

The first year of the EEU, however, was a rocky one. None of the benefits promised with the establishment of the EEU materialized in 2015. On the contrary, internal trade between the EEU members actually declined by 36% in the first three months of 2015, compared to the same period the previous year. Trade between Kazakhstan and the EEU declined by 21% in the first quarter of 2015. [89] This trend continued and the trade shrinkage with EEU countries reached 27.7% during January–November 2015, according to the statistics department of Kazakhstan's Economics Ministry.

In addition, a trade war unfolded between Russia and Kazakhstan with frequent seizures of tons of beef, poultry, milk and chocolate coming from Russia, and cheese and other dairy products coming from Kazakhstan. Behind mutual accusations of not meeting food standards was actually the 47% devaluation of the Russian *ruble* against the Kazakh *tenge* in 2014 alone. The *ruble* inflation made Russian goods extremely cheap on the Kazakh market, thus pushing local producers out. Kazakhstan's exports, on the other hand, became expensive for the markets in Russia, Belarus and Armenia, leading to a sharp decline in exports. [90]

The collapse of the Russian *ruble* caused the devaluation of the Kazakhstani *tenge*. The first sharp devaluation of the *tenge*—by 19% in February 2014—came as a result of Russian *ruble* devaluation the previous year by 8%. Kazakhstan buys from Russia 38% of its imported goods. The National Bank of Kazakhstan acted without warning causing shock and anger among Kazakh citizens who held savings in *tenge* and loans in dollars. Although the government announced it would spend one trillion *tenge* ($5.4 billion) from the National Welfare Fund to stimulate the economy, this measure was a drop in the ocean.[91]

By the end of 2014, foreign currency holdings skyrocketed in Kazakhstan, prompting the government to urge state companies to shift their holdings from dollars into the national currency. But in 2015, some experts estimated that 90% of retail deposits were still held in foreign currencies. The National Bank reported in January 2015 that non-performing loans made up 23.55% of total loans nationwide.[92] The share of non-performing loans had dropped from 31.4% (worth $22.7 billion) the previous year, but this reduction failed to approach the National Bank's target of cutting them by half in a year.[93]

Kazakhstan's GDP growth slowed from 4.1% during the first nine months of 2014 to an estimated 1% during the same period in 2015, according to the World Bank. The scope of the crisis was comparable to the effects of the 2009 global economic crisis in the country—trade volumes shrank to the same levels as in 2009 and GDP growth dropped again to about 1%. In addition, foreign direct investment (FDI) inflows declined and the overall external balance deteriorated, putting downward pressure on the *tenge*.[94]

Kazakhstan's economy was one of the hardest-hit in Eurasia by rapidly falling oil prices. According to the U.S. Energy Information Administration, Kazakhstan exported about 1.73 million barrels of oil per day in 2015, twice as much as Azerbaijan.[95] In 2014, the country's oil exports accounted for 69% of total exports, while petroleum products and natural gas constituted 6% of exports; three quarters of all exports are tied in some way to oil production. Oil revenues accounted for 60% of Kazakhstan's budget and made up 33% of its GDP. [96] According to the International Monetary Fund (IMF), Kazakhstan cannot cover government spending at oil prices below $58 per barrel, as projected in 2015. [97] As a result of the devastating effect of declining global oil prices, *Bloomberg* placed Kazakhstan in the world's top ten worst performing economies, with reduced growth forecasts that plunged to just 1.2% in mid-2015 (from 10% in 2000–2007). Total export revenue declined by about 35%, leading to budget revisions three times: in October 2014, the budget was redrawn to assume an oil price of $80 per barrel, then in early 2015—at $50 per barrel, and again at the end of 2015, when oil prices dropped to under $40. The World Bank projects Kazakhstan's economy will grow by barely 1% in 2016, while the Economist Intelligence Unit now has the country falling into recession.[98]

Russia has been traditionally a major trade partner for Kazakhstan. Although it does not hold first place in total trade volumes (the EU has the largest share), Russia is the main destination for Kazakhstan's non-oil exports. According to the Kazakhstani government, the average annual volume of trade between the two countries is about $21 billion. Russian companies are involved in the development of Kazakhstan's largest hydrocarbon deposits, but Western oil majors have the leading investments in the sector. Nevertheless, more than 5,600 enterprises in the country actively work with Russian capital.[99]

On the foreign policy front, the sharp confrontation between Russia and the West resulting from Moscow's actions in Ukraine initially challenged Kazakhstan's multi-vector foreign policy. East-West polarization was again growing, undermining the well-balanced foreign policy approach of all Central Asian states. Astana's attempts to neutralize this new polarization by restraining from taking a clear stand on the Ukrainian events backfired with its Western partners. Some observers expected Kazakhstan would be forced to make a choice between the West and Russia and will ultimately choose Russia.[100] But a few months after the annexation of Crimea, it became clear that Astana would seek to maintain independence in its foreign policy decisions. Firstly, Kazakhstan refused to implement counter-sanctions against the West, as Russia demanded; secondly, it boosted relations with Ukraine with mutual presidential visits and developing an action plan for cooperation and trade; thirdly, Astana signed an Enhanced Partnership and Cooperation Agreement with the EU, and sought to enhance relations with the US; and finally, Kazakhstan's government refused to boycott Turkey as Moscow demanded after a Russian fighter jet was downed for violating Turkey's airspace.

Kazakhstan's decision to uphold its multi-vector foreign policy, regardless of Kremlin pressure, derives from the geopolitical environment of a newly independent state located in a rivalry-torn Central Asia, between the former colonizer Russia and an economically strong China, lacking access to international seas. It is also a policy that originates in the traditions of Kazakh society, largely founded on clan-based patronage networks. The way the state leadership has managed the various competing or even acrimonious kinships is very similar to its approach to foreign policy: balancing relations with often competing or confrontational world actors, but without taking sides. The same approach is evident in the government's dealing with ethnic minorities, where careful management of grievances and aspirations has thus far produced inter-ethnic stability domestically.

By the fall of 2015, Kazakhstan had accelerated cooperation with Ukraine to the extent that the presidents of the two countries, Nursultan Nazarbayev and Petro Poroshenko, signed a road map for cooperation for the next two years. During the meeting, the two sides discussed ways to strengthen cooperation in trade, the coal industry, transport and logistics, and agriculture. They also shared views on urgent issues of the international agenda, including the situation in southeastern Ukraine and progress in the Minsk agreements. The Ukrainian president congratulated Nazarbayev on the 550th anniversary of the Kazakh khanate, a symbol of statehood and Kazakhstan's deep historical roots.[101]

Stressing that Kazakhstan maintained relations with a number of countries, including Turkey, China, India, Pakistan, Afghanistan,

Ukraine, Russia, Japan, as well as the US and EU, Kazakhstan's Foreign Minister Erlan Idrissov said at the end of 2015: "Kazakhstan does not adopt the position of a silent detached observer in the implementation of someone else's strategy. Our country is successful in making its own independent way in the world. We purposefully build good relationships and establish strong economic contacts with large and small states in the East and West, North and South. We work closely with Russia and China. Europe is our largest trading partner, and the US is the second largest foreign investor after Europe."[102]

Uzbekistan

Uzbekistan has been the most resistant to Russian political influence among the Central Asia states. Even under the Soviet system, Tashkent enjoyed the reputation in Moscow of having a mind of its own: Uzbekistan was resentful of demands to increase cotton production and of the Kremlin's efforts to uproot Islamic tradition. Moreover, it rejected attempts to appoint Russians to leading positions (the leader of the Uzbek Communist Party was consistently an Uzbek). After independence, Uzbekistan became even more unpredictable in its relations with Russia as well as with other countries in the region. Uzbekistan is critical for the regional powers Russia and China, but also for the US and the EU, because of its central geographic position, large population, and diverse natural resources. A doubly landlocked country, Uzbekistan is located in the heart of Central Asia and shares borders with all states in the region, plus Afghanistan.

Although Russia remains Uzbekistan's leading economic partner and an important factor in its foreign and security policy, Moscow does not enjoy the same leverage and political influence in Tashkent as it does in other Central Asian capitals. The Russian minority is gradually shrinking due to emigration and low birth rates, falling to under 3% of the total population of 31.5 million.[103] Uzbekistan is not a member of the Russian-led security bloc, the Collective Security Treaty Organization (CSTO), and prefers to take part instead in the China-led Shanghai Cooperation Organization (SCO). It refuses to join the Eurasian Economic Union (EEU) and is cautious about becoming a member of the EEU's free trade zone. Uzbekistan's President Islam Karimov has criticized the EEU, warning of a loss of political independence for the former Soviet countries.[104]

Though President Karimov's behavior is often seen as erratic, it tends to reflect well-calculated policy to preserve his country's sovereignty, particularly by offsetting any Russian attempt to regain influence in Uzbekistan. While Tashkent evidently implements a similar approach regarding other international actors, such as China and the West, Karimov seems to view the threat from Moscow as much more serious. As a result, Tashkent is the Central Asian capital most courted by Moscow. The latest gesture by Russian President Putin was a large debt write-off in December 2014—Uzbekistan will pay only $25 million of the $890 million it owes Russia. In exchange, Tashkent will consider taking part in a free trade agreement with the Eurasian Economic Union. The deal also included more Russian investments in strategic sectors of Uzbekistan's economy and new lines of credit for Russian arms and military technology.[105]

Uzbekistan has joined some of the groupings of former Soviet states, such as the Commonwealth of Independent States (CIS) and the SCO, but it usually carefully observes developments before making a decision and sometimes changes it later. For example, Uzbekistan became a founding member of the SCO in 2001, but it was not part of its predecessor, the Shanghai Five, established in 1996. It signed the Collective Security Treaty (CST) in 1992 (also known as the Tashkent Treaty), but did not renew it in 1999. When the CST was transformed into CSTO in 2002, Uzbekistan refrained from joining. There was logic in this decision, as by that time Uzbekistan had become an ally of the United States and NATO, following the September 2001 terrorist attacks in the US.

A few weeks after 9/11, Uzbekistan agreed to host the US Air Force at the Karshi–Khanabat Airbase (K2) to support the US-led *Operation Enduring Freedom* in Afghanistan. But four years later, Tashkent requested the base vacated, despite continuing concerns about security in Afghanistan. A combination of factors contributed to this development; not least pressure by Russia and China, which oppose US military presence in Central Asia. The Shanghai Cooperation Organization called in July 2005 for the US and its coalition partners in Afghanistan to set a timetable for withdrawing from several Central Asian countries, prompting comments by Gen. Richard B. Myers, chairman of the Joint Chiefs of Staff, that Russia and China are bullying the Central Asian nations. The two big SCO members had indeed enlisted the presidents of Uzbekistan, Kyrgyzstan, and Tajikistan to co-sign the declaration.[106]

Another factor for the US airbase closure was Tashkent's wariness of American presence in the country, following the "colored revolutions" in Georgia, Ukraine, and Kyrgyzstan, which Moscow blamed on the West. Suspicions amplified as Washington increased criticism of Uzbekistan's human rights record and, in 2004 and 2005, withheld $28.5 million of US military and economic aid, as a result of human rights concerns.[107] Tensions in bilateral relations intensified after the Uzbek security forces shot and killed hundreds of civilians during an insurgency outbreak in the city of Andijan, in 2005, when armed rebels, allegedly Islamists, broke into a high-security prison, captured the municipal building and took a number of hostages, and finally used civilians as human shields.[108]

While Western governments and human rights organizations legitimately criticized Uzbek authorities for using lethal force against civilians, some of them also incorrectly portrayed the incident as a crackdown on anti-regime protests. Russia and China, however, offered support to Tashkent, claiming that the Uzbek authorities' reaction during the Andijan events was an internal matter. Not surprisingly, Tashkent switched alliances again and joined the Russia-led CSTO a year later, in 2006.

Uzbekistan's CSTO membership, however, remained nominal, since the country abstained from ratifying any agreement adopted by the organization or taking part in joint military exercises. In June 2012, Tashkent suspended its participation in the CSTO and left the organization by the end of the year. The departure put Uzbekistan in a peculiar position vis-à-vis its neighbors Kazakhstan, Kyrgyzstan and Tajikistan, all of which are members of the security alliance. In case of a security crisis in the region, they would be able to turn to the CSTO for protection, while Uzbekistan would be left out. Moreover, in case of a conflict between Uzbekistan and a CSTO member state in Central Asia, the security alliance might step in to protect the member state, while Tashkent would have to seek allies elsewhere. At the same time, by maintaining strong bilateral security cooperation with the CSTO leader—Russia—Uzbekistan would be in a position to block CSTO intervention against itself in a potential regional conflict.[109] It seems, however, that Tashkent does not see the CSTO as a credible actor in Central Asia. The organization has proven ineffective after failing to intervene in the 2010 crisis in Kyrgyzstan, caused by ethnic clashes between Uzbeks and Kyrgyz in the southern region of Osh.

Meanwhile, in 2012, Tashkent adopted a new Foreign Policy Doctrine designed to guard the country from foreign interference. The document does not allow the deployment of foreign military bases on the territory of Uzbekistan, forbids the participation of the country in any military blocs or international peacekeeping missions, and rejects the mediation of any external power in regional conflicts in Central Asia.[110]

Since then, the CSTO has tried to establish a mechanism of cooperation with Uzbekistan and also Turkmenistan, but they have not responded to proposals about uniting the efforts of the special services to jointly fight against common threats, nor have they agreed to discuss offers of potential aid by the CSTO collective forces in case it is needed. CSTO Secretary General Nikolay Bordyuzha concluded in 2015 that his organization has practically no working relationship with either Uzbekistan or Turkmenistan.[111] Apparently, the Russian invasion of eastern Ukraine has alarmed these two Central Asian countries and made them even more cautious in their security relations with Moscow.

Nevertheless, Uzbekistan's bilateral military cooperation with other states continued, including with the US after a rapprochement between Washington and Tashkent. Since 2009, Uzbekistan has served as a vital part of the Northern Distribution Network (NDN), a key transit corridor along which Western militaries shipped supplies to the ISAF mission in Afghanistan and subsequently its successor, *Operation Resolute Support.* All three NDN railways lines ran through Uzbekistan and Kazakhstan, making the two countries essential for continuing NATO operations in Afghanistan and bringing significant benefits to their economies. In June 2015, Russian Prime Minister Dmitry Medvedev shut down the "Northern Line of Communication," consisting of two railway lines going through Russia. The southern NDN "Central Line of Communication" is still operational as it bypasses Russia completely, running through Uzbekistan and Kazakhstan and crossing the Caspian Sea via rail ferries to Azerbaijan and Georgia.[112] Medvedev's decree, although not seriously affecting current NATO operations in Afghanistan, which reverted to using exclusively the southern NDN line, had a negative economic impact on Uzbekistan and Kazakhstan. These Central Asian republics lost a significant portion of their income from transit fees.

In the beginning of 2015, the US government decided to transfer hundreds of armored vehicles to Uzbekistan as part of their military cooperation. The transfer involved some 308 Mine Resistant Ambush Protected Vehicles (MRAP), to be used for defensive purposes as well as to improve border security and counter-narcotics operations.

Reportedly, the deal marked the largest transfer of US military equipment to a Central Asian country.[113] The Uzbekistan-NATO partnership was also resumed, following a decline in relations after the Andijan events. In 2013, Uzbekistan agreed its first Individual Partnership Cooperation Program with NATO, and the Alliance opened a NATO Liaison Office in Tashkent.

Uzbekistan's official reaction to the annexation of Crimea was clearly negative. Tashkent cited the United Nations Charter and the UN Declaration on the Principles of International Law, stating that it firmly and invariably adheres to the principles of "settling international disputes by peaceful means and refraining in international relations from the threat or use of force against the territorial integrity or political independence of any state." The statement of the Ministry of Foreign Affairs called for immediate negotiations between Ukraine and Russia to resolve the conflict.[114]

The Russian public apparently disapproved of Uzbekistan's position and abstention from voting on the UN resolution rendering the March 14 referendum in Crimea illegitimate. Many called for sanctions against Uzbekistan and deportation of the nearly two million Uzbek migrant laborers working in the Russian Federation.[115] Labor migration is one of Uzbekistan's major vulnerabilities to pressure by Moscow and a channel for the Kremlin to insert political leverage.

Another serious vulnerability for Tashkent is the Republic of Karakalpakstan, an autonomous region in Uzbekistan's northwest. Nominally, Karakalpakstan has the constitutional right to hold a referendum and secede, but the Supreme Assembly of Uzbekistan (the *Oliy Majlis*) can veto a breakaway decision. The Russian annexation of Crimea underscored the volatile situation in this region, attached by Stalin to the Uzbek Soviet Socialist Republic (SSR) in the last stages of national delimitation in the Soviet Union in 1936. Subsequently devastated by the ecological catastrophe of the Aral Sea, overrun by poverty and neglected by the central authorities, Karakalpakstan has seen appeals for separation made by various local movements since 1990. Although not expressed publically by the authorities, Tashkent was clearly concerned that if it recognized the result of the referendum in Crimea, this could foment separatist drives at home. In fact, the declaration of independence of Kosovo in February 2008 was followed by similar calls in Karakalpakstan.[116]

Soon after Russia took Crimea, leaflets started appearing in Karakalpakstan, signed by a previously unknown group, *Alga Karakalpakstan Azatlyk Harakati (Forward Karakalpakstan Freedom Movement)*. The authorities detained several activists for distribution of leaflets calling for a referendum on Karakalpakstan's independence. Analysts say that the activity was a grassroots effort, connected with the developments in Crimea and Eastern Ukraine. *Alga Karakalpakstan* posted a statement on the Facebook page of the Uzbek opposition movement *Birdamlik*: "The people of Karakalpakstan do not agree with the foreign and domestic policies of Karimov's regime. Karakalpaks are eager to join Russia. By culture and language, Karakalpaks are closer to Kazakhs but will the [Kazakhstani] president support the freedom and independence of the Republic of Karakalpakstan? If we hear a good signal from the Kremlin, Karakalpakstan is ready to raise the Russian flag."[117]

Although the movement reportedly emerged from below, it provides Moscow with a strong card to use against the Uzbek government, if the latter fails to comply with Russian demands. The dire social, economic and health predicament of Uzbekistan's largest region, coupled with drastically reduced remittances from Russia and Kazakhstan, where many local residents have migrated for jobs, has created a combustible environment that could destabilize Central Asia at large. Just a nod of support from Russia and a bit of financial backing could increase demands for independence, compel people to protest in the streets, and prompt Tashkent to use its enormous security service apparatus to crush the movement. Karakalpakstan activists have already accused Karimov's regime of genocide against the people of the region for failing to address the environmental and health problems and promote economic development.

Potential clashes between Karakalpakstan's population and the police would not only destabilize Uzbekistan, but would also derail its current cooperative relationship with the US and NATO and could also give rise to Islamic movements calling for a Caliphate. Such a scenario might push Tashkent into Moscow's hands because the authoritarian regime of President Karimov would need protection to survive. As China would be unwilling to become involved in the internal political problems of any of its partners, Moscow would also succeed in distancing Beijing from Tashkent. In fact, the ethnic card in Karakalpakstan, but also in the Ferghana Valley, where Uzbeks live alongside Kyrgyz and Tajiks, seems to be the most effective instrument of subversion Moscow could use in Uzbekistan, if the regime continues to be recalcitrant and seek stronger partners either eastward or westward.

On the other hand, the Russian minority has been rarely used by Moscow as a political tool against Tashkent. The situation of Uzbekistan's Russians has been on Moscow's agenda only when relations with Tashkent deteriorate. Russians in Uzbekistan currently make up less than 3% of the total population, down from over 12.5% in the 1970s. The 1989 census found that Russians numbered 1.65 million, or 8.3% of the population, most of them living in Tashkent and other urban centers. Interestingly, while the Russian minority in Uzbekistan had grown by only 10% (158,000) between 1970 and 1989, the total population of Uzbekistan had increased by 40% (7.85 million) reaching almost 20 million.[118] There has been no official population census in Uzbekistan since the dissolution of the Soviet Union. After independence, the Russian population decreased by half and shrank to about 800,000 due to migration, while the total population of Uzbekistan swelled to over 31.5 million (a one-third increase in 25 years).[119]

Russian out-migration started in 1989, following the pogroms against the Meskhetian Turks in the Ferghana Valley, which alarmed the minority populations. Economic reasons soon replaced the initial political reasons for migrating to the Russian Federation; but lately, discrimination is named as the main motivation for departure. The Russian press has claimed that the position of Russians and Russian speakers is rapidly deteriorating across Central Asia, but that they are under most intense pressure in Uzbekistan. [120] Russian minority representatives complain that they are often fired without cause or explanation, paid less than their Uzbek co-workers, lose their housing, and face prison if they raise the issue about the status of ethnic Russians in Uzbekistan. Analysts point out that the low birth rates among Russians are an indication of their sense of insecurity and lack of hope for the future of their communities in Uzbekistan. The Russian minority is annoyed by government actions such as changing street names from Russian to Uzbek, or building a museum in memory of the victims of communist repressions—the only one in Central Asia—which they perceive as a museum of Russian occupation. The status of the Russian language has also declined, with most Russian-language schools closed down. Uzbekistan's Russians blame Russian President Putin for ignoring their plight and sacrificing their interests to maintaining good relations with Tashkent.[121]

Moscow's aggression in Ukraine, however, changed the atmosphere in Uzbekistan, giving hope to local Russians and making the authorities fearful of a similar attack on their country. This worry prompted the government to introduce a peculiar requirement for all broadcast facilities in the country. Shortly after Moscow-backed separatists captured and started broadcasting from several TV stations in eastern Ukraine, the Uzbek government ordered that all locally based TV and radio stations must rig their transmitters with explosive devices for immediate destruction in case the station were to fall into hostile hands. The National Security Service of Uzbekistan introduced additional security measures to prevent potential invasion via ventilation pipes and shafts. Furthermore, live programming, including news coverage, was also banned.[122]

On the economic front, Uzbekistan is extremely vulnerable to the deteriorating Russian economy. According to the Uzbek Foreign Ministry, Russia is Uzbekistan's number one foreign trade partner, with turnover between the two countries exceeding $8.3 billion dollars in 2013. Russian investments worth over $600 million were channeled into Uzbekistan—mostly the oil and gas industry, telecommunications, and production engineering.[123] The Russian company Lukoil boosted investment in Uzbekistan by 38% in 2013, to $660 million. Lukoil is working on three projects in Uzbekistan: Kandym-Hauzak-Shady, South-West Gissar and Ustyurt.[124] During Putin's visit to Tashkent in December 2014, Lukoil gave assurances that it would continue investing in the Kandym gas condensate field, in the Bukhara region, adding an additional $5 billion over the next 25 years.[125]

Uzbekistan is a member of the CIS free trade zone since 2014, when Russia finally ratified the 2011 protocol. The agreement exempts Uzbekistan from import duties on trade with other members. Members of the free trade zone are Armenia, Belarus, Kazakhstan, Kyrgyzstan, Moldova, Russia, Tajikistan and Ukraine, until Russia suspended the latter's membership when Kyiv signed an association agreement with the EU.[126]

By the end of 2015, remittances from Russia dropped by 60%, compared to 2013, when the Uzbek economy was boosted by $7.88 billion coming from migrant workers.[127] Remittances contributed almost 14% to the country's gross domestic product in 2013.[128] Now this amount hovers around $3 billion, or under 5% of GDP.[129] The main reason for diminishing remittances from Russia is considered to be the weakening value of the Russian ruble, which, by January 201,6 depreciated 55% compared to November 2013. As the dollar appreciated 121% compared to the Russian currency, the dollar value of remittances earned in rubles dropped significantly.[130] The official exchange rate of the Uzbek som is down by only 25%, which does not fully reflect the real depreciation of the Russian ruble.

The inadequate official devaluation of the Uzbek som makes Uzbek goods on the Russian market more expensive than they were before the war in Ukraine. Illustratively, sales in the Russian Federation market of cars produced by the joint GM Uzbekistan automobile plant dropped by 47% in 2015, threatening the American-Uzbek carmaker with significant losses. [131] Although Moscow's counter-sanctions against the West opened opportunities for higher demand of Uzbek agricultural goods on the Russian market, the devaluation of the ruble and shrinking purchasing power of Russian consumers dashed this hope.

According to the Russia's Federal Migration Service, as of January 2015, 2.2 million Uzbek citizens resided in Russia, down from 2.7 million in August 2014. About 81% percent of those migrants are of working age. Studies have shown that over the years the typical Uzbek migrant has become younger, less educated, and more motivated to succeed in foreign countries. When they return to their home country, the overall level of skills will rise. [132] As Uzbekistan expects many migrant workers to return home from Russia, it will be very important to provide them with proper jobs and business opportunities.

Despite hardship caused by the financial crisis in Russia, Uzbekistan's economic growth prospects are still stable, with a high GDP growth of 8% in 2015 and a forecasted growth in 2016 between 6.5% and 6.9%. Rising public investment and increased government spending are expected to help the economy overcome current drawbacks; the pace of growth may recover in 2017. [133] The Uzbek government also undertook a large privatization initiative that is expected to bear results in the next several years.

For Uzbekistan, like for the majority of Central Asia, the most promising alternative to economic dependence on Russia is China. In the wake of Russian aggression in Ukraine, Tashkent hastily began seeking a stronger alliance with Beijing. Criticizing international organizations for failing to enforce a strict observance of international law, Uzbekistan's President Islam Karimov called for support to the Chinese President Xi Jinping's proposals on developing a new security concept in Asia.[134] Uzbekistan subsequently entered into a strategic partnership agreement with China, which included jointly building the Silk Road Economic Belt.[135]

In August 2014, the two countries' presidents signed a joint declaration and strategic partnership development program for 2014–2018. The agreement included not only economic development plans, but also strengthening mutual political trust and security cooperation. The economic development plan gave priority to line D of the China–Central Asia natural gas pipeline from Turkmenistan through Uzbekistan, Tajikistan and Kyrgyzstan to China. Reportedly, *Gazprom* will abandon purchasing gas from Uzbekistan, due to reduced demand in Europe, and by 2021 China will become the main destination for Uzbek gas. The country produces around 63–65 bcm/a, but consumes 50 bcm domestically. Its export capacity has been under 15 bcm/a, half of which was sold to Russia.[136]

While pursuing closer economic relations with China and other partners, such as South Korea, Japan, Turkey and Europe, may not be a triggering point for Moscow to exert pressure on Tashkent, developing stronger security cooperation with other major actors could be very risky short term. Moscow can use not only internal political problems against Karimov's government, but it can also try to exacerbate Tashkent's uneasy relationships with other countries in the region. Tensions over water between Uzbekistan and the two upstream states, Kyrgyzstan and Tajikistan, have been among Moscow's arsenal of subversion. Russia has often used the water conflicts to its advantage. In order to keep Tashkent in check, Moscow has supported large hydropower projects in the two upstream, water-rich countries. Building large dams in the mountains will deprive Uzbekistan of much-needed water for agriculture downstream. More importantly, open conflicts over water have the potential to destabilize the entire region.

Kyrgyzstan

After two consecutive dictators were replaced through violent uprisings in 2005 and 2010, Kyrgyzstan succeeded in holding three peaceful elections—for parliament in October 2010, president in October 2011, and again parliament in 2015. Nevertheless, the country remains dangerously unstable because of internal regional divisions, inter-ethnic problems, a weak central government, corruption, and overwhelming economic and political dependence on Russia.

The 2010 riots in Bishkek were followed by violent interethnic clashes in the country's south, between the Kyrgyz majority and the ethnic-Uzbek minority, resulting in 470 deaths and 300,000 displaced ethnic Uzbeks.[137] Fierce competition for the spoils of the drug trafficking industry has resulted in political power struggle in southern Kyrgyzstan and became the main reason for the interethnic clashes in June 2010. The events in Osh demonstrated how easily the button of ethnic sentiment can be pushed by a powerful political figure who is threatened with loss of control—in Kyrgyzstan's case, allegedly, the associates of the deposed president Bakiyev felt threatened with losing political power and access to the profits of corruption and drug smuggling.

The failure of the justice system to hold the perpetrators accountable constituted additional proof that state institutions are weak and underdeveloped. The ethnic violence in 2010 gave rise to Kyrgyz nationalism that is increasingly becoming part of politics and is considered a high security risk for the country and the region.[138]

Since 2014, the Russian economic recession has brought hardship to the mountainous Central Asian country. The last country to join the Eurasian Economic Union, Kyrgyzstan could be the first to leave, if not for its pro-Russian leadership. None of the promises for economic development and benefits from joining the EEU came to fruition. On the contrary, the Kyrgyz economy suffered heavy losses from the economic downturn in Russia, a drastic fall in remittances, and reduced trade within the EEU. More importantly, EEU membership negatively affected Kyrgyzstan's trade with neighboring China, due to higher customs duties and increased prices of previously cheap Chinese goods.

Kyrgyzstan had benefited from becoming a warehouse for the import and re-export of consumer goods from neighboring China to other CIS countries. Low import tariffs between the two WTO members have allowed Kyrgyz and Chinese traders to develop a profitable economic activity. Import and resale of "bazaar goods" is also enabled by a 2004 government regulation, allowing individuals to pay customs duties and tax based on the weight of goods, not their value. The two biggest markets in Central Asia are located in Kyrgyzstan, Dordoi outside of Bishkek and Kara-Suu near the southern city of Osh, reportedly employ 20% of Kyrgyzstan's work force, directly or indirectly.[139] By joining the EEU, Kyrgyzstan was taking the risk of endangering a huge enterprise that was providing livelihood to a large part of the population.

Kyrgyzstan was hesitant to join the EEU, expecting more Russian economic assistance as well as relaxed procedures for Kyrgyz labor migration to Russia. Bishkek demanded large subsidies, exemption from various rules, a special status for the wholesale markets as free trade zones, and benefits for 400 commodity items for a period of five to ten years, as well as other concessions from EEU members. The authorities claimed that these measures are necessary to offset disadvantages caused by ceasing re-exporting goods from China. Taking into account Kyrgyzstan's lower wages compared to Russia and Kazakhstan, Bishkek also wanted to prevent further economic and political instabilities in the poor and restless Central Asian country.[140] Nevertheless, Bishkek joined the Union in August 2015 as the "right step" that would bring important economic and social benefits, Prime Minister Joomart Otorbaev claimed.[141]

Kazakhstan and Belarus were not enthusiastic about admitting economically weak Kyrgyzstan to the EEU since the country has little to contribute, but would be a serious burden to wealthier members. They finally consented when Russia agreed to cover most of Kyrgyzstan's accession cost, notably $200 million to upgrade its customs infrastructure. Moscow also promised a $1 billion financial injection to the newly established Russian-Kyrgyz Development Fund (RKDF), slated to support local business development and compensate Kyrgyzstan for economic losses caused by its accession to the EEU. The fund received only $350 million of the promised funds and it is not clear whether there will be another tranche, causing frustration among the country's leadership.[142]

Kyrgyzstan is heavily dependent on Russia, both economically and politically. Moscow has primarily used two tools to keep the country in line: threats and bribes. Convincing Bishkek to join the EEU was one example of how these tools work in synchrony—Moscow promised to accommodate Kyrgyz migrant workers in Russia by providing registration and jobs, but when the Kyrgyz authorities still hesitated whether to take the plunge, the Kremlin threatened for Kyrgyz migrants with hardship. Naturally, the promised benefits seemed a better deal, regardless of the expected shut down of re-exports of Chinese goods.

But remittances fell by 30%, and trade within the EEU declined significantly by the end of 2015 compared to 2013, before the sharp decline in oil prices and Western sanctions against Moscow contributed to a reduction in economic activity in Russia. [143] According the World Bank, remittances in 2013 accounted for 31% of Kyrgyzstan's gross domestic product.[144] Moreover, Kyrgyzstan is the second most remittances-dependent country in the world, with some 700,000 migrant laborers working mostly in Russia and some in Kazakhstan.[145]

Total trade turnover between Kyrgyzstan and Kazakhstan dropped by almost half, and trade with Russia also considerably declined. The main reason was currency devaluation in both countries, but also the fact that Kyrgyzstan was no longer able to re-export Chinese consumer goods to other EEU members. In addition, Russia's conflicts with Ukraine and Turkey spoiled trade relations with these two countries, which were large trade partners of Kyrgyzstan.[146]

Over the years, Russia has provided significant financial assistance to Kyrgyzstan, including $185 million aid to support budget operations between 2010 and 2015, a grant of $150 million and a $300 million loan on terms of official development assistance in 2009, along with a $180 million debt write off. In 2012, Moscow agreed to forgive $489 million of Kyrgyzstan's sovereign debt.[147] This financial support has not been free, as Moscow has always calibrated its assistance toward achieving a particular political goal. When in 2009, in addition to other financial incentives, Moscow promised to subsidize the Karambata-1 dam on the Naryn River with $2 billion aid package, it had one goal in mind—to have the US air base at Manas expelled from Kyrgyzstan. The Russian plan failed, however, because the Americans agreed to the increased rent from $17.4 million to $60 million a year, and the base was allowed to stay. The then-President Kurmanbek Bakiyev decided to benefit from both, the Russian subsidies and the American rent payments, a large part of which was going to his family's pockets, as became clear later. Allegedly, the Kremlin did not forgive him for this double crossing. According to some reports, the 2010 riots in Bishkek were instigated by Moscow with the purpose of deposing Bakiyev and installing a pro-Russian leader. A few weeks before the protests, Russian television stations aired scathing reports portraying Bakiyev as a repugnant dictator, while Moscow suspended the promised financial aid and eliminated subsidies on gasoline exports to Kyrgyzstan, causing a price hike.[148]

Russian financial support and investment plans were resumed when the government of Almazbek Atambayev came to power in 2011. As Russia fell under Western sanctions in Europe, Russian companies continued expanding in unaffected countries, such as Kyrgyzstan. *Gazprom* acquired the state gas company, in 2014, for the symbolic price of $1 and vowed to invest over $500 million to upgrade its infrastructure in the first five years. The Russian company also assumed the Kyrgyz gas company's debt of $40 million. Gazprom also announced plans to start exploration of gas fields in Kyrgyzstan. Moreover, Russian state-owned *Rosneft* signed a deal in 2014 to invest up to $1 billion for a stake of at least 51% in Manas International Airport.[149]

Russia was the sole investor in two large hydropower projects: the Upper Naryn cascade project and the Kambarata-1 hydropower plant. The Upper Naryn cascade consists of four hydropower plants, estimated to cost $700 million, while Kambarata-1, a mega-hydropower plant fiercely objected to by neighboring Uzbekistan, is estimated to cost $2 billion. But at the end of 2015, President Atambayev announced that Russia has not made any investments, because of the ongoing economic stagnation. The Ministry of Economy confirmed that Russia is unable to secure project financing. Western sanctions have impacted Russia's ability to access international financial markets. Therefore, such large investments are put on the backburner or simply scrapped. After months of frustration with the Russian side, Atambayev concluded that Russia might never have planned to actually fund these hydropower projects.[150] Bishkek subsequently canceled the investment agreement with Russia, but Kyrgyzstan was left with the bill for $40 million already spent by RosHydro on the Upper Naryn project.[151] Other investment plans may also be scrapped if Russian economic problems continue.

Tajikistan

Tajikistan's authoritarian system is extremely weak and vulnerable, undermined by widespread poverty, rampant corruption, sporadic domestic insurgency, and the growing appeal of militant Islam. In addition, Tajikistan has had problems with a domestic insurgency deriving from political rivalries dating back to the civil war of 1992–1997. Recent political conflicts have stemmed from the authorities' crackdown on the political opposition, as President Emomali Rahmon managed to remove from the government and the parliament all of his opponents from the former United Tajik Opposition. This has led to armed clashes, ambushes, and whole-scale military battles between insurgents and government security forces in the last several years.

Of all the Central Asian republics, Tajikistan is most exposed to terrorist incursions because of its 1,300-kilometer-long poorly protected border with Afghanistan. Much of this frontier runs through remote and difficult terrain, allowing smugglers, political and religious extremists, and terrorists to travel across it, to and from Afghanistan.

Security in and around Tajikistan has become a major concern for Russia, particularly with the spread of Islamist ideology among the Tajik youth and the recently established presence of Islamic State militants in Afghanistan. Tajik fighters who joined the IS in Syria have made video message threats not only to Dushanbe, but also to Moscow. [152] Furthermore, drugs worth billions of dollars pass through Tajikistan en route to Russia and China every year. The trafficking is not sufficiently addressed by the authorities, ostensibly because of vested interests of government officials in the profits or levies of the narcotics trade. The illicit drug trade is estimated to constitute as much as one-fifth of the country's GDP. [153]

The domestic security situation started to deteriorate in 2008 and quickly escalated to military battles between well-trained insurgents and inadequately equipped government security forces. Tajik security forces were dealt a blow by local warlords and a small insurgency group in the Rasht Valley, in 2010–2011. The violence crippled the State Security Committee's Alpha anti-terrorist unit and cost the National Guard many casualties. [154] The violence in the Badakhshan region in the summer of 2012 was linked to both narcotics trafficking and discontent among the local Pamiri population with their political marginalization. [155] Penetration of the Islamic State's ideology has further undermined trust in the security services, particularly following the defection of Gen. Gulmurod Khalimov, head of the Special Assignment Police Unit (OMON), to the IS in Syria in April 2015. [156] Khalimov was among the best-qualified high-ranking security officers in the country; he had received extensive training in the US as well.

More recent security incidents included armed clashes involving Tajikistan's security forces on September 4–5, 2015, which resulted in a number of deaths in the vicinity of Dushanbe and Dushanbe International Airport. The government blamed the political opposition for the events and declared the Islamic Renaissance Party of Tajikistan (IRPT) as a terrorist organization, arresting and putting on trial 13 of its members. Rakhmon's crackdown on the opposition party had started earlier, when he effectively ousted the IRPT from parliament, following an election in March 2015 riddled with violations. The party was banned a few days before clashes broke out around Dushanbe. [157]

Militarily, Tajikistan is Moscow's stronghold in Central Asia, hosting Russia's largest non-naval military base in a foreign country, with an estimated total strength of around 7,000 soldiers. The 201st Motorized

Rifle Division, subordinated to Russia's Central Operational Strategic Command, is headquartered in Dushanbe since the end of the Soviet-Afghan War. During the Tajik civil war, the Russian division played a critical role in supporting the pro-Communist Popular Front against the Democratic and Muslim Opposition. Without its support, President Emomali Rakhmon would not have come to power. Subsequently, the 201st Motorized Rifle Division became part of the CIS Collective Peacekeeping Force in Tajikistan, which was unable to obtain a peacekeeping status under the United Nation's jurisdiction, precisely because the 201st had fought against one of the sides in the civil war.

The 201st Motorized Rifle Division is organized into three motorized rifle regiments: the 92nd in Dushanbe, the 191st in Qurghonteppa, and the 149th in Kulob. The base in Kulob is expected relocate to a facility near Dushanbe in 2016. The Russian 670th air group and 303rd separate helicopter squadron are reportedly deployed at Ayni Airbase and equipped with Su-25 aircraft, Mi-24 and Mi-8 helicopters, although a formal agreement for the use of Ayni has not yet been finalized.[158] Ayni Airbase was completely renovated by India in the period 2004–2010, but Tajikistan's government, under pressure from Russia, refused to allow Indian or US air contingents to use the base.[159] In October 2013, Dushanbe ratified an agreement with Moscow to extend the deployment of the Russian military contingent in Tajikistan by three decades, until 2042.

The Russian government does not pay Tajikistan for hosting the 201st division, but Moscow promised, in 2004, to invest $2 billion in Tajik hydroelectric projects and infrastructure, as part of a bilateral basing and security accord. The promise was only partially fulfilled when Russian companies completed the construction of the Sangtuda–1 Hydroelectric Power Plant, which produces 15% of Tajikistan's electricity. Dushanbe has made clear that Moscow will have to pay to use the Ayni Airbase.[160]

The Russian military used to patrol Tajikistan's border with Afghanistan until 2005, when Dushanbe assumed control of its border security. As Moscow and the Central Asian capitals grow increasingly concerned about security threats stemming from Afghanistan, Russia has been trying to redeploy its border guards to the Tajik border. Although Tajik President Rahmon claims that fighting is taking place along 60% of the Tajik-Afghan border, and about 800 fighters from Tajikistan have joined the IS, Dushanbe rejects a new dispatch of Russian military troops to its borders. Tajikistan insists that Russia and the CSTO should only provide technical assistance to its border security service. [161] The next-best solution for Russia is the establishment of a rapid reaction border patrol formation within the CSTO that could be deployed in case of "a crisis situation on the external borders." This decision was made at the CIS Kazakhstan in October 2015 as part of the program for cooperation in strengthening border security of member states 2016–2020.[162]

In 2014, Russian Defense Minister Sergei Shoigu called the 201st division one of Russia's most important bases. He vowed that the base would be reinforced and equipped with the latest military technology to be fully prepared to deal with any threat in the lead-up to the withdrawal of NATO forces. [163] In the wake of the Crimean annexation, however, the Tajik public did not seem convinced that the reinforcement was aimed at preventing threats from Afghanistan. In fact, the largest group (45%) of all survey participants believed the reinforcement was intended to provoke a crisis in Central Asia, and 24% attributed the reinforcement to compensation for Russia's losses in Syria and Ukraine.[164]

In January 2015, Russian Deputy Defense Minister Anatoliy Antonov stressed that Russia and Tajikistan faced common challenges and threats. He told Tajik Defense Minister Lieutenant General Sherali Mirzo in Dushanbe that Tajikistan was Russia's outpost in the fight against terrorism, and, by providing assistance to the armed forces of Tajikistan, the Russian Defense Ministry was enhancing Russia's security.[165] Three months later, the commander of the 201st division said that Russia would increase the number of troops stationed in Tajikistan from 5,900 to 9,000 over the next five years, and add more military equipment through 2020. It also transpired that Russia was prepared to grant Tajikistan $1.2 billion in military aid.[166]

While the official explanation for increasing Russia's military presence in Central Asia is fear of terrorism spillover from Afghanistan, some analysts conclude that it is rather the result of Moscow's standoff with the West and competition for military domination in a key region such as Central Asia.[167] Such a conclusion is logical and consistent with Moscow's objectives in its flanks, but it is only partially true. The worsening situation in Afghanistan presents a real concern for Russia, which remembers its defeat in the Soviet-Afghan war. On the one hand, Moscow wants NATO to leave the region as soon as possible, but on the other hand it wants the Alliance to succeed in securing Afghanistan—the opposite would leave Russia with an insurmountable problem in its back yard. Tajikistan is a key state in the efforts to contain militant penetration from Afghanistan. Thus, Moscow's pledges to send more troops, equipment and money to Tajikistan are due to both genuine fear for its own security and a desire to portray itself as the savior of the region, the undisputed leader in Central Asia that trumps China and the US.

Russia's problem, however, is its lack of financial capabilities to sustain such a role in Central Asia in light of low oil prices and Western-imposed sanctions after its intervention in Ukraine in March 2014. Consequently, the January 2016 announcement that Russia would be downsizing its 201st division to a brigade came as no surprise. The news broke just three months after Russia confirmed plans to expand its military presence in Central Asia at the CIS summit in October 2015. A brigade typically consists of 3,000 to 5,000 troops, which in the best-case scenario would be half the number of military personnel announced in 2015. The official line of the Russian Central Military District is that the reorganization of the 201st division will reduce its numerical strength but increase its mobility.[168] Nonetheless, the fact that the reorganization started immediately leads to the conclusion that the actual reason is probably tied to the expected 5% cuts to the Russian defense budget in 2016.[169]

Public perception of Russian soldiers in Tajikistan has also grown negative following the murder of a young Tajik woman by a Russian officer on the territory of the military base in November 2015. A year earlier, a Tajik taxi driver was killed by two Russian soldiers, who were subsequently sentenced to lengthy prison terms.[170]

Analysts observe that, along with the drastic decrease of the Russian minority since the civil war, an intensive de-Russification process has taken place in Tajikistan. The government took down all memorials to Lenin and, in 2015, dismantled the 24-meter-high monument to Soviet power. Authorities have also renamed many streets that had Russian names in the capital Dushanbe, eliminated all Russian-language signs, and reduced the number of hours of Russian language in schools. In addition, citizens are required to use their national language in contacts with officials and adopt Tajik surnames without Slavic suffixes—for example, the president changed his name from Rahmonov to Rahmon.[171]

Most of these changes were determined by the fact that the Russian minority dramatically shrank and may be even extinct in the next two decades. Most of Tajikistan's Russians have emigrated as a result of the violence and civil war in the 1990s. By April 1993, approximately 300,000 or 77% of the Russian population of Tajikistan had left the country, according to the Russian Federal Migration Service.[172] In the 2000 census, Russians represented only 1.1% of the total population of the republic, or just over 68,000 people. Today, one can estimate their still-falling numbers at approximately 50,000 people.[173]

While Russia has lost virtually all of its influence regarding the Russian population in Tajikistan, Moscow is reportedly trying to create another line of division in the society and a potential lever against Dushanbe. During the 2012 violence in Gorno-Badakhshan Autonomous Region, the Russian media called for protecting Russian citizens in that region. According to the state census, there are no ethnic Russians in this part of the Pamir Mountains. However, Russia is offering citizenship to the local population to create a "Russian enclave" inside Tajikistan that it could take over in the future, according to Tajik commentators.[174] Some observers contend that up to 10,000 Gorno-Badakhshan residents held Russian passports at the time of Russian border guards' withdrawal in 2005.[175] Tajikistan is the only Central Asian republic that has a dual citizenship agreement with Russia. Social media users claim that half of the 250,000 residents of Gorno-Badakhshan have Russian passports today, but this number seems greatly exaggerated—different sources put Tajikistanis with dual citizenship between 80,000 and 100,000 nationwide, with most of them residing in Russia. After the annexation of Crimea, some commentators argued that a scenario of a takeover of the Pamir region is particularly likely in case of a Western-supported "revolution" in Tajikistan that could be used by Russia to divide Tajikistan and take over Gorno-Badakhshan by arranging fake elections and a referendum similar to that in Crimea.[176]

The scarcely populated Gorno-Badakhshan makes up nearly 45% of Tajikistan's territory but is home to only 3% percent of the country's population. Most of the 250,000 people living there are followers of Ismailism, a branch of Shia Islam, while most Tajiks are Sunni Muslims. They speak their native Pamiri languages, along with Tajik and Russian.

Russia maintained military presence in Gorno-Badakhshan since the late 19th century, when the region voluntarily joined the Russian Empire. It ended in 2005, when Dushanbe asserted control over the Tajik-Afghanistan border. President Rahmon was firm in rejecting Russia's offer to extend the border patrolling agreement, stating that "The border is a symbol of the state's independence, it is unheard of for the border of one nation to be protected by border guards from another."[177]

The presence of Russian troops, however, was providing jobs and higher wages to the local population, creating a bond between the region and Moscow. Subsequently, unemployment in the poor mountainous region increased and the disconnect between the central government and the local population deepened, as corruption related to narcotics trafficking penetrated the Tajik border guard service and the Drug Control Agency. Violent clashes between the police and the local population in 2012 and 2013 led to further discontent with the government that could be exploited by Russia to establish control over the region and return its border guards to the Tajik-Afghanistan border. The number of Russian passport-holders can serve as a justification for such an intervention, particularly if confrontations between Tajik authorities and the population continue.

Economically, Tajikistan is heavily dependent on Russia, mostly through trade and remittances from migrant labor, which reportedly accounted for half of Tajikistan's GDP in 2013.[178] According to the World Bank, Tajikistan is the world's most remittances-dependent country, with over 93% of its labor migrants working in Russia. It is the poorest Central Asian republic; its domestic situation is potentially explosive because of public dissatisfaction with low living standards and widespread corruption, which has impeded economic development and political reform. For a long time, labor migration played a critical role in easing unemployment and reducing poverty, but the economic downturn in Russia has slashed remittances and sent many laborers home. In 2015, remittances from Russia decreased by $1.966 billion, or 46%, compared to 2014.[179] Official estimates put labor migrants at one million, but unofficial assessments point to about two million people, making the country extremely vulnerable to both Russian economic instability and Moscow's political manipulation.

Turkmenistan

Turkmenistan has managed to limit Russian influence in domestic affairs and the energy trade, but it remains vulnerable to Moscow in the Caspian Sea, both in terms of security and energy transit. The country's neutrality status allows it to avoid participation in many of the regional groupings established by Russia—EEU, CSTO, or SCO. Turkmenistan is an associate member of the CIS, but has not ratified the 1993 CIS charter, although it participates in meetings and held the chairmanship of the CIS in 2012.

Turkmenistan's announcement in 2011 of plans to increase deliveries to China, participate in the Turkmenistan–Afghanistan–Pakistan–India (TAPI) gas pipeline, and work with the EU to build a trans-Caspian pipeline to Europe, caused a desperate reaction by the Kremlin, accompanied by outright threats of a "Georgian scenario" by semi-official Kremlin spokespersons. [180] In October 2011, then-President Dmitry Medvedev tasked his Energy Minister Sergei Shmatko and *Gazprom* CEO Aleksey Miller to draft proposals to resist the EU's Nabucco (now the Southern Gas Corridor) and Trans-Caspian gas pipeline projects. Turkmenistan's Foreign Affairs Ministry expressed its "bewilderment at Russian official structures' attitude toward Turkmenistan's advancing cooperation with the EU, a normal cooperation between equal partners on the energy markets." Turkmenistan declared that its cooperation with European energy partners would continue. [181]

The new Central Asia–China gas pipeline, which starts in Turkmenistan, has broken Russia's monopoly over gas transport in the region. It has also changed drastically Ashgabat's position vis-à-vis Moscow. Turkmen leaders started exhibiting confidence in price negotiations with Russia as well as in responding to pressures from the Kremlin regarding Ashgabat's cooperation with the EU on the trans-Caspian pipeline to Europe. [182]

Turkmenistan's largest gas field, South Yolotan, was developed with the help of a $4 billion loan from China provided in 2009. In November 2011, Beijing and Ashgabat signed a deal that will allow Turkmenistan to supply China with 65 bcm of natural gas per year, or over 50% more than the initially agreed 30 bcm per annum in 2007.[183] The deal challenged Russia's position as the main buyer of Turkmen gas at the time and subsequently pushed out Russia from Turkmenistan's gas market. In 2015, Russia ceased buying Turkmen gas due to price disputes, Gazprom's non-payment of received volumes, and the decreased demand for Russian gas in Europe.[184]

Using Beijing's new pipelines, Ashgabat already exports as much gas as it used to transit through Russia—Gazprom bought 40 bcm/a of gas from Turkmenistan in 2008, China's imports of Turkmen gas were boosted to 40 bcm/a in 2015. Currently, the Turkmenistan–China natural gas pipeline system consists of three branches with a total capacity of 55 bcm a year to transfer gas from Turkmenistan as well as gas from other Central Asian states. Another branch of the pipeline will be built in 2016, increasing the total capacity to 85 bcm a year.[185]

Endnotes

[1] President Putin's speech before the Russian Duma, March 18, 2014, http://en.kremlin.ru/events/president/news/20603.

[2] For detailed information on military activities see: Matthew Stein, *Compendium of Central Asian Military and Security Activity*, Fort Leavenworth: Foreign Military Studies Office, May 22, 2015, http://fmso.leavenworth.army.mil/documents/Central-Asian-Military-Events.pdf.

[3] About the *Hartland Theory* see H. J. Mackinder, "The Geographical Pivot of History," *The Geographical Journal*, Vol. 23, No. 4, April 1904, pp. 421–437, https://www.jstor.org/stable/1775498?seq=1#page_scan_tab_contents.

[4] European Commission trade statistics,
http://ec.europa.eu/trade/policy/countries-and-regions/countries/china/;
Simon Denyer, "In Central Asia, Chinese inroads in Russia's back yard,"
The Washington Post, December 27, 2015,
https://www.washingtonpost.com/world/asia_pacific/chinas-advance-into-central-asia-ruffles-russian-feathers/2015/12/27/cfedeb22-61ff-11e5-8475-781cc9851652_story.html.

[5] André Loesekrug-Pietri, "Why Europe Can't Afford to Ignore China's New Silk Road," *World Economic Forum*, November 16, 2015,
https://www.weforum.org/agenda/2015/11/europe-china-new-silk-road/.

[6] See testimony of Michael Clarke, "Looking West: China and Central Asia," Hearing before the U.S.-China Economic and Security Review Commission, One hundred and Fourteenth Congress, March 18, 2015,
http://www.uscc.gov/Hearings/hearing-looking-west-china-and-central-asia.

[7] Speech by H.E. Xi Jinping, President of the People's Republic of China at Nazarbayev University in Astana, September 7, 2013,
http://www.fmprc.gov.cn/ce/cebel/eng/zxxx/t1078088.htm.

[8] Simon Denyer, "China bypasses American 'New Silk Road' with Two if its Own," *The Washington Post*, October 14, 2013,
https://www.washingtonpost.com/world/asia_pacific/china-bypasses-american-new-silk-road-with-two-if-its-own/2013/10/14/49f9f60c-3284-11e3-ad00-ec4c6b31cbed_story.html.

[9] Initially, the Customs Union wanted to become a collective member of WTO, a proposal immediately rejected by the organization. Subsequently, as a result of its accession to the Customs Union in 2010, Kazakhstan increased more than half its import tariffs that were already negotiated with other WTO members. In addition, WTO had to negotiate not only with Astana, but also with the central authority of the Russian-led trade block, the Eurasian Economic Commission in Moscow. Kazakhstan eventually became a WTO member in November 2015. See Iana Dreyer and Mike Collier, "Eurasian Economic Union Complicates Kazakhstan's Final WTO Accession Bid,"*BNE IntelliNews*, March 25, 2015,

http://www.intellinews.com/eurasian-economic-union-complicates-kazakhstan-s-final-wto-accession-bid-500445484/?source=belarus&archive=bne.

[10] Stephen Blank, "Russia Losing Ground Across Central Asia," *Eurasia Daily Monitor* Volume 13, Issue 26, February 8, 2016, http://www.jamestown.org/single/?tx_ttnews%5Btt_news%5D=45077&no_cache=1#.Vt18wsc4lsM; Umida Hashimova, "Kyrgyzstan Determined to Pursue Its Hydropower Plans With or Without Russia," *Eurasia Daily Monitor*, Volume: 13 Issue 10, January 15, 2016, http://www.jamestown.org/single/?tx_ttnews%5btt_news%5d=44990&no_cache=1#.Vt19Zcc4lsN; "Правительство Кыргызстана постановило отказаться от межправительственного соглашения с Россией о строительстве Камбаратинской ГЭС и Верхне-Нарынского каскада ГЭС," *Kloop.kg*, December 31, 2015, http://kloop.kg/blog/2015/12/31/kyrgyzstan-denonsiruet-soglashenie-s-rossiej-o-stroitelstve-ges/.

[11] "General Assembly Adopts Resolution Calling upon States Not to Recognize Changes in Status of Crimea Region," United Nations, March 27, 2014, http://www.un.org/press/en/2014/ga11493.doc.htm; "Mixed Regional Response to Crimea Annexation," *Economist Intelligence Unit*, March 27, 2014, http://www.eiu.com.

[12] James Kitfield, "U.S. Sources: Russia Forging Alliance with Taliban," *Yahoo News*, February 12, 2016, https://www.yahoo.com/news/u-s--sources--russia-forging-alliance-with-taliban-201058133.html?ref=gs; "Islamic State gaining ground in Afghanistan: UN," *AFP*, September 25, 2015, https://www.yahoo.com/news/u-s--sources--russia-forging-alliance-with-taliban-201058133.html?ref=gs.

[13] US Congress, Senate, Senate Armed Services Committee and Senate Armed Services Committee, Worldwide Threat Assessment of the US Intelligence Community: Hearings before the Senate Armed Services Committee and Senate Armed Services Committee, Statement for the Record by James R. Clapper, Director of National Intelligence, 114th Cong., February 9, 2016, p. 19, https://fas.org/irp/congress/2016_hr/020916-threat.pdf.

[14] Sami Yousafzai, "A Taliban-Russia Team-Up Against ISIS?" *The Daily Beast*, October 26, 2015, http://www.thedailybeast.com/articles/2015/10/26/a-taliban-russia-team-up-against-isis.html.

[15] Fozil Mashrab, "Eurasian Union's Expansion Falters Amid Russia's Economic Woes," *Eurasia Daily Monitor*, Volume 13, Issue 42, March 2, 2016, http://www.jamestown.org/single/?tx_ttnews%5Btt_news%5D=45160&tx_t tnews%5BbackPid%5D=7&cHash=941df08ef9e8a6c42fbc27a5f39455a0#.Vt 3DP8c4nR0.

[16] On China's *Marching Westward* concept and *Grand Western Development Strategy* see Zhang Xiaotong and Marlen Belgibayev, "China's Eurasian Pivot," *The ASAN Forum*, December 1, 2014, http://www.theasanforum.org/chinas-eurasian-pivot/.

[17] Hillary Clinton, "Remarks at the New Silk Road Ministerial Meeting," New York City, New York, September 22, 2011, http://www.state.gov/secretary/rm/2011/09/173807.htm.

[18] Alexander Frost, "The Collective Security Organization, the Shanghai Cooperation Organization, and Russia's Strategic Goals in Central Asia," *China and Eurasia Forum Quarterly* vol. 7, no. 3, Central Asia-Caucasus Institute & Silk Road Studies Program, October 2009, pp. 83–102.

[19] Marcin Kaczmarski, "Russia Attempts to Limit Chinese Influence by Promoting CSTO-SCO Cooperation," *CACI Analyst*, October 17, 2007, http://www.cacianalyst.org/publications/analytical-articles/item/11497-analytical-articles-caci-analyst-2007-10-17-art-11497.html?tmpl=component&print=1.

[20] Richard Weitz, "Russia, China, and Central Asia: Time for Decision," Ther Asan Forum, December 23, 2015, http://www.theasanforum.org/russia-china-and-central-asia-time-for-decision/#a42.

[21] Edward Wong, "China Quietly Extends Footprints into Central Asia," *New York Times*, January 2, 2011, http://www.nytimes.com/2011/01/03/world/asia/03china.html?pagewanted=all.

[22] Speech by H.E. Xi Jinping, President of the People's Republic of China at Nazarbayev University in Astana, September 7, 2013, http://www.fmprc.gov.cn/ce/cebel/eng/zxxx/t1078088.htm.

[23] Dmitry Gorenburg, "External Support for Central Asian Military and Security Forces," SIPRI/ Open Society Foundations, January 2014, http://www.sipri.org/research/security/afghanistan/central-asia-security/publications/SIPRI-OSFno1WP.pdf.

[24] "Kazakhs Protest Against China's Growing Influence," *RFE/RL*, January 30, 2010, http://www.rferl.org/content/Kazakhs_Protest_Against_Chinas_Growing_Influence/1944085.html.

[25] International Monetary Fund, *Regional Economic Outlook: Caucasus and Central Asia*, October 2015, http://www.imf.org/external/pubs/ft/reo/2015/mcd/eng/pdf/cca1015p.pdf; Holly Elliyat, "Why China's Slowdown Should Not Worry Russia," *CNBC*, November 3, 2015, http://www.cnbc.com/2015/11/03/chinas-slowdown-should-not-worry-russia.html.

[26] Heather A. Conley and Caroline Rohloff, "The New Ice Curtain: Russia's Strategic Reach to the Arctic," CSIS, August 2015, http://csis.org/files/publication/150826_Conley_NewIceCurtain_Web.pdf.

[27] Stephen Blank, "China Shapes a New Asian Order," *Atlantic-Community.org*, October 2, 2009, http://www.atlantic-community.org/index/view/China_Shapes_a_New_Asian_Order.

[28] Zhou Yan and Wang Qian, "Turkmenistan to Expand Natural Gas Supply to China," *China Daily*, November 25, 2011, http://www.chinadaily.com.cn/bizchina/2011-11/25/content_14159921.htm.

[29] "Turkmenistan Supplied 125 bcm of Gas to China," *Natural Gas Europe*, September 28, 2015, http://www.naturalgaseurope.com/turkmenistan-supplied-125-bcm-gas-to-china-25610.

[30] Catherine Putz, "Russia's Gazprom Stops Buying Gas from Turkmenistan," *The Diplomat*, January 6, 2015, http://thediplomat.com/2016/01/russias-gazprom-stops-buying-gas-from-turkmenistan/.

[31] Michael Levyveld, "China-Russia Project Stalls as Energy Prices Plunge," *Radio Free Asia*, January 25, 2016, http://www.rfa.org/english/commentaries/energy_watch/china-russia-01252016152633.html.

[32] Linda Jakobson, Paul Holton, Dean Knox and Jingchao Peng, *China's Energy and Security Relations with Russia: Hopes, Frustrations and Uncertainties*, Stockholm: Stockholm International Peace Research Institute, October 2011, pp. 26–28.

[33] *Ibid*, pp.29–31.

[34] Michael Lelyveld, "Doubts Rise on Russia-China Gas Deal," Radio Free Asia, April 6, 2015, http://www.rfa.org/english/commentaries/energy_watch/doubts-rise-on-russia-china-gas-deal-04062015110032.html.

[35] *Ibid.*

[36] "China Says to Offer $10 Billion in Loans to SCO Member States," Reuters, June 6, 2012, http://www.reuters.com/article/us-china-sco-loans-idUSBRE85602920120607.

[37] John C. K. Daly, "Analysis: China Increases Stake in Kazakh Energy Assets," *UPI*, April 28, 2009, http://www.upi.com/Business_News/Energy-Industry/2009/04/28/Analysis-China-increases-stake-in-Kazakh-energy-assets/51441240959501/.

[38] Chris Rickleton, "By Opposing SCO Development Bank, Is Russia Biggest Loser?" *EurasiaNet.org*, March 25, 2015, http://www.eurasianet.org/node/72701; "Russia proposes to create SCO development bank," *The Caspian Times*, December 1, 2015, http://www.thecaspiantimes.com/russia-proposes-to-create-sco-development-bank/.

[39] Vladimir Putin, "New Integration Project for Eurasia – A Future Which is Being Born Today," in Russian, *Izvestia*, October 3, 2011, www.izvestia.ru/news/502761.

[40] Pew Research Center, *Confidence in Democracy and Capitalism Wanes in Former Soviet Union*, Washington, DC: Pew Research Center, December 5, 2011, http://www.pewglobal.org/2011/12/05/confidence-in-democracy-and-capitalism-wanes-in-former-soviet-union/.

[41] Richard Weitz, "Putin's Plan for Eurasia," *Analyst, CACI Analyst*, Central Asia-Caucasus Institute, November 16, 2011, http://www.cacianalyst.org/?q=node/5667.

[42] Margarita Assenova, "Kazakhstan Expands Economic Cooperation with Russia, but Guards Own Interests," *Eurasia Daily Monitor*, Volume 10, Issue 207, November 18, 2013, http://www.jamestown.org/single/?tx_ttnews%5Btt_news%5D=41646&no_cache=1#.Vt4zJMc4nVo.

[43] Erica Marat, "Russia Seeks Long-Term Military Presence In Tajikistan and Kyrgyzstan', *Eurasia Daily Monitor*, Volume 8, Number 174, September 22, 2011, http://www.jamestown.org/programs/edm/single/?tx_ttnews%5Btt_news%5D=38436&cHash=ad2e1380973746a723ae4a92df4050e2; Abdujalil Abdurasulov, "CIS summit: Russia to Bolster Central Asia Military," *BBC*, October 16, 2015, http://www.bbc.com/news/world-europe-34538051.

[44] Evgeniya Chaykovskaya, "Russia to Extend Tajikistan Military Base Lease by 50 Years," *The Moscow News*, September 2, 2011, http://themoscownews.com/international/20110902/188999237.html.

[45] Catherine Putz, "Why Is Russia Cutting Troops in Tajikistan?" *Russia Insider*, February 5, 2016, http://russia-insider.com/en/politics/why-russia-cutting-troops-tajikistan/ri12652.

[46] *World Drug Report 2010, UNODC* United Nations Office on Drugs and Crime (UNODC), https://www.unodc.org/documents/wdr/WDR_2010/1.2_The_global_heroin_market.pdf.

[47] *World Drug Report 2010*; *World Drug Report 2015*; "In-depth Mid-Term evaluation of the Regional Programme for Afghanistan and Neighbouring Countries 2011–2015," UNODC, March 2015, http://www.unodc.org/documents/evaluation/indepth-evaluations/2015/RP_Afghanistan_Neighbouring_Countries_In-Depth_Evaluation_Report_April_2015.pdf.

[48] Alexander Gabuev and Kabay Karabekov, "Almazbek Atambayev Starts Fulfilling Promises to Russia," in Russian, *Kommersant*, November 18, 2011, http://kommersant.ru/doc/1818153.

[49] Abdujalil Abdurasulov, "CIS summit: Russia to Bolster Central Asia Military," *BBC*, October 16, 2015, http://www.bbc.com/news/world-europe-34538051.

[50] Alexander Gabuev and Kabay Karabekov, "Almazbek Atambayev Starts Fulfilling Promises to Russia," in Russian, *Kommersant*, November 18, 2011, http://kommersant.ru/doc/1818153.

[51] "Central Asian Armies Start Exercises to Counter Potential Arab Spring-style Unrest," *Telegraph*, September 20, 2011, http://www.telegraph.co.uk/news/worldnews/asia/tajikistan/8777123/Central-Asian-armies-start-exercises-to-counter-potential-Arab-Spring-style-unrest.html.

[52] Ted Galen Carpenter, "Caught in the Middle: Beijing's Reaction to US-Russian Tensions," *ChinaUSFocus.org*, November 10, 2014, http://www.chinausfocus.com/foreign-policy/caught-in-the-middle-beijings-reaction-to-us-russian-tensions/#sthash.5cCDXe21.dpuf.

[53] See more about the Russian minorities in Central Asia in Sébastien Peyrouse, *The Russian Minority in Central Asia: Migration, Politics, and Language*, Occasional Paper #297, Woodrow Wilson International Center for Scholars, 2008, https://www.wilsoncenter.org/sites/default/files/OP297.pdf; Alexander Shustov, "Русский Мир Средней Азии Сжимается," *Nezavisimaya Gazeta*, February 1, 2016, http://www.ng.ru/courier/2016-02-01/11_asia.html; Paul Goble, "Ethnic Russians Leaving Central Asia and With Them, Putin's Hopes for Influence," *Eurasia Daily Monitor*, Volume 13, Issue 22, February 2, 2016, http://www.jamestown.org/programs/edm/single/?tx_ttnews%5btt_news%5d=45053&tx_ttnews%5bbackPid%5d=827&no_cache=1#.VuIJ-Mc4nR1.

[54] Fabio Belafatti, "Ethnic Tensions in Central Asia: Autochthonous and Russian Minorities," *Geopolitika*, October 3, 2014, http://www.geopolitika.lt/?artc=6569.

[55] George Voloshin, "Russian-Kazakhstani Relations: A Return of Moscow's Neo-Imperialist Rhetoric," *Eurasia Daily Monitor*, Volume 11, Issue 38, February 27, 2014, http://www.jamestown.org/regions/centralasia/single/?tx_ttnews%5Bpointer%5D=6&tx_ttnews%5Btt_news%5D=42026&tx_ttnews%5BbackPid%5D=53&cHash=13ea51189321a0e0a16cd64733c63f0f#.Vua5u5MrLfY.

[56] Dmitry Shlapentokh, "Kazakhstan and the EEU," CACI Analyst, March 4, 2015, http://www.cacianalyst.org/publications/analytical-articles/item/13156-kazakhstan-and-the-eeu.html.

[57] Simon Denyer, "China bypasses American 'New Silk Road' with Two if its Own," *The Washington Post*, October 14, 2013, https://www.washingtonpost.com/world/asia_pacific/china-bypasses-american-new-silk-road-with-two-if-its-own/2013/10/14/49f9f60c-3284-11e3-ad00-ec4c6b31cbed_story.html; "Major Outcomes of the Foreign Policy Activities of the Republic of Kazakhstan in 2015 and Priorities for 2016," Speech by Erlan Idrissov, Minister of Foreign Affairs of Kazakhstan, December 30, 2015, http://www.mfa.kz/index.php/en/component/content/article/17-minister-

s-blog/5601-major-outcomes-of-the-foreign-policy-activities-of-the-republic-of-kazakhstan-in-2015-and-priorities-for-2016.

58 Syed Adnan and Athar Bukhari, "Cooperative threat reduction: Case study of Kazakhstan – Analysis," *Eurasia Review*, June 13, 2011, http://www.eurasiareview.com/13062011-cooperative-threat-reduction-case-study-of-kazakhstan-analysis/.

59 David E. Hoffman, "How U.S. Removed Half a Ton of Uranium From Kazakhstan," *The Washington Post*, September 21, 2009, http://www.washingtonpost.com/wp-dyn/content/article/2009/09/20/AR2009092002881.html?sid=ST2009092002315.

60 ATOM Project official website, http://www.theatomproject.org/en/.

61 "Прецедент 'Защиты Русскоязычных Граждан в Крыму' Крайне Опасен, Поэтому в Вопросах Украины Казахстан не Может Встать на Сторону России - Эксперты," CA-NEWS, March 12, 2014, http://ca-news.org/news:1102573.

62 The White House, https://www.whitehouse.gov/the-press-office/2014/03/10/readout-president-s-call-president-nazarbayev-kazakhstan.

63 Official website of the Kazakh President (Akorda), http://www.akorda.kz/ru/events/international_community/phone_calls/page_216113_telefonnyi-razgovor-s-prezidentom-rossiiskoi-federatsii-vladimirom-putinym.

64 "В вопросе противостояния Запада и России необходимо «остыть» и отойти от обвинений, угроз и санкций - Президент РК Н.Назарбаев," March 25, 2014, *KazInform*, http://inform.kz/rus/article/2642060; Joanna Lillis, "Kazakhstan: Ukraine Crisis Cements Astana In Russia's Orbit," *EurasiaNet*, April 1, 2014, http://www.eurasianet.org/node/68218.

65 The statement was subsequently taken off the website of Kazakhstan's Ministry of Foreign Affairs, but remained on the website of Kazakhstan's

embassy in Moscow. "Statement by the Ministry of Foreign Affairs of Kazakhstan on the Referendum in Crimea," March 18, 2014, http://www.kazembassy.ru/en/mpolitika/6681-2014-03-18-16-10-33; "MFA's Statement on Referendum in the Crimea," *KazInform.kz*, March 19, 2014, http://mfa.gov.kz/en/#!/news/article/13803.

[66] Joanna Lillis, "Kazakhstan: Ukraine Crisis Cements Astana In Russia's Orbit," *EurasiaNet*, April 1, 2014, http://www.eurasianet.org/node/68218.

[67] Committee on Statistics, Ministry of National Economy of the Republic of Kazakhstan, Population by Ethnicity on January 1, 2014, http://www.stat.gov.kz.

[68] "Kazakh Foreign Ministry Protests Zhirinovsky Comments," *RFE/RL*, February 24, 2014, http://www.rferl.org/content/kazakhstan-zhirinovsky/25275475.html; "Kazakhstan's Foreign Ministry to send a note to Russia," *TengriNews.kz*, February 20, 2014, http://en.tengrinews.kz/politics_sub/Kazakhstans-Foreign-Ministry-to-send-a-note-to-Russia-26193/; George Voloshin, "Russian-Kazakhstani Relations: A Return of Moscow's Neo-Imperialist Rhetoric," *Eurasia Daily Monitor*, Volume 11, Issue 38, February 27, 2014, http://www.jamestown.org/regions/centralasia/single/?tx_ttnews%5Bpointer%5D=6&tx_ttnews%5Btt_news%5D=42026&tx_ttnews%5BbackPid%5D=53&cHash=13ea51189321a0e0a16cd64733c63f0f#.Vua5u5MrLfY.

[69] Bruce Pannier, "A Tale Of Russian Separatism In Kazakhstan," RFE/RL, August 3, 2014, http://www.rferl.org/content/qishloq-ovozi-kazakhstan-russian-separatism/25479571.html.

[70] Law of the Republic of Kazakhstan on Languages, Article 4, July 1997, http://www.usefoundation.org/view/780.

[71] Constitution of the Republic of Kazakhstan, Section I, Article 7, http://www.wipo.int/wipolex/en/text.jsp?file_id=256278.

[72] *Ibid.*

[73] On the Russians in Kazakhstan see Martha Brill Olcott, *Kazakhstan: Unfulfilled Promise?* (Revised Edition), Carnegie Endowment for International Peace, 2010; Sébastien Peyrouse, "Nationhood and the Minority Question in Central Asia. The Russians in Kazakhstan," *Europe-Asia Studies*, Vol. 59, No. 3, May, 2007, pp. 481–501; Sébastien Peyrouse, *The Russian Minority in Central Asia: Migration, Politics, and Language*, Occasional Paper 297, Washington, DC: Woodrow Wilson Center for International Scholars, 2008, https://www.wilsoncenter.org/sites/default/files/OP297.pdf; Mikhail Alexandrov, *Uneasy Alliance: Relations Between Russia and Kazakhstan in the Post-Soviet Era, 1992–1997*, Greenwood Press, 1999.

[74] Ian MacWilliam, "Kazakhs Protest Cossack Border Guards," The Moscow Times, April 17, 1997, http://www.themoscowtimes.com/news/article/kazakhs-protest-cossack-border-guards/308552.html.

[75] Martha Brill Olcott, *Kazakhstan: Unfulfilled Promise?* (Revised Edition), Carnegie Endowment for International Peace, 2010, p.79–80.

[76] Igor Rotar, "The Cossack Factor in Ukrainian War," *Eurasia Daily Monitor*, Volume 11, Issue 149, August 13, 2014, http://www.jamestown.org/single/?tx_ttnews%5Btt_news%5D=42747; George Voloshin, "Kazakhstani Cossacks in Media Spotlight Because of Ukraine Crisis," *Eurasia Daily Monitor*, Volume 11, Issue 147, August 11, 2014, http://www.jamestown.org/single/?tx_ttnews%5Btt_news%5D=42739.

[77] "Казаки Казахстана: Россия заплатит нам за геноцид!" (Cossacks of Kazakhstan: Russia Will Repay Us for the Genocide), *Yvision.kz (blog)*, May 30, 2013, http://yvision.kz/post/355094.

[78] Daniel Sneider, "Russian Politicians Stump with Nationalist Rhetoric," *The Christian Science Monitor*, November 29, 1993, http://www.csmonitor.com/1993/1129/29013.html.

[79] Sébastien Peyrouse, "Nationhood and the Minority Question in Central Asia. The Russians in Kazakhstan," 2007.

[80] Committee on Statistics, Ministry of National Economy of Kazakhstan, Population by Ethnicity on January 1, 2014, http://www.stat.gov.kz.

[81] Committee on Statistics, Ministry of National Economy of Kazakhstan, Population, http://www.stat.gov.kz.

[82] Compare with the case of Macedonia, where the Albanian minority represents 25% of the population. An armed insurgency in 2001 pushed the government to implement sweeping constitutional and legal reforms to provide for adequate minority rights and political representation for the Albanians. On the one hand, Macedonia is comparable to Kazakhstan as a young state that came out of the breakup of a federation (Yugoslavia). On the other hand, the Albanian minority in Macedonia is young, dynamic and growing, while the Russian minority in Kazakhstan is shrinking, aging, and losing the young and better-educated to emigration. However, there is a significant difference in the absolute numbers: the sheer size of 3.7 million Russians in Kazakhstan is hardly comparable to about 500,000 Albanians in Macedonia. Regardless of the differences, the presence of a larger than 20% strong minority in any nation state requires widespread provisions for securing adequate political representation, including access to elected positions, public sector jobs, proportionate inclusion in law enforcement and representation in the judiciary.

[83] Michael Birnbaum, "In Kazakhstan, Fears of Becoming the Next Ukraine," *The Washington Post*, May 2, 2015, https://www.washingtonpost.com/world/europe/in-kazakhstan-fears-of-becoming-the-next-ukraine/2015/05/01/10f7e73c-e878-11e4-8581-633c536add4b_story.html?tid=a_inl; "Kazakhstan Toughens Punishment for Separatism," *TengriNews*, April 8, 2014, http://en.tengrinews.kz/laws_initiatives/Kazakhstan-toughens-punishment-for-separatism-252777/; Catherine Putz, "Separatism Charge Lands Young Kazakh in Jail," *The Diplomat*, November 19, 2015, http://thediplomat.com/2015/11/separatism-charge-lands-young-kazakh-in-jail/.

[84] Всероссийский молодёжный форум «Селигер-2014», Kremlin.ru, August 29, 2014, http://kremlin.ru/events/president/news/46507.

85 Joanna Lillis, "Kazakhstan Makes Geopolitical Point With Statehood Celebrations," *EurasiaNet*, September 11, 2015, http://www.eurasianet.org/node/75036.

86 *Interfax, Tengrinews.kz*, October 25, 2013.

87 "Kazakhstan May leave EEU if its Interests are Infringed: Nazarbayev," *TengriNews*, August 27, 2014, http://en.tengrinews.kz/politics_sub/Kazakhstan-may-leave-EEU-if-its-interests-are-infringed-255722/; David Trilling, "As Kazakhstan's Leader Asserts Independence, Did Putin Just Say, 'Not So Fast'?" *EurasiaNet*, August 30, 2014, http://www.eurasianet.org/node/69771.

88 Julia Kusznir, "Russia's borders: Moscow's long alliance with Kazakhstan is strong but not unbreakable," *The Conversation*, January 20, 2015, http://theconversation.com/russias-borders-moscows-long-alliance-with-kazakhstan-is-strong-but-not-unbreakable-36457.

89 "Товарооборот стран ЕАЭС в I квартале упал на 21%" (Trade Turnover in EEU declined by 21% in the First Quarter of 2015), *News.am*, May 5, 2015, http://news.am/rus/news/266881.html.

90 Vladislav Vorotnikov, "Kazakhstan and Russia in Meat Dispute," *Global Meat News*, April 30, 2015, http://www.globalmeatnews.com/Industry-Markets/Kazakhstan-and-Russia-in-meat-dispute; Sergei Gretsky, "Hanging in The Trade Balance: Is Free Trade a Curse for Kazakhstan?," *CACI Analyst*, June 10, 2015, http://cacianalyst.org/publications/analytical-articles/item/13228-hanging-in-the-trade-balance-is-free-trade-a-curse-for-kazakhstan?.html.

91 Birgit Brauer, "The Cost of Black Tuesday for Kazakhstan," *CACI Analyst*, March 19, 2014, http://www.cacianalyst.org/publications/analytical-articles/item/12934-the-cost-of-black-tuesday-for-kazakhstan.html.

92 "Bank Deposits Show Kazakhs Fear Another Devaluation," *BNE InteliNews*, February 12, 2015, http://www.intellinews.com/bne-chart-bank-deposits-show-kazakhs-fear-another-devaluation-

500443657/?source=kazakhstan&archive=bne; Nate Schenkkan, "Impact of the Economic Crisis in Russia on Central Asia," Russian Analytical Digest, No. 165, March 17, 2015, http://www.css.ethz.ch/content/dam/ethz/special-interest/gess/cis/center-for-securities-studies/pdfs/RAD-165.pdf.

[93] Birgit Brauer, "The Cost of Black Tuesday for Kazakhstan," *CACI Analyst*, March 19, 2014.

[94] "Kazakhstan: Adjusting to Low Oil Prices, Challenging Times Ahead," The World Bank, Fall 2015, http://www.worldbank.org/en/country/kazakhstan/publication/economic-update-fall-2015.

[95] U.S. Energy Information Administration, http://www.eia.gov/forecasts/steo/pdf/steo_full.pdf.

[96] Najia Badykova, "A New Era for Caspian Oil and Gas," CSIS, February 13, 2015, http://csis.org/publication/new-era-caspian-oil-and-gas.

[97] "Caucasus and Central Asia: Oil Price Decline and Regional Spillovers Darken the Outlook," International Monetary Fund, May 2015, https://www.imf.org/external/pubs/ft/reo/2015/mcd/eng/pdf/cca0515.pdf.

[98] Nate Schenkkan, "A Perfect Storm in Central Asia," January 22, 2016, http://foreignpolicy.com/2016/01/22/a-perfect-storm-in-central-asia/.

[99] Malika Rustem, "Putin's State Visit Reconfirms Kazakh-Russian Strategic Partnership," Eurasia & World, October 18, 2015, http://astanatimes.com/2015/10/putins-state-visit-reconfirms-kazakh-russian-strategic-partnership/.

[100] Ainis Razma, "The Geopolitics of Central Asia after the Annexation of Crimea in 2014," Lithuanian Annual Strategic Review, Volume 13, Issue 1, Pages 125–143, December 2015, http://www.degruyter.com/view/j/lasr.2015.13.issue-1/lasr-2015-0007/lasr-2015-0007.xml.

101 "Kazakh, Ukrainian Cooperation Road Map Signed In Astana," Interfax-Kazakhstan, October 9, 2015, https://www.interfax.kz.

102 "Major Outcomes of the Foreign Policy Activities of the Republic of Kazakhstan in 2015 and Priorities for 2016," Speech by Erlan Idrissov, Minister of Foreign Affairs of Kazakhstan, December 30, 2015, http://www.mfa.kz/index.php/en/component/content/article/17-minister-s-blog/5601-major-outcomes-of-the-foreign-policy-activities-of-the-republic-of-kazakhstan-in-2015-and-priorities-for-2016.

103 "Население Узбекистана превысило 31 миллион," (The Population of Uzbekistan Exceeded 31 Million), *Gazeta.uz*, March 16, 2015, https://www.gazeta.uz/2015/03/16/statistics/; Worldometers, http://www.worldometers.info/world-population/uzbekistan-population/; Sébastien Peyrouse, *The Russian Minority in Central Asia: Migration, Politics, and Language*, Occasional Paper 297, Washington, DC: Woodrow Wilson Center for International Scholars, 2008, https://www.wilsoncenter.org/sites/default/files/OP297.pdf.

104 "Uzbek President Slams Russia-led Economic Union," AFP, May 29, 2014, www.afp.com.

105 "Russia Cozies Up to Uzbekistan With $865 Million Debt Write-Off," *The Moscow Times*, December 10, 2014, http://www.themoscowtimes.com/article.php?id=513096.

106 Ann Scott Tyson, "Russia and China Bullying Central Asia, U.S. Says," The Washington Post, July 15, 2005, http://www.washingtonpost.com/wpdyn/content/article/2005/07/14/AR2005071401768.html.

107 Jim Nichol, *Uzbekistan's Closure of the Airbase at Karshi-Khanabad: Context and Implications*, Congressional Research Service, October 7, 2005, UNT Digital Library. http://digital.library.unt.edu/ark:/67531/metacrs7519/.

108 Margarita Assenova, "Uzbekistan Is Running Out of Time," *Internationale Politik*, no. 3, 2005, pp. 56–60. Vol. 6, No. 3, Fall 2005, p. 52–

56; Shirin Akiner, *Violence in Andijan, 13 May 2005: An Independent Assessment*, Central Asia-Caucasus Institute & Silk Road Studies Program, 2005, http://www.silkroadstudies.org/resources/pdf/SilkRoadPapers/2005_akiner_violence-in-andijan-13-may-2005.pdf; AbduMannob Polat, Reassessing Andijan: The Road to Restoring U.S.-Uzbek Relations, The Jamestown Foundation, June 2007, http://www.jamestown.org/uploads/media/Jamestown-Andijan_01.pdf.

[109] Farkhod Tolipov, "Uzbekistan Without the CSTO," *CACI Analyst*, February 20, 2013, http://www.cacianalyst.org/publications/analytical-articles/item/12652-uzbekistan-without-the-csto.html.

[110] Zabikhulla Saipov, "New Foreign Policy Strategy Paper Codifies Uzbekistan's Reluctance Toward Restrictive Alliances," *Eurasia Daily Monitor*, Volume 9, Issue 153, August 10, 2012, http://www.jamestown.org/single/?tx_ttnews%5Btt_news%5D=39759&no_cache=1#.VwsmHBIrLfY; Farkhod Tolipov, "Uzbekistan's New Foreign Policy Concept: No Base, No Blocks but National Interests First," *CACI Analyst*, September 5, 2012, http://cacianalyst.org/?q=node/5829.

[111] Olga Sokolay, "Николай Бордюжа: Казахстан – генератор идей в сфере коллективной безопасности" (Nikolay Bordyuzha: Kazakhstan—Generator of Ideas in Collective Security), *Vlast.kz*, March 18, 2015, https://vlast.kz/politika/nikolaj_bordjuzha_kazahstan_generator_idej_v_sfere_kollektivnoj_bezopasnosti-10203.html.

[112] John C. K. Daly, "Russia Shutters Northern Distribution Network," *Eurasia Daily Monitor*, Volume 12, Issue111, June 15, 2015, http://www.jamestown.org/programs/edm/single/?tx_ttnews%5Btt_news%5D=44034&cHash=a612458b880c0fa6959388e9b2380789#.VxJKgRIrLfY.

[113] Navbahor Imamova, "US-Central Asia/Uzbekistan: Exclusive Interview with Daniel Rosenblum, Deputy Assistant Secretary of State for Central Asia," *Voice of America*, January 21, 2015, http://www.amerikaovozi.com/a/us-central-asia-dan-rosenblum-interview/2607884.html.

[114] "The Position of the Republic of Uzbekistan on the Situation in Ukraine and the Crimean issue," Ministry of Foreign Affairs of the Republic of Uzbekistan, March 25, 2014, http://www.mfa.uz/en/press/news/2014/03/1529/.

[115] Umida Hashimova, "Online Commentary in Uzbekistan Divided on Crimea," *Eurasia Daily Monitor*, Volume 11, Issue 82, May 2, 2014, http://www.jamestown.org/single/?tx_ttnews%5Btt_news%5D=42307&no_cache=1#.VwquLRIrLfY; "Узбекистан не признал Крым частью России," (Uzbekistan Did Not Recognize Crimea as Part of Russia), *OpenTown.org*, March 26, 2014, https://www.opentown.org/news/30853/.

[116] Gulnoza Saidazimova, "Uzbekistan: Shadowy Group Agitates For 'Free Karakalpakstan'," *RFE/RL*, April 5, 2008, 6 http://www.rferl.org/content/article/1079744.html.

[117] Ainis Razma, " The Geopolitics of Central Asia after the Annexation of Crimea in 2014," *Lithuanian Annual Strategic Review*, Volume 13, Issue 1, Pages 125–143, December 2015, http://www.degruyter.com/view/j/lasr.2015.13.issue-1/lasr-2015-0007/lasr-2015-0007.xml; Slavomír Horák, "Separatism in Uzbekistan? Karakalpakstan after Crimea," CACI Analyst, may 21, 2014, http://cacianalyst.org/publications/analytical-articles/item/12979-separatism-in-uzbekistan?-karakalpakstan-after-crimea.html.

[118] All-Union Census 1970 and 1989, National Composition of the Population of the Republics of the USSR, *Демоскоп Weekly*, Demoscope.ru, http://demoscope.ru/weekly/ssp/sng_nac_89.php?reg=4.

[119] Sébastien Peyrouse, *The Russian Minority in Central Asia: Migration, Politics, and Language,* 2008; "Население Узбекистана превысило 31 миллион," (The Population of Uzbekistan Exceeded 31 Million), *Gazeta.uz*, March 16, 2015.

[120] "Русские в Узбекистане: хуже некуда," (The Russians in Uzbekistan: Worse than Ever), Rosbalt, April 1, 2013, http://www.rosbalt.ru/exussr/2013/04/01/1112454.html.

[121] Paul Goble, "Ethnic Russians in Uzbekistan Under Pressure to Leave," *Window on Eurasia*, April 3, 2013, http://windowoneurasia2.blogspot.com/2013/04/window-on-eurasia-ethnic-russians-in.html.

[122] Bruce Pannier, "Uzbek Broadcasters Set to Self-Destruct," *RFE/RL*, http://www.rferl.org/content/qishloq-ovozi-uzbekistan-broadcasters-self-destruct/25361053.html.

[123] "Uzbek-Russian trade hits record high in 2013 - envoy," 12uz.com, March 1, 2014, http://www.12uz.com.

[124] "Lukoil Boosts Investment in Uzbekistan 38% to $660 mln in 2013," Interfax, March 11, 2014, Interfax, http://interfax.com/.

[125] Paolo Sorbello, "Yes, Uzbekistan is Putin's Friend," The Diplomat, December 15, 2014, http://thediplomat.com/2014/12/yes-uzbekistan-is-putins-friend/.

[126] "Duma Ratifies Protocol to Include Uzbekistan in CIS Free Trade Zone," *Interfax*, Mar 21, 2014, http://www.interfax.com/.

[127] Central Bank of Russia, Personal Remittances by CIS countries in 2011-2015, http://www.cbr.ru/Eng/statistics/?PrtId=svs.

[128] TradeEconomics.com, http://www.tradingeconomics.com/uzbekistan/gdp.

[129] Central Bank of Russia, Personal Remittances by CIS countries in 2011-2015.

[130] Central Bank of Russia, Official Exchange Rates RUB/USD, http://www.cbr.ru/.

[131] "Продажи GM Uzbekistan в РФ за 11 месяцев снизились на 47%" (Sales of GM Uzbekistan in Russia for 11 months dropped by 47%), *Gazeta.uz*, December 8, 2015, https://www.gazeta.uz/2015/12/08/gmuz/.

132 Ziyodullo Parpiev, "Who is behind remittances? A Profile of Uzbek Migrants," UNDP, March 5, 2015, http://www.uz.undp.org/content/uzbekistan/en/home/ourperspective/ourp erspectivearticles/2015/03/05/who-is-behind-remittances--a-profile-of-uzbek-migrants.html.

133 "Asian Development Outlook (ADO) 2016: Asia's Potential Growth," Asian Development Bank, March 2016, http://www.adb.org/countries/uzbekistan/economy; "Caucasus and Central Asia: Oil Price Decline and Regional Spillovers Darken the Outlook," Internationa Monetary Fund, May 2015, https://www.imf.org/external/pubs/ft/reo/2015/mcd/eng/pdf/cca0515.pdf.

134 Demir Azizov, "Uzbek President Says Trust is Most Important Element in Strengthening Int'l Cooperation", Trend, May 22, 2014, http://en.trend.az/regions/casia/uzbekistan/2276997.html.

135 "China and Uzbekistan Sign Agreement on Jointly Building the Silk Road Economic Belt," Ministry of Commerce, People's Republic of China, June 18, 2015, http://english.mofcom.gov.cn/article/newsrelease/significantnews/201506/2 0150601016814.shtml.

136 "Узбекистан снизит поставки газа в Россию и увеличит в Китай," (Uzbekistan will Reduce Gas Supplies to Russia and Increase to China), RIA Novosti, August 10, 2014, http://ria.ru/world_economy/20141008/1027447820.html#ixzz46BuRQg8E.

137 Kyrgyzstan Inquiry Commission, *Report of the Independent International Commission of Inquiry into the Events in Southern Kyrgyzstan in June 2010*, May 3, 2011, http://www.k-ic.org/en/news/364-kic-final-report-published.html.

138 *Kyrgyzstan: An Uncertain Trajectory*, International Crisis Group, Europe and Central Asia Briefing N°76, September 2015, http://www.crisisgroup.org/en/regions/asia/central-asia/kyrgyzstan/b076-kyrgyzstan-an-uncertain-trajectory.aspx.

[139] Roman Mogilevskii, "Re-export Activities in Kyrgyzstan: Issues and Prospects," Working Paper 9, University of Central Asia, 2012.

[140] Richard Weitz, "The Customs Union and Eurasian Union: A Primer," in S. Frederick Starr and Svante Cornell editors, *Putin's Grand Strategy: The Eurasian Union and Its Discontents*, September 2014, http://www.silkroadstudies.org/publications/silkroad-papers-and-monographs/item/13053-putins-grand-strategy-the-eurasian-union-and-its-discontents.html; Victoria Panfilova, "The Customs Union is bursting but not expanding," Vestnik Kavkaza, October 27, 2013, http://vestnikkavkaza.net/analysis/politics/46840.html.

[141] "Kyrgyz PM Says Joining Customs Union Is 'Right Step'," RFE/RL's Kyrgyz Service, April 17, 2014, http://www.rferl.org/content/kyrgyz-pm-says-joining-customs-union-is- right-step/25352983.html.

[142] Fozil Mashrab, "Eurasian Union's Expansion Falters Amid Russia's Economic Woes," *Eurasia Daily Monitor*, Volume 13, Issue 42, March 2, 2016, http://www.jamestown.org/single/?tx_ttnews%5Btt_news%5D=45160&tx_t tnews%5BbackPid%5D=7&cHash=941df08ef9e8a6c42fbc27a5f39455a0#.V xWfdRIrLfY.

[143] Central Bank of Russia, Personal Remittances by CIS countries in 2011-2015, http://www.cbr.ru/Eng/statistics/?PrtId=svs.

[144] World Bank, Personal Remittances Received, http://data.worldbank.org/indicator/BX.TRF.PWKR.DT.GD.ZS.

[145] "Migration and Remittances: Recent Developments and Outlook," The World Bank, October 2015, http://pubdocs.worldbank.org/pubdocs/publicdoc/2015/10/1027614453531 57305/MigrationandDevelopmentBrief25.pdf.

[146] Fozil Mashrab, "Eurasian Union's Expansion Falters Amid Russia's Economic Woes," *Eurasia Daily Monitor*, March 2, 2016.

[147] "Experts Estimate Amount of Financial Aid of Russia to Kyrgyzstan since 2008," 24.kg, April 2, 2016, http://www.eng.24.kg/economics/179154-news24.html; George Voloshin, "Looming Long-Term Economic Problems Stem From Kyrgyzstan's EEU Membership," *Eurasia Daily Monitor*, Volume 13, Issue 28, February 10, 2016, http://www.jamestown.org/programs/edm/single/?tx_ttnews%5Btt_news%5D=45086&cHash=01d74b039c6f72ce6e69663a6f266d19#.VxXUuxIrLfY.

[148] Philip P. Pan, "Russia is said to have fueled unrest in Kyrgyzstan," The Washington Post, April 12, 2010, http://www.washingtonpost.com/wp-dyn/content/article/2010/04/11/AR2010041103827.html.

[149] Stefanie Ott, "Russia tightens control over Kyrgyzstan," The Guardian, September 18, 2014, http://www.theguardian.com/world/2014/sep/18/russia-tightens-control-over-kyrgyzstan.

[150] Umida Hashimova, "Kyrgyzstan Determined to Pursue Its Hydropower Plans With or Without Russia," *Eurasia Daily Monitor*, Volume 13, Issue 10, January 15, 2016, http://www.jamestown.org/single/?tx_ttnews%5Btt_news%5D=44990&no_cache=1.

[151] "Russia Gives Kyrgyzstan $30M Lifeline," *EurasiaNet*, March 6, 2016, http://www.eurasianet.org/node/77676.

[152] *Joanna Paraszczuk*, "Tajik IS Militants Threaten 'Jihad' At Home (Or Even In The Kremlin)," *RFE/RL*, March 23, 2015, http://www.rferl.org/content/tajikistan-isis-islamic-extremism-threats/26915731.html.

[153] Jim Nichol, *Tajikistan: Recent Developments and U.S. Interests*, Congressional Research Service, September 25, 2013, p. 19, https://www.fas.org/sgp/crs/row/98-594.pdf.

[154] International Crisis Group, *Tajikistan: The Changing Insurgent Threats*, Asia Report N°205, Bishkek and Brussels: International Crisis Group, May 24, 2011, p. 7, http://www.crisisgroup.org/~/media/Files/asia/central-

asia/tajikistan/205%20Tajikistan%20-
%20The%20Changing%20Insurgent%20Threats.pdf.

[155] Zohra Ismail-Beben, "Framing the conflict in Khorog," *Registan*, July 27, 2012,
http://registan.net/2012/07/27/framing-the-conflict-in-khorog/.

[156] Contradicting reports claimed first that Gen. Gulmurod Khalimov was killed during an airstrike in Syria in June 2015 and later that he was relocated to a training camp in Iraq to prepare jihadists for attacks in Europe. See: "Gulmurod Khalimov Update – His Militant Views May Not Be a Recent Development," *Independent Strategy and Intelligence Study Group*, July 22, 2015, http://isisstudygroup.com/?p=7760.

[157] "Shuttered Tajik Islamic Party Branded As Terrorist Group," RFE/RL, September 29, 2015, http://www.rferl.org/content/tajikistan-islamic-party-terrorist-organization/27277385.html.

[158] Matthew Stein, *Compendium of Central Asian Military and Security Activity*, Fort Leavenworth: Foreign Military Studies Office, May 22, 2015, http://fmso.leavenworth.army.mil/documents/Central-Asian-Military-Events.pdf.

[159] Catherine Putz, "Will There Be An Indian Air Base In Tajikistan?" *The Diplomat*, July 15, 2015, http://thediplomat.com/2015/07/will-there-be-an-indian-air-base-in-tajikistan/.

[160] Alexander Sodiqov, "Russia Pressed To Pay For Its Military Base In Tajikistan," *Eurasia Daily Monitor*, Volume 9, Issue 47, March 7, 2012, http://www.jamestown.org/single/?no_cache=1&tx_ttnews%5Btt_news%5D=39107#.V0iQUpMrJPM; John C. K. Daly, "Tajikistan Entertains Indian Offer For Air Base," *Silk Road Reporters*, July 17, 2015, http://www.silkroadreporters.com/2015/07/17/tajikistan-entertains-indian-offer-for-air-base/.

[161] "Пограничники быстрого реагирования" (Rapid Reaction Border Guards), *Kommersant*, October 16, 2015, http://www.kommersant.ru/doc/2834943.

[162] *Ibid.*

[163] "Russian 201st Military Base in Tajikistan Ready to Deal with External Threats," *TojNews*, February 27, 2014, http://tojnews.org/taj/.

[164] "Tajikistanis Evaluate Russian Military Base Reinforcement," *TojNews*, March 6, 2014, http://tojnews.org/taj/.

[165] Russian Defense Official Says His Country to Help Bolster Tajik Armed Forces," *ITAR-TASS*, January 27, 2015.

[166] "Overall Strength of Russian Base in Tajikistan Will Reach 9,000 Servicemen by 2020," *Asia-Plus*, April 4, 2015, http://news.tj/en/news/overall-strength-russian-base-tajikistan-will-reach-9000-servicemen-2020; "Why Russia Will Send More Troops to Central Asia," *Stratfor*, April 11, 2015, https://www.stratfor.com/analysis/why-russia-will-send-more-troops-central-asia.

[167] "Why Russia Will Send More Troops To Central Asia," *Stratfor*, April 11, 2015.

[168] "Russian Military Base in Tajikistan to be Downsized," *Asia-Plus Online*, January 30, 2016, http://www.asiaplus.tj.
[169] *"Russia Will Cut Defense Budget by 5 Percent in 2016, RIA Reports,"* *Reuters*, March 6, 2016, http://www.reuters.com/article/us-russia-defense-budget-idUSKCN0W80TL.

[170] "Russian Officer Suspected of Killing Tajik Woman Ruled Sane," *Asia-Plus*, February 2, 2016, http://news.tj/en/news/russian-officer-suspected-killing-tajik-woman-ruled-sane.

[171] Paul Goble, "Moscow's Failure to React to Tajikistan's De-Russification Said Reflection of Larger Problems," *Window on Eurasia*, April 30, 2016, http://windowoneurasia2.blogspot.com/2016/04/moscows-failure-to-react-to-tajikistans.html.

[172] Paul Kolstoe, *Russians in the Former Soviet Republics*, London, Hurst & Company/ Indiana University Press, 1995, p. 198,

https://www.academia.edu/5499030/Russians_in_the_former_Soviet_repub
lics.

173 All-Union Census 1970 and 1989, National Composition of the Population of the Republics of the USSR, *Демоскоп Weekly*, Demoscope.ru, http://demoscope.ru/weekly/ssp/sng_nac_89.php?reg=4.

174 "Khatlon Press Online Supports Russia's 'Aggressive' Behavior Toward West," *Khatlon Press*, March 6, 2014, http://www.khatlonpress.tj/.

175 Gulnora Amirshoeva, "Tajiks Alarmed by Russian Troop Withdrawal," *IWPR*, February 21, 2005, https://iwpr.net/global-voices/tajiks-alarmed-russian-troop-withdrawal.

176 "Facebook Users Fear Russia Could Use 'Ukraine Option' in Tajikistan," March 12, 2014, https://www.facebook.com/groups/platformatj/.

177 Gulnora Amirshoeva, "Tajiks Alarmed by Russian Troop Withdrawal," *IWPR*, February 21, 2005.

178 David Trilling, "Tajikistan: Migrant Remittances Now Exceed Half of GDP," *EurasiaNet*, April 15, 2014, http://www.eurasianet.org/node/68272.

179 Central Bank of Russia, Personal Remittances by CIS countries in 2011-2015, http://www.cbr.ru/Eng/statistics/?PrtId=svs.

180 Vladimir Socor, "Bluff in Substance, Brutal in Form: Moscow Warns Against Trans-Caspian Project," *Eurasia Daily Monitor*, vo. 8, no. 217, November 30, 2011, http://www.jamestown.org/single/?no_cache=1&tx_ttnews%5Btt_news%5D=38723.

181 "Ashgabat Not Happy with Moscow's Attitude toward trans-Caspian Pipeline Project," in Russian, *Interfax-Azerbaijan*, October 19, 2011, http://interfax.az/view/476239; Turkmenistan Ministry of Foreign Affairs, Press Release, *Turkmenistan State News Service*, October 18, 2011.

[183] Zhou Yan and Wang Qian, "Turkmenistan to Expand Natural Gas Supply to China," *China Daily*, November 25, 2011, http://www.chinadaily.com.cn/bizchina/2011-11/25/content_14159921.htm.

[184] Catherine Putz, "Russia's Gazprom Stops Buying Gas from Turkmenistan," *The Diplomat*, January 6, 2015, http://thediplomat.com/2016/01/russias-gazprom-stops-buying-gas-from-turkmenistan/.

[185] "Turkmenistan Supplied 125 bcm of Gas to China," *Natural Gas Europe*, September 28, 2015, http://www.naturalgaseurope.com/turkmenistan-supplied-125-bcm-gas-to-china-25610.

7. Conclusion: Russia's Future and Western Responses

This concluding chapter will consider the potential for internal instability in the Russian Federation that will impact on Moscow's expansionist project, examine Western responses to Russia's drive for regional re-imperialization, and offer several concrete policy recommendations for Western governments.

Instead of confronting Russia's mounting economic, social, ethnic, demographic, and regional troubles, the Putin administration has increasingly incited anti-Western sentiments and engaged in foreign policy offensives to distract and mobilize Russian society. As the economy continues to decline and state revenues diminish, the country could be faced with several domestic convulsions. However, such scenarios will not necessarily lessen the Kremlin's imperial ambitions but could actually inflame them, as a more desperate regime tries to effectively pursue its foreign policy while preventing instability and state disintegration.

Since Russia's invasion of Ukraine and annexation of Crimea in 2014, official Western perceptions of the Putin administration have changed dramatically. It is now more accurately viewed as a revisionist, revanchist, and aggressive regime instead of a pragmatic and cooperative power. Unlike during the Cold War status quo and the post–Cold War rapprochement, the consequences of the conflict between Russia and the West will be less predictable and stable. This will have repercussions for the future of NATO and the EU, by testing their political unity and strategic reach, as well as their willpower and capabilities vis-à-vis a belligerent Russia. Washington must also consider the prospect of a Russian implosion if imperial overstretch is coupled with long-term economic decline, growing social unrest, and territorial fracture. This would have major consequences for nearby regions and for Western institutions.

Russia's Uncertain Future

Moscow's pan-regional assertiveness disguises Russia's mounting domestic problems, generated by a combination of deteriorating economic, social, demographic, ethnic, and regional conditions. The official crackdown on civil society, independent organizations, and Western influences is part of a broader strategy to eliminate dissent and increase support for President Vladimir Putin at a time of alleged national danger in which an assortment of foreign scapegoats are animated by state propaganda. Russia's propaganda camouflages the failings of the Putinist system and blames its problems on an assortment of external enemies.

Some observers perceive creeping chaos in Russia that will increasingly affect its key institutions. For instance, the FSB and other security agencies may become less disciplined, with some elements not necessarily blindly implementing Kremlin policy.[1] Because of the fusion of state and economy, corruption has spread so deeply that it is reportedly factionalizing the security organs and making them more unpredictable and uncontrollable. This can result in spreading ungovernability despite the formal top-down structure of the Kremlin's "vertical of power" within Russia's "managed democracy."

The authoritarian system is growing brittle, as corrupt loyalists surround Putin without personal or ideological commitments to the President.[2] His ability to retain their loyalty rests above all on the

Kremlin's control of substantial financial resources. With the economy contracting and oil revenues decreasing, this system could collapse because budgetary cuts will need to be undertaken that will alienate members of Putin's inner circle. This could lead to an intense struggle for power and even a coup d'état by members of the elite who perceive a growing threat to their own security and wealth. Fissures may also appear between oligarchs reliant on international trade and investment and those who stand to gain from "import substitution" in the wake of the imposition of Western sanctions.

On the hard economic front, Russia fell into recession during 2015 and will remain so into 2016. The country has been battered by a combination of Western economic sanctions, the Kremlin's ban on the import of agricultural products from the EU, and a plunge in the price of oil exports. In June 2015, Russia's economic development ministry revised its GDP forecast for 2015 from a projected growth of 1.2% to a drop of 0.8%. In July 2015, the IMF predicted that the 2015 slump in GDP would reach 3.4%.[3]

US and EU sanctions were imposed during 2014 on dozens of Russian individuals and companies and several government-owned banks. As a result of these fiscal sanctions, state-owned banks have no access to credit in the West. Major Russian companies, including energy giants, are excluded from global capital markets and prevented from refinancing massive debts with Western lenders. They are now heavily reliant on the Russian state for dollar liquidity even though Russia's central bank is trying to conserve its foreign reserves.

The impact of Western sanctions was exacerbated significantly by a dramatic fall in global oil prices, from $110 a barrel in June 2014 to less than $50 a barrel in early 2015 and $42 a barrel by August 2015. In order to balance its budget, Russia needs oil prices at $80 a barrel, otherwise the economy will continue to contract. Indications are that crude prices will remain at under $60 a barrel through 2016, especially as Iranian supplies are likely to come on line. As a result of bad investments, incompetent calculations, and escalating Western sanctions, the Kremlin's favored company *Gazprom* is experiencing a steep decline in value. Since 2008, its market capitalization plummeted from $367.27 billion to $51.12 billion in August 2015.[4] This illustrates the fate of Russia's entire energy sector as the national economy shrivels.

Capital flight from Russia has also drastically accelerated: the net outflow reached $32.6 billion during the first quarter of 2015.[5] In June 2015, Russia's Central Bank forecast that capital flight could exceed $131 billion by the end of the year, resulting in severe losses in tax revenues and domestic investment. Russia's deteriorating market conditions have sparked an exodus of international investors.

At the end of June 2015, EU foreign ministers extended the sanctions from the end of July 2015 until the close of January 2016, voicing dissatisfaction with Moscow in honoring the Minsk ceasefire agreement in Ukraine.[6] The core of the sanctions consisted of a ban on 11 Russian state-owned oil companies, banks, and defense firms from raising money in the EU's capital markets or receiving loans from EU individuals or firms. Russia's authorities declared that the import ban on EU agricultural products would also remain in effect while Western sanctions were maintained. Putin signed an order to extend Moscow's counter-measures for a year, starting from June 24, 2015. The Kremlin imposed its own sanctions against the EU, erroneously calculating that European farmers' lobbies would pressure governments to rescind the sanctions against Russia. On September 2, 2015, the EU further extended the sanctions until March 2016 to maintain pressure on Moscow to fully implement the Minsk ceasefire, including withdrawing all of its forces from Ukraine and returning control to Kyiv of the Ukrainian side of the border with Russia.

The net effect of Putin's domestic and international policies will include a prolonged economic downturn, falling investments, diminishing living standards, rising unemployment, the withdrawal of migrant workers largely from Central Asia and the Caucasus, a decline in basic services and welfare benefits, and potential political, social, and regional unrest. According to the Economic Development Ministry, the economy contracted by 2.4% between January and April 2015.[7] For the first time since Putin took office, real incomes have shrunk, with the government expecting the decline to reach 9.8% by the close of 2015.

According to official statistics, more than three million Russians fell below the official poverty line in the first three months of 2015, as Russia's economy fell into recession.[8] The number of people living below the poverty line rose from 19.8 million to 22.9 million in the course of one year, or 15.9% of the total population. While millions of Russians sink into destitution, in August 2015 the government burned hundreds of tons of EU food that evaded the Kremlin-imposed sanctions. Officials claim that by destroying the contraband Russia's agricultural production will boom. The forbidden goods are presented as dangerous products designed to poison the Russian people.

Meanwhile, the cost of living continues to soar due to inflation spurred by steep falls in the value of the ruble, which pushed up the cost of imported products and components. By August 2015, the Russian currency had plummeted by 44.8% against the dollar in one year, and with oil prices showing no signs of recovery, the ruble will continue to slide into 2016.[9]

The economic cul de sac is exacerbated by an aging and crumbling infrastructure. This includes Russia's road and railway networks, electric power grid, and other energy distribution systems. The maintenance of this vital infrastructure is beset by problems, including official corruption that vastly raises costs, bureaucratic neglect and mismanagement, sloppy work habits, shrinking state funds, and the use of poor-quality materials. Budget cuts will also restrict Moscow's capabilities in its planned military re-armament program, although Putin's great power ambitions may preclude any downsizing and will reverberate negatively on state spending in other sectors.

On the regional front, growing public protests against declining economic conditions could contribute to ousting unpopular local governments. According to Moscow's Institute of Social Policy, because of shrinking federal funds governments in many of Russia's 85 regions (including the illegally annexed Crimea and Sevastopol in 2014) will have to impose drastic cutbacks in health, education, and housing, thus exacerbating social discontent.[10] In particular, several North Caucasus republics are almost completely dependent on revenues from the central government and are likely to suffer accordingly.

The economic crisis and decreasing state revenues will exacerbate the competition for resources in a growing number of federal units. This can become manifest in tensions and conflicts between regions, ethnicities, religious and occupational groups, and challenge the survival of incumbent regional governments. In some regions, whether containing ethnic-Russian or non-Russian majorities, drastic financial cutbacks could spark demands for political autonomy, separation from the federal structure, or the creation of larger regions combining several federal units that would disassociate themselves politically and economically from Moscow. Some federal regions could then seek closer economic ties with neighboring states, such as China and Japan, or with multi-national organizations such as the EU. This would increase the influence of several neighboring countries, reduce Moscow's leverage, and in some cases accelerate aspirations toward secession and statehood.

Kaliningrad is a valuable example where long-term economic decline will challenge Kremlin control.[11] The three nearby Baltic countries plan to exit Russia's unified energy system by 2020. Together with the closure of an energy plant in Kaliningrad, this could lead to the collapse of economic activity in the Moscow-controlled exclave. Moreover, in 2016 Kaliningrad's exports will no longer receive special treatment within the EU. As a result, some 900 enterprises in the region will close with 30,000 workers laid off. Putin ordered the government to accelerate the adoption of laws for the support of Kaliningrad's hard-pressed industries, but the government has little money to allocate to any region. If Moscow cannot deal with the crisis, the Kaliningrad economy will slide into a deeper recession. This may activate groups that either want a special relationship for the territory with the EU or even complete separation, independence, and statehood.

A strategy of structural reform and modernization of the Russian economy seems highly unlikely because of the absence of political will and a fear that this could dislodge the current regime. Other political possibilities for Russia include a popular revolt, similar to Ukraine in 2014, culminating in the election of a democratic and internationally responsible administration or the installation of a more predatory nationalist regime. Spreading social and regional unrest could also paralyze the central government and lead to Russia's fracture through administrative and territorial disintegration. Some Russian analysts are not convinced that economic deprivation will be sufficient to stimulate social revolt, as the public is largely passive and subservient to the state. Nonetheless, a combination of elite power struggles and regional dissatisfactions could undermine central control sufficiently to galvanize social protests in Moscow and other large cities in favor of regime change.

External factors could also have a negative impact on Russia's stability. For instance, growing criminality among the separatist leaders in the Donbas region of Ukraine is spilling over into Russia, with irregular fighters, criminal networks, and smuggled goods crossing the porous borders.[12] A huge spike in organized crime has been recorded in neighboring Russian oblasts and the security services are either in cahoots with the criminals or cannot control the separatists, with some implicated in a spate of assassinations of particularly bothersome warlords from Donbas.

The official encouragement of Russian ethno-nationalism, as evident in calls to defend Russian-speaking populations in neighboring states and to annex territories with sizeable ethnic-Russian populations, is likely to divide non-Russians from Russians and increase the appeal of anti-Muscovite nationalism. Furthermore, any attempts to transform the multi-ethnic Russian Federation into a Russian nation state, which could include the elimination of the 21 non-Russian ethno-national republics, can precipitate an escalation of ethnic and regionalist conflicts and provoke potential territorial fissures. In his comprehensive work on Eurasian polities, political scientist Henry E. Hale points out that seemingly strong authoritarian figures at the apex of the power pyramid can rapidly fall during a power struggle in the event of a major economic downturn or a loss in war.[13]

Mounting indignation over deteriorating economic conditions, coupled with the persistent denial of cultural, linguistic, and educational rights and the unrestrained corruption of the ruling elite, can also aggravate ethnic and religious conflicts. This would be especially explosive if Moscow turns to Russian nationalism or pan-Slavism to mobilize the public in the service of the regime. Russia's estimated 20 million Muslims are periodically used as a domestic scapegoat by Kremlin propaganda, largely because of the ongoing insurgency in the North Caucasus. The annexation of Crimea has added another 300,000 Muslim Tatars who can become an additional source of anti-state militancy.

About a quarter of Russia's population of 143 million are non-Russians, and in many regions resentment against Moscow's failing economic policies and repressive centralism is escalating. This is especially evident in the 21 ethnic republics, even where the titular ethnicity does not form a majority. In Siberia and the Far East, the ethnic-Russian population is steadily declining while the Chinese proportion is growing, together with their political aspirations. Beijing is investing in a number of Russian border regions, including the North Caucasus, at a time when federal budget allocations are drying up. Local authorities will benefit from Chinese investments and are likely to pursue more intensive contacts and bypass Moscow's interference. The option of sovereignty will thereby become increasingly attractive for several federal units.

Russia's financial troubles will negatively impact on its ability to continue supporting proxy regimes in separatist entities in Georgia, Moldova, and Ukraine. For instance, on June 17, 2015, the government of Abkhazia was informed that it would not receive a promised Russian aid payment of $91 million until 2016. [14] The legislature had passed Abkhazia's annual budget expecting to receive this sum. In Transnistria, where 70% of the annual budget relies on subsidies from Moscow, budget revenues have dropped 30% since 2014. Both entities may need to cut welfare payments, with the potential of social unrest that could destabilize them. Financial constraints are also reversing Russian real estate ownership in Bulgaria, Montenegro, and other locations, thereby reducing the extent of the "Russian World" in parts of Europe's east. In the immediate neighborhood, Russia's economic decline will become a strong disincentive for Russian-speaking populations to canvass for joining Russia and will undermine Putin's empire-building enterprise.

On the military front, in a display of global stature to compensate for its economic failures, the Putin clique is also engaged in the militarization of state and society. Russia's defense budget is rapidly growing. In 2014, it amounted to €55.5 billion, a substantial increase from €30.2 billion in 2010. In total, Moscow intends to spend €404 billion on the military between 2011 and 2020. Russian armed forces are also devoting significant resources to employing tactical and mobile nuclear missiles. This places Washington in a major dilemma whether to initiate a rearmament in US nuclear capacity in Europe or risk a Russian propaganda victory concerning NATO's vulnerabilities. Nonetheless, persistent Kremlin provocations and aggressive actions against neighbors could spark a renewed arms race with the West in which Russia, much like the Soviet Union, lacks the capacity to compete and could further bankrupt the economy.

The Kremlin is also unnerved by the prospect of an EU-US free trade agreement (the Transatlantic Trade and Investment Partnership—TTIP) that would weaken Russia's energy weapons as well as its economic stability. All EU members could ratify the accord by 2016.[15] It will bring benefits both to producers and consumers on both sides of the Atlantic by reducing the price of imported goods with the lifting of bureaucratic barriers and tariffs. There would also be improvements in access to services in banking, insurance, and telecommunications. Moscow supports organizations in the West that campaign against such a free trade accord, whether leftists, greens, nationalist, or anti-globalists. Analogies can be made with the activities of "pacifist" movements in the West during the 1970s and 1980s that were financed by Soviet intelligence agencies. The import of American shale gas and oil is now a major threat for Moscow, as the US exports these resources to states with which it has free trade agreements. Hence, the Americans can squeeze the Russians out of a sizeable portion of the European market. If US energy companies can operate more freely in the EU, this will further reduce Moscow's revenues.

On the neighborhood front, deteriorating economic conditions are also affecting Russia's closest allies in the EEU. For instance, public protests in Armenia in June 2015 over the raising of electricity prices were symptomatic of brewing dissatisfaction with economic conditions and anger over corruption and unaccountability in the Armenian government.[16] Russian oligarchs with ties to the Kremlin monopolize big business in Armenia and the electricity network is wholly owned by Inter-RAO, a Russian energy company whose chairman, Igor Sechin, is a close friend of Putin.

Central Asian countries are also experiencing the effects of Russia's economic decline and the fall in the value of the ruble.[17] For example, remittances of workers from Tajikistan laboring in Russia have dropped precipitously since 2014. Migrant remittances are equivalent to almost half of Tajikistan's GDP. It is estimated that remittances sent from Russia to the CIS countries via money transfer agents in March 2015 fell by about 42% compared to March 2014. Many migrants are now returning home with dim economic prospects. For instance, money sent home by Armenians working in Russia is a vital means of survival for many families; about 21% of Armenia's economy relies on such remittances.[18]

Russia is also a major trading partner for the Central Asian economies, and exports to Russia have significantly contracted. Moreover, the decline of the ruble depreciates the Central Asian currencies, depletes their currency reserves, and raises the risks of inflation. In addition, the drop in global oil prices has impacted on Kazakhstan, a major oil producer, by significantly reducing its exports and tax revenues and diminishing its fiscal reserves. In the meantime, China is making greater inroads into Central Asia through trade and investment, especially in large infrastructure projects. It is also purchasing increasing amounts of Caspian Basin fossil fuels that will further divert the Central Asian economies away from Russia.

In one of his four alternatives for Russia's future, international relations scholar Richard J. Krickus outlines how the country could rapidly contract or even disintegrate, only in a much more violent manner than the collapse of the Soviet Union in 1990–1991.[19] Elaborating on this scenario, the prospects could include: violent power struggles between members of the ruling elite; the collapse of central authority; growing popular unrest because of falling living standards and shortages of products; regional turmoil generated by growing opposition to Moscow's policies; military mutinies and the creation of private armies that splinter the country's defense structure; gang warfare between criminal organizations that increase chaos and ungovernability; the escalation of inter-ethnic disputes over power, territory, and resources; the proliferation of ethnic, religious, regional, and economic fiefdoms largely independent of the capital; an upsurge of violent jihadism among radicalized Muslims in different parts of the Federation, especially in the North Caucasus and the Middle Volga; the growth of terrorism, sabotage, and the destruction of Russia's infrastructure; civil war in several parts of the country in escalating struggles for statehood; and the danger that weapons of mass destruction could fall into the hands of non-state militants. Such scenarios could also spill over and destabilize several countries along Russia's strategic flanks.

Western Responses

The chill in the West's relations with Moscow in the wake of the Russia-Ukraine war resembles a new Cold War, except that its results will be more difficult to anticipate. The Cold War was a frozen condition that left Europe divided between NATO and the Soviet Bloc while both sides avoided direct confrontation. The new epoch can be defined as a Shadow War in which the West and Russia are in perpetual competition to exert their influence and pursue their interests. Russia presents the most persistent security threat to the West because President Vladimir Putin's neo-imperial goals undermine the stability of several regions from northern Europe to Central Asia, challenge NATO as a security provider, and undercut the EU project. Russia also establishes a dangerous precedent for other ambitious powers that may seek to test NATO and US resolve.

There are three fundamental principles of the escalating Shadow War. First, Russia's rulers no longer depict the country as a European state. They define Russia as a separate "Eurasian pole of power" defending itself against Western encroachment, proud of its anti-Americanism, and playing a vanguard role among all authoritarian or expansive governments that reject US influence.

Second, there is no longer a clear division of Europe into Western and Russian spheres. Instead, the stage is set for a prolonged struggle over states that are under pressure to join the Russian zone but whose populations are divided or whose governments do not possess the power to resist Moscow. The Kremlin even endeavors to subvert and suborn countries that are members of NATO and the EU, such as Bulgaria and Hungary. For instance, corrupt business deals with state officials are intended to influence the governments to adopt international positions favorable to Russia's foreign policy.

And third, various kinds of weapons are employed in the Shadow War to undermine the adversary, whether via energy, investment, propaganda, cyberspace, corruption, blackmail, or various paramilitary and military tools. Although US and EU officials claim that there is no zero-sum competition with Russia over the allegiance of any country, in reality the protagonists are competing over the future international alignments of a string of states in the Wider Europe and Central Asia.

Putin's Russia denounces Western policy as conflicting with its own historical and geostrategic claims that the post-Soviet countries form an essential part of the "Russian World" and must return under Moscow's umbrella. This would not only entail a loss of national sovereignty, but also the adoption of a value system based on statism and authoritarianism. Russia is better prepared for the new Shadow War, as evident in its current international offensives. Unfortunately, the West is only emerging from its post–Cold War illusions and misdirected "peace dividends," and needs to confront Moscow with the strength of its economic, political, cultural, social, intellectual, and security capacities.

The European flank of NATO remains dependent on the US for its security, as its defense expenditures have been seriously depleted. Without American involvement, Europe would be unable to deter an increasingly belligerent Russia. Europe's demilitarization over the last decade has coincided with Russia's military buildup. [20] The US provides 70% of all NATO defense spending, while Europe's contribution to NATO's military capability is at less than 25%, and the figure is dropping. Several countries have decimated their equipment to such an extent that they may be incapable of deploying more than a few thousand troops in the event of war. Meanwhile, Russia is rearming to the tune of $700 billion over the next decade and plans to introduce the next generation of armor, aircraft, and missiles and to modernize its nuclear forces.

Two fundamentally contrasting strategies exist for US and NATO policy toward a resurgent Russia: imperial accommodation or trans-Atlantic assertiveness. In the former approach, a number of Putin appeasers or those urging patience and non-escalation have been proposing another "reset" or even a "détente" with Moscow. [21] They operate on the premise that Russia possesses some distinct special interests toward its numerous neighbors that Washington should acknowledge. [22] Suggestions have even been made about a "grand bargain" that would concede Crimea to Russia and allow Moscow to assert its "national interests" throughout the former Soviet Union, in return for Kremlin support in combating the Islamic State (IS) *jihadists* in Syria. In practice, as evident in Russia's foreign policy since Putin assumed power, Russia's "national interests" include determining its neighbors' foreign and security policies, dominating their economies, deciding on their administrative structures, formulating their constitutions, regulating the extent of their territories, and selecting their international alliances.

An accommodationist approach that concedes some special "national interests" to Russia is not only unacceptable to all independent states that emerged from the Soviet Union and the Soviet bloc, but it also whets Moscow's appetite for further imperial aggrandizement. Paradoxically, consenting to Russia's aggressive and asymmetrical "national interests" toward neighbors is more likely to result in a collision with NATO and the EU than a more dynamic approach. If the Kremlin operates with the conviction that it has a relatively free hand to methodically undermine countries along its borders, this can result in serious miscalculations when it overreaches by provoking a regional crisis and sparking conflicts with neighbors who are Alliance members; this would precipitate a direct war with NATO.

Some policymakers and analysts put forward three additional arguments in favor of accommodation with Moscow despite its aggressive neighborhood policy: business interests, problem-solving, and Russia's seemingly inevitable decline. First, powerful business lobbies in Germany, France, and other EU states view sanctions imposed on Moscow for its attack on Ukraine as a temporary measure that will be lifted so that lucrative economic investments can be resumed. This has been most evident in two agreements signed by Berlin and Moscow in the natural gas sector at the Vladivostok economic forum on September 4, 2015. [23] The first involves construction of the Nord Stream Two pipeline along the Baltic seabed; the second will result in Gazprom's full takeover of Wintershall's gas marketing business and gas storages in Germany. In return, Wintershall will acquire a minority stake in a Siberian gas field. These agreements will significantly increase Germany's reliance on Russian gas for consumption, transit and storage.

In a second accomodationist argument, it is claimed that Russia is a valuable partner in resolving various regional crises outside Europe. Instructively, disclosures made in September 2015 that Moscow had dispatched an expeditionary force together with military aid to Syria demonstrated that Russia's cooperation had limited value and could actually be counter-productive for US policy. In October 2015, Russia conducted air strikes in Syria that were not directed against the Islamic State (IS) *jihadists* but included opposition forces supported by the West. Putin's primary objective was to prop up the regime of President Bashar al-Assad in Damascus and thereby guarantee Russia's ongoing military and intelligence presence in the country.

A third position held by some Western officials and analysts simply dismisses Russia as a declining power toward which little action needs to be taken. It contends that Putin is not a strategist and will defeat himself without the need for any significant Western offensive against Moscow. Such a deterministic approach ignores the prospect that even during a period of economic decline Russia can create significant damage to its neighbors, inject itself into unstable regions such as the Middle East, and undermine Western security and cohesion. An inadequate policy response to Russia's revanchism serves to reinforce Western complacency and encourages further hawkishness by Moscow. Moreover, the most effective way to ensure Russia's global decline and retreat from its neo-imperial project is through an activist policy that hastens such a process.

In contrast to an accommodationist approach, trans-Atlantic assertiveness toward Russia will include both tests and benefits for the future of the NATO alliance and the EU structure. For instance, it will impact directly on the role of the EU in its agenda for closer association in the Eastern neighborhood. It will test the political unity of the Union in the face of Moscow's aggressive empire building, its growing pressure on vulnerable European capitals, and its blatant disregard of international norms. No one can be certain whether EU member states will bear prolonged sanctions against Russia and mount an effective defense of the EU's and NATO's eastern flank. Conversely, they may succumb to compromises in order to pacify Moscow and inadvertently encourage future Kremlin ambitions.

At the very least, a trans-Atlantic commitment is needed to strengthen the state sovereignty, national institutions, and market economies of all former Soviet bloc countries and republics bordering Russia, particularly NATO partners such as Ukraine, Georgia, Moldova, and Azerbaijan. The strategic standoff with Moscow will also provide an opportunity for Washington to consolidate the defense of key allies in the region, including Poland, Romania, and the three Baltic States. Washington will need to factor in the changing security perceptions of several Central and East European allies since the Ukrainian crisis erupted. A range of measures has already been initiated or implemented to more effectively protect the security of each NATO ally, but much more needs to be accomplished in the coming years.

The overriding question in Tallinn, Riga, and Vilnius is whether NATO can respond adequately and swiftly to defend its most exposed members. In terms of conventional military threats, it is essential to have an effective tripwire by ensuring the presence of soldiers from various NATO members, including the US, on a permanent basis in these countries. Moves in this direction, through air policing units, regular training and military exercises, and the creation of small bases to accommodate the planned NATO Rapid Reaction Force, were taken as the war in Ukraine unfolded during 2014. But fears remained that these measures relied more on symbolism than substance and without a more permanent stationing of international NATO forces and equipment among the frontline states they could be quickly overrun by a Russian assault. At a mini-NATO summit in Bucharest on November 4, 2015, nine states—Bulgaria, the Czech Republic, Estonia, Hungary, Latvia, Lithuania, Poland, Romania, and Slovakia—signed a joint declaration calling on NATO to maintain a permanent presence in the region to deter Russian aggression.

NATO has drawn up defense plans for Poland, Estonia, Latvia, and Lithuania, including guarantees of NATO's military response to outside attacks. East Central Europe (ECE) and the Baltic region have also gained more regular NATO military exercises. Deliberations have also intensified over the potential hosting of US and NATO military infrastructure. However, at the NATO Summit on September 4–5, 2014, Alliance leaders did not endorse the positioning of permanent bases in the ECE region despite the urging of Warsaw and the three Baltic governments. Instead, they agreed to create a spearhead contingent within the existing NATO Response Force (NRF)—a Very High Readiness Joint Task Force (VJTF). Once formed, it would be capable of deploying at short notice along NATO's periphery and would consist of land, air, maritime, and Special Operations Force components.

The VJTF is to include 4,000 troops trained to move on 48 hours' notice to hotspots in any NATO member state. Nonetheless, it would be too small to counter the massive military might Russia has deployed along its western frontier.[24] The spearhead force is to be part of a wider NATO response force of 13,000 to 30,000 troops that could take weeks to deploy in a crisis. It will benefit from equipment and logistics facilities pre-positioned in ECE and Baltic countries, but the troops will not be permanently stationed in the region.[25] The force could evidently be used as a mobile tripwire when dispatched to a threatened state. However, at this early stage in its planned deployment, it is difficult to estimate the effectiveness of a relatively small VJTF contingent in deterring either the subversion or outright invasion of a NATO member by Russia.

On February 5, 2015, NATO decided to establish six command centers in Estonia, Latvia, Lithuania, Poland, Romania, and Bulgaria.[26] They will plan contingencies and organize exercises, and will be key for connecting national forces with NATO reinforcements. They will be used for logistics, reconnaissance, and planning missions, and contain permanent multinational staffs consisting of between 300 and 600 persons in each center.[27] The multinational headquarters for the command and control centers will be located in Szczecin, on Poland's Baltic coast. NATO Supreme Allied Commander, General Philip Breedlove, proposed that Szczecin expand its existing base to help NATO respond faster to any threat posed by Russia.[28] Several NATO allies backed the general's plans to store weapons, ammunition, and ration packs to enable a sudden influx of thousands of NATO troops in the event of a crisis. Multinational Corps Northeast was formed in 1999, at Szczecin, as NATO's only multilateral corps thus far, consisting of Polish, German, and Danish units.

Among other NATO measures, 600 soldiers from the US Army's 1st

Cavalry Division deployed to Poland and the Baltic states in October 2014 for three-month training exercises.[29] This was part of Operation Atlantic Resolve designed to foster interoperability through small-unit and leader training. In addition to ground forces, the US sent F-16 combat aircraft to Poland and participated in NATO air policing missions over the Baltic states. In June 2015, Washington decided to store heavy weapons, including tanks and infantry fighting vehicles, in Poland that could be used in training exercises and outfit one brigade in the event of war. Up to 5,000 NATO troops could be equipped with the weapons, thus enabling a rapid reaction brigade to deploy at short notice. This decision precipitated a furious response from Russian officials who claimed that NATO was moving closer to Russia's borders, failing to point out that Moscow had provoked the build-up by significantly reinforcing its military presence close to NATO's borders.

US Defense Secretary Ashton Carter announced on a visit to Estonia, on June 23, 2015, that the US would deploy heavy weapons, including 250 tanks, armored vehicles, and howitzer artillery guns, in Bulgaria, Estonia, Latvia, Lithuania, Poland, and Romania.[30] Each set of equipment would be enough for a battalion of 750 soldiers. The equipment would be moved around the region to help in training and improving mobility. The positioning of military hardware without the presence of US troops is premised on the assumption that the local armed forces would be capable of defending the country for a sufficient period of time from a Russian assault to allow for the timely arrival of American and other NATO units.

The Chairman of the US Joint Chiefs of Staff, General Martin Dempsey, has also asserted that America's military is ready to ensure the deployment of high alert forces within 48 hours to NATO countries bordering Russia.[31] If this is insufficient to stem a Russian attack, then Washington will be ready to use additional force to protect its allies.

The increasing intensity of NATO's Baltic airspace policing mission is also related to the growing activity of Russian fighter aircraft in the region's airspace. Fighter jets of different NATO member states have been patrolling the Baltic skies since 2004, as the three Baltic nations do not have airplanes suitable for guarding their air space. NATO also increased its presence and military activities in the Black Sea in the wake of the Ukraine crisis.

As part of a new strategy, more NATO countries have deployed either warships or surveillance vessels to the Black Sea since January 2014.[32] NATO officials are also considering deploying a missile defense system to protect Europe from attacks from the Middle East and Russia.[33] Calls for such an expansion to the system have been growing in Poland, Lithuania, Estonia, and Latvia. After Putin announced on June 16, 2015, that Russia would place 40 new nuclear-armed intercontinental ballistic missiles into service, NATO Secretary General Jens Stoltenberg described the move as "dangerous saber-rattling."

Washington has accused Moscow of testing a new ground-launched cruise missile, breaking the Intermediate-Range Nuclear Forces (INF) Treaty that Presidents Ronald Reagan and Mikhail Gorbachev signed in 1987. NATO allies are to review their preparedness for a nuclear standoff with Russia in response to Moscow's threats.[34] They are expected to hold an additional meeting of NATO's Nuclear Planning Group, a body established in the 1960s to co-ordinate defense plans against the Soviet Union. Some NATO officials also believe that the alliance should resume nuclear drills to rehearse a potential counterattack against a threatening Russia.

Policy Recommendations

In the wake of the escalating confrontation between the West and Russia, policy recommendations for Washington and the EU capitals need to focus on consolidating a dynamic trans-Atlantic alliance, repelling and deterring a belligerent Russia, implementing a concerted counter-subversion strategy, ensuring the security of all states bordering Russia, and preparing for a potential implosion of the Russian Federation.

Multi-Regional Policy Agenda

- Develop a long-term trans-Atlantic policy toward states that were formerly part of the Soviet Union but are not currently NATO or EU members. Such an agenda should be based on the following principles: maintaining the independence and territorial integrity of all countries; preventing and deterring any single power from dominating the political or economic systems of neighbors or determining their foreign and security policies; pursuing closer political, economic, legal and institutional relations with Western states and multi-national organizations; and setting targets for eventual institutional integration into NATO and the EU for all countries that qualify for and seek membership.

Threat Monitoring

- Anticipate Moscow's actions through enhanced intelligence gathering and information sharing. This requires more intensive and extensive monitoring of threats emanating from Russia, especially in the use of its multi-pronged arsenal of subversion against neighboring states. Western intelligence services should also seek to determine to what extent Moscow's operations to undermine and destabilize neighbors are controlled and coordinated by the Kremlin's presidential administration and what roles are played by specific individuals. One must be careful not to assume that Moscow is behind every instance of neighborhood instability. Indeed, it serves Kremlin objectives to create the impression that it possesses extensive influences in all nearby states, thus underscoring its power and omnipresence. Instead, it is necessary to closely monitor the precise arenas where Moscow is engaged in subversive actions against its targets.

- Map and document Russia's propaganda resources and Moscow-financed media agencies, agents of influence, and political parties throughout Europe that are pro-Kremlin in orientation.[35] Expose and publicize the links of Western organizations, foundations, agencies, NGOs, journalists, politicians, and academics with Russia's various state agencies and Kremlin-connected individuals.

- Coordinate US-European counterintelligence operations, in which every suspected Russian agent is expelled. This would send a powerful political message and disrupt Russia's intelligence operations, including the recruitment of spies and agents of influence in Western states.

- Monitor the transfer of Russian weapons to nonstate militias along Russia's flanks by increasing espionage work against insurgent groups and disclosing their connections to Moscow. This should also include information concerning the support provided by Russia's intelligence agencies to international terrorist networks.

Informational Campaigns

- Bolster expertise to analyze specific cases of Moscow's disinformation.[36] This will require linguistic and area expertise, the restoration of the National Defense Education Act (NDEA) Title VI program, and the development of career paths in government that allow individuals to pursue a full career without shifting outside their area of expertise. It will also require the restoration of government translation programs such as the

Foreign Broadcast Information Service (FBIS) that comprehensively cover developments inside Russia and among countries bordering Russia.

- Invest in defensive strategic communications in order to counter the Kremlin's false narratives. [37] While Russia's propaganda messages are relatively simple and emotional, the West's are often too complex regarding the conflict with Russia and therefore lack the same broad public appeal. [38] Western policy makers should focus on developing several key themes in their communications approach, such as providing a compelling narrative exposing Russia's disinformation, fostering skepticism toward Russia's media outlets, and exposing the Kremlin-financed support network in the West. The Western narrative should focus on the values of individual freedom, democracy and the rule of law.

- Neutralize Moscow's disinformation campaigns through media channels delivering alternative messages, including international broadcasting to Russian-speaking audiences in all post-Soviet states. [39] This should include Internet and satellite television broadcasting. Riga and Tallinn are developing Russian-language media to counter Kremlin disinformation campaigns targeting Russian-speakers. They need a positive message that they are Europeans and welcome in the host states, while contrasting their situation with declining economic conditions inside Russia.

- Increase the availability of television from EU countries to Europe's East. For example, the Nordic states plan to create a Russian-language TV station for Russian speakers in Estonia and Latvia. They possess significant experience in combining entertainment with news and competing with TV channels broadcast from Russia. Also needed are courses on media literacy for schools and aspiring journalists.

- Target Russia for a new international broadcasting effort, directly to home satellite television, in Russian and other languages of the Russian Federation.[40] There is little coverage of domestic news within Russia, as Moscow's propaganda does not discuss the economic, demographic, and regional crises in the country. Such an initiative should also aim at de-imperializing the mentality of the Russian public that still believes the Kremlin narrative that Russia is a great power. Psychological de-imperialization among the British, French, and other empires was a long process that eventually brought dividends. In Russia, the process has failed to be undertaken since the collapse of the Soviet Union.

• Promote use of English in all post-Soviet states to help displace Russian as a second language. Kazakhstan's President Nursultan Nazarbayev has reportedly ruled that students will not only study English but also study all subjects in English in the last two years of their schooling. Such policies should be encouraged across the region, as they will undermine the assertions of Putin's "Russian World" toward neighboring territories on the basis of common language and culture.

International Ostracism

• Isolate the Russian government internationally through diplomatic, institutional, and economic measures. Diplomatically, US and EU leaders must consistently insist that by occupying any part of Ukrainian territory, together with portions of Georgia and Moldova, Russia violates numerous international accords, beginning with the UN Charter, and will not be treated as an equal partner or a credible international interlocutor. The West must focus on Russia's vulnerabilities, including denying access to Western capital and assets by the pro-Putin Russian elite. Many more names could be added to the sanctions list, including government ministers, parliamentarians, senior state bureaucrats, regional and municipal leaders, businessmen, journalists, and academicians with ties to the Kremlin.

Economic Instruments

- Accelerate the development of the European Energy Union in order to reduce Moscow's ability to manipulate oil and gas supplies as leverage against Western states.[41] Gazprom and other Russian companies should be competitively pushed out of Europe's energy market, thus seriously depleting Kremlin export earnings and political influences. In an important move in this direction on July 10, 2015, fifteen EU and Energy Community countries in Central and South East Europe signed a Memorandum of Understanding to work together in accelerating the construction of missing gas infrastructure links.[42] This will involve resolving the remaining technical and regulatory obstacles that hinder the development of a fully integrated regional energy market.

- Avoid EU institutional engagement with the Eurasian Economic Union (EEU), as this would lend the organization credibility and legitimize Russia's empire building.[43] Instead, the EU should develop closer bilateral economic and political relations with countries that have been incorporated into the Eurasian Union— Belarus, Kazakhstan, and Armenia—but may seek future alternatives.

- Boost regional development in countries with sizable and compact Russian minorities that may be susceptible to Kremlin-induced separatism. For instance, in Latvia economic development is mostly concentrated in the Riga region, while much of the rest of the country suffers chronic underdevelopment and high unemployment. This can increase Moscow's subversive influence in the Latvian countryside.[44] Latvia, Estonia, Ukraine,

Moldova, and other states can cooperate in these endeavors and learn lessons from each other's experiences.

NATO Enhancement

- Underscore that a strong NATO alliance is the backbone of European security and preclude proposals for a European Army, which simply dilutes and distracts from the only capable multinational Western security organization. [45] A European Army would not only siphon off NATO's already limited assets and resources and diminish its capabilities, but it would also trigger rivalries between Europe and North America over the deployment of military forces. It could also split Europe between countries committed to close security relations with the US and states at a safe distance from Russia that see little need for American security guarantees. Such an outcome would, in effect, grant Moscow a strategic victory over NATO.

- Amend the Washington Treaty, especially Article 5, and the definition of an attack on a NATO member state. This needs to reflect the challenges associated with contemporary warfare to include non-state actors, externally generated insurgencies, cyber attacks, information warfare, and other forms of subversion aimed at undermining state independence or truncating its territory.

- Revive NATO's fundamental mandate and ensure that capabilities match commitments in defending Alliance members. Needed are stronger national capabilities that increase the costs of any Russian attack. [46] Europe must engage in military modernization and be capable of defending its border rather than operating with the traditional formula based on retaliation and the extended deterrent provided by the US. Local forces must possess the ability to protect their own borders and increase the costs of aggression even if they cannot win the conflict unaided. In particular, NATO needs to place greater emphasis on ensuring the ability of frontline states to defend themselves during the critical, early phases of a limited war.

- Prepare for a wide assortment of unconventional threats among frontline NATO states. This must include penetrating intelligence gathering; detection, early warnings, and rapid preparations for a foreign assault; effective communications between central and local governments; comprehensive border controls; consolidation of a professional and loyal police force; and capabilities to pursue intensive and prolonged anti-guerrilla operations. There must also be a focus on conventional warfare. According to Adrian Bradshaw, NATO's deputy supreme commander, the Alliance should prepare for a Blitzkrieg-type assault by Russia on east European member states and not be sidetracked by "hybrid" or low intensity attacks.[47]

- Strengthen the defense of frontline states. Each NATO state bordering Russia requires three fundamental elements: adequate infrastructure and prepositioned equipment to allow for speedy deployment of indigenous and other NATO forces; early warning of Russian subversion and covert attack; and capable forces that can respond quickly to an assault on a country's territorial integrity. Each state also needs the positioning of US and West European forces on a permanent basis as a tripwire against potential Russian attack. In addition to enhancing their defensive capabilities, front line states also need an offensive component that can threaten Russia's aggressive operations by targeting the enemy's staging areas, airports, radar installations, sea and river ports, and logistical nodes.[48] Defensive capabilities alone are unlikely to be sufficient to deter a military assault.

- Ensure NATO capabilities to move troops between West, Central, and East European states and to converge different units from various NATO countries by improving infrastructure connections, such as railways. This also requires that SACEUR possesses the authority to make quick decisions without prolonged consultations. Since Moscow's assault on Ukraine, NATO has taken initial steps to bolster the defense of vulnerable members by adding combat aircraft support to NATO's Baltic air policing mission, dispatching a dozen F-16 fighters to Poland, and deploying AWAC reconnaissance aircraft in Poland and Romania. Washington needs to station Patriot missile batteries in the three Baltic states, conduct more regular NATO exercises, transfer military equipment and reposition NATO bases from West to Central Europe. In this equation, US forces in Europe must be relocated and retrained to adopt a forward presence on the "eastern front." General Philip Breedlove, NATO's Supreme Allied Commander for Europe, has called Moscow's conquest of Crimea a "paradigm shift" that requires a fundamental rethinking of where American forces are located and how they are trained.

- Demonstrate NATO's vitality by admitting Montenegro into the Alliance following the membership invitation issued in December 2015, as well as by pushing Greece to enable Macedonia to enter NATO under its temporary name, the Former Yugoslav Republic of Macedonia (FYROM). The Warsaw Summit in July 2016 will also be a timely occasion to offer NATO Membership Action Plans (MAP) to Bosnia-Herzegovina, Georgia, and Ukraine and to confirm that they will also join the Alliance at a future date. NATO also needs to pursue closer military cooperation with Moldova, Azerbaijan, and Armenia to prevent their potential capitulation to Russia's incessant pressures.

Ensuring Imperial Indigestion

- Provide the Ukrainian military with sufficient means to make any further aggression by Moscow increasingly costly.[49] The White

House and Congress must commit serious money to Ukraine's defense, including $1 billion in military assistance each year until 2017. It must also provide lethal assistance, including counter-battery radars and other defensive weapons. Ukraine's government has so far unsuccessfully appealed for US military aid. An under-armed army is more likely to encourage a Russian invasion than a force capable of resisting military assault.

• Preclude the digestion of any occupied territories by Moscow by making such an operation expensive and painful. This will require Western defense aid to Ukraine, Georgia, and other states threatened by Moscow. Priorities must include intelligence sharing, technology for cyber defense, and secure military command and control. Ukraine's army needs technical assistance as well as combat equipment to resist Russian military incursions, and Kyiv must develop a credible territorial defense force that would make any occupation protracted and costly. Training for Ukraine's recently formed National Guard in territorial defense and in insurgency and counter-insurgency operations remains critical. In all NATO Partnership for Peace states bordering Russia, assistance in constructing more effective territorial defense forces, security services, and law enforcement bodies will improve their resilience to Moscow's subversion.

• Avoid the political pitfalls of negotiating with Russia over territories that Moscow has carved out of neighboring states, whether through proxies (as in Ukraine's Donbas) or dissatisfied local politicians (as in Georgia's Abkhazia and South Ossetia). Washington and Brussels have been complicit in pushing Kyiv to amend its constitution and provide a special constitutional status to rebel-held areas in Donbas. Such short-sighted moves to attain a temporary peace will provide credibility to the separatist groups, legitimize Russia's war of aggression against Ukraine, and encourage the Kremlin to prepare subsequent acts of political subversion and territorial partition.[50] It may also stimulate ethno-territorial secession in the broader region, undermine Western security guarantees, and challenge a number of European borders from which Moscow will profit. Simmering conflict in Donbas will preoccupy governments and mediators, enable Moscow to encroach on Ukraine's sovereignty, and threaten to reignite a renewed war similarly to what has been witnessed in Georgia, Azerbaijan, and Moldova.

Systemic Transformation

• Thwart Russia's expansionist ambitions by undermining the Putinist regime. A strategy needs to be developed to weaken Kremlin control over the Russian Federation, not only through sanctions and isolation but also by supporting minority rights, regional self-determination, and national independence movements from Kaliningrad to Chukotka and from Karelia to Dagestan. Washington and Brussels must consistently assert that if the current administration is not replaced with a non-imperialist and pro-democratic successor, Russia will increasingly face ethnic and religious conflicts and territorial fracture. Russia's numerous ethnic groups should be encouraged to preserve their culture, language, heritage, and history, while promoting their autonomy and self-determination. This is consistent with Western support for individual freedom, democracy, and human rights inside Russia. Paradoxically, Moscow's annexation of Crimea means that the West does not recognize Russia's claimed borders, signaling that it may no longer accept the legitimacy of Moscow's "inner empire."

• Assess the possible consequences of a chaotic end to the Putinist system and prepare contingencies for the conflicts that this may generate and the opportunities that this will provide for the West.[51] In particular, Russia's neighbors must be shielded from the most destabilizing scenarios of civil conflict and the country's violent disintegration. A peaceful change of leadership or a bloodless dissolution of the Russian Federation would be the preferable alternatives to a civil war that could spill over the country's borders.

In his drive to expand Russia's territorial possessions and zones of influence, Putin is likely to miscalculate. Authoritarian rulers often believe they are invincible when they achieve early triumphs, as with Moscow's annexation of Crimea or truncation of Georgia. Paradoxically, Putin's attempts to construct a new Russia-centered dominion will accelerate the country's decline. An overstretched Russia, facing growing economic problems cannot withstand a prolonged conflict with the West, with a multitude of neighbors, or within its own borders. The turmoil engendered by Putin's push for empire can have a direct impact on the stability of the Russian Federation. An economically and militarily overstretched Russia will witness escalating domestic economic, social, political, and regional turmoil and present even more menacing challenges for Western policy. The question is how can the West capitalize on Russia's economic weaknesses, multi-ethnic turmoil, and regional disquiet to enable the Russian population to replace the Putinist system as peacefully and quickly as possible.

Ultimately, the uncertainty over Russia's future may be resolved through two possible scenarios: either Russia transforming itself into a responsible international player without neo-imperial aspirations toward its neighbors, or the Russian Federation fracturing with the emergence of a smaller and weaker Russia that can eventually co-exist with Europe's democracies and multi-national institutions. Given the ongoing collision with Ukraine and the Kremlin's extensive imperial aspirations, the first scenario seems highly unlikely for the foreseeable future. In light of the policies pursued during the Putin presidency at a time of prolonged economic decline, the latter scenario seems more probable, although the timescale and multi-regional impact of a Russia implosion remains highly unpredictable. This would be a timely and strategically critical subject for a future in-depth study.

Endnotes

[1] Pavel K. Baev, "Free Rein of Special Services Makes Russia Ungovernable," *Eurasia Daily Monitor,* March 9, 2015, Volume 12, Issue 43.

[2] Alexander Motyl, "Goodbye, Putin, Why the President's Days Are Numbered," Foreign Affairs, February 5, 2015, http://www.foreignaffairs.com/articles/142840/alexander-j-motyl/goodbye-putin.

[3] Elena Popina and Ye Xie, "Investors Flee Russia as Morgan Stanley Sees Long Market Chill," Bloomberg Business, July 26, 2015, http://www.bloomberg.com/news/articles/2015-07-26/investors-flee-russia-as-morgan-stanley-sees-long-market-chill.

[4] For data on the decline of Gazprom see "Russia: Gazprom, a Behemoth No More," August 3, 2015, http://www.eurasianet.org/node/74501.

[5] "Russia: Massive Capital Flight Continues," *The Moscow Times,* May 1, 2015, http://www.themoscowtimes.com/article/520112.html.

[6] Laurence Norman, "EU Extends Economic Sanctions on Russia Until End of January," June 22, 2015, *The Wall Street Journal,* http://www.wsj.com/articles/eu-extends-economic-sanctions-on-russia-until-end-of-january-1434960823.

[7] Lack of Action Questions Forum's Reform Agenda," Johnson's Russia List, June 19, 2015, http://russialist.org/lack-of-action-questions-forums-reform-agenda/.

[8] The Moscow Times, June 11, 2015, www.themoscowtimes.com.

[9] Cheap Oil Drags Down Russia's Ruble," CNN Money, August 18, 2015, http://money.cnn.com/2015/08/17/investing/russia-ruble-currency-slide/index.html.

[10] Paul Goble, "Financial Instability in Russia's Regions Already 'Worse than Default,' Zubarevich Says," Window on Eurasia – New Series, June 11, 2015, http://windowoneurasia2.blogspot.com/2015/06/financial-instability-in-russias.html.

[11] Paul Goble, "New East-West Tensions Leave Kaliningrad Out In The Cold," Window on Eurasia - New Series, October 31, 2014, http://windowoneurasia2.blogspot.com/2014/10/window-on-eurasia-new-east-west.html.

[12] Adrian Karatnycky, "Putin's Warlords Slip Out of Control," The New York Times, June 9, 2015.

[13] Henry E. Hale, Patronal Politics: Eurasian Regime Dynamics in Comparative Perspective, Cambridge University Press, 2015, p. 84.

[14] Matthew Czekaj, "Russia's Bankrupting Empire," Eurasia Daily Monitor, Volume 12, Issue 121, June 29, 2015, http://www.jamestown.org/single/?tx_ttnews[tt_news]=44093&tx_ttnews[backPid]=7&cHash=4943b3783c312dfa3f0b07912a293854#.VY_xY6b9qxKBy.

[15] Wespazjan Wielohorski, "Moscow's Worst Nightmare Is Called TTIP," Gazeta Polska, Warsaw, October 15, 2014, http://www.gazetapolska.pl/.

[16] "Armenia Protests: Electricity Price Hike Suspended," BBC News, June 27, 2015, http://www.bbc.com/news/world-europe-33301689.

[17] Alexander Kim, "It's All About the Ruble: How to Resolve the Looming Regional Economic Crisis in Central Asia?" Eurasia Daily Monitor, July 6, 2015, Volume 12, Issue 125.

[18] Zaur Shiriyev, "The Protests and Energy Interdependence in Armenia: View From Baku," Eurasia Daily Monitor, July 7, 2015, Volume 12, Issue 126.

[19] Richard J. Krickus, "Russia After Putin," Strategic Studies Institute and US Army War College, May 2014, pp. 62–66, http://www.StrategicStudiesInstitute.army.mil/.

[20] Andrew A. Michta, "Europe's Russia Denial," Politiko, July 25, 2015, www.politico.eu/article/europe-russia-denial-ukraine-baltics-central-europe-attack.

[21] For an in-depth account of Putin's appeasers and accomplices among US academics and former officials see James Kirchick," How a US Think Tank Fell for Putin, The Daily Beast, July 27, 2015, www.thedailybeast.com/articles/2015/07/27/how-a-u-s-think-tank-fell-for-putin.html?via=mobile&source=email.

[22] See for example, Leslie H. Gelb, "Russia and America: Toward a New Détente," The National Interest, June 9, 2015, www.nationalinterest.org/feature/russia-america-toward-new-detente-13077?page=8. As Gelb notes, "It is totally unrealistic, however, to think that the West can gain desired Russian restraint and cooperation without dealing with Moscow as a great power that possesses real and legitimate interests, especially in its border areas." According to this kind of explanation, all of Russia's neighbors simply have the status of "border areas" rather than being independent states with their own national interests.

[23] Vladimir Socor, "Nord Stream Expansion Agreed, Wintershall Swapped to Gazprom (Part One)," Eurasia Daily Monitor, Volume, 12, Issue, 162, September 10, 2015.

[24] Mark MacKinnon, "Protect Baltic States, Not Ukraine, NATO Told Ahead Of Summit," http://www.theglobeandmail.com/news/world/protect-baltic-states-not-ukraine-nato-told-ahead-of-summit/article20296698/.

[25] "NATO Response Force, At The Centre Of NATO Transformation," October 2, 2014, www.nato.int/cps/en/natolive/topics_49755.htm.

[26] "NATO To Unveil Strengthened Eastern Europe Defense," AFP (North European Service), February 5, 2015, Brussels, http://www.afp.com/en/home.

[27] "NATO Will Set Up Five New Bases In Eastern Europe, Including One in Romania," Adevarul Online, Bucharest, September 2, 2014, http://www.adevarul.ro.

[28] "NATO To Expand Polish Base In Response To Russian Threat," Euractiv, July 25, 2014, http://www.euractiv.com/sections/global-europe/nato-expand-polish-base-response-russian-threat-303713.

[29] "US To Rotate 600 Troops, Heavy Weapons In Baltics, Poland," Tallinn, August 14, 2014, http://www.bns.ee.

[30] "US Announces New Tank and Artillery Deployment in Europe," BBC News, June 23, 2015, http://www.bbc.com/news/world-europe-33238004.

[31] "US. Army Ready To Respond To Russia In 48 Hours, In Event Of Its Attack On NATO,"Joinfo, June 25, 2015, http://joinfo.com/world/1002670_u-s-army-ready-to-respond-to-russia-in-48-hours-in-event-of-its-attack-on-nato.html.

[32] "NATO Boosts Black Sea Presence Amid Ukraine Crisis," Hurriyet Daily News Online, Istanbul, July 12, 2014, www.hurriyetdailynews.com. According to the Montreux Convention, all NATO countries taking part in Black Sea activities must comply with certain stipulations, including limited scope, non-provocation toward Russia, and confinement to the western and southern parts of the Black Sea.

[33] "Baltic Fears -- NATO Debates Directing Missile Shield Against Russia," Spiegel on Line, Hamburg, August 25, 2014, http://www.spiegel.de.

[34] Matthew Holehouse, "NATO Updates Cold War Playbook as Putin Vows to Build Nuclear Stockpile," The Telegraph, June 25, 2015,

www.telegraph.co.uk/news/predictions/politics/11697512/Nato-updates-Cold-War-playbook-as-Putin-vows-to-build-nuclear-stockpile.html.

35 Vitalii Usenko and Dmytro Usenko, "Russian Hybrid Warfare: What are Effects-Based Network Operations and How to Counteract Them," http://euromaidanpress.com/2014/11/05/russian-hybrid-warfare-what-are-effect-based-network-operations-and-how-to-counteract-them/.

36 Paul Goble, "Hot Issue – Lies, Damned Lies and Russian Disinformation," Jamestown Foundation, August 13, 2014, http://www.jamestown.org/single/?tx_ttnews%5btt_news%5d=42745#.VXi b4Cgx85Q.

37 Keir Giles, Philip Hanson, Roderic Lyne, James Nixey, James Sherr, and Andrew Wood, "The Russian Challenge," June 4, 2015, Chatham House, London, http://www.chathamhouse.org/publication/russian-challenge?dm_i=1TYG,3FSEV,DOYKRT,CAZM8,1#.

38 Ben Nimmo, "Anatomy of An Info-War: How Russia's Propaganda Machine Works, And How To Counter It," Central European Policy Institute, May 15, 2015, http://www.cepolicy.org/publications/anatomy-info-war-how-russias-propaganda-machine-works-and-how-counter-it.

39 A new Russian-language TV news program was launched in October 2014 to provide audiences in countries bordering Russia with a balanced alternative to the disinformation produced by Russia's media outlets. See "New TV Show Brings 'Facts, not Lies,' to Russian Speakers," Radio Free Europe/ Radio Liberty, Washington DC, October 14, 2014, http://www.rferl.org/content/release-new-tv-show-brings-facts-not-lies-to-russian-speakers/26631532.html. "Current Time" ("*Nastoyashchee Vremya*") is a joint production of *Radio Free Europe/Radio Liberty* and the *Voice of America*, undertaken in partnership with public and private broadcasters and Internet portals in Georgia, Estonia, Latvia, Lithuania, Moldova and Ukraine. The project began with a 30-minute daily program, but plans were in place to expand programming and satellite and online distribution by the end of 2015.

[40] Paul Goble, "Putin is Waging War While the West is Talking Sanctions," Window on Eurasia – New Series, July 27, 2014, http://windowoneurasia2.blogspot.com/2014/07/window-on-eurasia-putin-is-waging-war.html.

[41] Mark Galeotti, "Time for a New Strategy in Russia," Foreign Affairs, August 4, 2015, https://www.foreignaffairs.com/articles/russia-fsu/2015-08-04/time-new-strategy-russia.

[42] Sofia, BTA Online, 10 July 10, 2015, http://www.bta.bg. EU Commission Vice-President Maroš Šefčovič and EU Commissioner Miguel Arias Cañete signed the Memorandum of Understanding, together with Energy Ministers from Austria, Bulgaria, Croatia, Greece, Hungary, Italy, Romania, Slovakia, Slovenia, Albania, Macedonia, Serbia and Ukraine. Bosnia-Herzegovina and Moldova were due to sign at a later date.

[43] Joseph Dobbs, "The Eurasian Economic Union: A Bridge to Nowhere?" Policy Brief, European Leadership Network, March 4, 2015, p. 6, http://www.europeanleadershipnetwork.org/the-eurasian-economic-union-a-bridge-to-nowhere_2498.html.

[44] Jānis Bērziņš, "Introduction," Russia's New Generation Warfare in Ukraine: Implications for Latvian Defense Policy, Policy Paper No.2, April 2014, National Defence Academy of Latvia, Center for Security and Strategic Research, p. 10, http://www.naa.mil.lv/~/media/NAA/AZPC/Publikacijas/PP%2002-2014.ashx.

[45] COL Douglas Mastriano and LTC Derek O'Malley (Editors), Project 1704: A US Army War College Analysis of Russian Strategy in Eastern Europe, an Appropriate US Response, and the Implications for US Landpower, March 26, 2015, p. 8, http://www.strategicstudiesinstitute.army.mil/pubs/display.cfm?pubID=1274.

[46] Jakub Grygiel and Wess Mitchell, "Limited War is Back," The National Interest, August 28, 2014, http://nationalinterest.org/feature/limited-war-back-11128.

[47] "NATO Must Prepare For Russian Blitzkrieg, Warns UK General, Sam Jones," The Financial Times, February 20, 2015, http://www.ft.com/cms/s/0/204ecbb8-b913-11e4-a8d0-00144feab7de.html#axzz3T4y1NKb5. Deploying overwhelming force at short notice is now a hallmark of Russian military exercises. For example, Russia's 2013 Zapad war games involved the rapid mobilization of 25,000 troops in Belarus and Kaliningrad in preparation for a conflict with a NATO state.

[48] Jakub Grygiel, "Arming Our Allies: The Case for Offensive Capabilities," Parameters 45(3) Autumn 2015, http://www.strategicstudiesinstitute.army.mil/pubs/parameters/issues/Autumn_2015/7_Grygiel.pdf.

[49] Steven Pifer and Strobe Talbott, "Ukraine Needs America's Help," The Washington Post, January 29 2015, http://www.washingtonpost.com/opinions/ukraine-needs-more-help-from-the-west/2015/01/29/462b1ea4-a71b-11e4-a7c2-03d37af98440_story.html.

[50] Janusz Bugajski, "West Legitimizes Ukraine's Division," Europe Edge, CEPA, August 18, 2015, http://rtcg.me/vijesti/svijet/101097/zapad-legitimizuje-podjelu-ukrajine.html.

[51] Keir Giles, Philip Hanson, Roderic Lyne, James Nixey, James Sherr, and Andrew Wood, "The Russian Challenge," June 4, 2015, Chatham House, London, http://www.chathamhouse.org/publication/russian-challenge?dm_i=1TYG,3FSEV,DOYKRT,CAZM8,1#.

Appendix I: Maps of Vulnerable Flanks

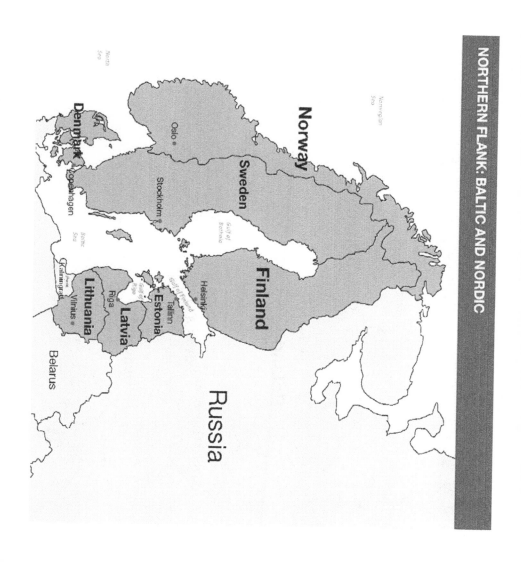

NORTHERN FLANK: BALTIC AND NORDIC

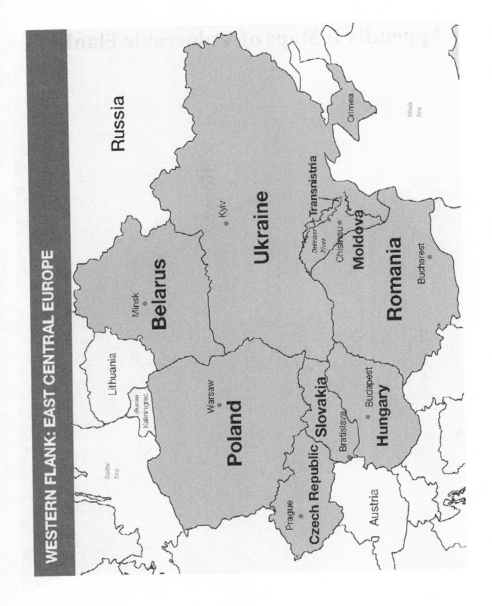

501

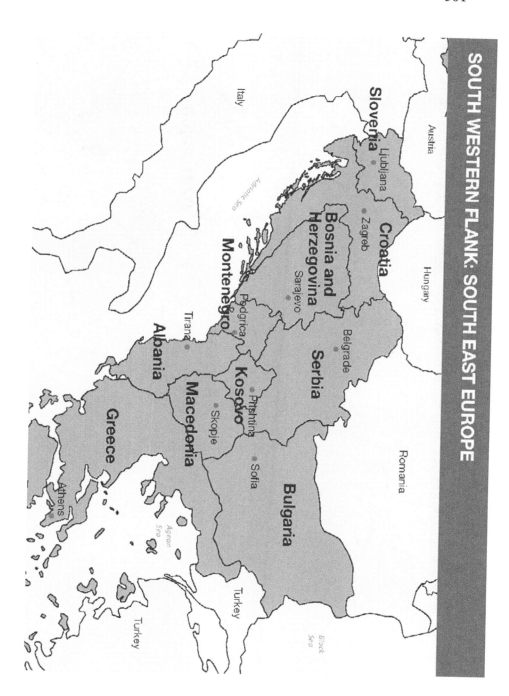

SOUTH WESTERN FLANK: SOUTH EAST EUROPE

502

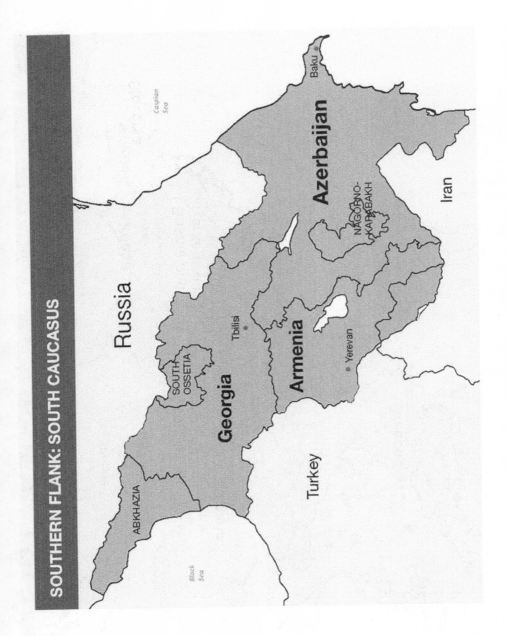

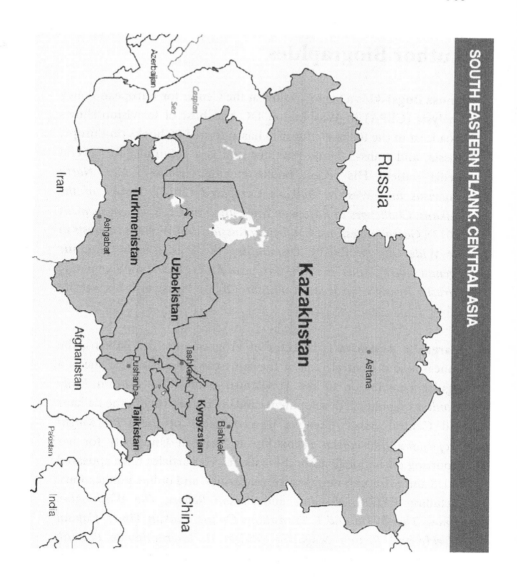

Author Biographies

Janusz Bugajski is a Senior Fellow at the Center for European Policy Analysis (CEPA) in Washington DC and host of television shows broadcast in the Balkans. Bugajski has authored 20 books on Europe, Russia, and trans-Atlantic relations and is a columnist for several media outlets. His recent books include *Conflict Zones: North Caucasus and Western Balkans Compared* (2014), *Return of the Balkans: Challenges to European Integration and U.S. Disengagement* (2013), *Georgian Lessons: Conflicting Russian and Western Interests in the Wider Europe* (2010), *Dismantling the West: Russia's Atlantic Agenda* (2009), *America's New European Allies* (2009); and *Expanding Eurasia: Russia's European Ambitions* (2008). Please visit his website at http://www.jbugajski.com/.

Margarita Assenova is Director of Programs for the Balkans, the Caucasus and Central Asia at the Jamestown Foundation. She is a regular contributor to the Jamestown publication *Eurasia Daily Monitor* on political developments and energy security in the Balkans and Central Asia. Assenova is a recipient of the *John Knight Professional Journalism Fellowship* at Stanford University for her reporting on nationalism in the Balkans. Her articles have appeared in US and European newspapers, magazines, and online publications, including *RFE/RL Newsline* and *Balkan Report*, *The Washington Times*, *The World and I*, *Transitions Online*, *Balkan Times*, *Capital Weekly* and *Reason Magazine (Bulgaria)*, *Internationale Polititik (Germany)*, *World Finance Review Magazine (UK)*, *and Future Prospects (UAE)*. She authored book chapters and journal articles on security, energy, and democracy published by CSIS Press, Brassey's, Freedom House, Bertelsmann Foundation Publishers, the University of New Haven and the Jamestown Foundation. She is the co-editor of *Azerbaijan and the New Energy Geopolitics of Southeastern Europe*, published by the Jamestown Foundation in June 2015.